£50.00

The Institute of British Geographers
Special Publications Series

31 Diffusing Geography

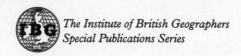 *The Institute of British Geographers*
Special Publications Series

EDITORS: Felix Driver, Royal Holloway, London University and Neil Roberts, Loughborough University

Diffusing Geography
Essays for Peter Haggett

Edited by A.D. Cliff, P.R. Gould,
A. G. Hoare and N.J. Thrift

BLACKWELL
Oxford UK & Cambridge USA

Copyright © Institute of British Geographers 1995

First published 1995

Blackwell Publishers Inc.
238 Main Street
Cambridge, Massachusetts 02142, USA

Blackwell Publishers Ltd
108 Cowley Road
Oxford OX4 1JF
UK

Library of Congress Cataloging-in-Publication Data
Diffusing geography : essays for Peter Haggett / edited by A. D.
  Cliff . . . [et al.].
      p.   cm. – (The Institute of British Geographers special
  publications series: 31)
    Includes bibliographic references and index.
    ISBN 0–631–19534–3 (acid-free)✓
    1. Geography. 2. Haggett, Peter. I. Haggett, Peter. II Cliff,
A. D. (Andrew David) III. Series: Special publications series
(Institute of British Geographers) : 31
G62.D53 1995
910–dc20   94–31610
                                            CIP

British Library Cataloguing in Publication Data
A CIP record for this book is available from the
British Library

Typeset in 10 on 12 pt Plantin
by Archetype, Stow-on-the-Wold, Glos
Printed in Great Britain by Hartnolls Ltd, Bodmin, Cornwall

This book is printed on acid-free paper.

As befits the man, formal photographs of Peter Haggett are few and far between. But this one shows Peter in the summer of 1984 at the time he began his period as Vice-Chancellor of the University of Bristol.

Contents

viii   *Contents*

Part III Medical Geography

Part IV Pacific Studies

Part V Geography and Higher Education

Part VI Peter Haggett: A Career in Geography

Plates

Figures

Tables

Acknowledgements

The editors wish to thank the numerous friends and colleagues of Peter's in Britain and around the world without whose help this *Festschrift* could not have been produced. One of the hallmarks of the lists of acknowledgements in Peter's many books is the generous tribute he has always paid to the unsung heroes whose background work is critical in putting together any book of this kind. So we have a special word of thanks to say to our support team in Bristol and Cambridge. These include (in alphabetical order): Frances Barker, Timothy Cliff, Keith Crabtree, Simon Godden, Brenda Haggett, Sarah Howell, Kit Leighton-Kelly, Tony Philpott and, crucially, Margaret Reynolds who has been Peter's secretary for his entire Bristol career. Finally, our gratitude is due also to our publishers, Blackwell, and especially that Earl of Rochester, John Davey, who has been one of Peter's partners in crime from their association at Edward Arnold. A grant from the University of Bristol has helped to defray some of the publication costs.

A Celebration

This book is a *festschrift*, a form of publication which may suggest these days a certain degree of esotericism, a 'writing within' a rather closed and specialized group. Nothing could be further from the truth. Just listen to the word: *fest schrift*, a festival writing, a celebratory writing, above all a joyous writing to honour with smiles and gratitude the accomplishments of a geographer, a counsellor of slowly acquired and carefully sifted wisdom, and a delightful human being. It is written by friends, some of them former students, who have had the privilege of sharing with him three or four remarkable decades in the history of geography.

The essays vary widely in approach, subject matter, and informing preconceptions, yet all in their different ways touch upon and celebrate themes in the life of Peter Haggett himself, themes and experiences that constitute the six parts of this book. Either alone, or in the company of 'well-beloved' colleagues, he has made great contributions to geography's methodological development, to locational analysis, to medical geography, to Pacific studies, and to geography in higher education. But, as the sixth and last theme discloses, his efforts have frequently borne good fruit far beyond the immediate discipline he has explored with such passion, fascination and delight. His contributions, to what John Henry Newman called in the title to his great book *The Idea of the University*, range from the guidance of students, memorable lectures, and service as a Vice-Chancellor, to membership on national boards responsible for things as varied as university funding and radiation protection. Internationally, he has been adviser to universities literally around the world, a visiting scientist at major research centres, and one of the first two geographers admitted to the new Academia Europaea. It is not difficult to write with an air of festivity for such a person.

But the six parts and themes are only the warp of this book, the basic strings stretched on the frame to provide the structure from start to finish, from cover to cover. Weaving back and forth through time, building the pattern and design that is still growing, is the weft of Peter's own research themes, different threads of different colours, yet all joined and connected together from the first throw of the geographical shuttle in the county of his birth, to the most recent gold medal at Stockholm. Picking out long threads of private thinking from publications, from those occasions of 'making public', is dangerous work. The appearance of an idea in print always has a prior origin, sometimes years before. Still, the general trend is not difficult to see, and that is precisely where the thread starts, with a method for separating out a general trend across a region from the specificities of particular places. Trend surface analyses start in 1963 and continue for 15 years, used with great imagination as a tool to examine such disparate questions as vegetation and settlement patterns in Brazil, the geomorphological intricacies of the Breckland in East Anglia, and the difficulties involved in inter-regional comparisons.

But this method of spatial decomposition and simplification, recalling John Stuart Mills's 'Method of Residues', is neither a philosopher's nor a geographer's stone. Its adaptation to delimit isochronic lines of pioneer settlement in Brazil suggests a dynamic element of movement in the human world at rates not normally visible in the slower processes of growth and erosion in biological and physical phenomena. Things move, goods, ideas, and people themselves, and they move in real regions structured by the human presence, not across the smooth and isotropic spaces of the theoreticians. Around 1967, networks appear as a prominent research focus, and these 'connectivity structures' guide research and thinking for another 15 years, cutting across the human and physical divisions of the field, a distinct counter-trend at the time to making these two traditional components of geography more and more separate, distinct, and uninforming of each other. From stream networks, to roads in Portugal, from networks of connections shaping the passage of measles in Iceland, to an examination of formal graph theoretic measures and their geographical utility, the moving shuttle begins to weave other patterns in the unfolding cloth of research.

Some of the things guided by network structures are the diseases that afflict all living things, especially those carried by Pestilence, whose pale horse knows the intricate pathways all too well. By 1969, the first paper in medical geography appears, a research theme that continues prominently to the present day. No one has done more to remind the epidemiological and medical professions that epidemics always exist in space as well as time, that they always have a hideous geography to complement their destructive history. From Iceland to the islands in the South Pacific, different networks at different geographical scales carry the measles virus, whose passage discloses in turn the often unobservable structures of immediate human interaction.

Such studies are not simply an academic interest; historical processes over geographical space are investigated to see if they can help us make educated guesses about the future. By 1971, regional forecasting appears as another explicit theme, and no one believes that only seven years later Peter's contributions were 'from the touchline', comments from a spectator, rather than as a player on the field. By 1963, the threads of medical geography, networks, and regional forecasting overlap to produce papers tackling the enormous, and always uncertain, task of predicting where a disease will move next.

And so questions of intervention and control appear, not simply in scientific papers, but through consultant reports and joint recommendations for WHO, the international organization that has designated, after the worldwide elimination of smallpox, that measles is one of the next diseases to be destroyed. Intervention, control, and involved caring for health usually take place outside of academic walls, often in national and international councils where persuasion may be slow and difficult, and judgements sometimes hesitant on sound and reasonable grounds. It is a measure of the respect with which he is held by the larger scientific and medical communities that Peter has served not simply as a consultant to international committees, but also as a member of Britain's National Radiological Protection Board.

But there is one further thread to trace in this remarkable and still unfolding career: he is above all a teacher, and a remarkable one at that, not just in the seminar room and lecture hall, but in the widest sphere of public education in the earth and social sciences, most especially the field of geography itself. It is no accident that the reforms he catalysed in the geographical curriculum of the schools in the 1970s are producing such high-quality students for the university in the 1990s, or that geography is 'oversubscribed' as a field of study. Many attest to his direct influence through his basic text, *Geography: A Modern Synthesis*, first appearing in 1972, and now in German, Italian, Spanish and Russian. But behind this basic pedagogic work lie the Madingley Lectures of 1965, and their *Models in Geography* in 1967 (also in Russian, Spanish, and Portuguese), and the results of his own teaching at Cambridge, the 1965 publication of *Locational Analysis in Human Geography* (in Russian, German and French). Geography, geographical teaching, and geographical research are very different today compared to 40 years ago when he started as an undergraduate at Cambridge, and many of the differences and advances are due to his long-term influence as a teacher. How he has touched many of us can be seen in the chapters that make up this book, each of which is written by a close colleague of Peter's, past or present.

In Part I, David Harvey reminds us that not all methodology these days need be algebraically expressed or computer-driven. On the contrary, reflection on the various paths towards knowledge points to marked contrasts in the initial stances and 'taken for granteds', from which research can be generated to illuminate an old and continuing problematic in geography – the interlocked and reciprocal question of process and form. Dialectical thinking, as a chosen approach to a spiralling dynamic of reciprocity, is itself constructed in different ways at different times, reflecting the larger embedding conditions of a society. With a formal history going back to Aristotle, it is pinned down by Hegel to a rather strict and constraining definition in the early nineteenth century, from which it begins to wriggle loose in the works of Marx. Harvey himself has opened the space for dialectical thinking in his own consideration of Marx's writings and the possibilities they hold for creating a deeper understanding of our world.

Peter Gould approaches methodological questions from a different perspective, linking them to the always difficult and uncertain task of teaching. What ways (*hodos*), to geographical knowledge are worth emphasizing in teaching so that the informing spatial perspective of the geographer infuses inquiry, yet does not create methodological automatons who cling to certain approaches like a child clutching a comforting blanket? Where is the balance between approaches so abstract and theoretical that students are bewildered by their sense of unreality, and those increasing calls for 'thick description', that send most students off to sleep with their drowning detail from which no coherent pattern seems to emerge? How can one investigate the human world in its physical setting without reifying both for the purposes of analysis? How can the abstract method be taught with concrete example to give students possibilities for enquiry rather than intellectual strait-jackets? The jolts of eureka in our litera-ture, the examples that illuminate in a lightning flash of understanding, reach our students too slowly, and too often point uncertainly from the specific instance to the larger possibilities they contain for enquiry.

Yet a third, and very different perspective on choosing paths to knowledge, is given by Torsten Hägerstrand, who reminds us of the effects of concrete human action in a concrete physical world by dusting off and polishing up the old and often romanticized concept of 'landscape'. In his hands, all cleaned up and intellectually presentable once again, 'landscape' reaches back to an older Ratzelian sense of human action embedded in a physical world, each in reciprocal relation to the other. As a concrete example, Galileo and his famous experiment on timing falling bodies (on which Newton drew so heavily) becomes a centrepiece of the essay. But, asks Hägerstrand, what about the materials of the experiment, and all the things and thoughts that had to be 'in place' before they could be brought together and assembled in that particular configuration? What prior acts of tool-making, smelting, glass-blowing and other crafts, let alone the centuries of thinking about time, cause and effect, had to be 'present' for such a disturbing event, a *physical* event whose intellectual consequences would resonate to our own times? Every human action – prepar-ing a meal, planting a flower, bicycling to work . . . breathing a tubercular breath – changes the landscapes of our world, those near and immediate, and others thousands of miles away. As he notes, 'Our meaningful actions bring with them "meaningless" change'.

A second major thread of the warp is locational analysis, a topic as variously approached as methodology itself. The four papers in this section reflect that variety; the first two are formal, while the second two address locational problems in a more empirical vein. Neil Wrigley begins by revisiting two of the classic topics in the statistical theory of locational analysis – the modifiable unit problem and the associated issue of ecological fallacy. Statisticians have known for some 60 years that correlation and regression results calculated from areal data are affected by the sizes of the units for which they are computed (the modifiable unit problem). In addition, it is not possible to make inferences about individual behaviour from results calculated from data that represent areal aggregations of those individuals (the ecological fallacy). Many solutions to these problems have been unsuccessfully proposed. Wrigley describes a new weighting approach and outlines how appropriate weights may be constructed and used to mitigate the effects.

In the second paper, Bill Macmillan exemplifies the formal approach and tradition, and its development over the past three decades, by grounding spatial interaction firmly in the economic realm. Yet in the theoretical structure there is a nagging lacuna that needs to be closed: how are constrained individual choices at the microlevel, and the setting of prices at the macrolevel of an entire economy, to be integrated into a general theoretical structure capable of handling locational and interaction problems? These are directly connected, since choices about residences and employment opportunities are related daily by those interactive flows we call the 'journey-to-work'. It is not surprising that such work builds on some of the earliest modelling in entropy maximization and residential choice, but it extends these approaches by demonstrating their inconsistencies and asymmetries, while showing that these questions are both resolvable and computable within discrete choice theory.

In a different, empirical vein, Michael Chisholm considers the highly current locational question of Britain in relation to the European Community. Is location on the geographical periphery of Europe an irreducibly damaging 'fact' for which Britain has no choice and no way of overcoming? In brief, is Britain geographically doomed by costs of access so high that competitiveness is inevitably reduced? In a wider union, does this mean that investments will go more and more to the centre, so depriving Britain of their concomitant power to create jobs in a country with already distressingly high levels of unemployment? For over 40 years, the proportion of Britain's trading with Europe has steadily increased, with a related decline in traffic to the rest of the world. Trading distances and costs to market have been greatly reduced, so that today a locational disadvantage with respect to Europe can be considered trivial. The same conclusion holds internally; the much vaunted advantage of the south-east and London is often more than offset by lower costs of other factors of production. Costs of accessibility can be virtually disregarded, implying that economic performance is predicated on other things than geographical location.

The final essay in locational analysis, by Paul Cloke, focuses on a lesser known element of Peter Haggett's work which concerns surveys of rural communities in the English county of Somerset. The essay describes this work both in terms of its own value and as a springboard for some thoughts on the changing philosophical and methodological relations between social science research and rural planning. There appear to have been three moments of change in these relations: those achieved by Bracey himself; the resistance to traditional research–planning relations that arose as part of the turn towards political economic approaches; and, third, the struggle to include qualitative accounts of lay discourses of rural lifestyle in the planning process.

In Part III, essays on medical geography, the 'research shuttle' of Peter's own inquiries produces a sharply defined pattern. Andy Cliff and Keith Ord are his long-time partners in research from the earliest Bristol days over a quarter of a century ago, and they focus upon the important question of how frequently epidemics are likely to return, and how they may be damped down, and perhaps even eliminated one day, by intervention strategies. Eliminating a disease is difficult, even one like measles which requires only human hosts, not because it is immunologically infeasible, but because political will and the distribution of economic resources make it difficult to push regions under the endemic thresholds below which the virus cannot sustain itself. So the question then becomes: can we point to those areas most at risk for a new epidemic, and intervene with what resources we have in geographically specified immunization programmes? Such spatio-temporal forecasting is difficult on a global scale, because infected people can move over great distances in very short times these days, but the regionally tested models seem capable of further extension.

In a dramatic scale and disease shift, Matt Smallman-Raynor, another, more recent collaborator, focuses on AIDS in a geographically concentrated homosexual community, the Castro and adjacent districts of San Francisco. Already the HIV has created an epidemic of such severity that deaths in the city now exceed those of the 1906 earthquake. After testing a series of questions relating homosexual membership and poverty to the acquisition of HIV by sexual and intravenous drug transmissions, the further question arises as to whether it is possible to construct a space–time model to predict the future course of the epidemic. Most models to date have focused exclusively on the time domain, and have been totally aspatial. While limited to annual time slices, because of confidentiality constraints, the spatio-temporal modelling by the expansion method is suggestive of directions to predict over both space and time the future course of the epidemic in the heterosexual population, the now rapidly growing third wave after the homosexual and IV drug communities.

The third essay in medical geography, by Tony Gatrell, examines the possibility of modelling cancers in a framework of a geographical information system (GIS) for analysing incidences recorded as point patterns. Such possibilities, of working directly with point data, would overcome the difficult question of spatially aggregated areas which are always arbitrary, so that any statements must be cautiously related to the specific units used in the analysis. In fact, postal codes with a spatial resolution of 100 metres are required, but for all practical purposes they are so 'fine grained' that they can be considered point patterns. Analyses of such point patterns in an epidemiological framework are not easy, and require clustering procedures which are capable of comparing cases of a particular illness with measures derived from 'controls' of healthy people. Nor are the expressions particularly tractable analytically, so that permutational approaches must often be Monte Carloed out. The trick is to develop an analytical approach so closely coupled with GIS capabilities that the 'system' constitutes a practical method for examining many disease distributions – in this case, cancers of the larynx and prostate.

Pacific Studies may seem a rather strange and different category if it moves thinking towards traditional regional geography, but these studies concern a part of the world long associated with Peter as a teacher, researcher, and adviser in New Zealand, Australia, Brunei, Hong Kong, Singapore, and Malaysia. Even if we were to confine our definition to the slice of 25° North to 40° South, and 100°–140° East, covered by Peter's own peregrinations, it is still a huge chunk of geographical space. But, as Gerry Ward shows, the sheer geographical size of the Pacific Basin may not really be the 'space' in which our thinking should be shaped today. Our late twentieth-century world is in 'tele-cost space' shaped not simply by cost, *per se*, but by costs that are themselves influenced by political and social factors, constraints on capacities that have to be rationed in some way, and even language and cultural differences that move French-speaking Polynesia far away from the geographically nearby Cook Islands. It is a strange, unstable space, in some cases fluctuating four times a day as the earth spins on its diurnal rhythm, waking up people in London, while others are going to sleep in Fiji. The result is a vast archipelago whose islands communicate in asymmetric, changing electronic spaces. If human communication is a crucial component of any human geography, in what space is it taking place, and how is it shaped by the strange wobbling geometry itself?

Pip Forer's analysis of two recent decades of dramatic change in New Zealand demonstrates how a small, supposedly dependent, economy behaves in a turbulent international economic and political climate. It has felt waves of change reaching its Pacific and Tasman shores from economic disturbances far off, and these waves have triggered a series of responses in New Zealand's trade patterns, the structures that produced them, and the economic environment upon which these depend. Each shock had its resulting differential regional impacts within the country, encouraging something of a back-to-rural-basics movement. But New Zealand also amplified these external influences in ways both distinctive and surprising, especially in the enthusiasm with which governments of both parties have stood previous economic programmes of protection on their heads, with further ramifications throughout the economy, society and polity.

A very different problem from this part of the world, but one closely comparable to a similar situation in the United States, is the manner in which vast rangelands will be used. John Holmes compares the complex land tenures and property rights controlling the multiple land uses over these quasi-public lands in Australia, New Zealand, and the United States. All three nations formulated policies in their earlier days, policies which are generating considerable public debate as new possibilities impinge upon once indigenous lands now subject to government leases and licences, some granted grudgingly, others with enthusiasm. Prominent among the arguments is a new concern for the environment, as overstocking strips away the protective covers of fragile ecosystems, aided and abetted by feral populations that can have an equally devastating effect on the land. There is also a growing sensitivity to aboriginal rights and values, as well as a recognition in mountainous areas (the Rockies and New Zealand's Alps and 'High Country') of the impact of recreation and tourism, forestry, and hydroelectric development.

The essays of Part V raise questions of a different genre, but one in which Peter has spent much of his professional life – the place of geography in higher education. Tony Hoare starts by putting a different twist to this question – for higher education itself has a geography, one shaped by public policies. British universities face change in a climate of great uncertainty and disruption, expanding as a whole to give greater access to students, while facing cuts from traditional funding sources. While the number of universities has increased markedly over the past ten years in Britain, their geographical 'reach' has shown only a marginal increase. All such expansions and changes work their way down to the local level, where they are evaluated in terms of compatibility to existing architectural forms and urban landscapes. In the case of some subjects, for example veterinary science, the larger agricultural geography of the country was reflected in the debates of consolidation, expansion, and closure. Finally, and in addition to all the debates about research and teaching functions, the students themselves produce a most human geography, one shaped by tradition and loyalty to one's home region, by the ability to attend from the parental home, and by the way the universities themselves appear to be splitting into one set dominated by research, and a second where teaching is the current focus of financial support.

Like four other geographical colleagues, Ron Johnston is now a British university Vice-Chancellor, and is literally in the thick of higher education at the national level. Drawing upon his own numerous analyses of national education policy, he notes the way in which the pressures of such policies can sway the directions of geographical inquiry and teaching as they become more applied and 'relevant' in economically lean times. The business of geography, so the underlying threnody went in the 1980s, was business; a major responsibility of the university was to supply the technologists demanded by potential employers responding in turn to 'the market'. Rather than making research and teaching slaves to market forces, such responses to robust realities would wean the universities away from national handouts, and thus enhance their academic freedom. Or so the Thatcher argumentation ran. Whether posited as accountability, new blood, assessment, or utility, the technological tail increasingly wagged the geographical dog. The human, not to say humane, dimensions of geographical enquiry received little encouragement, along with such other humanly focused disciplines as the arts and social sciences. It was not necessary to know too much about the social condition. Despite such pressures, often on one year and off the next, geography as a discipline rollercoasted with the trends, doing generally better by most measures than other disciplines. What the future holds is difficult to see.

A very different perspective is put forward by yet another Vice-Chancellor, Alan Wilson, who builds on an analytical approach he pioneered nearly 30 years ago – entropy maximization modelling. Noting how locational theory must eventually be capable of incorporating many different types of problems at many different scales, he turns to very general mathematical tools which hold promise for the eventual integration of subsystem components, as well as pointing to the rigorous data demands such 'social accounting' requires. *Geographically*, integration means connecting up separate regional components, each with their own particular and local intricacies, so that interactions of many types – goods, materials, people, money, even ideas (?) – must be incorporated into any global structure. As an example, Wilson takes the universities themselves as a 'system', each with potential areas of influence for attracting students, themselves characterized or 'indexed' by their intellectual or practical interests. But how are questions of supply (courses in medicine?) and demand (courses in Italian?) to be answered? And how do we evaluate effectiveness at delivering the required courses, and the efficiency with which they are delivered? What are the constraints on the system, constraints whose tightening and release shape the locational patterns and their connecting flows? All these questions point to focused empirical research which would help us to understand the complexities of a national university system much better than at present.

Last, but by no means least, Part VI focuses upon Peter himself. 'By no means least', because we suspect many readers will leaf through these final pages in a happy mood, and with a genuine sense of festivity, to read about the recreation of 'his' Cambridge by his collaborator (and co-conspirator?), Dick Chorley, and to appreciate the testifying paragraphs woven together by Nigel Thrift to limn Peter's remarkable geographical life. We forget too often that behind the formal publications and scholarly presentations there are wonderfully human biographies, full of chuckling anecdote, gentle concern, and sometimes moments of high and discouraging stress. We can all sympathize at the sight of a young lecturer being verbally chastised by a head of department for bringing geographical research at Cambridge into disrepute with those awful quantitative techniques, conducting himself in this disgraceful way in the august halls of the Royal Geographical Society. And we can all smile with him when, 21 years later, that same Society awards him its gold medal for precisely the contributions he has made! Sometimes you just have to outlive 'em.

Such backward glances over a life, marked properly at times with gentle nostalgia, but no regrets, are valuable today as reminders of other ways, other concerns, and other enthusiasms. 'Haggett's Cambridge', to use Dick Chorley's title, speaks of another world, very different from our own, and different for both good and ill. How the many aspects of that world of learning, teaching, and research will be evaluated today will vary with the reader, but they invite reflection on what we do today, most especially how we evaluate the people around us.

Nigel Thrift closes by drawing on, and drawing together, a stream of testimony from many who have worked with Peter over the years, some from his early school days which formed his first steps in geography. As he himself attests, these steps were on no Damascan road of instant conversion, but were the result of earlier years of landscape exploration and observation, watching birds, old *National Geographics*, exemplary teaching, and a distressing period of enforced immobility lightened by Charles Cotton's wonderful book on New Zealand. The steps follow pathways through Cambridge reminiscences, and lead to Bristol and other pathways around the globe so complex they would defy even his own network analysis! Yet, all along the way, it is clear he touched people with his own skills and enthusiasms, many acknowledging with gratitude his gentle support over difficult intellectual and academic times.

He is a geographer who has shaped geography with his own life, thought, and example.

PART I

Methodology

Plate I Among Peter Haggett's many contributions to the methodology of
Geography, the symbiotic relationship between spatial form and generating
process has been central. This plate, taken from the second edition of
Haggett's book, *Locational Analysis* (p.15), captures his view of the way in
which our interpretation of spatial form may change without changes in the
data. It is a theme picked up in detail in chapter 1 by David Harvey. Original
source: a section from an Escher drawing showing fish and birds *(Lucht en
Water, II)*, 1960.

1

A Geographer's Guide to Dialectical Thinking

D.W. Harvey

Regional organisation needs a constant movement of people, goods, money, information to maintain it; an excess of inward movements may be met by form changes (city expansion and urban sprawl) just as decreased movement may lead to contraction and ghost cities . . . The advantages of viewing the region as an open system are that it directs our attention towards the links between process and form, and places human geography alongside other biological and social sciences that are organising their thinking in this manner. (P. Haggett, *Locational Analysis in Human Geography*, p. 19)

The question of how to relate processes to forms is at the centre of Peter Haggett's quest to establish geography's position within the social and biological sciences. It was, therefore, no accident that he decided that his key point of entry into the understanding of geographical systems in his classic text *Locational Analysis in Human Geography*, lay in the study of *movement*. His continuing fascination with d'Arcy Thompson's *On Growth and Form* suggests, furthermore, a deep ontological commitment to the idea of transformative processes always at work in shaping the geometrical forms that provide the focus for his study of the geographical landscape.

The clarity of these aims still hits home, testifying to the extraordinary and quite revolutionary impact (as well as the deep resistance at the time) that Haggett's work has had on geographical thinking (my own included). But I here want to argue that the commitment to positivist method, outlined in Part II of *Locational Analysis*, exercised a restraining influence on the pursuit of the noble goals that Haggett sought to realize. In the end, the commonalty he established with the biological and social sciences was epistemological and reductive rather than guided by the extraordinary ontological insights that so inspired the opening gambit of *Locational Analysis*.

So what would have happened if Haggett had pursued a *dialectical* rather than a *positivist* vision of how to understand the relationship between process and form? One of the major sources of divergence between Haggett's work and my own is precisely captured in that contrast. So my purpose here is to sketch in how dialectical thinking operates within the field of geography to define a different path to the resolution of the process/form problem. In so doing I shall also pay some attention to how some work in the biological and social sciences, and much recent work in the humanities, has shifted into a more dialectical mode as a way of rethinking the process/form relation.

1 THE PRINCIPLES OF DIALECTICAL THINKING

The craft of dialectical reasoning is not well understood, let alone widely practised, in geography. This absence seriously impoverishes work within the discipline. Furthermore, non-dialectical readings, however well intentioned, of the dialectically constructed arguments which have emerged have generated widespread misinterpretations (sometimes wilfully so, as in Duncan and Ley's (1982) positivist misreading of several Marxian dialectical contributions to geography). It therefore appears useful to set out, as simply as possible, the general principles of dialectical reasoning, to explore its epistemological and ontological underpinnings and to illustrate by way of examples how such reasoning can be deployed to think through certain kinds of geographical problems. I should perhaps also add, that while Marx's own work was fundamentally dialectical in character, there is much Marxist argumentation which is either non-dialectical or (as in the case of analytical Marxism) overtly hostile to dialectics, and a whole tradition of dialectical thinking (most strongly influenced by Leibniz and Hegel though its origins go back at least to the Greeks) which is not Marxist.

The principles of dialectical thinking to which I shall appeal can most simply be stated in terms of ten basic propositions.

(1) Dialectical thinking prioritizes the understanding of processes, flows, fluxes, and relations over the analysis of elements, things, structures, and organized systems. Haggett's opening gambit in *Locational Analysis* is therefore deeply concordant with such a way of thinking. There is a deep ontological principle involved here, for dialecticians in effect hold that elements, things, structures, and systems do not exist outside of, or prior to, the processes and relations that create, sustain, or undermine them. For example, flows of capital (goods, money, people) and of people give rise to, sustain, or undermine cities in exactly the way that Haggett imagined. Epistemologically, the process of enquiry usually inverts this priority: we get to understand processes by looking either at the attributes of what appear to us in the first instance to be self-evident things or at the relations between them. Newton did not start with gravity, for example, but with the apple, his head, the earth, and the moon. Dialectical reasoning holds, however, that the seeming inevitability of this epistemological condition should get reversed when it comes to formulating abstractions, concepts, and theories about the world. The impact is here to transform the self-evident world of things with which positivism typically deals into a much

more confusing world of relations and flows manifest as things. Capital, in Marx's definition, is, for example, *both* the process of circulation of value (a flow) and the stock of assets ('things' like commodities, money, production apparatus) implicated in those flows. Money takes on all manner of 'thing like' forms but those 'things' (like coins or entries on a computer screen) only have meaning in terms of the processes of social production and exchange that validate them. Quantum theory similarly states that 'the same entity (for example, an electron) behaves under one set of circumstances as a wave, and in another set of circumstances as a particle' (Bohm and Peat, 1989, p. 40); that is, particles sometimes appear as 'things' and sometimes appear as 'flows'. Yet it took many years for physicists to recognize that these two conceptions were not incommensurable or mutually exclusive. Only when they did so could modern quantum theory begin to take shape. It has likewise proven very difficult for social scientists to abandon what Ollman (1993, p. 34) calls the 'common sense view' – erected into a philosophical system by Locke, Hume and others – that 'there are things and there are relations, and that neither can be subsumed in the other'.

This was a key step in thinking that Haggett did not take. And the implications are legion. As Raymond Williams (1977, p. 128) so cogently remarks, the more we treat the world as being made up of finished products separate from the continuous flow of experience out of which such products get created, so we reduce everything to the past:

> In most description and analysis, culture and society are expressed in an habitual past tense. The strongest barrier to the recognition of human cultural activity is this immediate and regular conversion of experience into finished products. What is defensible as a procedure in conscious history, where on certain assumptions many actions can be definitively taken as having ended, is habitually projected, not only into the always moving substance of the past, but into contemporary life, in which relationships, institutions and formations in which we are still actively involved are converted, by this procedural mode, into formed wholes rather than forming and formative processes. Analysis is then centred on relations between these produced institutions, formations, and experiences, so that now, as in that produced past, only the fixed explicit forms exist, and living presence is always, by definition, receding.

By this dialectical definition, Haggett often confined himself to doing historical geography, exploring relations between things rather than paying much closer attention to the continuous processes of formation, maintenance, and dissolution of things.

(2) Elements or 'things' (as I shall call them) are constituted out of flows, processes and relations operating within bounded fields which constitute structured systems or wholes. Here, too, in his turn to general systems theory, Haggett saw something very important. But a dialectical conception of both the individual '*thing*' and the *structured system* of which it is a part rests entirely on

an understanding of the processes and relations by which they are constituted. Put another way, the 'things' and systems which many researchers treat as irreducible and therefore unproblematic are always seen in dialectical thought as internally contradictory by virtue of the processes which constitute them. I am, for purposes of social theory, considered an individual within a social system and for certain restricted forms of enquiry such a supposition might appear entirely reasonable. But further inspection shows that I am a rather contradictory and problematic 'thing' created by all sorts of processes. My body contains a variety of life-supporting organs such as the heart, lungs, liver, and digestive system 'whose functioning is more or less automatic, and required by the fact that the body . . . is involved in the perpetual process of internal self-reconstruction' (Ingold, 1986, p. 18). The metabolic processes which permit that internal self-reconstruction to proceed entail exchanges with my environment and a whole range of transformative processes which are necessary for the maintenance of my bodily individuality. If the processes change, then the body is either transformed or ceases to exist. My sociality (for example, the acquisition of language and symbolic skills) is likewise built up through my capturing of certain powers which reside in social processes. Continuous reconstitution of those powers (with respect to mental faculties and symbolic skills, for example) is a process which is as perpetual as my life is long (we all know what it means to 'keep sharp' or 'get rusty' at what we do). To put the matter this way is not to view the 'thing' (or the system) as a passive product of external processes. What is remarkable about living systems is the way they capture diffuse (and often high entropic) energy or information flows and assemble them into complex but well-ordered (low entropic) forms. Human individuals, furthermore, have a remarkable capacity to capture and reorganize energy and information flows in ways which are inherently creative rather than passive. But the fact that they do so in no way challenges the ontological proposition that 'things' and systems are all constituted out of processes.

(3) 'Things' are always assumed 'to be internally heterogeneous at every level' (Levins and Lewontin, 1985, p. 272). This follows from the first two propositions but is worth stating explicitly. There are three major points to be made here:

(a) Any 'thing' can be decomposed into a collection of other 'things' which are in some relation to each other. For example, a city can be considered as a 'thing' in interaction with other cities, but it can also be broken down into neighbourhoods or zones which can in turn be broken down into people, houses, schools, factories, etc. which can in turn be broken down *ad infinitum.* The *ad infinitum* clause is very important because it says that there are no irreducible building blocks of 'things' for any theoretical reconstruction of how the world works. It then follows that what looks like a system at one level of analysis (for example, a city) becomes a part at another level, for example, a global network of world cities (again this was an insight that was not lost on Haggett or, for that matter, on Brian Berry (1964) whose celebrated essay title on 'Cities as systems within systems of cities' neatly captured the point). This idea has become very important in contemporary quantum physics where a fundamental guiding principle is that 'whatever we say a thing or structure is, it isn't' because 'there is always something more than what we say and something different' (Bohm and Peat, 1989, pp. 141–2). There is, as Levins and Lewontin (1985, p. 278) put it, 'no basement' since experience shows that 'all previously proposed undecomposable "basic units" have so far turned out to be decomposable, and the decomposition has opened up new domains for investigation and practice'. One implication is that it is legitimate to investigate 'each level of organization without having to search for fundamental units'. But the other implication, taken seriously in the dialectics of deconstruction, is that in principle all fixed and frozen categories are capable of dissolution. Critical practice in the humanities is very much guided these days, perhaps overly so, by concerns to dissolve fixed categories within conflicting fields and fluxes of socio-linguistic and representational practices.

(b) If all 'things' are heterogeneous (that is, contradictory) by virtue of the complex processes (or relations) which constitute them, then the only way we can understand the qualitative and quantitative attributes of 'things' is by understanding the very processes and relations which they internalize. This is what Ollman (1976) has been very explicit about in constructing his arguments concerning *internal relations*. But such arguments are now advanced in much of the ecological literature (see Eckersley, 1992, pp. 49–55; Naess, 1989, p. 79; Zimmerman, 1988). I, as an individual, cannot be understood except by way of the metabolic, social and other processes which I internalize. This implies, however, that I necessarily internalize heterogeneity and a bundle of associated contradictions. Contradiction is here understood in the sense given to the term by Ollman (1990, p. 49), as 'a union of two or more internally related processes that are simultaneously supporting and undermining one another' (cf., here also, Maurice Wilkins's (1987) discussion of the operation of principles of complementarity in microbiology and other spheres of science and creative endeavour).

(c) There is, however, a limitation to be put upon this argument. I as an individual, do not in practice internalize everything in the universe, but absorb mainly what is relevant to me through my relationships (metabolic, social, political, cultural, etc.) to processes operating over a relatively bounded field (my ecosystem, economy, culture, etc.). There is, however, no fixed or *a priori* boundary to this system. Where my relevant environment begins and ends is itself a function of the ecological, economic, and other processes which are relevant to me. Furthermore, the criteria of relevance are not independent of my own actions (the atmosphere relevant to my breathing, to take a trivial example, depends on whether I stay indoors all day, take a hike in the country or fly to Los Angeles). Setting boundaries – a problem with which Haggett himself frequently wrestled – with respect to space, time, scale, and environment then becomes a major strategic consideration in the development of concepts, abstractions, and theories. It is usually the case that any substantial change in these boundaries will radically change the nature of the concepts, abstractions, and theories. In geography we often encounter this problem in the form of the paradoxes generated by different scales of ecological correlation (cf. Haggett's answer on pages 4–9 of *Locational Analysis*).

(4) Space and time are neither absolute nor external to processes but are contingent and contained with them. There are multiple spaces and times (and space–times) implicated in different physical, biological and social processes. The latter all *produce* – to use Lefebvre's (1991) terminology – their own forms of space and time. Processes do not operate in, but *actively construct,* space and time and in so doing define distinctive scales for their development. Haggett broadly accepted a Newtonian view of space and time as absolute containers for action even when transformations showed the *relative* status of the metrics. A much more dialectical conception is given in Leibniz's attack upon Newton and in the *relational* conception of time and space that derives therefrom.

(5) Parts and wholes are mutually constitutive of each other. 'Part *makes* whole, and whole *makes* part' (Levins and Lewontin, 1985). This is, it seems to me, a principle which Giddens (1984) does much to promote in his very best writings on structuration theory (agency makes structure and structure makes agency) and it is, of course, a fundamental principle which operates across the whole breadth and range of Marx's work. To say that parts and wholes are mutually constitutive of each other is to say much more than that there is a feedback loop between them. In the process of capturing the powers that reside in those ecological and economic systems which are relevant to me, I actively reconstitute or transform them within myself even before I project them back to reconstitute or transform the system from which those powers were initially derived (again, to take a trivial example, I breathe in, I reconstitute myself by virtue of the oxygen I gain, and I breathe out and in so doing transform the atmosphere around me). Reductionist practices 'typically ignore this relationship, isolating parts as pre-existing units of which wholes are then composed' while some holistic practices reverse the preferential treatment.

(6) The interdigitation of parts and wholes entails 'the interchangeability of subject and object, of cause and effect' (Levins and Lewontin, 1985, p. 274). Organisms, for example, have to be looked at as both the subjects and the objects of evolution in exactly the same way that individuals have to be considered as both subjects and objects of processes of social change. The reversibility of cause and effect renders causally specified models (even when endowed with feedback loops) suspect. In practice, dialectical reasoning, precisely by virtue of its embeddedness in and representation of the flow of continuous processes, makes limited appeal to cause and effect argument.

(7) Transformative behaviour – 'creativity' – arises out of the contradictions which attach both to the internalized heterogeneity of 'things' and out of the more obvious heterogeneity present within systems. Heterogeneity, as both Ollman and Levins and Lewontin (1985, p. 278) insist, means more than mere diversity: 'the parts and processes confront each other as opposites, conditional

on the wholes of which they are parts'. Out of these oppositions, creative tensions and transformative behaviours arise. Becoming, to appropriate Hegel's language, arises out of the opposition between Being and Not-Being. In the dialectical view, opposing forces (matter and not-matter, positive and negative charges, repulsion and attraction, male and female, love and hate, life and death, etc.) lie at the base of the evolving physical, biological, and social world (Levins and Lewontin, 1985, p. 280).

(8) 'Change is a characteristic of all systems and all aspects of all systems' (Levins and Lewontin, 1985, p. 275). This is perhaps the most important of all dialectical principles and one which Ollman (1990) prioritizes above all else. The implication is that change and instability are the norm and that the stability of 'things' or systems is what has to be explained. In Ollman's (1990, p. 34) words, 'given that change is always a part of what things are, [our] research problem [can] only be *how, when,* and *into what* (things or systems) change and why they sometimes appear not to change.' Levins and Lewontin make a similar point:

> The dialectical view insists that persistence and equilibrium are not the natural state of things but require explanation, which must be sought in the actions of the opposing forces. The conditions under which the opposing forces balance and the system as a whole is in stable equilibrium are quite special. They require the simultaneous satisfaction of as many mathematical relations as there are variables in the system, usually expressed as inequalities among the parameters of that system.

Since transformative action – creativity – arises out of contradiction, it then follows that it can in principle be found anywhere and everywhere in the physical, biological, and social world. To put it this way does not imply, however, that all moments within some continuous process are equally significant. The theoretical and empirical research task is to identify those characteristic 'moments' and 'forms' (that is, 'things') embedded within continuous flows which can produce radical transformations or where, conversely, 'gatekeeping' or other mechanisms might be constructed so as to give a 'thing' or a system (such as a person, a city, a region, a nation state) qualities of identity, integrity and relative stability. The question of 'agency' in social and biological as well as in physical systems has to be formulated broadly in these terms.

(9) Dialectical enquiry is not itself outside of its own form of argumentation but subject to it. Dialectical enquiry is a *process* that produces *things* in the form of concepts, abstractions, theories and all manner of institutionalized forms of knowledge which stand in their own right only to be supported or undermined by the continuing processes of enquiry. There is, furthermore, a certain relationship implied between the researcher and the researched, a relationship which is not construed in terms of an 'outsider' (the researcher) looking in on the researched as an object, but one between two subjects each of which necessarily internalizes something from the other by virtue of the processes that operate. Observation of the world is, Heisenberg argued, inevitably intervention

in the world, in much the same way that deconstructionists will argue that the reading of a text is fundamental to its production. Marx similarly insisted that only by transforming the world could we transform ourselves and that it is impossible to understand the world without simultaneously changing it as well as ourselves. Dialectics cannot be superimposed on the world as an act of mind over matter (this was Engels's critical mistake, unfortunately replicated by Levins and Lewontin). The underlying unity of theory and social praxis, or for that matter of material and mental activities, can, it seems, never be broken, only attenuated or temporarily alienated.

(10) *Eduction* – the exploration of potentialities for change, for self-realization, for the construction of new totalities (for example, social ecosystems) and the like, rather than deduction or induction – the central motif of dialectical praxis. When Lösch, in his famous opening argument, concluded that our task 'is not to explain our sorry reality, but to improve it' and concluded with his vision of a science which 'like architecture rather than architectural history, creates rather than describes', he was bringing to bear a dialectical (albeit Hegelian) sense of creative science as the exploration of more rational and equitable worlds. It is in this sense that his (infamous) statement that if 'the model does not conform to reality then it is reality that is wrong' is to be understood. Dialectical enquiry necessarily incorporates, therefore, the building of ethical, moral, and political choices *(values)* into its own process and sees the constructed knowledges that result as discourses situated in a play of power. Values, for example, are not imposed as universal abstractions from outside but arrived at through a living process (including intellectual enquiry) embedded in forms of praxis and plays of power attaching to the exploration of this or that potentiality (in ourselves as well as in the world we inhabit). To the degree that a distinctively 'green value theory' has arisen in recent years (see Eckersley, 1992; Fox, 1990), for example, it must be seen as arising out of socio-ecological processes and plays of power. And this search for possibilities was always central to Raymond Williams's work, particularly in his novels, where he seeks again and again to recapture 'a sense of value which has won its way through different kinds of oppression of different forms . . . an ingrained and indestructible yet also changing embodiment of the possibilities of common life'. The search for those possibilities is contained within, rather than articulated after, the research process.

2   DIALECTICAL CONCEPTS, ABSTRACTIONS, AND THEORIES

There is a longstanding discussion in the literature as to whether the world is inherently dialectical or whether the dialectic is simply one convenient set of assumptions or logic to represent certain aspects of physical, biological, and social processes. The former view, which I shall call the strong version of dialectical argumentation, was powerfully promoted by Engels, most particularly in *The Dialectics of Nature* and *Anti-Dühring:* while Marx made no general statement on the subject, he certainly held that social processes at work under capitalism were inherently dialectical. This strong view has come in for considerable criticism in part because of its association with ideas of teleology and doctrines of emergence and immanence which appear almost deterministic in their evolutionary implications. The meaning of this controversy depends in part on how dialectics is represented in the first place. The rather mechanical rendering of Hegel's dialectic as just a matter of thesis, antithesis, and synthesis certainly suggests, when set down synchronically, a rather simplistic teleology (class struggle under capitalism necessarily gives rise to a classless socialism or, in the hands of Lösch, the chaos of the actual world confronted with rational entrepreneurialism gives rise to the rational landscape of freedom and the preservation of cultural roots provided the conditions for rational behaviour prevail). And there is no doubt that Engels in particular looked to the logical and idealist conception of dialectical argumentation set out in Hegel as his model and that he can therefore reasonably be accused of imposing a particular logical conception on the natural and social world. Marx, on the other hand, though he starts with Hegel, seems to have achieved a radical materialist transformation of Hegel's views (cf. Bhaskar, 1989, ch. 7). The way I have specified the dialectical argument above (which owes much to Levins and Lewontin as well as to Ollman), by focusing on the relationships between processes, things and systems, avoids many of the problems which Engels bequeathed and seems to be much more in accord with Marx's own practice (as I shall try to demonstrate below). I therefore see no reason to abandon the strong version of dialectics when formulated in this way. The *least* that can be said of it is that there is as much evidence for the argument that processes constitute things and systems in the natural and social world as there is evidence for any alternative proposition.

There is, however, an acute epistemological problem of how to present, codify, abstract and theorize the vast amount of information of seemingly incomparable status generated out of the kind of research programme which a dialectical stance mandates. The principles of dialectical enquiry as enunciated above (entailing multiple changes of scale, perspective, orientation, and the like, while internalizing contradictions, oppositions, and heterogeneity at every level), *should* generate a perpetual state of motion in our concepts and our thoughts. But the negative side of this flexibility and openness is that it appears to have little chance of producing anything except a vast panoply of insecure and shifting concepts and findings. For those unfamiliar with dialectical thinking, the seeming slipperiness of dialectical concepts elicits a good deal of scepticism, impatience, and distrust. The purpose of multiple approaches to phenomena is, however, to try and identify a restricted number of very general underlying processes which simultaneously *unify and differentiate* the phenomena we see in the world around us. In this sense, dialectics does seek a path towards a certain kind of ontological security, or reductionism – not a reductionism to 'things' but to common generative processes and relations.

This commitment to parsimony and generality with respect to processes (though not to things or systems) is common across a variety of fields, which range from David Bohm's work in quantum theory and its implications for physical, biological, social, and aesthetic forms (see Bohm, 1980; Hiley and Peat, 1987; Bohm and Peat, 1989), to Wilkins's (1987) pursuit of principles of complementarity and the union of opposites in fields as diverse as physics, molecular biology, psychology, music, and the visual arts, and Levins and Lewontin's work on dialectical biology, as well as Marx's dialectical materialism.

Perhaps one of the most interesting findings from such studies is that singular processes can give rise to highly diversified and highly complex as well as often quite unpredictable results. There are precedents for this kind of finding in spatial analysis. Lösch, for example, started with a very simple set of generative principles concerning the maximization of profit subject to monopolistic competition and economies of scale. From these principles he generated landscape patterns of remarkable spatial complexity (I note in passing how many geographers misinterpret his work to be about geometrical patterns directly when it is really about the variety of geographical patterns which can be produced out of a fairly simple set of generative principles). Work on fractals, chaos theory, and the like, illustrates how generative orders of even greater complexity can be developed out of simple rules of process. Bohm and Peat (1989, p. 157) argue, however, that the whole idea of such generative orders 'is not restricted simply to mathematics but is of potential relevance to all areas of experience'. They apply it to painting, musical composition, novel writing, as processes:

> In all this activity, what is crucial is that in some sense the artist is always working from the generative source of the idea and allowing the work to unfold into ever more definite forms. In this regard his or her thought is similar to that which is proper to science. It proceeds from an origin in free play which then unfolds into ever more crystallised forms.

In setting the generative principles to work in this way, Bohm and Peat come close to embracing a very dialectical view of human creativity, one that unifies art and science in a certain complementarity of opposites that, again, Haggett often overtly expresses a certain sympathy for as a basis for geographical work, without quite seeing how to do it other than to instantiate the fact–value distinction as a norm of geographical endeavour.

None of this means that underlying generative processes are easy to identify or specify. Indeed, the immense complexity of 'things' and systems which we encounter makes it particularly hard, given the epistemological problem that we must always start with 'things' and systems as they are, to identify underlying processes and to specify them exactly right. Furthermore, different processes intersect and intertwine – capital circulation and ecological processes intersect, for example – to create complex forms of environmental degradation; this requires either a reformulation of the idea of process under consideration or a means to describe how different processes can and do intersect. The emphasis on prioritizing process which I have here outlined suggests, however, that the search for order which has traditionally characterized Western science since the Renaissance is itself transformed from a search to classify and categorize things and the relations between things, into a search for generative principles which produce orders (that is, things and systems with definable quantitative and qualitative attributes) of different types.

3 RELATIONS WITH OTHER SYSTEMS OF THOUGHT

Dialectical thinking is one out of several possible modes of approach to understanding the human condition and the world in which human life unfolds. It is in many respects intuitively appealing, if only because we experience life as a process rather than as a 'thing' (or as an amalgam of 'things' and relationships between them), and because we are constantly having to cope with the problem of keeping the process going even in the very act of producing the many 'things' with which we surround ourselves. Furthermore, we are all acutely aware of what it means to become committed to the process of maintaining, developing, or letting go of the 'things' we create (such as dwellings, machines, money, skills). Academics surely also will recognize that how we learn is very different from what we write and that the written word often returns to haunt us as the power of a fixed 'thing', an alien force, that can rule our lives even no matter how hard we strive to go beyond. But intuitive appeal has never provided the only or even the main justification for accepting any particular set of epistemological or ontological assumptions as *the* basis for generating knowledge. Indeed, much of the success of Western science has been based upon the construction of counter-intuitive ways of thinking.

A primary opposing system of thought is given by the Cartesian rationality which was built into classical physics and has since become the basis of theorizing in many of the other natural sciences, in engineering, medicine, the social sciences, and philosophy (particularly of the analytic variety). Levins and Lewontin (1985, p. 269) categorize this mode in terms of 'four ontological commitments, which then put their stamp on the process of creating knowledge'. These four commitments are:

- There is a natural set of units or parts of which any whole system is made.
- These units are homogeneous within themselves, at least insofar as they affect the whole of which they are parts.
- The parts are ontologically prior to the whole; that is, the parts exist in isolation and come together to make wholes. The parts have intrinsic properties, which they possess in isolation and which they lend to the whole. In the simplest cases the whole is nothing but the sum of its parts; more complex cases allow for interactions of the parts to produce added properties of the whole.
- Causes are separate from effects, causes being the properties of subjects, and effects the properties of objects. While causes may respond to information coming from effects (so-called feedback loops), there is no ambiguity about which is causing subject and which is caused object. (This distinction persists in statistics as independent and dependent variables.)

This Cartesian view is widespread and it, too, has a certain intuitive appeal. We encounter 'things' (for example, individuals) and systems (for example, transport and communication networks) which appear to have a stable and self-evident existence so that it appears perfectly reasonable to build knowledge upon categorizations of them and upon the pattern of causal relations between them. From the dialectical point of view, however, this is to look at matters in an unduly restrictive and one-sided way. Levins and Lewontin go on, correctly in my view, to characterize the Cartesian view as an 'alienated' form of reasoning because it depicts a world in which 'parts are separated from wholes and reified as things in themselves, causes separated from effects, subjects separated from objects'. Marx was similarly critical of the 'common-sense' view which whenever 'it succeeds in seeing a distinction it fails to see a unity, and where it sees a unity it fails to see a distinction' and so 'surreptitiously petrifies' distinctions to the point where they become incapable of generating new ideas, let alone new insights into how the world works (cited in Ollman, 1990, p. 44). He would, doubtless, be equally scathing about the atomistic and causative reasoning which dominates in contemporary economics and sociology, the methodological individualism which pervades much of current political philosophy, and the like.

But it would be wrong, however, to view Cartesian and dialectical conceptions as fundamentally incompatible in *all* senses, as Capra (1982) and to some degree Levins and Lewontin (1985) tend to do. Cast in a more complementary light they can provide a fecund source of new ideas. In theoretical physics what were seen in the nineteenth century as radically incommensurable propositions 'that matter is in its essence of a particle nature, or that it is of a wave nature', were ultimately treated as a unity under the conception in quantum theory. Here, too, there is an intuitive rendition which makes for a common-sense reading. We all know what Heraclitus meant when he said that we cannot step into the same river twice, but we also all know that there is a sense in which we can return again and again to the banks of the same river. At this point, however, there may indeed arise some sort of claim for the superiority of the dialectical view, precisely because it allows for an understanding of 'things' and systems as if they are real and stable as a special case of the proposition that processes are always at work creating and sustaining 'things' and systems. The converse proposition appears not to hold, however. Cartesian thinking has a hard time coping with change and process except in terms of comparative statics, cause and effect feedback loops, or the linearities built into examination of experimentally determined and mechanically specified rates of change (as represented in differential calculus). And this was the broadly positivist programme of scientific thinking to which Haggett confined himself.

Ollman's (1990, p. 32) argument is particularly strong on this last point:

In the view which currently dominates the social sciences, things exist *and* undergo change. The two are logically distinct. History is something that happens to things; it is not part of their nature. Hence the difficulty of examining change in subjects from which it has been removed at the start. Whereas Marx . . . abstracts 'every historical form as in fluid movement, and therefore takes into account its transient nature *not less* than its momentary existence'.

4 DIALECTICAL APPLICATIONS – MARX'S CONCEPTION OF CAPITAL

I want here to look more closely at Marx's particular use of dialectical thinking. My purpose is not to argue whether he was right or wrong, but to illustrate *how* he puts dialectical thinking to work to understand capitalism as a social system defined and bounded by a process of capital circulation. His language in *Capital* directly signals adherence to a materialist dialectics in which the priority of process over thing and system is everwhere apparent. This is captured by his statement, cited above, that he aims to abstract 'every historical social form as in fluid movement' so as to take into account 'its transient nature not less than its momentary existence'. The prior commitment to process rather than to 'thing' or system could not be more plainly stated. Capital is directly concep-tualized, therefore, as a *process* or as a *relation* rather than as a 'thing'. It is viewed, in its simplest incarnation, as a flow which at one 'moment' assumes the 'form' of money, and at another assumes the 'form' of commodities or the 'form' of productive activity. 'Value', Marx writes, 'is here the active factor in a process, in which, while constantly assuming the form in turn of money and commodi-ties, it at the same time changes in magnitude, differentiates itself by throwing off surplus value from itself . . . Value therefore now becomes value in process, money in process and, as such, capital.' This process definition differs radically from that typically incorporated into neo-classical economics where capital is treated as an unproblematic (that is, non-contradictory) stock of assets (of things) with certain qualitative and quantitative attributes which, when set in motion by human agency, embody causative powers (for example, capital investment creates employment). Marx's point is not that there is no such thing as a stock of assets, but that we cannot understand what those assets are about, what they are worth or how they might be used without understanding the process in which they are embedded, in particular the process which gives rise to, reconstitutes, maintains, devalues or destroys them. When Marx argues that 'capital does' or 'capital creates' he is *not* arguing that a thing called capital has causal power, but that the process of capital circulation, understood as a whole, is at the centre of vital social transformations and for that reason has to be looked upon as embodying a powerful generative principle affecting social life (a proposition that even university faculties must surely better understand these days!).

We can understand this argument more generally by appeal to the following statement drawn from the *Grundrisse*:

> The conclusion we reach is not that production, distribution, exchange and consumption are identical, but they all form members of a totality, distinctions within a unity. Production predominates not only over itself, in the antithetical definition of production, but over other moments as well. The process always returns to production to begin anew. That exchange and consumption cannot be predominant is self-evident. Like-wise, distribution as distribution of products; while as distribution of the agents of production it is itself a moment of production. A definite

production thus determines a definite consumption, distribution and exchange as well as *definite relations between these different moments.* Admittedly, however, *in its one-sided form,* production is itself determined by the other moments. For example if the market (that is, the sphere of exchange) expands, then production grows in quantity and the divisions between its different branches become deeper. A change in distribution changes production, for example, concentration of capital, different distribution of the population between town and country, etc. Finally, the needs of consumption determine production. Mutual interaction takes place between the different moments. This is the case with every organic whole.

Those unfamiliar with dialectical ways of thinking will, quite reasonably, regard such a statement as obscure if not incredibly tautological (the obscurity in part derives from the fact that this was written as notes for Marx's own guidance and not as a definitive text designed to persuade a sceptical public). But if we track back to my initial representation of dialectical thinking, it becomes plain enough what Marx is saying. The reproduction of social life is being treated as a continuous process operating within certain bounds which define a totality or a whole. Under capitalism (as well as in certain other kinds of society) this process becomes internally differentiated so as to contain distinctive 'moments' of production, exchange, distribution, and consumption. When we look closely at any one of these 'moments' we find that it cannot be understood independently of the process as a whole which passes through all the other moments. Production, therefore, necessarily *internalizes* impulses and pressures emanating from consumption, exchange, and distribution. But to think of production only in those terms is to think of it 'one-sidedly'. We also have to recognize that production internalizes influences from itself (that is, it is non-heterogeneous and contradictory – this is why Marx says that production is 'antithetical' to itself) and that creative and transformative powers with respect to the process as a whole potentially reside within its domain. But that potentiality presumably resides elsewhere also. If we understand production in a broad sense to mean *any* transformative activity (no matter where it occurs), then plainly we are by definition asserting the 'predominance' of production over everything else. But Marx also insists that the point of maximum leverage, the point of maximum transformative capacity and, in the famous last instance, the 'moment' which exercises a 'determinant' transformative power over the system as a whole, lies within rather than without the domain of production. Transformative activities in other domains then only have relevance for the process as a whole in so far as they are internalized within the production moment.

Now if we read this passage in Cartesian terms, we might interpret Marx as saying that production as an independent entity causes changes in consumption, exchange and distribution. But this is exactly what Marx is *not* saying. He cannot say it, precisely because production, according to his conception, internalizes relations with all the other moments (and vice versa). Yet he *is* saying (and I am not concerned whether he was right or wrong) that *the* transformative moment in the whole process resides at the moment of production and that it is there where we have to concentrate our attention if we wish to understand the creative mechanisms by which the process (in this case the circulation of capital) is reconstituted, transformed or enhanced. How, in short, are the powers that reside in this process of capital circulation mobilized at the moment of production in such a way as to transform the system of which it forms but a fleeting and inherently unstable moment? This seems a perfectly reasonable question to ask. It is in principle no different from asking how does any one individual internalize certain powers that reside in their environment, creatively transform them and thereby change the course of history or of evolution?

There are all sorts of things to be said pro or contra the Marxian (or more broadly, the dialectical) view, of course. It may be, for example, that there are other 'moments' (such as reproduction and all that this entails) which ought to be incorporated in the schema or that his stress on the significance of *labour* in production as *the* radical point of departure for the transformation of both social relations and the relation to nature is overemphatic. But the fundamental point I want to insist on here is that critique of Marx (and of those Marxists who follow his dialectical procedures) should at least recognize what he is doing and how he is doing it and not read him or (mis)represent him unthinkingly through Cartesian, positivist, analytic, or even realist lenses.

Let us suppose, however, that Marx correctly captured the general process of capital circulation through his abstractions. It is then important to see how such a theoretical formulation is (a) elaborated upon and specified and (b) put to work as an 'explanatory' device.

With respect to (a) we find Marx building more and more specific versions of his argument concerning the circulation of capital in general by recognizing that different rules of circulation attach to different kinds of capital, such as industrial, money (finance), merchant, landed and even state capital (borrowings and taxation) while differences can also be specified according to the physical form of the capital (whether it is fixed, large scale, embedded in the land, etc.) and the peculiarities of organizational forms (joint stock companies, small businesses, land tenure conditions in agriculture, and the like). And the uncertain dynamics of class differentiation and struggle is a major source of uneven development, internalized contradiction and instability. The process of capital circulation in general is modified by the specific conditions of circulation which attach to different forms and conditions. Capital in general now has to be considered not as an undifferentiated unity but as something which is heterogeneous and often internally contradictory. The discovery of these internal differentiations depends on the historical, geographical, and theoretical interrogation of material circumstances (this is why Marx's dialectics have to be considered as coupled with a certain conception of materialism).

To elaborate on the theory in this way is not, however, to introduce a mass of *external* contingencies. The organization of firms or of nation states, to take just a couple of examples, is not an external event that interferes with a pure circulation process of capital. In each case it is to be conceptualized as a social form (a particular kind of entity or 'thing') which arises out of the circulation process and 'commands' a particular 'moment' in the circulation of capital. It has a shaping influence by virtue of the powers it internalizes and the creativity of the transformations (social as well as material) which it accomplishes. But its existence is embedded in the continuous flow of the process of which it is a part and, like any other entity, it internalizes contradictions, is heterogeneous, and inherently unstable by virtue of the complex processes which support, reconstitute, or develop it. The recent history of both firms and nation states would, I think, broadly justify such a view of their status. Lewontin (1982), incidentally, provides a similar interpretation for the mediating role of the organism (in the context of genetic mutations and environmental adaptations) in evolution.

The work of elaboration, further specification and better articulation of the theory is ongoing and can never be complete, if only because the world is always changing, in part *because of* the creative thoughts and activities generated by dialecticians. Theorizing, like any other process, is as continuous and transformative, as heterogeneous and as contradictory, as any other process which dialecticians confront. There is always plenty more to do and innumerable points of theoretical intervention to be examined and acted upon. The process of dialectical thinking and its application to human affairs has also to be produced, sustained, developed. The aim and objective of my own work (for example, *The Limits to Capital*) has in part been given over to identifying (dialectically) extensions to the theory and better specifying its operation with respect to time and space. But I would also want to better define the domains within which certain kinds of capitalistic processes operate and with what effects and to consider what kinds of transformative opportunities thereby arise to change the trajectory of social life.

Turning to (b), above, as an explanatory device, the theory does not operate as a simple predictor of events (states of things). It has to be viewed more as a set of generative and transformative principles, embedded in continuous processes, which, by virtue of internalized heterogeneity and contradiction, has the capacity to create all kinds of new but always transient states of things. Here, too, we encounter a major source of misunderstanding. To explain phenomena in terms of the circulation of capital certainly does not imply that all phenomena that lie within its domain have to be or are the same. Limiting and quite extraordinary situations could arise where this was indeed the case, but the generative and transformative principles embedded in the circulation process are such as to give rise to as many shapes and forms of social life (of commodities or of capitalist cities, for example) someone like Mandelbrot can generate through fractal methods. Yet there is an underlying unity to the production of such differences and that underlying unity sets limits on the nature of the differentiations which can be generated. Socialist social relations cannot, for example, be produced out of capitalistic generative principles.

The purpose of materialist enquiry is not to *test* in some positivistic or formal sense whether or not capital circulation exists (we know it does) but to show in what forms, over what domains (within what bounds) and with what effects it operates and what possibilities exist for transformative behaviour. Can we show, for example, that what is usually referred to as 'cultural production' lies within its domain or not? Are there circumstances in, for example, the circulation of capital through built environments or in the production of space which require us to rethink the specification of the process? Can we track the circulation of capital through state apparatuses and functions and what does this mean for our conception of the limits and potentialities of state power? What happens if capital circulation is barred from direct operation in certain sectors (for example, health care or education) or if it is suddenly liberated to flow into arenas formerly denied to it? In what ways and in what directions is social change promoted by capital circulation and in what respects can this be regarded as a stable rather than as an inherently unstable process?

In the instance of capital circulation (itself a loosely bounded domain of Marxist enquiry) the problem is to explore the forms and domains of operation, the *how* of generative and transformative principles at work. This implies a particular materialist research strategy. Treating nation states, for example, as homogeneous entities and examining their behaviour and performance according to a set of economic indicators is of limited value. The principles of dialectical thinking would suggest that the focus of enquiry should be on *how* nation states internalize powers (or lose their grip on such powers), in what ways they are heterogeneous and internally contradictory, and in what ways these internalized tensions result in the kind of creativity which leads to new configurations of activity, and, finally, in what ways such activities transform social life.

The charge that Marxists 'read off' from theory to reality is, from this perspective, sadly misplaced. This is not to claim that all Marxist enquiry of this sort is error free. Generative principles can get distorted, domains of operation can be imagined rather than substantiated, and materialist studies of actual processes are just as liable to get lost in a thicket of detail as any other kind of research. Through construction of generative principles and theories, Marxists themselves seek, of course, to change the world. But this does not imply that the results of enquiry will always be appropriate or that they can never be confused and destructive. Marxist argumentation cannot, any more than any other way of thinking, escape the dilemmas described by Bohm and Peat (1989, p. 57) as follows:

> We cannot impose any world view we like and hope that it will work. The cycle of perception and action cannot be maintained in a totally arbitrary fashion unless we collude to suppress the things we do not wish to see while, at the same time, trying to maintain, at all costs, the things that we desire most in our image of the world. Clearly the cost of supporting such false vision of reality must eventually be paid.

And, it is fair to comment, many have paid the cost of such a false vision on the part of Marxism. But then no other processes of thought can claim a mantle of untarnished virtue either. There is now a vast and quite intimidating terrain of theory and action to be fought over and the stakes involved are peculiarly high. Dialectical thinking, with its focus on change, has a strong claim to be at least one of the key modes of enquiry. Treating different modes of thought as complementary though antagonistic rather than as mutually exclusive and unrelated can, furthermore, yield creative insights. This is, in fact, an ancient principle that the Greeks understood well. 'The finest harmony is born from differences,' said Heraclitus, and 'discord is the law of all becoming'. Marx, likewise held that 'one-sided' representations are always restricting and problematic and that the best way to proceed was always 'to rub together conceptual blocks in such a way that they catch fire'. Perhaps a little rubbing in the right way can chart creative ways to think about socio-geographical and environmental change. I think this is the geni that Haggett let out of the bottle and the best the rest of us can do is to follow its wisps and trails wheresoever it leads us.

REFERENCES

Berry, B.J.L. (1964). 'Cities as systems within systems of cities.' *Papers and Proceedings of the Regional Science Association*, 13,147–63.

Bhaskar, R. (1989). *Reclaiming Reality*. London: Verso.

Bohm, D. (1980). *Wholeness and the Implicate Order*. London: Routledge & Kegan Paul.

Bohm, D. & Peat, F.D. (1989). *Science, Order and Creativity*. London: Routledge.

Capra, F. (1982). *The Turning Point: Science, Society and the Rising Culture*. New York, Simon & Schuster.

Duncan, J. & Ley, D. (1982). 'Structural Marxism and human geography: A critical assessment. *Annals of the Association of American Geographers*, 72, 30–59.

Eckersley, R. (1992). *Environmentalism and Political Theory: Towards an Ecocentric Approach*. London: University College London Press.

Engels, F. (1940 edn). *The Dialectics of Nature*. New York: International Publishers.

Engels, F. (1947 edn). *Anti-Dühring*. London: Lawrence & Wishart.

Fox, W. (1990). *Toward a Transpersonal Ecology: Developing New Foundations for Environmentalism*. Boston: Shambhala.

Giddens, A. (1984). *The Constitution of Society*. Cambridge: Polity Press.

Haggett, P. (1965). *Locational Analysis in Human Geography*. London: Edward Arnold.

Harvey, D. (1982). *The Limits to Capital*. Oxford: Basil Blackwell.

Hiley, B. & Peat, F. (eds) (1987). *Quantum Implications: Essays in Honour of David Bohm*. London: Routledge.

Ingold, T. (1986). *The Appropriation of Nature: Essays on Human Ecology and Social Relations*. Manchester: Manchester University Press.

Lefebvre, H. (1991). *The Production of Space*. Oxford: Basil Blackwell.

Levins, R. & Lewontin, R. (1985). *The Dialectical Biologist*. Cambridge, Mass.: Harvard University Press.

Lewontin, R. (1982). 'The role of the organism in evolution.' In H. Plotkin (ed.), *Learning, Development and Culture*. Chichester: Wiley.

Lösch, A. (1954). *The Economics of Location*. New Haven: Yale University Press.

Marx, K. (1967) *Capital*. New York: International Publishers.

Marx, K. (1973). *Grundrisse*. Harmondsworth: Penguin Books.

Naess, A. (1989). *Ecology, Community and Lifestyle*. Cambridge: Cambridge University Press.

Ollman, B. (1976). *Alienation: Marx's Conception of Man in Capitalist Society*. Cambridge: Cambridge University Press.

Ollman, B. (1990). 'Putting dialectics to work: the process of abstraction in Marx's method.' *Rethinking Marxism*, 3, 26–74.

Ollman, B. (1993). *Dialectical Investigations*. New York: Routledge.

Thompson, d'Arcy (1961 edn). *On Growth and Form*. Cambridge: Cambridge University Press.

Wilkins, M.H.F. (1987). 'Complementarity and the union of opposites.' In B. Hiley & F. Peat (eds) (1987). *Quantum Implications: Essays in Honour of David Bohm.* London: Routledge.

Williams, R. (1977). *Marxism and Literature.* Oxford: Oxford University Press.

Zimmermann, M. (1988). 'Quantum theory, intrinsic value, and pantheism.' *Environmental Ethics*, 10, 3–30.

2

Teaching the Spatiality of Geography Concretely with the Abstract

P.R. Gould

1 ON A PERSONAL NOTE: THINKING IS THANKING

Sometimes things do not fit neatly into boxes, including the titles of essays. But to be true to itself, thinking has to reflect the messiness of the world, even as we try to impose order upon it, and the title contains five words which refuse to let go of one another – teaching, spatiality, geography, concretely, and abstract. For me they form the vertices of a four-dimensional structure lying at the core of our discipline, and it does not take much imagination to see Peter in the middle of this topological simplex holding the vertices together – a bit like Leonardo's man spanning his circle with outstretched fingers and toes. Except, of course, Peter is decently clothed – naked emperors need not apply – and he has a tougher job. Holding a four-dimensional structure together when you are only three-dimensional yourself requires considerable dexterity and intellectual concentration, because at any one moment you have to let go of one of the vertices to secure the other four. May this rather strange imagery and thinking be my thanking, the *danken* in the *denken*, for all his efforts over the years to hold things together.

2 GEOGRAPHY

Since all the words are connected, it matters little where we begin to think our way around the structure, but recalling that West Country folk like Peter are called to geography by the gods, proper respect requires that we start with the

This essay was written in the small mountain village of Autrans in the Vercors from memory, and without any of the bibliographic resources normally available to scholarly writing. For this reason there are not, and cannot be, the usual footnoted references and acknowledgements. I hope the many who recognize their ideas will understand.

vertex Geography itself. Immediately we feel something close to an oxymoronic tension, because if we separate this highly integrative perspective on the world from the rest of our structure it seems to stand in isolation. And so, perhaps, it did 40 years ago when Peter began his career, or at least with such tenuous links to other ways of looking and thinking that it seemed severed and apart, contributing little from its own intellectual richness and potential to others. This distancing from a larger world of enquiry now appears to be due partly to external circumstances, and partly self-imposed. The external circumstances seem to be the culmination of a curious and damaging historical process of intellectual fragmentation that in the case of geography has yet to be properly explicated by intellectual historians in general, or by historians of the social sciences in particular. Something happened in that late eighteenth- and early nineteenth-century world to fray and abrade the filaments connecting geographic thinking to other modes of thought, especially the historical, the mode heightening the sense of movement and change along the temporal dimension. And by 'geographic thinking' I mean the inherent, essential, and quite properly taken-for-granted importance of incorporating the spatial dimensions of human existence into all enquiry. It is almost as though the convulsions of the age of geographic exploration had exhausted the capacity of European thought to think further, that the continuous geographic probing and exposing, literally unimaginable to an earlier fifteenth-century world, had so informed and radically changed Europe's life over 200 years that thinking in the spatial domain could go no further for the moment. Perhaps something analogous happened to physics in the latter half of the nineteenth century. After 200 years of the Newtonian paradigm there was little left to do except to tie up a few loose ends – akin to filling in a few blank areas on the map, essentially a mopping-up operation with the end in sight.

The fraying threads were abraded further in the nineteenth century by the emergence of the human sciences as these sloughed off as formal disciplines from the old mother lode of philosophy, in much the same way as the physical and biological sciences had defined themselves in the two centuries before. With roots in Vico, Condorcet, and other *philosophes* of the eighteenth century too complex to untangle here, it became thinkable to treat the human world in the distanced fashion that had proved so astoundingly capable of ordering and illuminating the physical and living worlds. Yet as these new, and even then increasingly specialized ways of enquiry became formalized and accepted as bodies of knowledge by the conservative university structures, so the spatial domain appears to have gone into concealment once again.

Now if it is not already implicitly clear, then let me make it explicit: these thoughts, and others that follow, are more of the nature of highly compressed speculations rather than definite assertions, thoughts for research rather than well-supported statements. So let me assert the theme again: something happened in that nineteenth-century world to hide the spatial domain from the then fresh and new ways of thinking about the human condition. This did not, and perhaps could not, happen in the physical world, where the ds/dt, d^2, and other algebraic expressions of space and time virtually defined huge areas of enquiry. It is unthinkable that physics could let go of the spatial domain – there would be no physics left. It happened less in the sciences of the living world, where the sensitivity of a Linné or a Darwin to geographic habitat and variation was never quite lost, and was still there to emerge with new force in ecological studies in the middle of the twentieth century. But in economics, political science, sociology, anthropology, and other offshoots, the dominance of the temporal domain over the spatial is more than just a passing curiosity of intellectual history. It constitutes an excision of thought, a denial of opportunity for thinking, that had, and continues to have, numbing consequences for these increasingly isolated disciplines, particularly in a world where a concern for human-environmental systems becomes more and more prominent for literally vital, that is life and death, reasons.

Why did this happen? Speculation one: in their emulation of the physical sciences, what we might call the social physics stage in which large areas of the social sciences are still stuck, the dynamics of the differential dt was absorbed but left the ds and all its spatial consequences behind. We can find a reason, if not an excuse, for such intellectual blindness. Here it is, as speculation two: in an age of revolution – technical, political, economic and social – thinking is almost forced to emphasize the temporal domain. Take the familiar three score years and ten: a person born in 1720 has seen 'a world turned upside down' by 1790 – the very tune played by Cornwallis's troops during their surrender at Yorktown. Born in 1790, a person by 1860 has seen a world so changed by technology that it was previously unimaginable. A Balzac, travelling for the first time on a train from Paris at the wicked speed of 50 kph, comments that the world races towards him, expands and disappears in a bewildering and blurred screen of impressions on either side. Can the human being survive such speeds if experienced too often? This is the time when we begin to hear comments that the world is shrinking, but the measures are always in *time* – around the world in 80 days. The inherent spatiality of technological change, the fact that everything with a history must always have a geography, still lies hidden from thought. As for 1860 to 1930, we are still children of those revolutions in aviation, electrification, and communication, electronic revolutions that follow ever-faster on the heels of one another. The conclusion? We live today in a spaceless world where there is no geography any more! There is no geography any more when it is precisely the quickening, dynamic, and always spatial structures of the human world that shape our lives. The AIDS virus knows this even if we do not. Sometimes we ignore the spatiality and dynamic geography of our world at our mortal peril. But notice that in acknowledging this how space and time in the human world have once again been conjoined. We have the capacity to be spatio-temporalists once more.

Forty years ago this capacity was not there. The severance of space and time begun in the nineteenth century had been completed in the twentieth almost as a self-inflicted wound. Time was for the historians, and history, despite the clichés, never repeated itself, although similarities could be found. Area, and its differentiation into places, was for geographers, and geography never repeated itself – even if southern California did have a Mediterranean climate. Some of the high gurus of the field, whose masterful works became objects of thoughtless adoration rather than critical catalysts to thought, even denigrated the efforts of their younger colleagues to inject an historical and dynamic element into their studies of regional development. Some even misused power to build and shape the barricades behind which geography, and its inherent, but too often latent sense of spatial dynamics, could safely wither away in intellectual isolation. In North America such 'withering away' was precisely what happened in some universities with high intellectual standards, and properly so. Properly so, because the generation that let geography as a formidable intellectual discipline slip from its grasp never received much support from its peers. You get intellectual respect and collegial support when you can show others, not the least your own students, that the spatial perspective illuminates and brings out of concealment things of importance that others do not see. Otherwise what is the point? In Europe, many wondered what geographers did except to teach others to be teachers of geography, not a dishonourable occupation, but hardly the *raison d'être* for a presence in the university.

'Changed, all changed', wrote the poet Yeats, about another sudden shift with a concomitant tightening of resolution. And here we enter dangerous ground, perhaps not for the first time. Like judiciously edited and ego-enhancing autobiographies, one should be properly suspicious of accounts of intellectual changes by those who were around at the time to participate. Predilections to self-serving have a tendency to assert themselves, like Robert Graves's 'Down, Wanton, Down!' But the alternative is to leave the field of interpretation entirely to those who came later, and who have already started to provide narratives that leave rapidly ageing participants of the 1950s and 1960s breathless with wonder at the far-reaching capabilities of the human imagination. Nor does projecting the multidimensional complexity of intellectual influences on to planar graphs help very much. Once in the literature they have a certain graphic stolidness that is difficult to budge.

Nevertheless, and despite all the qualifications of paradigmic shift, including outright denials, all – well, much – has changed. This is not the place for a detailed account, which requires in any case extensive scholarly inquiry properly grounded in contemporary intellectual history, but one only has to point to the immense vitality in geographic publishing to sense the radical change that has come about in the 40 years spanning the professional life of a Peter Haggett. And I certainly do not mean simply books with a technical content, but a broad spectrum of publications from the reflective and theoretical, to substantive contributions to cultural, historical, and what I can only call 'involved' geography. Fortunately, many of these are not written for specialists, but reach out to much wider professional and educated lay audiences, so infusing other fields with a sense of the importance of place within a larger and always interrelated space.

It is the spatiality of contemporary geography that others respond to, whether archaeologists, epidemiologists, urban historians, sociologists, and many others, often with an enthusiasm and excitement that geographers find slightly bewildering. The map, used with imagination and skill, still has a power to move, to make others say 'I never thought about it like that before', that surprises those who take it too often for granted. And in series, when a dynamic sequence of maps brings space and time together, joining spatiality and temporality once more, the effect is sometimes startling. A sequence showing the diffusion of AIDS from 1982 to 1990 in the United States caused one epidemiologist at the International Conference on AIDS in Amsterdam in 1992 to exclaim 'I think we have a new paradigm here!', while their publication in *Time* (31 August 1992), brought numerous requests from non-geographers to republish. In fact, the numbers and locations could have been given to teenagers as an exercise in drawing contour maps, and we recall that the map has been around since Babylon. A new paradigm? John Snow must be turning in his grave.

So it is the inherent but sometimes latent spatiality of geography that has renewed the field, a way of looking, thinking and writing with few if any precedents in the first half of the twentieth century. How and why did this happen?

3 SPATIALITY

There are still many who deny that anything particularly startling happened in the late 1950s and early 1960s to enlarge the possibilities for thinking in geography. So denigrating was the chorus challenging the claims to paradigmic shift that 20 years later I got cold feet myself and used a mealymouthed '(r)evolution' as an obsequious genuflection of which I am now somewhat ashamed. After all, in the same book, *The Geographer At Work*, the evidence was there in the very language that geographers used, and since we think in language the same dramatic rise in the use of the word 'spatial' reflected an equally dramatic change in thinking – at least among a good and generally energetic number of then young geographers. Indeed, it would be interesting to hear what other interpretation the new hermeneuticists could place upon this empirically grounded graphic 'text'. I am sure they will think of several: no one has ever accused them of a lack of imagination.

Like any revolution, new ways and forms are sought in a context of dissatis-factions with the old, and excesses of zeal are to be expected. These, it should be noted, can always be challenged to produce modifications and more modest claims, but such enthusiasms are worth orders of magnitude more intellectually than the smug platitudes and banalities preceding them. For within the latter, almost by definition, there is no hope of change, no opening to enlarge the horizons for thinking. Trapped within Kuhn's paradigms of 'normal science', thinking plods along following essentially prescribed, that is already written, ways. Any teacher who forgets this does so at the peril of stultifying the growth in his or her students.

Again, this is not a detailed intellectual history, but it is worth recalling that the deep dissatisfaction with traditional perspectives and modes of inquiry was expressed by young geographers steeped in the same traditional ways. I suggest that as undergraduates most of them accepted such traditional forms in the first years, hoping and assuming that things would become better and more intel-lectually challenging by the last undergraduate years, and certainly after the quantum change that surely must justify geography in graduate schools oriented to research and the production of new and worthwhile knowledge. There must be something justifying the existence of geography as an intellectually demanding discipline other than the almost ubiquitous diagrams of overlapping circles in presidential addresses showing geography tying together everyone else's work, or the equally static and atemporal intersecting planes that appeared in certain 'higher works' of the field. Either we had something to offer ourselves beyond an intellectual begging bowl to be filled with scraps from other disciplines, or we might as well become members of some other earth or human science and let geography go.

But to think this way, a sort of intellectual escapism, was precisely and paradoxically to find one's self back behind the *laager*, the circle of defensive and justificatory wagons that had been drawn so tightly in the first half of the century against imaginary hordes of savage colleagues in the university. In fact, the real problem was to straighten out the wagon train of geography, whip up the horses, and get it moving again across intellectually difficult, but always challenging terrain. This was not appreciated by many of those who had carefully constructed the defensive circle and had skulked inside to take defensive potshots at the savages who became more and more disinterested in such peculiar behaviour. With considerable justification, many savages suggested that wagon trains and unexercised horses should be left outside the walls of the university.

So I will submit my third speculation, to be subject one day to critical and thorough inquiry: what emerged as a focus, sometimes brazenly, sometimes incoherently, was the inherent, but non-exclusive spatiality of human existence in geography to match the inherent but non-exclusive temporality in history. That they should never have been split apart is obvious today, but certainly was not obvious then. Indeed, and as I have noted before, the dynamic potential of the temporal dimension was often explicitly excluded by the geographic tradition, or reduced to static and unconnected time slices across the spatio-temporal cube to make time and change non-intrusive, and so non-challenging elements. And here, essentially as a stage aside, I should note that this speculative narrative is concerned exclusively with human geography. The human-environmental theme to emerge and be renewed so prominently in the 1980s was still far off, except for a handful of geographers. As for physical geographers, they were quite happy then, as most of them still are today, ordering the world in the Newtonian framework.

But what I can only call the inherent spatiality of human affairs was creeping back into human thought along all sorts of then-obscure rivulets. In retrospect we can hardly be surprised that the texts of Christaller and Lösch were seized upon with such enthusiasm, or that the nineteenth-century models of von Thünen and Reilly were freshened up and reapplied. While Christaller's text still had a static feel to it, it left room for thinking to consider how such patterns came about and interacted. As for Lösch, the spatio-temporal framework is explicitly in everything from regional adjustments to the diffusion of price waves and depressions. Even in von Thünen, land use was not a static thing, as he knew perfectly well from the meticulous records he kept over 20 years as an estate manager in East Prussia. Weather, rotation schemes, applications of fertilizer, technology, improved breeding, diseases – all are variables producing a dynamic in the human use of the earth. Reilly's work on spatial interaction was refurbished, and 'gravity thinking' in one way or another still informs virtually every aspect of interactive modelling, despite the difficulties of gaining unequivocal interpretations to the numerical measures of distance effects. Even John Graunt was brought out from his mid-seventeenth-century hiding place, and new appreciation given to his concern for 'intrinsick' and 'extrinsick' factors of location.

It was not just spatiality that was flowing into the spaces created by enlarging the horizons, but temporality too. By the 1980s spatio-temporality so informs geographic thinking that it has become a taken-for-granted in specialities as wide ranging as scientifically informed medical geography to the humanistic implications of the geometry of landscapes in cultural geography. The sweeping arrows of a Meinig, the ordered spaces and landscapes of a Cosgrove, the informing and devastating spatial clusters of an Openshaw, the parametric adaptation to spatial structure in expansion methodologies of a Casetti, all stand in a world of research possibilities permeated today with genuinely spatial thinking. I submit that such spatiality was virtually unthinkable in the discipline 50 years ago, and I challenge the professional reader to find genuinely informing precedents before the middle 1950s. As for 'feminine space', it was nowhere in sight. That there might be a literally engendered woman's world, with a different geometric constraint and meaning, would have brought bemused looks from both women and men alike.

But 'spatiality' has an abstract feel to it, indeed is an abstraction of a high philosophical order. We see today that any human expression is in some quite profound sense an 'abstraction', despite the rather archaic calls to realism that echo with increasing faintness across the valleys of geography. The abstract, the willingness to distance oneself from the particular and seek some degree of generality, is an informing vertex of our rather strange four-dimensional struc-ture. How did this come to be emphasized?

4 THE ABSTRACT

In one sense, any move to describe, let alone analyse, requires a degree of abstraction, so a claim might be made here that really nothing new had appeared. Geographic texts, both written and graphic, had not only been in place for hundreds of years, but effectively defined the discipline. We already had those simplifications, compressions and abstractions of reality that this new-fangled and jargony generation were calling 'models'. After all, every map was a model: what was all the fuss about?

The fuss – and it was a fuss that effectively blocked the publication of new works in the 1960s, so producing in turn an explosion of new journals – the fuss seems to have been the production of numerical and algebraic 'texts' that were unfamiliar in the tradition, and therefore not geography. A few, more perspica-cious, not to say mature and relaxed geographers began to see such algebraic or numerically parameterized statements as alternative ways to find 'signals in the noise', to search for more general statements that might help us see those always unique events as particular instances of more general possibilities. Those with some genuine scientific and philosophical background saw such attempts as quite normal in the scientific tradition, and also wondered what all the fuss was about. Indeed, it is difficult to recapture the sense of tension that was felt by many at that time. There were some rather extreme claims that certain geometrically expressed laws determined human affairs, but these soon bumped into the problem that human beings can make choices to break any law written to describe them, even if it means dying for those choices. Still, and like many making more extreme claims, the 'geometers' left a residue of useful insights behind them.

And so regression lines, trend surfaces, components and factors, and a variety of other means of linear decomposition and ordering were imposed upon empirical observations of the human world. Great chunks of variance were absorbed by these linear functions, which were then displayed with proper pride as worthwhile geographic generalities; while residuals, unique and error factors, and aliased spectral components were thrown in the garbage can, or plotted in various graphical forms to display their worthless nature. Meaning, of course, that no one looking at them could give them any convincing interpretation. And if we realize today that even then God was not a linear mathematician, the imposed functional structures often did clarify considerable complexity, even if the clarification was only classificatory in nature. But then classification itself was another instance of partitional thinking that frequently imposed order by hacking tightly connected complexity apart and putting it into tidy little taxonomic boxes. And if the particular taxonomic algorithm you used did not give you what you wanted to see before you started, then there were always plenty of other algorithms around that probably would.

The deity's name was invoked above neither facetiously nor in vain. The abstraction produced by the mathematical ordering of human affairs generated feelings of disquiet from other than traditional quarters. There was an often unexpressed but informing undercurrent of moral outrage, and I think it is no accident that sharp questions about the reification of the human world were often posed by geographers with strong, though quite private religious convictions. They were not alone: others with an increasingly rich philosophical background also questioned the 'thingification' of the human being, and pointed out how such intellectual tidiness could be the joy of the bureaucrat with hands on the levers of power. It would take some time to clarify this issue, to realize that *any* mode of abstraction, including language, constituted a hierarchy of increasing reification, paralleled by a matching hierarchy of increasingly abstract spaces and concomitant geometries. But these insights, and the sensitivity to language itself, were to lie in the future, and they take us far beyond our present speculative narrative. The moral tension, however, remains with us in teaching, research, consulting, and every other area of intellectual endeavour. It is something to be lived with, agonizingly for some of us who see it as an inescapable part of being a thinking person. For others the problematic is not seen, or is dismissed as a precious posturing of a too sensitive soul. After all, we have to be realistic.

It was not only the numerical parameterization of functional descriptions that characterized moves to the abstract. Whether expressed in graphic or algebraic form, abstract modelling, as a means of description seldom seen in the discipline before, became not only increasingly acceptable, but increasingly required by those controlling the purse strings of agencies providing research grants. It was, after all, the scientific way to go, even if abstract models in geography meant, by definition, excising thought from place-specific variables. With a bit of residual adjustment here and there, von Thünen seemed to work at all sorts of scales around a world with agricultural economies at all stages of development, and from the North China Plain to Iowa you could see the hexagons of Southern Germany if only you knew how to look. Entropy maximizing approaches structured patterns of interaction with probability distributions so sharply peaked that they became, oxymoronically, determined to a degree such that no one cared about the differences. Anyway, if these residual differences were bothersome, they only pointed positively to bits of more refined information that might be incorporated, like blue- and white-collar subscripts. The abstract model was never in doubt, not the least because it was so difficult to find sufficiently refined bodies of data to test it. The same problem of verification appeared in models of dissipative structures, where verification itself takes on a double meaning of verifying whether a geographic system has ever bifurcated throughout its observable history, and verifying whether this could conceivably be a useful, that is illuminating, way of looking at the human world.

But all these ways, and many others, including all forms of normative and optimizing models, opened up possibilities for thinking about spatial arrangements, juxtapositions, and relations. They provoked new ways of looking, new angles and perspectives not only on the familiar stuff of geography, but also brought into view and into thinking wholly new things that never before had been subject to enquiry from a truly geographical perspective. New perspectives, new methodologies, and new sensitivities should provide new possibilities for illuminating our world, of bringing out of concealment that which has not been seen in the darkness. Except in mathematics itself, the abstract is only worth pursuing if it can illuminate the concrete instance. We must move our narrative to the adverbial and fourth vertex of our structure – concretely.

5 THE CONCRETE

There are social and other scientists, geographers among them, who eschew the concrete instance, process or event, who play with mathematical expressions or in computerized sandboxes for their own sake, and make rather superior noises to the effect that it is not their fault if their theory has outrun the data. Anyway, who needs data today when computers can vomit forth 'scenarios' from all the combinatorial sets of assumptions we care to shovel into our machines? Enough: I suggest we dismiss these pseudo-scientists out of hand and turn to more important matters. As geographers, of all varieties and interests, we have a common task ahead of us that is a condition of possibility of being human. It is to light up, illuminate, and come to a deeper understanding of this world in its spatial and temporal dimensions. Our concern ultimately is the concrete, no matter how rarified our abstract pathways and perspectives might appear in their methodological and ideological identities.

In fact, as our thinking moves to that vertex of the concrete, it has arrived at a piece of our topological structure that is so rich that it is impossible to convey much of it in a necessarily short essay and narrative. And yet the very attempt to choose outstanding examples raises interesting, not to say teasing questions. In picking out examples that make thinking people say with a touch of eureka 'Why, I never thought about in that way before!', what is it that we pick out from the jewel box of geography and hold out for others to admire? Granted everything about the interpretations we impose, the hermeneutic stances we take, the personal interests and predilections that turn us on to some things and off to others, why – I suggest as another speculative question – why might there be considerable agreement about the illuminating power of some geographical studies and not others? What, and despite the caveats that hedge this specula-tion, what constitutes geographic eureka? Why do we close some books, and finish some articles, with a glow of excitement, and say to ourselves 'Hey, that's neat', meaning that we now see something in a way we did not see it before, and that this new insight somehow feels . . . true?

Is it just my imagination, or could there be carefully gathered and counted textual evidence to back my claim, that certain geographical texts get reprinted or used again and again because they have a special intellectual appeal? What is that intellectual appeal, and what does it call forth from us? I hope that picking out a few concrete examples to illustrate 'the concrete' will not appear invidious, but what is it that makes us thoughtful when we follow cholera with a Pyle through three epidemics in a nineteenth-century United States undergoing radical spatial restructuring? I suggest it is neither cholera nor the United States *per se*, but an illumination that spatial structure and spatial interaction are symbiotic reflections of each other, and that cholera is a traffic carried on this changing backcloth. You can say all this abstractly, and people will nod their heads and forget to think about it and with it. But make it concrete, real cholera moving in a real but changing geographic space, and you start thinking of other possibilities.

For example, when a Watts goes to the Gambia to look at rice schemes, who really cares about rice schemes and who really cares about the Gambia? What resonates here is the illumination of a common event, and often a common tragedy, in the Third World. A global economic system, informed (or should it be misinformed?) by often well-meaning, but sometimes greedy 'experts', can touch down like a tornado at specific places and alter not just agricul-tural production and land use, but relations between men and women, young and old, and even language itself. Travel linguistically with a Pred through nineteenth-century Stockholm, and you understand *concretely* how language reflects human life. Like old tools hanging in agricultural museums that make you wonder what they could have been used for, so old words get hung up on pegs, covered with dust, and disappear from use. Makes yer think don't it?

And then a Ley makes you think, about invisible landscapes in cities, wholly real to those whose movements are informed by ridges of danger and valleys of safety, and all too visible landscapes of graffiti that mark boundaries of human violence. Why do such mental maps have such appeal across many disciplinary boundaries; why do those maps of the pathetically constrained black and hispanic worlds in Los Angeles get published again and again? For maps, just as much as written text, are called upon repeatedly to make us thoughtful. A series showing the disappearance, the reverse diffusion of the otter in France has an intellectual bite no textual description could achieve. We can see the effects of pollution with our own eyes, and we know what is going on underneath as once sparkling rivers turn into chemical soups whose ingredients amplify and concentrate up the aquatic food chain. And surely it is the maps of Openshaw's GAM (Geographical Analytical Machine), those simple black blobs on a white background, that carry the intellectual punch for all the brilliant ingenuity of their construction. For they not only announce like a dark angel the effects of radioactivity on children, but discover another but equal danger where no one suspected one before. And what is the deeper symbolism of that 'black on white' in our culture? Might the colours be reversed in China and Japan, or appear in orange in Ghana, where the colours of death are informed by quite different cultures? Why, since Harley's brilliant essays on cartographic deconstruction, do we approach maps today in ways that were closed to us before? What else might he have helped us to see before his recent and tragically early death? Why, no matter what our own ideological stance, do we resonate with Harvey's essay on a symbolic landscape containing a Sacre Coeur?

We dismiss much geographic description and analysis with a 'who cares?' Yet these, and many other written, graphic, and mathematical 'texts' we cannot dismiss. Is it because they make us care? That in their 'ringing true' they also pluck that chord of caring in each of us that constitutes another condition of possibility for being human? We are in deep philosophical water? Of course we are: we are thinking about what it is to be a caring geographer trying to illuminate the human condition. What other water should we be in? But while we cannot pursue this thread further at the moment, notice something: these 'concrete abstractions' of geographic research have a wide appeal precisely because they illuminate not just themselves, by which I mean the particular subject matter intrinsic to them, but make us think towards other possibilities – other movements, diseases, landscapes, dangers, symbols, and so on. In their very concreteness about the particular they give us more abstract perspectives to think with. And to give intellectual perspectives to think with means we have landed on the last vertex of our geographical simplex – teaching.

6 TEACHING

What is worth teaching? Anyone who has taught and cares about teaching knows this is the most important and agonizing question. Whether designing a new course or seminar, or thinking through one given before in light of new examples and developments, not to say new audiences, it is the most difficult question to answer. You can never be quite sure beforehand that you have got it right, that you have made the right choices. Perhaps, in the last analysis, good teachers can only share their own enthusiasms, although this response still begs the question: what is worth teaching? This is worth a book in itself, one written by a teacher, *not* by a professional pedagogue, but let me take one anxiety of my own to stand for all the complexity a full response might require.

I worry today that we are not giving our students enough to think *with*, recognizing immediately the terrible trap in providing a perspective, a framework, a methodology, *une grille* – iron bars that can frame a way of looking, and yet at the same time bar the way to other forms of thinking. There is nothing we can do about this potential contradiction and the tension it produces except to live with it and be sensitive to it. This means that even as we give a way of seeing, a method of approaching a particular topic, we must point out constantly the dangers of taking a single path. We all know people who have taken and clung to a single perspective, ideological or methodological, and recognize that they have been stuck there. No one wants to teach intellectual stagnation.

I emphasize methodology as worth teaching, but only if it is understood that its abstractions constantly encounter the concrete exercise, example, and counter-example. Teaching methodologies, teaching *ways* of looking, *ways* of approaching topics, gives someone a freedom to move in 'problem space' that makes teaching, and therefore learning, a liberating experience. The *grille*, the framework is there, but as one of many choices to be made, not as bars to imprison thinking. You have to be able to see, concretely with example after example, how we might think of transforming space abstractly. Otherwise you never think of turning Iceland inside out to see measles diffusing smoothly and contagiously instead of jumping around the map. And once you can think abstractly *with* this concrete example, perhaps it occurs to you that Latin American cities, with their outer rings of slums and *favelas*, are nothing more than North American cities turned inside out, like the inner-to-outer movements in cat's cradle. You have to be able to think 'signal-in-the-noise' before decompositional searching for variance is seen as the common thread through all regression, trend surface, component, harmonic and similar forms of analysis. You have to think 'spatial structure' in its simpler forms before moving to spatio-temporal analysis in which a general relationship in time can adapt its parameters to region and place. You have to think the possibility of using information in spatial series to tighten up predictions of what the next maps of AIDS in the Bronx are going to look like in time. You have to think what normative patterns might look like under optimal and optimizing assumptions before you can create a sort of intellectual touchstone of comparison. You have to think spatio-temporal process, and let all diffusion studies illustrate the fact that traffic moving on a backcloth raises questions of what structures might be guiding the movements. You have to think classification, yes; but then immediately think what those partitional algorithms are doing, how the order imposed too frequently comes from shredding tightly connected structures (as every librarian knows), and that it is always we, with our always limited imaginations, who impose the order. After 100 urban factorial ecologies we discover the structure of the census they have all used.

Teaching, all teaching, is dangerous work. For some, the privilege of being able to share those enthusiasms is what makes life worth living.

7 ON A PERSONAL NOTE: THANKING IS THINKING

At the risk of embarrassing him let me point to Peter's two score years as a professional geographer, for they constitute a fine example of how it is possible to hold those vertices together – somehow! Called to geography, under circumstances only he knows how trying, he was a major force in renewing that sense of spatiality inherent in geography. His research is a record of a series of abstract approaches, perspectives and methodologies, but always applied to illuminate the concrete instance. As for teaching, he has shaped geography at all levels, from the school curriculum to graduate work. In 1965, I wrote what some considered to be a too extravagant review of his first book, *Locational Analysis in Human Geography*. I reread it recently and would not change a word, for I can still feel the surge of excitement he gave us by pulling together what were then a plethora of apparently disconnected examples, so showing us a coherence and structure that few of us saw at the time. As for teaching as a lecturer, several of his former students, now prominent geographers themselves, have told me of a common experience. While listening to a lecture of Peter's, always modestly presented but with crystal clarity, many students became so entranced by the apparent simplicity of what they thought were complex ideas that they took few notes. 'Only later', they said, 'as we came to reconstruct the ideas and review them, did we wonder what the hell he actually said!'

But they were all smiling as they told me.

3

Action in the Physical Everyday World

T. Hägerstrand

Our actions leave traces in the physical world. We produce things and bring about states of a sort that nature does not shape on its own. Most traces have a short duration. Others lead to more lasting changes. In most cases there is a limited and comprehensible purpose behind specific actions. In addition, most actions – possibly all – have consequences which were not taken into account in the moment of action. It is quite easy to discover such unintended consequences in the immediate neighbourhood. Consequences with a wide reach and a slow course are more difficult to grasp.

Today there is a growing awareness of the fact that the added volume of human actions is in some cases leading to problems which may become disastrous if they are not deflected in new directions or else totally avoided.

There is a growing body of work on the most visible of these emerging problems which tries to identify, rank and counteract them. This undertaking is presently dominated by workers in the geosphere and biosphere sciences. In order to fill out the picture we also need to focus more directly on the human and societal side of the matter. We need to look more closely at how our ways of life in their entirety are related to the material reality. What happens when we consciously and unconsciously make our traces? What impacts are perhaps unavoidable, given the kind of creatures that we are, and what could be otherwise and less disturbing in the long run? We must keep in mind that it is an illusion to believe that human society can isolate itself from nature. The best we can hope for is a reasonably safe co-evolution.

When speaking about actions it comes to mind that there exists a whole family of theories concerned with the human being as an actor. This field is cultivated by philosophers, linguists, social psychologists, sociologists, and others. The dominant question seems to be how purposeful human action is at all possible in a world otherwise governed by physical causality. From whence comes our feeling of freedom and how free are we in fact? A related question concerns how the actor is connected to the environment in his or her doings. A short summary answer is given in a symposium report on the structure of action: 'Human action necessarily is situated; it occurs in a context' (Ginsburg, 1980, p. 333). So far so good. However, it is striking how tightly the boundary is drawn around the actor. There is only a social context and this only in a very abstract form. Neither the actor nor his or her partners are considered as living bodies. And there are neither tools nor other things as support or as material to work on.

Historians are also clearly preoccupied with the nature of action even if, as a rule, they do not theorize about the matter. R.G. Collingwood was a brilliant exception. He is an interesting author because he moves beyond the mental and social in order to consider real world changes in general. The following is a central formulation of his:

> The processes of nature can . . . be properly described as sequences of mere events, but those of history cannot. They are not processes of mere events but processes of actions, which have an inner side, consisting of processes of thought; and what the historian is looking for is these processes of thought. All history is the history of thought. (Collingwood, 1949, p. 215)

The distinction between 'actions' and 'mere events' refers to the seemingly different ways in which the two kinds of occurrences are set in motion. On the other hand, the formulation gives the impression that actions and mere events are easy to disentangle in the real world. How else could history be only the history of thought? The position sounds odd to an old-fashioned geographer. Perhaps a literal interpretation is a misunderstanding of what Collingwood wanted to say. Nevertheless, once again this kind of abstraction seems to suppress everything of the context located beyond the mental and social realms.

There is at least one philosopher who prefers to view the actor and his or her context in a radically different manner. In a paper called *The Agent and his World* Jacob Meløe asks about 'the smallest possible section of our world that necessarily forms a part of a single practical operation, or the smallest intelligible system within which an operation is intelligible' (translated from Norwegian according to Londey, 1984, p. 426). The use of the word 'operation' instead of 'action' underlines that attention has moved from speech-acts towards manipulation of objects in the material world. Meløe's answer is that such a framing must show an agent-in-the-landscape. He gives a simple and striking example: 'Consider, for example, a man who is chopping firewood with an axe. Imagine then that we take away the axe, but that otherwise we make no changes. What we are left with is not just an implementless operation, but an unintelligible gesture. The implement is in this sense internal to the operation' (Meløe, 1973, p. 133). Then, to chop wood is of course only a part of a much longer series of connected operations which convert the living tree in the forest into fuel in a stove. Again, according to Meløe (p. 134): 'Every form of operation gets its identity from its place in the total system of our forms of operation.'

The concept of landscape is familiar to geographers. Meløe's use of the word, however, is somewhat exceptional. As a rule it has referred to what one sees when looking beyond the immediate vicinity towards a wider environment. This tradition means that the finer details of human operations are passed over – and so also are the finer details of natural events – in favour of the more large-scale aggregated sediments of human actions and natural processes. On the other hand, if we accept Friedrich Ratzel's dictum that geography should deal with the totality of things which fill the surface of the earth, there is no smallest mixture of things in the everyday world which could not be called a landscape. If we are really aiming at understanding how our actions make traces in the world, Meløe's interpretation is the only applicable one.

Operations do not relate only to preceding and subsequent operations. They may also start because of signals from 'mere events'. Operations also have 'mere events' in their train, or they alter the conditions for such events.

It is not only operations which require a landscape to be comprehensible. Also 'sequences of mere events' are always bound to landscapes where entities act causally on each other because of their relative positions. Even investigations undertaken in the laboratory need an appropriately arranged landscape. This has to be specified in a satisfactory description of any experiment. Otherwise it cannot be repeated.

The conceptual distinction between actions and mere events is clearly not obliterated by the fact that both have to take place in landscapes. The fundamental difference between finality and causality remains. The landscape, however, makes clear how the two types of occurrences intertwine, even if they come about differently. People who make a journey for some purpose may transmit an infection without knowing it, so causing an epidemic, that is a sequence of mere events. An epidemic must be classified as such despite its close relation to human behaviour.

Where the human being is present there is also a point of intersection between two spheres of the world. One is made up of more or less coherent patterns of meaning. The other is the sphere of bodily existence with all its things and movements, containers and timings. Both are implacably united in the landscape. To combine the agent and his or her landscape, as well as the mere event and its landscape, calls not only for making operations and events comprehensible, but also for the full registration of conditions and consequences.

At this point one may well have reason to ask in what sense pure social structure and relations have to do with tangible landscapes. When structures and relations are mediated by things the connection is obvious. But what about social communication by words, the strongest shaping force in a society? The answer is that a society is not just minds in communication but also bodies. Two individuals cannot engage in unmediated conversation without first placing themselves – or having been placed – within earshot of each other. This requires navigation in the landscape. Also, only observation of behaviour presupposes mutual presence. Books, mail, and telecommunications, on the other hand, are means which correspond to the axe of the woodcutter.

Behind all its abstract characteristics a society is a set of persons, engaged in forming ever-changing configurations with respect to each other. The relative positions only partially reveal purpose, compared to what a craftsman using tools and materials does more fully. We have to include words as tools in order to get the complete picture. If we do, they also become components of the landscape, strongly affecting actions and events. Social communication plays a role in the anthroposphere similar to the role of climate in the biosphere. That the immense flow of words can only be sampled does not contradict their importance.

The circumstance that the spatial and temporal configuration of communicating people only exposes fragments of exchanged meanings, when viewed from the outside, does not mean that the configuration as such is unimportant. To an agent his particular presence inside the configuration defines what experiences he can make and what actions he can undertake. There are no social situations that are free from physical positioning in a landscape. 'The world, unfortunately, is real', Jorge Luis Borges said.

So far the term landscape has been used as if the meaning of the term is unproblematic. This, of course, is not the case. The term has been understood in several different ways, particularly in the German and Nordic languages (Hard, 1969), and some versions are loaded with romanticism. Particularly confusing has been the double meaning of scenery and area with certain scenic characteristics. Some geographers have used the term for the totality of things and forces forming a piece of land territory. Russian geographers seem to think in that direction when they define geography as the study of the 'landscape mantle'. Such interpretations may seem strange in English, where traditionally an emphasis on the visual seems to predominate. They may also appear strange and impossible as an object of research. What something can one possibly say about everything?

On the other hand, when we speak about environment or milieu, we don't just refer to the visual but to what is totally – or at least potentially – there. In specific cases only a sample of what is present needs to be taken into account, but this sample comes from what is there, and we do not know what until it has revealed itself. When a person is attacked by a virus or happens to hear a piece of information, the source must have been present in the vicinity at least some time before. We are in fact accustomed to being embraced by a thereness, complete with known and unknown phenomena. A totality of beings and events is after all thinkable, somewhat like the very useful concept of infinity in mathematics.

Why call the totality landscape and not just environment or milieu in the ordinary way? The reason is that these two concepts logically postulate someone or something as its centre. They are monocentric. Hence to speak of the human environment in general is strictly taken to be impossible. There is no one human environment; everyone has his or her own. We are all parts of each other's environments. We need instead to have an image of a multitude in which the fact of overlapping and interacting individual environments is the main problem to consider.

Something in that all-embracing direction of thought must have loomed in the minds of those who introduced the concept of ecosystem (Tansley, 1935; Odum, 1959) which means 'everything living and its life-environment in an area'. At least in theory, this definition includes people as biological beings. In practice, conscious and creative people with their elaborate technology are only peripherically integrated. Landscape, on the other hand, includes without question both nature and society plus technology as the bridge.

So, finally, when we are interested in how our doings change the world, it is impossible to think of Meløe's landscape as something less than everything that potentially may come to be affected by human operations, including also human minds. To call this intractable totality a landscape is motivated by the fact that we have to do with something historically given, in its mixtures and arrangements resembling what we see from an outlook tower. Nevertheless, a reservation about the terminology is in order. The totality includes much more than can be observed from any one point, and much that can only be indirectly observed. Therefore, a different term would be preferable. It is, however, hard to find a suitable alternative. Ordinary thinking has never needed this broad conception, and thus a word for it has never been invented.

Let us now, after these preliminary considerations, take a closer look at how a selected action (operation) relates to its landscape. The purpose is to introduce a case through which one can make some observations about meaningful action as related to the part of the landscape which makes it comprehensible and to the parts beyond. In principle any operation would do, but since some are more significant than others, it is most tempting to dwell upon a case of indisputable importance.

Galileo's experiment with accelerated motion is one of those undertakings in history which has had a thorough-going consequence for science, techology and society, and indirectly probably for nature as well. Galileo himself published a rather detailed description. Through this description we can get a picture both of how he designed his experiment and of how much of its necessary landscape he included in his report.

When modern physics began, motion was at the centre of interest. 'To be ignorant of motion is to be ignorant of nature', Aristotle had declared (Drake, 1978, p. 8). This Galileo did not doubt, but he felt that the time had come to test traditional ideas about motion, for example, those concerning the speeds of freely falling bodies. Watches were not yet accurate enough for measuring very short times. Therefore Galileo had to figure out how to 'dilute' and make measurable the fall of a round body by making it slow on an inclined plane. His own story about the experiment runs as follows.

A piece of wooden moulding or scantling, about 12 cubits long, half a cubit wide, and three finger-breadths thick, was taken; on its edge was cut a channel of little more than one finger in breadth; having made this groove very straight, smooth and polished, and having lined it with parchment, also as smooth and polished as possible, we rolled along it a hard, smooth, and very round bronze ball. Having placed this board in a sloping position, by lifting one end some one or two cubits above the other, we rolled the ball, as I was just saying, along the channel, noting, in a manner presently to be described, the time required to make the descent. We repeated this experiment more than once in order to measure the time with an accuracy such that the deviation between two observations never exceeded one-tenth of a pulse-beat. Having performed this operation and having assured ourselves about its reliability, we now rolled the ball only one-quarter the length of the channel; and having measured the time of its descent, we found it precisely one-half of the former. Next we tried other distances, comparing the time for the whole length with that for the half, or with that for two-thirds, or three-fourths, or indeed for any fraction; in such experiments, repeated a full hundred times, we always found that the spaces traversed were to each other as the square of the times, and this was true for all inclinations of the plane, i.e. of the channel, along which we rolled the ball. We also observed that the times of descent, for various inclinations of the plane, bore to one another precisely that ratio which, as we shall see later, the Author had predicted and demonstrated for them.

For the measurement of time, we employed a large vessel of water placed in an elevated position; to the bottom of this vessel was soldered a pipe of small diameter giving a thin jet of water, which we collected in a small glass during the time of each descent, whether for the whole length of channel or for part of its length; the water thus collected was weighed, after each descent, on a very accurate balance; the differences and ratios of these weights gave us the differences and ratios of the times, and this with such accuracy that although the operation was repeated many, many times, there was no appreciable discrepancy in the results.

The epoch-making outcome of Galileo's experiment was that he was able to describe a physical process in mathematical terms. This remarkable achievement will be ignored until further notice. To begin with, the purpose is not to address the evolution of physics but to look at the experiment from a quite different angle: a human operation as a subset of its landscape.

We have to deal with an arena divided in two parts, on the one hand the reported arrangement and on the other a wider neighbourhood about which Galileo is silent, just like every storyteller. The strength of the descriptive verbal language is that it sets the spotlight on selected items, leaving what is supposed to be self-evident in the dark. This means that the involved landscape is left out as a coherent whole.

The experimental setting is a 'cell of local order' in the larger landscape. We find in this cell the experimenter himself and (probably) assistants, with ideas in their heads, skills in their hands, plus an assortment of things of various shapes and substances. Assume now that the artist is asked to make a picture illustrating the story. He would have to add a lot from his own imagination. Different artists would amplify the text differently with respect to many details. However, in one respect they would have to agree in order to produce a credible picture of the experiment. They must place every separate body in *touch* with other bodies in a correct way.

Touch – or contact – is the most fundamental and general relation we encounter, directly with the body and indirectly by experiencing its importance in the living and non-living world around us. The only method by which Galileo could ascertain that his ball and parchment were smooth was to pass his finger-tips over their surface. More than that, his whole structure required a suitable order of joinings, that is, components in close contact from the floor and upwards.

Space is what bodies cannot share. The closest relation involving no or only elastic deformation is contact. By grasping things with the hands and placing them in contact according to some idea or plan, we can make constructions which nature is unable to bring about on its own. Contact is at the root of all technology. It is obviously also an internal reality. Minds and hands must somehow be in touch for purposeful action to happen. All this is of course obvious, since we learn its elements as exploring toddlers before we learn the names of things. It is less obvious – or at least seldom brought into the open – that the configuration of contacts extends out into the wider landscape. Nature is in its own purposeless way held together as an immense configuration of things in long-term or transient contact. Trees stand upright because their roots are held in place by grains in the ground. An esker is a huge mass of grains of sand and gravel pressed against each other by gravitation. Predators must reach and grasp prey in order to survive. And prey must flee or hide to avoid that very sort of contact. Viewed in this perspective a landscape is not just a visual panorama but a configuration of contacts between countless existents, each with their own 'life-history' of encounters.

The above observation is not complete until we go further and note that natural as well as man-made existents have different shapes and sizes, different strengths, and different surface characteristics. Irregular shapes in contact form cavities between them. These interspaces are small down at ground level, bigger and less rigid between herbs, blades of grass and bushes above the ground, still bigger between trees in the forest as well as between inner and outer walls in human settlements, and finally one single open sphere above the tree-tops and roofs.

Taken together the hierarchy of connected interspaces makes up one pure and nameless three-dimensional form. It is the only really unifying component of the total landscape mantle. It is not empty. It is filled with either water or air. Light, on the other hand, meets a more space-specific filtering on its way through air and water.

The extremely convoluted surface at which the air/water-body is in contact with the aggregate of non-living and living things is the locus of a large part of the processes now under investigation in the Global Change Program. Critical chemical and mechanical exchanges take place there, whether we think of the foliage of plants or the walls of buildings and the pavings of streets.

The surface is not a fixed structure. It is changing all the time. As new contacts are established between entities of any kind, they necessarily expose non-committed parts of their bodies towards the void. Changes, however, take place at widely different rates. These differences are essential for maintaining diversity. Here is an area wide open for investigation. So far as the living part is concerned there currently exists no evolutionary theory incorporating the concomitant ecological transformation (Stenseth, 1986, p. 130). The problem is that most species have to survive in micro-landscapes made up of other species. A single tree is a world of living creatures. This leads to extremely complex mutual relations. Another growing worry is the lack of coherent ideas about the place of humans and their technology in the total landscape of mixed existents in configurations of contact. Without overcoming these drawbacks it is difficult to establish norms about how to inhabit our planet.

Some general aspects of human operations in the total landscape can be picked up by a further look at Galileo's experiment. It is assumed that he actually performed it in the way he describes, but one should keep in mind that several trials and much scribbling down of triangles and figures preceded the final solution (Drake, 1978).

A fundamental idea behind experimentation is to keep unwanted influences absent or at least constant. Galileo did his utmost to remove friction. The groove was made straight, the surface smooth and the ball hard and shiny. He could not do away with air resistance, but its effect was clearly insignificant in view of the manner in which time was measured. Galileo's studies of pendulums fit in here. They were bodies in motion without contact with a support. Galileo does not mention a further circumstance, obvious as it was. The test-area as such must be left undisturbed by rain and wind and manipulation by undesired visitors. It is easy to meet these requirements in a society with buildings and property rights.

Experimental settings are not the only things that need to be protected from unwanted influences. The same is the case with all crystallization processes in which components have to be brought into contact in an orderly fashion. In living nature we find territories and nests as protective devices. Perhaps eggs and wombs of mothers are the most effective solutions evolution has come up with. However, one must assume that variability in nature would be much smaller than it is so far were it not for one further means of protection. Since movement takes energy, space itself wards off contact. Space as such isolates and that is a positive but underestimated fact for the survival of species and the well-being of human beings. The latter point is well demonstrated by Cliff and Haggett (1989).

Protection from unwanted influences while work is going on is one thing. The other side of the coin is that the operation would have been impossible without contributions from a larger surrounding landscape. The wood must have been brought in from a tree felled there, the parchment from some goat or calf, the ball of bronze came originally from copper and tin, mined in one or two places, and the water from a well in the vicinity. The groove in the wood had to be made with the aid of a chisel and hammer, or else some special sort of plane. It took paste to fix the parchment. Still more things were probably necessarily involved and in addition human labour.

The removal of the needed substances from nature and their further design and transport caused some permanent changes in the original locations, admittedly insignificant but unavoidable. The point is not the magnitude but the observation that an actor's landscape contains a much broader range of broken and created contacts between entities than is consciously present in the minds of him or herself and his or her readers or listeners. In science our ability to abstract from material conditions has been taken very far. In the end the whole experiment is reduced to a mere formula.

Turning our attention towards the time dimension we can view the experiment as the convergence of three different histories. The first of these concerns the ancient debate about the nature of motion. Opinions differ concerning Galileo's dependence on earlier thinking. His references show that he was familiar with the works of Aristotle, Euclid, Archimedes, and some other classics. But there is no evidence that he picked up his ideas from these authorities. More interesting to note is that his father, a musician and musical theorist, made experiments with weights on strings, showing mistakes in the prevailing number theory of intervals (Drake, 1978, pp. 16–17). Galileo was then 22 years old. Participation could well have inspired his own later experimentation as well as making him think about movements of pendulums.

The second historical aspect was that Galileo could use products of quite advanced pre-scientific techniques. Practitioners of these techniques knew how to produce bronze, round balls, smooth parchment and good balances. Also, the woodworking tools must have represented very old ideas. In these early days of science, techniques came first and discoveries later. It has probably, to a large extent, remained that way.

The origin of materials and equipment can be looked at as a process in two steps. The first critical event is when something comes into being for the first time, in nature or in culture. The second event is when the particular items in use began to grow or were fabricated. The final time-related observation has to do with this stage. By that point we are no longer in the somewhat fluid world of ideas but back in the material landscape. All the tangible things that are needed must be available at the right moment. They must physically exist and be within social, economic, and geographical reach.

On the other hand, they cannot be available unless they have had their necessary gestation period. It takes decades for a tree to be ready for felling. Production of bronze and balls of bronze goes faster, but it likewise takes its time. And the production also needs equipment, manufactured still earlier, just as no trees grow unless there are seeds or saplings from older trees to start with. Nothing comes from nothing. Biology, as well as technology, is linked with the past. This means that before the experiment actions and events had taken place at other locations and times, unrelated to the experiment and to each other. Strange as it sounds the experiment made traces before it had happened. This is a normal feature of human operations when you view them as whole space/time configurations in the landscape.

A more common perspective is to ask about what happened subsequently. Galileo's equipment must have been put away somewhere. Perhaps his inclined plane became firewood, ashes and smoke. The ball may still exist in some box or lie waiting for an archaeologist in the ground. And so on. The slight material remains of the experiment were of course *per se* unproblematic. Their continued existence somewhere and in some form was nevertheless unavoidable, as is the disregarded case of all things involved in our actions.

If the immediate traces in the material landscape of Galileo's experiment were negligible, ramifications in the realm of thought were more extensive. Galileo was a pioneer in several fields other than those related to the fall of bodies. Nevertheless, this part of his work represents his major methodological legacy. He made experiments the backbone of physical science, and gradually natural science in general, and he showed the power of mathematical reasoning.

The continuation belongs to the history of thought, to remind us of Collingwood's distinction. The purpose of looking at Galileo's experiment, however, was not to contribute to that story. It was instead to place it in the context of the physical everyday world and attract attention to the necessary relation between an operation and the landscape. This relation not only makes the operation intelligible. It is also a source of change beyond the intended meaning of the operation. Most of that is so self-evident that we ignore it. 'The aspects of things that are most important for us are hidden because of their simplicity and familiarity' (Wittgenstein, 1976, p. 50).

Galileo's thought was unique; his use of things not at all exceptional, if we disregard how he arranged them. Every meal we prepare and eat, every garment we put on, every trip we make with the car, transforms the landscape in the sense that some things are removed from their contacts in some locations and placed in new contacts in other locations. We are movers of matter all the time, just like water and wind. Our meaningful actions bring with them 'meaningless' change.

Human beings as matter-movers were of no particular significance as long as the species occupied a limited niche in the total landscape. On the whole, this was still the case in the time of Galileo. We are many more now. And, in addition, since then – and not least because of the science-and-technology age Galileo launched – our individual capability to transform the landscape through every-day action has multiplied many times over. Air and water and our own bodies interact with new kinds of surfaces in a world in which space isolates less and less. The problem of finding a proper balance between the world's biomass and its new technomass in ways which still leave a livable everyday for human beings requires, amongst other things, that the hidden aspects of situated actions are brought out into the open.

REFERENCES

Cliff, A.D. & Haggett, P. (1989). 'Spatial aspects of epidemic control.' *Progress in Human Geography*, 13, 313–47.
Collingwood, R.G. (1949). *The Idea of History*. Oxford: Oxford University Press.
Drake, S. (1978). *Galileo at Work. His Scientific Biography*. Chicago: Chicago University Press.
Galileo, G. (1636). *Dialogues Concerning Two New Sciences*. Translated by H. Crew and A. de Salvio. New York: Macmillan, 1914.
Ginsburg, G.P. (ed.) (1980). 'Epilogue: A conception of situated action.' In M. Brenner (ed.), *The Structure of Action*. Oxford: Oxford University Press, 313–50.
Hard, G. (1969). 'Die Diffusion der Idee der Landschaft.' *Erdkunde*, 23, 249–64.
Londey, D. (1984). 'The agent in a Northern landscape.' *Inquiry*, 27, 425–38.
Meløe, J. (1973). 'Aktøren og hans verden.' *Norsk Filosofisk Tidsskrift*, 8, Årgang, no. 2, 133–43.
Odum, E.P. (1959). *Fundamentals of Ecology*. Philadelphia: Saunders.
Stenseth, N.C. (1986). 'Darwinian evolution in ecosystems: a survey of some ideas and difficulties together with some possible solutions.' In J.L. Casti and A. Karlqvist (eds), *Complexity, Language, and Life: Mathematical Approaches*. Berlin: Springer-Verlag, 105–45.

Tansley, A.G. (1935). 'The use and abuse of vegetational concepts and terms.' *Ecology*, 16, 284–307.

Wittgenstein, L. (1976). *Philosophical Investigations*. Translated by G.E.M. Anscombe. Oxford: Oxford University Press.

PART II

Locational Analysis

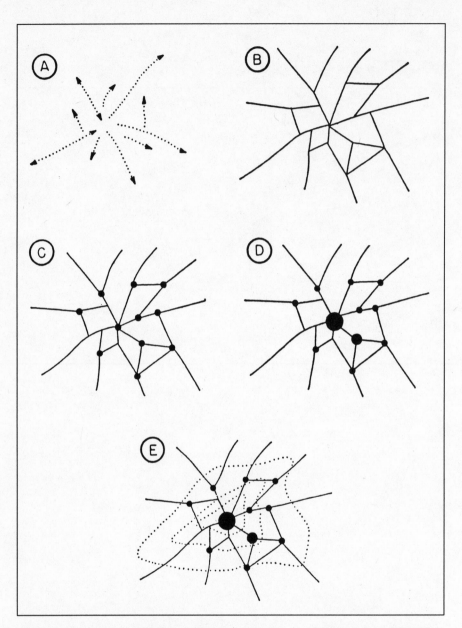

Plate II One of the most reproduced of Peter's diagrams is his original five-fold conception of locational analysis in human geography. This follows a logical progression from flows between areas (A), to networks for the flows (B), through to the settlement nodes on the networks (C), the hierarchical size-ordering of the nodes (D), and culminates finally with the surfaces upon which events take place (E). The diagram, drawn in Peter's own fair hand, appeared initially in the first edition of *Locational Analysis* (1965, p.18) and was used as the organizing framework for that book.

4

Revisiting the Modifiable Areal Unit Problem and the Ecological Fallacy

N. Wrigley

1 INTRODUCTION

In 1979, at a joint Royal Statistical Society/Institute of British Geographers Conference held at the University of Bristol, Openshaw and Taylor presented a now famous paper on the modifiable areal unit problem in spatial analysis. In that paper, they distinguished two interrelated aspects of the problem which they labelled the *scale problem* and the *aggregation* (or *zoning*) *problem*. They also presented results of large-scale simulation experiments which highlighted both the pervasiveness and the stubbornness of the scale and zoning problems. Several of the participants in the original Bristol conference have, over the years, found themselves drawn back time and time again to the Openshaw and Taylor results. Peter Haggett, for example, has revisited those results in both his *The Edges of Space* (1981) paper, and in *The Geographer's Art* (1990, ch. 3).

What is it then that has drawn geographers back to the Openshaw and Taylor paper on so many occasions? In simple terms, it must be that the modifiable areal unit problem remains so stubbornly 'unsolved'. But, beyond that it is surely because the Openshaw and Taylor results can be read in two fundamentally different ways. Spatial analysts of a 'pessimistic' disposition have long taken the Openshaw and Taylor results as indicating that the life of the spatial analyst will be complicated for all time by the aggregation effects arising from the fact that much of the data used in spatial analysis is based on areal units that are modifiable. They have painted a rather bleak picture in which 'the modifiable areal unit problem is shown to be essentially unpredictable in its intensity and effects' (Fotheringham and Wong, 1991, p. 1025) and have suggested that results of modifiable areal unit problem experiments are 'rather depressing in that they provide strong evidence of the unreliability of *any* multivariate analysis undertaken with data from areal units' (Fotheringham and Wong, 1991, p. 1025). In contrast, spatial analysts of an 'optimistic' disposition have read the Openshaw and Taylor results in a totally different way. They have drawn attention to the empirical regularities uncovered by Openshaw and Taylor – to the intriguing evidence of the Gaussian shape of the distribution of the correlation coefficient across alternative zonings at a given scale of analysis, to the variance of that distribution increasing with scale, and to the tendency for the range of variability of the correlation coefficient to be sensitive to the level of spatial autocorrelation – and have remained convinced that one day a statistical framework would be found that would account for, or at the very least exploit, those regularities. Envisaged in ideal form, such a framework would take the form of an elegant and parsimonious statistical theory which would embrace all previously observed empirical regularities. More realistically, however, such a framework would most probably provide merely a *practical* method of continuing to conduct statistical analysis of areal-unit data in the presence of, and making allowance for, the interrelated scale and zoning aspects of the modifiable areal unit problem.

My reading of Peter Haggett's continuing fascination with the modifiable areal unit problem places him firmly in the camp of the 'optimists'. How else is it possible to read such statements as:

If the problems of estimating and correcting for spatial effects were the only concern for quantitative geography, then it would rank as a useful but somewhat sombre intellectual activity. Fortunately there is a reverse side to the coin. For although the awkward, multilevel, anisotropic world we study may pose problems for our sister disciplines in making space-free generalizations, those same problems provide a resource for geography itself. A world without boundary or autocorrelation problems would be one with little geographic interest. (Haggett, 1981, p. 61)

At a time, then, of re-emergent interest in the modifiable areal unit problem amongst spatial analysts, and of new research initiatives in both North America and the UK linked to the arrival of the 1990s census data, it seems an appropriate moment to revisit the modifiable areal unit problem and the intrinsically associated issue known as the 'ecological fallacy'. In this chapter, I will review some of the most recent work in the field, and will celebrate Peter Haggett's unquenched 'optimism' concerning this fascinating and longstanding challenge via the presentation of a new approach to the problem.

2 DEFINITIONS

The *scale problem* is the tendency, within a system of modifiable areal units, for different statistical results to be obtained from the same set of data when that information is grouped at different levels of spatial resolution (for example, census districts, counties, regions). Classically the problem has been observed in the magnitude of the correlation between variables increasing as the size of the areas involved in the analysis increases. For example, Openshaw and Taylor (1979) studied the association within the state of Iowa, USA, between percentage vote for Republican candidates in the congressional election of 1968, and the percentage of population aged 60 and over in the 1970 US Census. When they computed the correlation at the level of the 99 constituent counties in Iowa, the value they obtained for the correlation coefficient was +0.345. However, when they grouped the 99 counties into six larger functional regions, the coefficient they obtained increased to +0.713. This tendency of correlation coefficients to increase in magnitude as the size of the areal unit involved increases has been known since the work of Gehlke and Biehl (1934) and Yule and Kendall (1950). Yule and Kendall, for example, considered the correlation between yield per acre of wheat and yield per acre of potatoes across 48 agricultural counties in England in 1936. As table 4.1 shows, as the counties were grouped successfully into a smaller number of units the correlation coefficient increased successively from +0.2189 to +0.9902. As a result, Yule and Kendall concluded that, in practice, it was possible 'to produce any value of the correlation from 0 to 1 by choosing an appropriate size of the unit of area for which we measure the yields' (p. 311). Hence correlations have 'no absolute validity independently of [the areal] units, but are relative to them' (p. 312).

Table 4.1 Correlation coefficients between yields per acre of wheat and potatoes in grouping of 48 English agricultural counties, 1936

No. of units	Correlation coefficient
48	0.2189
24	0.2963
12	0.5757
6	0.7649
3	0.9902

Source: Yule and Kendall (1950, pp. 310–11)

The *zoning problem*, in contrast, relates to the variability in results obtained within a set of areal units as a function of the various ways those units can be grouped *at a given scale*, and *not* as a result of variation in the size of those areas. Thus, for any scale of analysis (any specified number of zones) there are many many ways of defining the boundaries of those zones. Figure 4.1, for example, taken from the work of Arbia (1989), shows two alternative zonings of Italy each at the scale of 32 areal units. Similarly, figure 4.2, from the work of Clark (1991), shows two alternative proposals for subdividing Los Angeles County into five 'Supervisor Districts'. One zoning (figure 4.2a) was designed to increase the opportunity of Hispanics to elect a representative of their choice. The other zoning (figure 4.2b) is an example in which Los Angeles County has been divided into five Supervisor Districts without the inclusion of this 'Hispanic opportunity district' element.

Openshaw and Taylor (1979) demonstrated that, *at any given scale*, the zoning problem is likely to be sufficiently strong to ensure that a wide range of statistical results are obtained. For example, in their consideration of the correlation between Republican voting and percentage of the population aged 60 and over in Iowa, they showed that if the 99 constituent counties were grouped together

Figure 4.1 Two alternative zonings of Italy at the scale of 32 areal units
(*Source*: redrawn from Arbia, 1989)

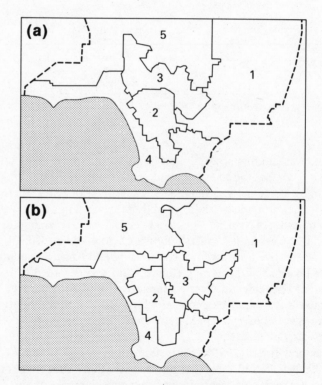

Figure 4.2 Two alternative proposals for subdividing Los
Angeles County into five 'Supervisor Districts'
(*Source*: adapted from Clark, 1991)

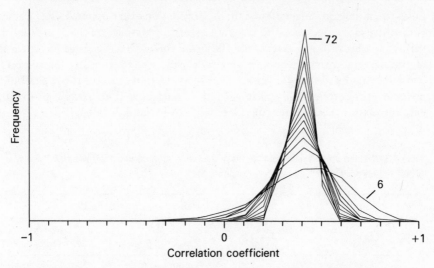

Figure 4.3   Frequency distributions of correlation coefficients at different scales
(*Source*: Openshaw and Taylor, 1979, figure 5.1, p. 131)

into 24 larger contiguous districts, and then all possible zonings at the 24-district scale were considered, the correlation coefficient ranged in value from a maximum of +0.979 to a minimum of −0.811, implying very different substantive interpretations.

In practice, the scale and zoning problems interact. In the case of the Iowa data, using simulations of 10,000 alternative zonings at different scales, Openshaw and Taylor were able to demonstrate (see table 4.2) that the spread of results associated with the zoning problem increased (decreased) as the size of the areas involved in the analysis increased (decreased). Moreover, they were able to display the frequency distributions of the correlations across the alternative zonings at each given scale (see figure 4.3).

In addition, the zoning problem interacts with spatial autocorrelation. In the case of the Iowa data, Openshaw and Taylor were able to demonstrate that

Table 4.2   Maximum and minimum values of the correlation coefficient between Republican voting and percentage of the population aged 60 and over in Iowa

Spatial scale (no. of units)	Zoning effect (min. r)	Zoning effect (max. r)
6	−0.999	0.999
12	−0.984	0.999
24	−0.811	0.979
36	−0.745	0.949
48	−0.548	0.886
60	−0.349	0.777
72	−0.059	0.703

Source: Openshaw and Taylor (1979, table 5.2, p. 130)

positive spatial autocorrelation in the X (population over 60) and Y (Republican voting) variables reduces the magnitude of the zoning problem; that is, the variability of results at a given scale. Table 4.3 shows that the range of variability of the correlation coefficient is generally wider, at each scale, for X and Y variables that exhibit negative spatial autocorrelation than for those exhibiting positive autocorrelation, whilst X and Y variables that exhibit no spatial autocorrelation assume intermediate range-of-variability values.

Table 4.3   Maximum and minimum values of the correlation coefficient (Iowa data) when spatial autocorrelation varies

| No. of units | Spatial autocorrelation in X and Y | | | | | |
| | Negative | | Nil | | Positive | |
	(min. r)	(max. r)	(min. r)	(max. r)	(min. r)	(max. r)
6	−0.99	0.99	−0.99	0.99	−0.99	0.99
12	−0.97	0.99	−0.99	0.99	−0.99	0.99
24	−0.98	0.99	−0.90	0.99	−0.89	0.98
36	−0.93	0.98	−0.80	0.98	−0.61	0.93
48	−0.87	0.96	−0.66	0.95	−0.39	0.89
54	−0.85	0.95	−0.52	0.91	−0.32	0.88

Source: Openshaw (1984b, table 11, p. 22)

Finally, the intrinsically associated problem of the *ecological fallacy* arises when areal-unit data are the only source available to the researcher but the objects of study are individual-level characteristics and relationships. Because of the scale component of the modifiable areal unit problem, correlations measured using areal-unit data will usually be greater in absolute magnitude than the unknown individual-level correlations and, as we have seen above, may even differ significantly in sign. It follows, therefore, that inferences about individual-level relationships drawn from areal-unit results will normally be highly suspect.

These dangers have been recognized for a considerable time. Gehlke and Biehl (1934), for example, questioned the value of areal-unit level correlations (such as those derived at the scale of census tracts) for 'causal' analysis, and noted that 'a relatively high correlation might conceivably occur by census tracts when the traits so studied were completely dissociated in the individuals or families of those traits' (p. 170). Robinson (1950) followed this by providing a now classic empirical demonstration of such dangers, in a study of correlation between racial group and illiteracy in the USA. He termed the areal-unit (group) level correlation, the *ecological correlation*, and since that time the inappropriate inference of individual-level relationships from areal-unit results has been termed the *ecological fallacy*.

More recently, Openshaw (1984a) has been able to provide an indication of the typical range of ecological fallacy problems in census data analysis via an analysis of 122,342 household census records for the city of Florence, Italy. These data, which represent a 100 per cent census of all households in the city, were collected by the Regional Government of Tuscany at the same time as the official 1971 Italian Census, and they contain information about 40 variables. Using these data, Openshaw was able to compute 780 pairwise correlations between the 40 census variables at each of two levels: the individual household level, and the census district level (when the 122,342 household records were aggregated into 484 census districts). Table 4.4 shows the cross-tabulation of these correlation coefficients. In the important central section of the table, where the data are most numerous, it can be seen that, typically, only 20 to 30 per cent of the values of the census-district (ecological) correlations fall into the same category as the individual-level correlations. The off-diagonal elements of the table indicate, therefore, the scale of the ecological fallacy problem. Usually the census-district correlations are simply stronger (greater in absolute magnitude) than the individual-level correlations. For example, in the row corresponding to individual-level correlations in the range +0.2 to +0.4, 82 per cent of area-level correlations are stronger (with 55 per cent lying in the range +0.6 to +0.8). But the incidence of shifts in sign is also disturbingly high. For example, in the row corresponding to individual-level correlations of *negative* sign −0.2 to 0.0, no less than 39 per cent of area-level correlations show *positive* signs, with a substantial 16 per cent lying in the range +0.2 to +0.6.

Table 4.4 Cross-tabulation of individual- and area-level correlations, Florence, Italy

Individual correlations: from / to	Census district correlations: from / to										No. of pairwise correlations in category
	−1.0/ −0.8	−0.8/ −0.6	−0.6 −0.4	−0.4/ −0.2	−0.2 0.0	0.0 0.2	0.2/ 0.4	0.4/ 0.6	0.6/ 0.8	0.8/ 1.0	
−1.0/−0.8	100										1
−0.8/−0.6											0
−0.6/−0.4			100								2
−0.4/−0.2	2	19	31	24	17	6					83
−0.2/0.0		1	7	21	32	23	14	2			603
0.0/0.2			1	6	10	28	28	22	3		78
0.2/0.4							18	27	55		11
0.4/0.6								100			1
0.6/0.8									100		1
0.8/1.0											0
No. of pairwise correlations in category	3	21	72	154	214	167	106	33	10	0	780

Figures in table body represent percentages of row totals.

Source: Openshaw (1984a, table 1, p. 20)

Moreover, when assessing Openshaw's results it should be noted that they represent the typical range of ecological fallacy problems *at fixed or given levels* of the scale and zoning components of the overall modifiable areal unit problem. Clearly, there are an infinite number of ways of defining the boundaries of 484 census districts in Florence, each of which would produce a version of table 4.4. Likewise, table 4.4 could also be replicated for each of many different scales of census district. Despite the message of such results, however, routine analysis of census area data is often used in the formulation of urban policy responses to individual/household-level sociological problems of deprivation, deviance, and so on, with considerable ecological-fallacy risks.

3 SOME RECENT INVESTIGATIONS

The Openshaw and Taylor (1979) paper set a precedent in spatial analysis for studies of the modifiable areal unit problem which are essentially empirical and involve large-scale numerical experiments on the effects of scale change and zoning-system change. In this section, the contrasting conclusions of two recent research projects which have adopted this approach will be considered.

3.1   The modifiable areal unit problem in multivariate analysis

The majority of research on the modifiable areal unit problem has focused on univariate or bivariate data. Correlation coefficients and the parameter estimates of bivariate regression models have been the statistics which have dominated empirical investigations of the scale and zoning problems. Despite this, however, it is multivariate analysis of areal data, particularly the routine 'feeding of census data into canned multiple regression programs . . . to formulate urban policy' (Fotheringham and Wong, 1991, p. 1029) which presents the greatest dangers. Recently, Fotheringham and Wong (1991) have explicitly considered scale and zoning sensitivity in multivariate analysis. They have argued that, at this stage of knowledge, there is little possibility of anticipating analytically the effect of scale change or zoning-system change on parameter estimates in multivariate analysis. As a result, their work follows the Openshaw and Taylor tradition of empirical analysis and numerical simulation in its examination of scale and zoning effects in the calibration of standard multiple regression and logit regression models.

The base-level information for Fotheringham and Wong's research consisted of 1980 US Census data for 871 block groups in the Buffalo Metropolitan area. These base-level data were then aggregated successively into 800, 400, 200, 100, 50 and 25 areal units and, at each given scale, standard multiple regression and logit regression models containing four explanatory/predictor variables were fitted for each of 20 alternative zoning systems. In addition, the zoning issue was further explored via a fuller analysis of models fitted to 150 alternative zonings at one given scale (that corresponding to 218 census tracts).

Clear evidence of scale and zoning effects emerged in the estimation of the models. Figure 4.4 shows that the goodness-of-fit statistic of the 4-variable regression model varies systematically with scale – increasing as the data are aggregated, and mirroring the results typically found in bivariate regression. Moreover, several of the parameter estimates of the multiple regression and logit models vary systematically with scale. Likewise, the results are clearly

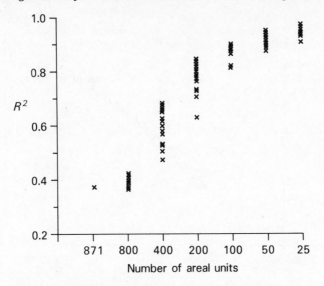

Figure 4.4   Variations in R^2 from a four-variable regression model with scale changes
(*Source*: redrawn from Fotheringham and Wong, 1991)

highly sensitive to zoning effects. Figure 4.5 shows, for example, the range of parameter estimates for one variable (percentage of the population in the census area aged over 65 years) across the 150 alternative zonings at the 218 census tracts scale. The vertical axis shows the t value (parameter estimate divided by its standard error) for each parameter estimate. In this case it can be seen that whilst most of the estimates are not significantly different from zero (and thus lie in the range $-1.96 \leq t \leq +1.96$), several are significantly negative, and two are significantly positive – suggesting very different substantive interpretations.

The sensitivity of multivariate models to variations in scale and zoning systems is clear from Fotheringham and Wong's results. However, because the interaction between changes in the variances and covariances of the explanatory/response variables cannot easily be anticipated, they were not able to predict just which of the parameter estimates of their models would be most severely affected or the direction of any systematic effects. Moreover, they could find no simple link between the level of spatial autocorrelation of a variable and its sensitivity to the modifiable areal unit problem. As a result, they concluded (pp. 1041–2) that their results 'are rather depressing' and that 'the effects of the modifiable areal unit problem, in multivariate analysis, unlike those in the unvariate and bivariate analysis, are essentially unpredictable.'

3.2 Developing 'rules of aggregation'

Not all spatial analysts would accept, however, the rather negative conclusions which Fotheringham and Wong drew from their research. Some researchers have taken the view that the way forward is to move away from real world data sets and empirical analysis with possibly misspecified models, to a more

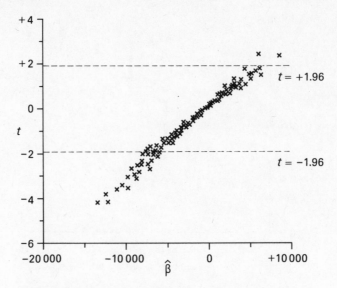

Figure 4.5   Range of parameter estimates for one variable across 150 alternative zonings at 218 census tracts scale (*Source*: redrawn from Fotheringham and Wong, 1991)

controlled environment – an idealized world in which computational experiments can be designed to isolate scale and zoning effects and to hold constant all other possible effects in a fashion that would be impossible with real world data. These researchers argue that only in such controlled environments can we truly explore the existence and nature of scale and zoning effects.

Recently Amrhein (1994) has begun to report the results of a series of experiments along these lines. In this work he first generates idealized populations, of 10,000 individuals free from any extraneous, uncontrolled process-based information. Each individual in a population is located at one of 10,000 addresses on a continuous surface – the addresses being generated first by a uniform distribution and then a normal distribution. Each individual (address) is then endowed with randomly generated observed values for two socio-economic variables (again using, first a uniform, then a normal distribution). As a result, there are four idealized populations based on the combinations of distributions used to generate the addresses and the values of the socio-economic variables assigned to each address – that is, uniform–uniform, uniform–normal, normal–uniform, and normal–normal. Summary parameter values for these idealized populations are stored as the 'true' population parameters.

Following the generation in this way of populations which contain 'no useful process-based information', Amrhein captures scale effects by partitioning the continuous space (that is, aggregating the 10,000 individuals) into first 100 then 49 and then 9 square equal-area zones. At each of these scales, zoning effects are then captured by taking 100 trials (in the case of the 100-zone scale) or 50 trials (in the case of the 49- or 9-zone scales). Tables 4.5 and 4.6, and figure 4.6, offer a selection of results from Amrhein's immensely rich experimental design.

Tables 4.5A and 4.5B report results on mean values of Variable 1 (Variable 2 results are similar and are not shown), whereas tables 4.6A and 4.6B and figures 4.6A and 4.6B report results on the correlations of Variables 1 and 2. To understand these tables, first consider table 4.5A which shows the mean values of Variable 1 obtained across the various scale levels. Under column B (headed Sample), 0.500 is the average mean of Variable 1 calculated from the 100, 49 or 9 zonal means in each trial – each trial (of which 100 or 50 were conducted at the various scales) being one in which 10,000 observations generated using a uniform-uniform distribution combination have been aggregated into 100, 49 and 9 equal-area zones. Table 4.5B then reports the standard deviations of the trial-specific values underlying each of the average statistics reported in table 4.5A. The way to read tables 4.5A and 4.5B is to compare population and sample values, that is, pairs of columns – A with B, C with D. Any observed difference between pairs of columns in table 4.5A represents a scale effect, whilst any difference between pairs of columns in table 4.5B represents a zoning effect.

It can be seen from table 4.5A there is no evidence of scale effects in the mean values of the variables. Likewise, table 4.5B indicates that the results reported in table 4.5A are very stable and that there are no apparent zoning effects (that is, differences arising under repeated trials).

In contrast, tables 4.6A and 4.6B – which report the results for correlation coefficients and which should be read in a similar fashion to tables 4.5A and 4.5B – provide clear evidence of scale and zoning effects. For example, in the case of the 9-zone scale (normal-uniform case), the average sample correlation coefficient is –0.09 compared to 0.0 in the population – that is, a clear scale effect is present. Moreover, across the trials, the standard deviation of this correlation coefficient is 0.374, suggesting clear zoning effects and implying that the expected correlation coefficient at this 9-zone scale is –0.09 plus or minus 0.374. That is to say the expected correlation coefficient lies between +0.284 and –0.464. Moreover, the scale-effect and zoning-effect trends in tables 4.6A and 4.6B are systematic, increasing in severity with decreasing numbers of zones and paralleling Openshaw and Taylor's (1979) results. Amrhein also finds similar results in the case of regression parameter estimates.

Figures 4.6A and 4.6B show these scale and zoning effects in a more immediate way. In these diagrams (for the representative cases of the uniform–uniform and normal–uniform experiments) the vertical bars connect together the highest and lowest correlation coefficients encountered in each experiment, whilst the small horizontal bar represents the average correlation coefficient obtained from the 100 or 50 trials in the experiment. It can be seen that zoning effects increase dramatically between 49 and 9 zones, rendering the results of any particular empirical study of very little value. Yet as Amrhein (1994) points out, there are countless published examples in the literature of studies using correlation results from 9 or 10 census regions.

On the basis of these findings obtained in a controlled experiment for a set of data constructed specifically to remove any extraneous process-based information, Amrhein feels able to challenge the spirit of Fotheringham and Wong's rather bleak view of the pervasiveness and unpredictability of scale and zoning

Table 4.5 Summary statistics (Variable 1) from each of Amrhein's experiments

Distribution used to generate addresses	No. of zones	A Average mean			
		Distribution used to generate variable values			
		Uniform		Normal (0, 1)	
		A Population	B Sample	C Population	D Sample
Uniform	100	0.500	0.500	−0.001	−0.001
	100w[a]	0.500	0.500	−0.000	−0.000
	49	0.500	0.500	−0.004	−0.004
	49w				
	9	0.500	0.500	−0.001	−0.001
	9w				
Normal	100	0.500	0.500	−0.000	−0.000
	100w	0.500	0.500	−0.000	−0.000
	49			0.000	−0.001
	49w	0.500	0.500	−0.001	−0.001
	9			−0.001	−0.001
	9w	0.500	0.500	• 0.001	−0.001
		B Standard deviations of the means			
Uniform	100	0.003	0.003	0.009	0.009
	100w	0.003	0.003	0.010	0.010
	49	0.004	0.004	0.010	0.011
	49w				
	9	0.003	0.003	0.010	0.010
	9w				
Normal	100	0.003	0.500	0.010	0.013
	100w	0.003	0.500	0.011	0.011
	49			0.011	0.011
	49w	0.003	0.500	0.009	0.009
	9			0.009	0.010
	9w	0.003	0.500	0.009	0.009

[a] *w* indicates the sample average statistic is generated by weighting the zones by the number of observations. The unweighted result is simply the arithmetic mean of the 100, 49 or 9 zonal statistics.

effects. Although the work discussed above is only the first of a series of experiments, and the further experiments planned are necessary to consider the interaction of changing scales, changing processes, and the extent to which various assumptions underlying certain statistics are affected by scale and zoning, Amrhein believes that certain 'rules of aggregation' can be identified. These rules are of the following type:

1 There is no reason to expect means of variables to display pronounced scale or zoning effects.
2 Variances are likewise unlikely to display pronounced scale effects beyond those expected due to the decrease in the number of observations as the size of the areal units increases. However, scale-specific variance values

Table 4.6 Correlations (Variable 1 on Variable 2) from each of Amrhein's experiments

		A Average correlation coefficient			
		Distribution used to generate variable values			
		Uniform		Normal (0, 1)	
Distribution used to generate addresses	No. of zones	A Population	B Sample	C Population	D Sample
Uniform	100	0.001	-0.009	0.000	0.008
	100w[a]	0.001	0.000	0.003	-0.004
	49	0.000	0.020	0.002	0.005
	49w				
	9	0.003	0.046	-0.002	0.019
	9w				
Normal	100	-0.000	-0.011	-0.001	0.039
	100w	0.002	-0.015	0.000	-0.010
	49			0.002	0.014
	49w	-0.001	-0.022	-0.000	0.001
	9			0.001	-0.001
	9w	0.000	-0.090	-0.001	0.042
		B Standard deviations of the correlation coefficients			
Uniform	100	0.011	0.091	0.010	0.117
	100w	0.010	0.109	0.010	0.106
	49	0.010	0.128	0.012	0.140
	49w				
	9	0.011	0.414	0.010	0.365
	9w				
Normal	100	0.010	0.140	0.010	0.132
	100w	0.009	0.143	0.010	0.135
	49			0.010	0.172
	49w	0.011	0.175	0.010	0.170
	9			0.010	0.381
	9w	0.009	0.374	0.011	0.385

[a] *w* indicates the sample average statistic is generated by weighting the zones by the number of observations. The unweighted result is simply the arithmetic mean of the 100, 49 or 9 zonal statistics.

cannot be imputed to other scales without adjusting for the change in the number of reporting units.

3 Populations with high variances tend to exhibit more pronounced zoning effects than do populations with smaller variances.

4 Regression parameter estimates display scale effects that increase systematically with decreasing numbers of zones (that is, as the size of the areal units increases).

5 Standard deviations of regression parameter estimates display pronounced zoning effects. The standard deviations increase to a point at which the parameter estimates fail to provide reliable information (based on the expectation).

6 Correlation coefficients exhibit pronounced scale and zoning effects. As

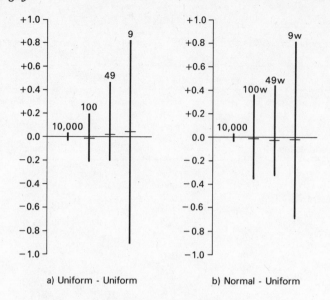

Figure 4.6   Scale and zoning effects for correlation
coefficients in Amrhein's experiments
(*Source*: adapted from Amrhein, 1994)

the size of the areal units increases (number of zones decreases) correlation coefficients increase in range to the point where the range and standard deviation of the values which might be observed converge systematically on the span of possible values (+1 to −1) of the statistic.

Amrhein's view is that such 'rules of aggregation' provide a starting point for further controlled experiments and that these experiments, in turn, might offer the predictability of scale and zoning effects sought by Fotheringham and Wong for the case of multivariate analysis. His view is that although there might be a long way to go before scale and zoning effects can easily be purged from the data encountered in spatial analysis, it 'is of some comfort to know that we can proceed in an orderly fashion'.

4 A NEW APPROACH

The findings of recent research, particularly Amrhein's (1994) proto 'rules of aggregation' suggest that scale and zoning effects and the associated problem of the ecological fallacy are beginning to be far better understood by geographers than at the time of Openshaw and Taylor's Bristol paper of 1979. The world of the spatial analyst is beginning to appear far less bleak and unpredictable than some analysts would suggest. Yet outside Geography, Statistics, and the confines of quantitative social science more generally, ignorance of these problems is still as widespread as ever. Moreover, ever easier, more widespread, access to small area census data (for example, in CD-ROM form), and the spreading of GIS technology with its inherent capacity to facilitate simplistic analysis of areal data, has substantially increased the real risk posed by these problems. The dilemma is that, 15 years on from Openshaw and Taylor's paper, whilst the understanding of such problems by geographers may have been deepened and enriched, two major hurdles still remain to be overcome.

The first hurdle is the lack of an adequate statistical framework for treating these problems, and the lack of clearly formulated statistical models which can embrace the empirical regularities uncovered by geographers working on these problems in the Openshaw and Taylor tradition. Indeed, a typical statistician's view is provided by Steel and Holt (1993) when they state that 'whilst aggregation effects have been studied empirically in many studies, the lack of a clearly specified statistical model has limited the interpretation of these studies'. That is not to say, however, that no efforts have been made to provide such a model. Beginning with the work of Goodman (1959), there have been several attempts across the social sciences to suggest a way forward. More recently, Arbia (1989) has proposed a framework which attempts to take account of the spatial configuration of the data (size, interconnectedness and dependence of the areal units, etc.) in establishing a relationship which leads from group-process (areal unit) observations to estimates of individual process characteristics. Using this framework he has demonstrated, for example, that scale effects on correlation coefficients depend upon various combinations of six elements which derive from the spatial configuration of the data: the two spatial autocorrelations, the cross-variance, the lagged cross-covariance, the size of the areal units, and the connectedness of the areal units. Unfortunately, Arbia's framework involves several very restrictive assumptions, notably stationarity of the stochastic spatial processes at the individual level and uniform covariances.

The second hurdle is the lack of a *practical* method which can be offered to researchers for using areal data to draw meaningful inferences about individual/household-level relationships. Given confidentiality and other restrictions on the availability of individual-level data, many researchers have no option other than to attempt such inference on the basis of small area census information, yet what they crave is a straightforward method of adjusting their area-level results to yield estimates of the underlying individual-level processes. Despite the enhanced understanding of the scale, zoning and ecological fallacy problems which geographers have achieved since the Bristol conference of 1979, the question of what practical methods can be suggested appears as intractable as ever. Indeed, some geographers regard the enterprise as impossible. For example, Openshaw (1984a) quotes Langbein and Lichtman's (1978, p. 61) view that 'investigators will find no philosopher's stone for transmuting information about groups into conclusions about individuals'.

Recently, however, a team of statisticians and geographers at the University of Southampton (Holt, Steel, Tramner, and Wrigley) have attempted to demonstrate the value of an alternative approach to the aggregation/ecological-fallacy problems. This approach, which derives from the work of Steel (1985), tackles both of the remaining hurdles in a direct fashion. That is, it attempts: (a) to provide the missing statistical framework as well as clearly specified statistical models; and (b) to provide the practical method necessary to adjust

area-level statistics to produce reasonable estimates of the underlying individual-level relationships. By taking advantage of recent developments in statistical
theory relating to inference in populations with group structures, and by
judicious incorporation of a strictly limited amount of exogenous individual-
level information within an innovative theoretical framework, it can be shown
that group-level (census district) data can in fact be used to provide practical
estimates of individual-level parameters and relationships. How then does this
new approach operate?

4.1 A conceptual framework

Consider the situation in which there is a finite population of N individuals/
households, each individual i having an associated set (vector) of characteristics/
variables of interest, y_i, but that the researcher has available information only
on the area/group-level values of those variables based on a sample of individuals in each of the census areas (n_g individuals in the g-th census area). Instead
of y_i, the researcher will therefore have available only vectors of sample mean
values; for example, in the case of the g-th area, where s denotes the sample,

$$\bar{y}_{gs} = \frac{1}{n_g} \sum_{i \in g,s} y_i .$$

(4.1)

To explore relationships between the variables, the researcher must therefore
rely upon the area-level variance–covariance matrix

$$\bar{S}_{yys} = \frac{1}{(m-1)} \sum_{g \in s} n_g (\bar{y}_{gs} - \bar{y}_s)(\bar{y}_{gs} - \bar{y}_s)'$$

(4.2)

where m is the number of areas, and $\bar{y}_s$ is the overall sample mean.

To understand the new approach proposed, it is necessary to ask why this
area-level variance–covariance matrix, $\bar{S}_{yys}$, is unlikely to be a reasonable
estimator of the desired individual-level variance–covariance matrix, Σ_{yy}, and
hence why statistics such as correlation coefficients computed on the basis of
the area-level variance–covariance matrix will normally provide unreliable
inferences concerning the individual-level relationships. The answer to this
question relates to the fact that $\bar{S}_{yys}$ will only approximate to Σ_{yy} if individu-
als/households with similar characteristics are scattered randomly over space.
This, however, is unlikely to be the case for individuals/households with similar
characteristics will tend to be grouped together in some fashion. That is to say,
a particular census area will tend to contain individuals/households that are
more alike than those in another census area. This positive clustering effect is
often accepted as an empirical fact but, as Steel (1985) suggests, there are at
least three explanations for its occurrence.

1   Some 'process' has and/or continues to operate, either when the groups
    are formed or through migration. That is to say, similar individuals/house-
    holds are constrained by the operation of the housing market into certain
    areas or, alternatively, choose to migrate into certain areas.

2 Individuals in the same group/area may be subject to similar external influences. For example, there may be some 'contextual' variable affecting all individuals in the area. Alternatively, some common influence may have operated in the past, the effects of which are still felt.

3 Individuals interact with each other and influence each other, and the frequency/strength of such interaction is likely to be greater between individuals in the same area than between individuals in different areas.

In practice, it is rather difficult to separate out these three potential influences on positive clustering as more than one may be operating in any given situation. For example, individuals may migrate into an area because of a contextual variable and that contextual variable may then affect the individuals' future behaviour. What is clear, however, is that any resolution of the aggregation/ecological-fallacy problems via a statistical modelling approach must explicitly incorporate this grouping/clustering effect into the model structure.

Previous attempts to provide the statistical framework required can be summarized as concentrating upon either explanations 1 or 2 of the clustering effect. In contrast, the new approach gives priority to explanation (1) – that is, to the 'grouping process' – and tackles the aggregation/ecological-fallacy problems via a model structure in which the group formation process is assumed to be represented by a set of auxiliary or 'grouping' variables, z_i. These variables can be thought of as being those which in some sense characterize the areas, that is, those individual-level variables whose distributions are not random across areas because of processes which operated when the groups were formed, or because of selective migration.

This new approach is due to Steel (1985) who developed a general theoretical framework for statistical analysis of populations with group structure rooted in methods developed by the Southampton statisticians to facilitate multivariate analysis of data from complex sample surveys (see Skinner, Holt, and Smith, 1988). From that work comes a simple 'grouping process' model which can be used to provide the statistical framework to tackle the aggregation/ecological-fallacy problems.

4.2 A model structure and its implications

In a finite population of N individuals/households, assume that each individual has an associated vector of variables of interest y_i, a vector of auxiliary/grouping variables z_i, and a vector c_i that indicates which area a particular individual is located in (that is, $c_i = [0, \ldots 1, \ldots 0]$ a vector with zeros in all positions except the one corresponding to the area in which the individual is located). The finite population of values can then be represented by the matrices $y = [y_1, \ldots, y_N]$, $z = [z_1, \ldots, z_N]$ and $c = [c_1, \ldots, c_N]$, and these matrices can be taken to be realizations of the random matrices Y, Z, and C, say.[1]

Given this finite population and the assumption that the 'grouping variables', z_i, in some sense characterize the areas, Steel (1985) suggests a simple model structure to account for variation in the characteristics/variables of interest between areas which takes the form:

$$E(\mathbf{Y}_i \mid \mathbf{z}, \mathbf{c}) = \mu_{\mathbf{y} \cdot \mathbf{z}} + \beta_{\mathbf{y}\mathbf{z}} \mathbf{z}_i$$

$$\text{var}(\mathbf{Y}_i \mid \mathbf{z}, \mathbf{c}) = \Sigma_{\mathbf{y}\mathbf{y} \cdot \mathbf{z}} \qquad (4.3)$$

$$\text{cov}(\mathbf{Y}_i, \mathbf{Y}_j \mid \mathbf{z}, \mathbf{c}) = \Delta_{\mathbf{y}\mathbf{y} \cdot \mathbf{z}} \quad \text{if } \mathbf{c}_i = \mathbf{c}_j$$

$$= 0 \quad \text{otherwise.}$$

In this model notice that:

1 The conditional expectation of $\mathbf{Y}_i$ depends only on the values of the grouping variables for individual i and is independent of both the area/group to which the individual belongs and the values of the grouping variables for other individuals.
2 The conditional variance is the same for all individuals in the population.
3 The conditional covariance between any two individuals depends on whether or not they are in the same area/group (that is, it captures residual within-group/intra-area covariance), but conditional cross-covariances between individuals in different areas are assumed to be zero.

In addition, notice that the model structure allows for the inclusion of 'contextual' variables, affecting all individuals in an area. That is to say, $\mathbf{z}_i$ can take the same value for every individual in the area ($\mathbf{z}_i = \mathbf{z}_g$ for all i in g). Moreover, the model structure can be generalized, if required, to allow $\Sigma_{\mathbf{y}\mathbf{y} \cdot \mathbf{z}}$ and $\Delta_{\mathbf{y}\mathbf{y} \cdot \mathbf{z}}$ to differ between areas/groups (for example, according to size of area), and to allow for non-zero covariances between individuals in different areas.

Although the structure of model (4.3) is of intrinsic interest in its own right, the important point about this grouping model as far as the aggregation/ecological fallacy problems are concerned relates to the properties of the standard estimators which can be produced from it. These estimators offer insight into the relationship between the area-level variance–covariance matrix, $\mathbf{S}_{\mathbf{y}\mathbf{y}\,\mathbf{s}}$, and the individual-level variance–covariance matrix, $\Sigma_{\mathbf{y}\mathbf{y}}$, and suggest a method of adjusting the area-level variance–covariance matrix to obtain the desired area-level estimator,

$$\hat{\Sigma}_{\mathbf{y}\mathbf{y}} \text{ of } \Sigma_{\mathbf{y}\mathbf{y}}.$$

In particular, it can be shown (Steel, 1985, p. 176; Steel and Holt, 1993) that given $\mathbf{z}$ and $\mathbf{c}$ and sampling issues aside, the conditional expectation of the area-level variance–covariance matrix takes the form:

$$E[\mathbf{S}_{\mathbf{y}\mathbf{y}\,\mathbf{s}} \mid \mathbf{s}, \mathbf{z}, \mathbf{c}] = \Sigma_{\mathbf{y}\mathbf{y}} + \beta_{\mathbf{y}\mathbf{z}}' (\mathbf{S}_{\mathbf{z}\mathbf{z}\,\mathbf{s}} - \Sigma_{\mathbf{z}\mathbf{z}}) \beta_{\mathbf{y}\mathbf{z}} + (\bar{n}^* - 1) \Delta_{\mathbf{y}\mathbf{y} \cdot \mathbf{z}}, \qquad (4.4)$$

where $\bar{n}^*$ is effectively the average sample size per area. From this equation, it can be seen that the conditional expectation of the area-level variance–covariance matrix is made up of the individual-level variance–covariance matrix, Σ_{yy}, adjusted by two additive 'bias' components. The first of these takes account of aggregation effects amongst the grouping variables, whilst the second takes account of residual within-group/intra-area correlations (that is, the conditional intra-group/area correlations given the grouping variables). Moreover, if the grouping variables do in fact characterize the areas in the sense of accounting for a significant proportion of variation in the y_i variables between areas, then it follows that $\Delta_{yy \cdot z}$ will be very small and the bias will derive mainly from the first component.

What this result implies is that, given suitable grouping variables, it is feasible to consider using $\bar{S}_{yys}$ to derive the required area-level estimator of the individual-level variance–covariance matrix. Equation (4.4) demonstrates that the bias in using $\bar{S}_{yys}$ to estimate Σ_{yy} due to the grouping variables is $\beta_{yz}' (\bar{S}_{zzs} - \Sigma_{zz}) \beta_{yz}$, so it follows that if $\beta_{yz}' (\Sigma_{zz} - \bar{S}_{zzs}) \beta_{yz}$ is added to $\bar{S}_{yys}$, the term due to the grouping variables will be removed.

The crucial question becomes, therefore, is it possible to calculate the bias term associated with the grouping variables? Fortunately, the answer is 'yes', subject merely to two extra conditions:

1 That the grouping variables are available on the area-level data file, thus allowing $\bar{S}_{zzs}$ to be calculated.
2 That some additional individual-level information is available, say from a sample s_0, which can be utilized to provide an unbiased estimate, termed S_{zzs_0}, of the variance–covariance matrix of the grouping variables Σ_{zz}.

Steel and Holt (1993) show that, given that these two extra conditions are satisfied, the required area-level estimator of the individual-level variance–covariance matrix Σ_{yy} can then be calculated from the area-level data using the expression

$$\hat{\bar{\Sigma}}_{yy} = \bar{S}_{yys} + \bar{B}_{yz}' \left(S_{zzs_0} - \bar{S}_{zzs} \right) \bar{B}_{yz} \tag{4.5}$$

where $E(\bar{B}_{yz} \mid z, c) = \beta_{yz}$. Having derived this vital area-level estimator, the aggregation/ecological fallacy problems are then essentially overcome. Aggregation bias due to selectivity or migration effects acting through individual level variables (the major bias component) has been removed leaving only residual intra-group/area correlation. The area-level estimates,

$$\hat{\bar{\Sigma}}_{yy} ,$$

of the components of the individual-level variance–covariance matrix can then be fed into all the formulae of the usual multivariate statistics – correlation coefficients, regression parameter estimates, and so on – allowing, for the first time in spatial analysis, a theoretically sound but practical method of deriving inferences about individual-level relationships from area-level data.

4.3 Some practical considerations

In theoretical terms, this new approach proposed by Steel (1985) appears to offer considerable advantages to the wide range of researchers faced with the need to use areal data to draw inferences about individual/household-level relationships. But, how in practice are such researchers to proceed? In particular, how are they to derive the vital individual-level variance–covariance matrix, S_{zzs_0}, via which the judicious amount of exogenous information essential to operationalize the approach is inserted into the theoretical structure? Clearly, obtaining such exogenous information is not likely to be a practical proposition for the majority of researchers.

At the conclusion of the ESRC-funded research programme at the University of Southampton (Holt and Wrigley, 1992) it is hoped that, at least for the UK, published tables of the required S_{zzs_0} variance–covariance matrices will be available in a variety of formats. These tables will be the key to operationalizing the approach, and it is hoped that their production may involve the cooperation of the Office of Population Censuses and Surveys. However, simply stating that tables will ultimately be available to researchers begs the question of how the Southampton team will initially identify the grouping variables and derive first estimates of the required variance–covariance matrices.

This aspect of the Southampton work is based around the availability for the first time in the UK of a public-use Sample of Anonymized Records (SAR) from the 1991 Census. (For the background to the development of the SAR see Wrigley (1990), and Marsh et al. (1991), and for a description of the SAR see Marsh and Teague (1993).) The SAR provides both 1 per cent and 2 per cent samples of individual British census records, from which it is possible to derive large individual-level variance–covariance matrices, denoted S_{yys_0}, of y, the census variables of interest. In practice, the grouping variables, z, are likely to form a subset of y. Ideally, they should be relatively few in number and relatively invariant to the choice of census variables in y.

To help identify these grouping variables, Steel (1985) suggests that the eigenvalues

$$\hat{\Theta}_1 \geq \ldots \hat{\Theta}_k \geq \ldots \geq \hat{\Theta}_p$$

of the matrix

$$S_{yys_0}^{-1} \, \bar{S}_{yys} \tag{4.6}$$

should be calculated as well as the associated eigenvector matrix $\hat{D}_y$ such that

$$\hat{D}_y \, \bar{S}_{yys} \, \hat{D}_y = \text{diag} \, (\hat{\Theta}_k) \quad \text{and} \quad \hat{D}_y \, S_{yys_0} \, \hat{D}_y = I. \tag{4.7}$$

In the Southampton work, the first element of equation (4.6) will be the inverse of an appropriate 1991 Census SAR variance–covariance matrix, whilst the second element will be the equivalent area-level variance–covariance matrix derived from the 1991 Small Area Census Statistics (SAS).

The new set of variables defined by the transformation

$$\mathbf{u}_i = \hat{\mathbf{D}}_\mathbf{y}\,\mathbf{y}_i \tag{4.8}$$

are termed the *canonical grouping variables* (CGVs) by Steel (1985), and are those variables which have successively maximum ratios of between-group to total variance, and which are uncorrelated with each other. The original variables which should be investigated as the possible 'grouping variables', $\mathbf{z}$, are those for which the loadings on the CGVs are 'significantly' different from zero, for CGVs whose eigenvalues are 'significantly' different from 1.

Once the grouping variables have been identified in this or other ways currently being explored by the Southampton team, then the required estimates of $\mathbf{S}_{\mathbf{zz}\,s_0}$ can be derived for insertion into equation (4.5). However, this stage of the Southampton team's research involves a considerable amount of painstaking empirical analysis which will not be completed until the latter period of 1994. What is clear already, however, is that a number of important insights into the aggregation issue can be derived from a consideration of the covariances between the CGVs and the original variables, and some of these issues are taken up by Steel and Holt (1993).

Following the completion of this empirical analysis,[2] British researchers faced in the future with just area-level census data and who wish to draw inferences about individual-level relationships will not need to repeat the Southampton work but will be able to use, directly, either of the following methods.

1 They will be able to derive the required $\hat{\Sigma}_{\mathbf{yy}}$ matrix from equation (4.5), on the basis of the standard area-level values of the identified $\mathbf{z}$ variables, plus an appropriate published estimate of $\mathbf{S}_{\mathbf{zz}\,s_0}$ based upon the Southampton research (or, alternatively, based upon improved versions of these matrices which OPCS may ultimately agree to provide on the basis of the $\mathbf{z}$ variables identified in the Southampton research).
2 They may be able to derive a version of the $\hat{\Sigma}$ matrix based solely on the first q most important CGVs. However, in this case the values of the CGVs would need to be made available externally (by the Southampton team or Census Offices) for each of the census areas in the researcher's analysis. The practicality/likelihood of this suggestion has yet to be established.

5 CONCLUSION

In *The Geographer's Art* (1990, p. 68), Peter Haggett identified three continuing tasks in spatial analysis. First, 'the precise identification of spatial effects separating those which are significant from those which are trivial'. Second, a flagging of 'those areas where errors may be large and solutions difficult'. Third, the development of 'analytical methods which build in corrections'. The resurgence of interest in the modifiable areal unit/ecological fallacy problems amongst spatial analysts in the early 1990s is focused precisely on the three tasks which Haggett identified.

The work of Amrhein, Fotheringham and others (for example, Wong with

Fotheringham, Flowerdew with Amrhein, and Hunt (1993) with Boots), cast in the Openshaw/Taylor tradition of large-scale numerical experiments, takes up the first two challenges. It is already clear that, as a result of this work, the differential impact of scale and zoning effects and the dimensions of the associated problem of the ecological fallacy are beginning to be understood with more precision than at the time of Openshaw and Taylor's Bristol paper in 1979. In addition, as this chapter demonstrates, the third task which Haggett identified is also the subject of considerable research effort. Indeed, the method being investigated in the ESRC-funded research at Southampton is driven by an explicit attempt to provide an analytical framework which permits a practical method of adjusting/correcting area-level statistics to produce reasonable estimates of the underlying individual-level relationships.

Haggett (1990, p. 69) concluded his analysis of the tasks of spatial analysis by suggesting that in attempting to balance 'the space-correcting tasks within quantitative geography [by] those which exploit spatial effects as one of the central planks of geographical research . . . new alliances with colleagues in mathematics, and in particular, those in statistics, [need] to be forged.' It is particularly appropriate to finish this chapter by noting, therefore, that the value of the new approach to the aggregation/ecological fallacy problems presented above, which derives from the work of the statisticians, Steel and Holt, is being tested and operationalized by a team which involves an alliance of statisticians and geographers. In a very real sense the new approach marks the 'return to old roots' which Haggett advocated.

NOTES

1 Note that in this chapter, this local notational convention for matrices of finite population values will be adopted for consistency with the work of Steel and Holt.
2 Initial results based upon three trial areas of the UK (Reigate, Manchester, Isle of Wight) are highly promising and were reported at the Association of American Geographers Conference, March 1994 (Steel, Holt, Tramner, and Wrigley, 1994).

REFERENCES

Amrhein, C.G. (1994). 'Searching for the elusive aggregation effect: evidence from statistical simulations.' *Environment and Planning A*, 26.
Arbia, G. (1989). *Spatial Data Configuration in Statistical Analysis of Regional Economic and Related Problems.* Dordrecht: Kluwer.
Clark, W.A.V. (1991). 'Geography in court: expertise in adversarial settings.' *Transactions of the Institute of British Geographers*, NS16, 5–20.
Fotheringham, A.S. & Wong, D.W.S. (1991). 'The modifiable areal unit problem in multivariate statistical analysis.' *Environment and Planning A*, 23, 1025–44.
Gehlke, C.E. & Biehl, K. (1934). 'Certain effects of grouping upon the size of the correlation coefficient in census tract material.' *Journal of the American Statistical Association Supplement*, 29, 169–70.

Goodman, L.A. (1959). 'Some alternatives to ecological correlation.' *American Journal of Sociology*, 64, 610–25.

Haggett, P. (1981). 'The edges of space.' In R.J. Bennett (ed.), *European Progress in Spatial Analysis*. London: Pion, 51–70.

Haggett, P. (1990). *The Geographer's Art*. Oxford: Blackwell.

Holt, D. & Wrigley, N. (1992). 'A new approach to the aggregation issue in census data analysis.' Research project No. A507 26 5013 funded by UK Economic and Social Research Council.

Hunt, L. (1993). 'Scale and aggregation effects upon factor analysis when observations are areal units.' Paper presented at 1993 Annual Meeting of The Canadian Association of Geographers, Carleton University, Ottawa, Canada.

Langbein, L.I. & Lichtman, A.J. (1978). *Ecological Inference*. Beverly Hills, CA: Sage.

Marsh, C. & Teague, A. (1993). 'Samples of anonymized records from the 1991 Census.' In Dale, A. and Marsh, C. (eds), *1991 Census Users' Guide*. London: Her Majesty's Stationery Office.

Marsh, C., Skinner, C.J., Arber, S., Penhale, B., Openshaw, S., Lievesley, D., Hobcraft, J., & Walford, N. (1991). 'The case for samples of anonymized records from the 1991 Census.' *Journal of the Royal Statistical Society A*, 154, 305–40.

Openshaw, S. (1984a). 'Ecological fallacies and the analysis of areal census data.' *Environment and Planning A*, 16, 17–31.

Openshaw, S. (1984b). *The Modifiable Areal Unit Problem*. Concepts and Techniques in Modern Geography 38. Norwich: Geo Books.

Openshaw, S. & Taylor, P.J. (1979). 'A million or so correlation coefficients: three experiments on the modifiable areal unit problem.' In N. Wrigley (ed.), *Statistical Applications in the Spatial Sciences*. London: Pion, 127–44.

Robinson, W.S. (1950). 'Ecological correlations and the behaviour of individuals.' *American Sociological Review*, 15, 351–57.

Skinner, C.J., Holt, D., & Smith, T.M.F. (1988). *The Analysis of Complex Surveys*. Chichester: John Wiley.

Steel, D.G. (1985). 'Statistical analysis of populations with group structure.' University of Southampton, Department of Social Statistics, unpublished PhD dissertation.

Steel, D.G. & Holt, D. (1993). 'Analyzing and adjusting aggregation effects in multivariate statistical analysis.' Manuscript in preparation for *Journal of American Statistical Association*, Dept. of Social Statistics, University of Southampton.

Steel, D.G., Holt, D., Tramner, M., & Wrigley, N. (1994). 'Aggregation and grouping effects in UK census data.' Paper presented at the 1994 annual conference of the Association of American Geographers, San Francisco, USA.

Wrigley, N. (1990). 'ESRC and the 1991 Census.' *Environment and Planning A*, 22, 573–82.

Yule, G.U. & Kendall, M.G. (1950). *An Introduction to the Theory of Statistics*. London: Griffin.

5

Computable Equilibrium and Spatial Interaction

W.D. Macmillan

1 INTRODUCTION

One of the many areas of the geographical literature to which Peter Haggett has made a major contribution is locational analysis. His 1965 book, *Locational Analysis in Human Geography*, was exceptional in both its scope and depth. It also had a significant influence on the debates in geography about the nature of the discipline. Amongst its topics were location, land use, and spatial interaction. The explanations of location and land use covered in the book drew, in one way or another, on assumptions about economic behaviour. The section on spatial interaction relied primarily on physical analogies. This difference of approach has been eroded steadily over the years as the economic basis of spatial interaction has been demonstrated with increasing clarity. The development of discrete choice theory, the linking of discrete choice to entropy maximization, and the introduction of the concept of group surplus maximization have been particularly important in this respect; see Wilson et al. (1981) for an excellent presentation of the key models and methods. Meanwhile, the economic foundations of location theory have improved. This has been due partly to a shift towards general equilibrium modelling and this shift has brought group surplus maximization models (with their focus on spatial interaction) and location and land use models closer together. There is, however, a significant gap that remains to be closed. The purpose of this chapter and a related paper (Macmillan, 1994) is to show how this can be done.

The problem of closure has two related aspects, both of which are concerned with the notion of completeness. The first has to do with the completeness of the treatment of the decision problem of individual economic agents: given a household budget, what happens to the residue after the discrete choice has been made? The second has to do with the completeness of the treatment of the economy as a whole: how is the complete set of prices determined on which individual choices depend and, given any feasible set of economic conditions, what will those prices and choices be?

To answer these questions, it is necessary to build a computable general equilibrium (CGE) model incorporating discrete choices.[1] As the foundation for such a system is a model of the behaviour of individual economic agents, it is important to clarify the microeconomic assumptions that lie behind discrete choice theory. It is argued here that the terms *utility, benefit, surplus*, and *bid rent* tend to be used interchangeably in the discrete choice literature and that they should not be. An attempt is made in section 2 to clarify the meaning of these terms by considering three forms of the household decision problem: utility maximization; expenditure minimization; and bid-rent maximization. Section 3 takes the first two of these forms and examines their implications for modelling aggregate discrete choice.

In section 4, a classical geographical problem is considered, namely the residential location problem. The particular form of the problem chosen for examination is the Williams and Senior (1978) version of the Herbert and Stevens (1960) problem. This work adopts a group surplus maximization approach and helps to illustrate the nature of the gap between the location theoretic and spatial interaction schools. The original Herbert and Stevens model and its development by Wheaton (1974) and others, can be thought of as belonging firmly in the location theoretic camp, with its microeconomic explanatory form, and linear and quadratic programming model structures. Wilson (1969), Senior and Wilson (1974), and others established a parallel but closely related spatial interaction approach to residential location. The behavioural basis of this approach was transformed by the development of discrete choice theory, as noted above. Williams and Senior's paper, with its discrete choice-theoretic foundation, represents the closest convergence of the location theoretic and spatial interaction approaches. The key question examined in section 4 is whether or not their model is actually consistent, as claimed, with the establishment of a competitive market equilibrium, given the models of microeconomic behaviour presented in section 2. It is argued that it is not consistent as it stands. The argument is extended to Williams and Senior's employment location model which has a very similar form to the residential location model. Indeed, the two models are presented as alternative interpretations of the standard doubly-constrained gravity model. The apparent symmetry of this model with respect to housing and employment turns out to be one of the sources of the difficulties identified in section 4.

Section 5 shows how these difficulties may be overcome and section 6 contains the chapter's conclusions.

2 INDIVIDUAL DISCRETE CHOICE

In the literature on discrete choice theory, the terms *utility, benefit, surplus* and *bid rent* (or, more generally, *bid value*) tend to be used interchangeably. However, there are important differences among the concepts which these terms are intended to denote. These differences need to be understood before proceeding. They are revealed below through the consideration of three different formulations of an individual discrete choice problem.

The choice problem facing individuals or individual households is usually overlooked in discussions of discrete choice theory. This does not appear to be unreasonable on the face of it as a simple ranking of alternatives is sufficient to identify the problem's solution, namely, the alternative with the highest ranking. But how is the ranking determined? The standard answer is that it is based on utilities, surpluses or bid values. To see why this is, at best, incomplete, it is sufficient to compare the form of the discrete choice problem which appears to be implicit in discrete choice models with the standard continuous choice problem from the theory of the household. The latter involves a choice space over which a utility function and an expenditure function are defined: the choice problem can be solved either by fixing the expenditure level (thereby imposing a budget constraint) and maximizing utility, or by fixing a utility level and minimizing expenditure. The former involves a utility function but appears to make no use of an expenditure function. Consequently, it does not deal with the utility derived from expenditure on commodities other than that (or those) involved in the discrete choice.

It is easy enough to incorporate expenditure functions and, therefore, budget constraints into the discrete choice framework. When this is done, the differences among utility, benefit, surplus, and bid value become clear. What is more, the inadequacy of the bid-value concept is revealed. Three related formulations of a household choice problem will be used to demonstrate how income and expenditure can be melded with utility in a discrete choice context. Each of them involves a continuous composite commodity in addition to discrete commodities. In the utility maximizing version of the problem, the purchase of this commodity adds to the household's utility and allows the budget to be fully spent. Equivalent conditions are achieved in the two other problems. The addition of the composite commodity is necessary for the achievement of *completeness* in the household decision problem. Without it, there will generally be a gap between budget (or income) and expenditure from which the household receives no benefit.

2.1 Utility maximization

Consider first the following household decision problem:

$$\max_{x_k^0, \ldots, x_k^N} u_k = u^0 x_k^0 + \sum_{n=1}^{N} u_k^n x_k^n$$

subject to

$$p^0 x_k^0 + \sum_{n=1}^{N} p^n x_k^n \leq \overline{w}_k,$$

$$\sum_{n=1}^{N} x_k^n = 1,$$

$$x_k^n = 0 \text{ or } 1 \text{ for } n = 1, \ldots, N,$$

$$x_k^0 \geq 0,$$

where

$$u^0, p^0, \overline{w}_k > 0,$$

$$u_k^n, p^n > 0 \quad \forall n,$$

$$p^n < \overline{w}_k \quad \forall n,$$

and

$$\exists \, n' \text{ such that } (u_k^{n'} - u^0 p^{n'}/p^0) > (u_k^n - u^0 p^n/p^0) \, \forall n \neq n'.$$

In this problem, u_k is household k's (linear) utility function whose arguments are the discrete choice variables x_k^n for $n = 1, \ldots, N$ and the continuous variable x_k^0, which represents the demand for some composite good. For analytical convenience, it is assumed that the utility parameter associated with the continuous composite good does not vary across households, but those associated with the discrete alternatives do vary. In the first constraint (the budget constraint), p^0 is the price of the composite good, p^n is the cost or price of alternative n, and $\overline{w}_k$ is the household's wage income. The next two constraints ensure that one and only one discrete variable can be equal to one, implying that one unit of one and only one discrete commodity can be chosen. The last constraint and the first two sets of conditions on the parameters are self-explanatory. The third parameter condition ensures that whatever discrete alternative is chosen, some quantity of the continuous commodity will be acquired as well: if $x_k^n = 1$ then the maximum value of x_k^0 is $(\overline{w}_k - p^n)/p^0$ (from the budget constraint), so the maximum utility achievable when n is selected is $u^0(\overline{w}_k - p^n)/p^0 + u_k^n$. The last parameter condition ranks the utilities associated with each discrete alternative (the common $u^0 \overline{w}_k/p^0$ term cancels) such that n' is the optimal alternative. That is, the optimal solution is

$$x_k^{n'} = 1,$$

$$x_k^n = 0 \quad \forall n \neq n',$$

$$x_k^0 = (\overline{w}_k - p^{n'})/p^0.$$

Clearly, it is not necessary to have $u_k^{n'} > u_k^n \, \forall n \neq n'$ for n' to be the optimal alternative. Note also that by multiplying through by p^0/u^0, the *utility* ranking (in the last parameter condition) could be turned into an equivalent *surplus* ranking, where the surplus of alternative n, s_k^n, is given by

$$s_k^n \equiv b_k^n + \overline{w}_k - p^n$$

in which p^n is the cost and b_k^n is the *benefit* of alternative n, where the latter is defined to be equal to $u_k^n p^0/u^0$. Note that benefit is expressed in the same monetary units as cost. As $\overline{w}_k$ is common to all alternatives, the surplus ranking takes the form

$$b_k^{n'} - p^{n'} > b_k^n - p^n \ \forall n \neq n'.$$

If the cost term is disaggregated into rent, r^n, and commuting costs, c^n, this becomes

$$b_k^{n'} - r^{n'} - c^{n'} > b_k^n - r^n - c^n \ \forall n \neq n',$$

and, if wage income is not common to all alternatives, it alters to

$$b_k^{n'} + w^{n'} - r^{n'} - c^{n'} > b_k^n + w^n - r^n - c^n \ \forall n \neq n',$$

where w^n is the wage associated with alternative n.

It is worth dwelling on the distinction between, on the one hand, the utility parameters and benefit terms u_k^n and b_k^n, and on the other, the total utilities and surpluses of each choice package. Evidently, a ranking of the discrete alternatives in terms of u_k^n or b_k^n is not the same as a ranking based on the surpluses (involving terms of the form $[p^0(u_k^n/u^0) - p^n]$) or, equivalently, the total utilities (terms of the form $[u_k^n - u^0(p^n/p^0)]$). As these two sets of terms are functions of the price of the composite good, p^0, changes in p^0 can change the rankings. Conversely, the rankings also influence p^0. The rankings determine the choice of discrete alternative and the latter determines the demand for the composite good. In the aggregate, the distribution of choices of discrete alternatives across the population determines the aggregate demand for the composite good. This aggregate demand interacts with supply to determine p^0. Thus, the distribution of discrete choices influences the total utilities or surpluses. It follows that taking *utility*, *benefit*, and *surplus* as exogenous and interchangeable implies, at best, a partial equilibrium analysis based on extreme assumptions. A general equilibrium approach requires, as a minimum, the use of endogenously determined ranking terms, involving an endogenously determined continuous commodity price.

2.2 Expenditure minimization

Now consider the expenditure minimization problem associated with the above utility maximization problem. It takes the following form:

$$\min_{x_k^0, \ldots, x_k^N} w_k = p^0 x_k^0 + \sum_{n=1}^{N} p^n x_k^n$$

subject to

$$u^0 x_k^0 + \sum_{n=1}^{N} u_k^n x_k^n \geq \bar{u}_k,$$

$$\sum_{n=1}^{N} x_k^n = 1,$$

$$x_k^n = 0 \text{ or } 1 \quad \text{for } n = 1, \ldots, N,$$

$$x_k^0 \geq 0,$$

where

$$p^0, u^0, \bar{u}_k > 0,$$

$$p^n, u_k^n > 0 \quad \forall n,$$

$$u_k^n < \bar{u}_k \qquad \forall n,$$

and

$$\exists\, n' \text{ such that } (p^{n'} - p^0 u_k^{n'}/u^0) > (p^n - p^0 u_k^n/u^0) \,\forall n \neq n'.$$

The optimal solution to this problem is

$$x_k^{n'} = 1,$$

$$x_k^n = 0 \,\forall n \neq n',$$

$$x_k^0 = (\bar{u}_k - u^{n'})/u^0.$$

The expenditure ranking (the last parameter condition) is identical to the surplus ranking associated with the utility maximization problem (the expenditure ranking can be converted into the surplus ranking by multiplying through by -1). Thus, the only difference between the solutions to the two problems is in the value of x_k^0. Aggregate choice models based on these two microeconomic problems will, in general, yield different solutions because p^0 will be affected by aggregate demand for the composite commodity and different values of p^0 will yield different rankings of the discrete alternatives. However, if the exogenous utility in the expenditure minimization problem is equal to the optimal value of the objective function in the utility maximization problem and the equivalent condition is satisfied for expenditures, then the solutions will be the same. Thus, under certain conditions, the two approaches are interchangeable.

2.3 Bid rent maximization

Next, consider the problem of bid rent maximization. Bid rent is defined as the maximum amount a household with a given budget would be able to pay for a given house type in a given location whilst maintaining a specified level of utility. Before formulating the bid rent maximization problem, it is necessary to specialize the general cost of alternative n, p^n, as the sum of two elements, rental cost, r^n, and commuting cost, c^n. The problem can then be written

$$\max_{x_k^0, \ldots, x_k^N} \sum_{n=1}^{N} r^n x_k^n = \overline{w}_k - p^0 x_k^0 - \sum_{n=1}^{N} c^n x_k^n$$

subject to

$$u^0 x_k^0 + \sum_{n=1}^{N} u_k^n x_k^n \geq \overline{u}_k \,,$$

$$\sum_{n=1}^{N} x_k^n = 1 \,,$$

$$x_k^n = 0 \text{ or } 1 \quad \text{for } n = 1, \ldots, N \,,$$

$$x_k^0 \geq 0 \,,$$

where

$$p^0, u^0, \overline{u}_k > 0,$$

$$u_k^n, p^n > 0 \quad \forall n,$$

$$u_k^n < \overline{u}_k \qquad \forall n,$$

and

$$\exists \ n' \text{ such that } (c^{n'} - p^0 u_k^{n'}/u^0) > (c^n - p^0 u_k^n/u^0) \ \forall n \neq n'.$$

Maximizing

$$\overline{w}_k - p^0 x_k^0 - \sum_{n=1}^{N} c^n x_k^n$$

is identical to minimizing

$$p^0 x_k^0 + \sum_{n=1}^{N} c^n x_k^n,$$

so that this problem differs from the expenditure minimization problem in only one respect: c^n appears in place of p^n in the objective function and last parameter condition. Bid rent maximization can be thought of, therefore, as a special case of expenditure minimization in which only non-rental expenditure is minimized. This difference is sufficient to ensure that the optimal alternative will differ, in general, from the optimal alternative in the expenditure minimization and utility maximization problems. The optimal bid rent is $\overline{w}_k - p^0 (\overline{u}_k - u_k^{n'}) / u^0 - c^n$ since the optimal value of z is $(\overline{u}_k - u_k^{n'}) / u^0$. The restriction of bid rent maximization to non-rental expenditure makes it unattractive as a behavioural concept. There are also significant problems in reconciling bid rents with market rents in competitive markets. Similar problems exist with the use of bid wages. It will be argued below that the Williams and Senior housing choice model (which uses bid rents) and employment choice model (which uses bid wages) both need to be recast as simple surplus maximization models, where surplus is defined as in section 2.1.

3 AGGREGATE DISCRETE CHOICE THEORY

In the random utility form of (aggregate) discrete choice theory, it is assumed that each individual makes a deterministic decision based on a (utility) ranking of discrete alternatives but that the observer/modeller has incomplete knowledge of the values assigned to alternatives by members of the decision-making population. In the multinomial logit model, it is assumed that the utility terms, u_k^n, have independent, identical, double-exponential distributions with mean u^n and parameter λ. It can be shown that this implies that the expected value of the utility of the discrete choice made by a randomly selected individual is

$$\sum_{n \in N} \left(u^n P^n - \tfrac{1}{\lambda} P^n \ln P^n \right)$$

such that

$$\sum_{n \in N} P^n = 1, \quad P^n \geq 0 \quad \forall n,$$

where P^n is the probability of selecting an individual who has chosen discrete alternative n from the set of available discrete alternatives N.

In the individual decision problems discussed above, some quantity of a continuous composite commodity is chosen as well as a discrete alternative. If x^0 is the demand for the composite commodity by the population as a whole and u^0 is the utility term associated with this composite commodity by all households, then the expected contribution from this source to the utility of a randomly selected individual is $u^0 x^0 / K$, where K is the population size. Thus, the total expected utility for a randomly selected individual is

$$\frac{u^0 x^0}{K} + \sum_{n \in N} \left(u^n P^n - \frac{1}{\lambda} P^n \ln P^n \right).$$

Aggregating over the population yields the welfare function

$$u = u^0 x^0 + K \sum_{n \in N} \left(u^n P^n - \frac{1}{\lambda} P^n \ln P^n \right).$$

If the total demand for discrete commodity n is x^n, this expression can be reformulated as

$$u = u^0 x^0 + \sum_{n \in N} \left(u^n x^n - \frac{1}{\lambda} x^n \ln \frac{x^n}{K} \right),$$

whilst the probability restriction becomes

$$\sum_{n \in N} x^n = K, \quad x^n \geq 0 \quad \forall n.$$

The probability restriction is an essential part of the apparatus for deriving the multinomial logit (MNL) model. Because of the presence of the continuous composite commodity, an expenditure function is also required. Defining p^0 to be the price of the continuous composite commodity and p^n to be the price of discrete alternative n, the MNL formula may be generated by solving the problem

$$\max \ u = u^0 x^0 + \sum_{n \in N} \left(u^n x^n - \frac{1}{\lambda} x^n \ln \frac{x^n}{K} \right)$$

subject to

$$p^0 x^0 + \sum_{n \in N} p^n x^n \leq \overline{w},$$

$$\sum_{n \in N} x^n = K,$$

$$x^0 \geq 0, \quad x^n \geq 0 \quad \forall n,$$

where $\overline{w}$ is aggregate income so that the first constraint is an expenditure or budget constraint. From the Kuhn–Tucker conditions for this problem, it can be shown that

$$x^n = \frac{K \exp\left[\lambda\left(u^n - \gamma p^n\right)\right]}{\sum_{n'} \exp\left[\lambda\left(u^{n'} - \gamma p^{n'}\right)\right]}$$

and

$$(u^0 - \gamma p^0)\, x^0 = 0 .$$

If it is assumed that $(\overline{w}/K) > p^n$ for all n (so that all members of the population have some disposable income after paying for their discrete choice), the positivity of u^0 implies that $x^0 > 0$, so that $\gamma = u^0/p^0$. Thus, the exponents in the above equation for x^n are utility ranking terms (see the ranking expressions in section 2.1). Changing the exponents into a benefit ranking form transforms the equation into

$$x^n = \frac{K \exp\left[\dfrac{\lambda u^0}{p^0}\left(b^n - p^n\right)\right]}{\sum_{n'} \exp\left[\dfrac{\lambda u^0}{p^0}\left(b^{n'} - p^{n'}\right)\right]} \tag{5.1}$$

where $b^n \equiv p^0 u^n / u^0$.

This expression can also be generated by solving the aggregate expenditure minimization problem

$$\min\ w = p^0 x^0 + \sum_n p^n x^n$$

subject to

$$u^0 x^0 + \sum_{n \in N} \left(u^n x^n - \frac{1}{\lambda} x^n \ln \frac{x^n}{K}\right) \geq \overline{u},$$

$$\sum_{n \in N} x^n = K,$$

$$x^n \geq 0 \quad \forall n,$$

provided that $\overline{u}$ is large enough to ensure that each decision-maker chooses a positive quantity of the composite commodity. This condition can be satisfied only approximately because the double exponential distribution tails off asymptotically.

If the cost term p^n is expanded into rental and commuting costs, equation (5.1) becomes

$$x^n = \frac{K \exp\left[\dfrac{\lambda u^0}{p^0}\left(b^n - r^n - c^n\right)\right]}{\displaystyle\sum_{n'} \exp\left[\dfrac{\lambda u^0}{p^0}\left(b^{n'} - r^{n'} - c^{n'}\right)\right]} . \tag{5.2}$$

If alternatives differ in terms of wage and commuting cost, but not rent, the expression becomes

$$x^n = \frac{K \exp\left[\dfrac{\lambda u^0}{p^0}\left(b^n + w^n - c^n\right)\right]}{\displaystyle\sum_{n'} \exp\left[\dfrac{\lambda u^0}{p^0}\left(b^{n'} + w^{n'} - c^{n'}\right)\right]} , \tag{5.3}$$

whilst differences in both wages and rents imply that

$$x^n = \frac{K \exp\left[\dfrac{\lambda u^0}{p^0}\left(b^n + w^n - r^n - c^n\right)\right]}{\displaystyle\sum_{n'} \exp\left[\dfrac{\lambda u^0}{p^0}\left(b^{n'} + w^{n'} - r^{n'} - c^{n'}\right)\right]} . \tag{5.4}$$

4 DISCRETE CHOICE AND THE DOUBLY CONSTRAINED SPATIAL INTERACTION MODEL

These observations will be put to work after considering the Williams and Senior (1978) residential and job choice interpretations of the fully constrained spatial interaction model. Their argument is as follows.

Whereas the singly constrained model has a clear-cut residential choice or job choice interpretation in a home-work interaction context because of the asymmetric form of the constraints . . . , the symmetric constraints [of the doubly constrained model] . . . imply that both interpretations are possible, so to speak, simultaneously. (Williams and Senior, 1978, p. 263)

4.1 The residential location model

The housing market (residential choice) interpretation is said to be a generalization of the Herbert–Stevens model allowing for dispersion of preferences in the residential choice-making population. It involves the maximization of a locational surplus function subject to two sets of constraints:

$$\max_{T_{ij}^{mn}} \sum_{ijmn} \left[\left(R_{ij}^{mn} - c_{ij} \right) T_{ij}^{mn} - \frac{1}{\lambda^n} T_{ij}^{mn} \ln \frac{T_{ij}^{mn}}{D_i^m E_j^n} \right] \tag{5.5a}$$

subject to

$$\sum_{jn} T_{ij}^{mn} = D_i^m \quad \forall im, \tag{5.5b}$$

$$\sum_{im} T_{ij}^{mn} = E_j^n \quad \forall jn, \tag{5.5c}$$

$$T_{ij}^{mn} \geq 0 \qquad \forall ijmn, \tag{5.5d}$$

where, according to the authors,

T_{ij}^{mn} is the number of persons working in jobs of type n in zone j who live in a house of type m in zone i;

R_{ij}^{mn} is the mean bid rent associated with a house of type $\{i, m\}$ and with $\{j, n\}$ type workers;

D_i^m is the stock of houses of type $\{i, m\}$;

E_j^n is the number of jobs of type $\{j, n\}$;

c_{ij} is the cost of travel from i to j.

This program is said to establish 'a market equilibrium based on competitive bidding'.

It is easy to show that the optimal value of T_{ij}^{mn} in the above problem is given by

$$T_{ij}^{mn} = D_i^m E_j^n \exp \left[\lambda^n \left(R_{ij}^{mn} - c_{ij} - \rho_i^m + \omega_j^n \right) - 1 \right]$$

where ρ_i^m and ω_j^n are the dual variables associated with the housing and employment constraints respectively. When combined with the employment constraint after summing over i and m, this expression implies that

$$T_{ij}^{mn} = \frac{D_i^m E_j^n \exp \left[\lambda^n \left(R_{ij}^{mn} - c_{ij} - \rho_i^m \right) \right]}{\sum_{i'm'} D_{i'}^{m'} \exp \left[\lambda^n \left(R_{i'j}^{m'n} - c_{i'j} - \rho_{i'}^{m'} \right) \right]}. \tag{5.6}$$

In the interpretation of Williams and Senior, ρ_i^m is the rent on housing of type m in location i, and ω_j^n is said to represent a consumer surplus accruing to locators. The appearance of D_i^m in equation (5.6) is justified by reference to a general discrete choice probability formula

$$P_{ji} = \frac{a_i \exp [\lambda(u_i - c_{ji})]}{\sum_{i'} a_{i'} \exp [\lambda(u_{i'} - c_{ji'})]}$$

where u_i is said to be the mean value of the *utility* gained from performing an activity at location i from zone j, and c_{ji} is the associated travel cost. The term a_i is said to be the *a priori* probability that the activity will be performed in zone i. In the residential choice model, Williams and Senior say that a_i is proportional to the housing stock D_i^m.

4.2 Some criticisms

For equation (5.6) to carry a discrete-choice, residential-location interpretation, it should have the same form as equation (5.2) but it differs in two respects: the presence of the D_i^m terms and the interpretation of R_{ij}^{mn} as bid rent. The precise interpretations given to T_{ij}^{mn} and E_j^n are also open to criticism, as is the interpretation of ω_j^n.

Consider first the D_i^m terms. If equation (5.6) is to be interpreted as the outcome of a discrete choice process, these terms must be capable of playing a part in such a process. An individual who chooses alternative $\{i, m\}$ does so because he or she ranks $\{i, m\}$ above all other alternatives. The only role D_i^m could play is by influencing this ranking. To put it another way, the aggregate concept of attractiveness, which D_i^m can be thought of as representing, has to be convertible into a benefit term based on individual household preferences. If $b_i^{mn} \equiv \mu/\lambda^n \ln D_i^m$ (where μ is a conversion factor introduced to ensure dimensional consistency), equation (5.6) could be rewritten as

$$T_{ij}^{mn} = \frac{E_j^n \exp [\lambda^n(R_{ij}^{mn} + b_i^{mn} - c_{ij} - \rho_i^m)]}{\sum_{i'm'} \exp [\lambda^n(R_{i'j}^{m'n} + b_{i'}^{m'n} - c_{i'j} - \rho_{i'}^{m'})]}. \tag{5.7}$$

This equation makes some sense behaviourally. The term b_i^{mn} could be interpreted, conventionally enough, as a measure of the attractiveness of alternative $\{i, m\}$, in benefit terms, to workers employed in job n.

It follows that equation (5.6) could be altered to conform to the required specification but not without some convoluted arguments. It would be simpler to reformulate problem (5.5) to produce the desired result directly.

The second problem with the Williams and Senior model is the interpretation of R_{ij}^{mn} as the mean bid rent associated with a house type $\{i, m\}$ and worker type $\{j, n\}$. Bid rent is a concept of little value at the best of times and is a positive nuisance here. The discussion in the last paragraph of section 2.3 suggests that, in the present context, the mean value of bid rent may be written as

$$w_j^n + b_{ij}^{mn} - c_{ij} - \overline{b} \tag{5.8}$$

where b_{ij}^{mn} is the mean benefit of housing type $\{i, m\}$ to workers of type $\{j, n\}$, w_j^n is the wage from job type $\{j, n\}$, c_{ij} is the associated commuting cost, and $\overline{b} \equiv p^0 \overline{u} / u^0$, which might be thought of as the target benefit level. Both m_j^n and $\overline{b}$ are independent of i and m so an aggregate discrete choice model derived from terms of the form of expression (5.8) would have only $(b_{ij}^{mn} - c_{ij})$ terms in the exponents. Thus, to interpret equation (5.6) as deriving from a process of bid rent maximization, R_{ij}^{mn} should be regarded as a benefit term (that is, it should be replaced, in effect, by b_{ij}^{mn}) and ρ_i^m should be deleted. Alternatively, if R_{ij}^{mn} was interpreted strictly as bid rent, as in expression (5.8), then equation (5.6) would become

$$T_{ij}^{mn} = \frac{D_i^m E_j^n \exp [\lambda^n(b_{ij}^{mn} - 2c_{ij} - \rho_i^m)]}{\displaystyle\sum_{i'm'} D_{i'}^{m'} \exp [\lambda^n(b_{i'j}^{m'n} - 2c_{i'j} - \rho_{i'}^{m'})]}$$

which has no apparent behavioural interpretation.

There is a further, more general, problem with the use of the bid rent concept in the context of distributed preferences. If the value of the benefit term for each alternative varies across the population according to some distribution, then bid rents will be similarly distributed. But a spatial equilibrium determined by bid rent maximization is supposed to have properties which make this unacceptable. In Alonso's work, from which the Herbert–Stevens model is supposed to take its theoretical underpinning, the following condition must be met for an equilibrium:

each area goes only to that use offering the highest net return per unit of land . . . [which] in turn implies three things
a) each household selects . . . that [housing–land bundle] yielding the highest net rent . . .
b) that household which locates in an area must have a net land rent at least as high as [the net land rent which could be offered at that location by] any household not located there,
c) if two households locate in the same area, their net land rents must be identical. (Wheaton, 1974)

Clearly, the last of these clauses would not be met with distributed preferences and the second could not be guaranteed either. What is more, this problem cannot be assumed away by modifying the definition of equilibrium. Suppose the actual rent for a given alternative was the mean of a distribution of bid rents. A decision-maker offering a bid lower than the mean would fail to be located. It would be necessary to increase the bid to the mean. Similarly, a decision-maker offering more than the mean could reduce the bid to the mean. The idea that bid rents can be distributed is simply inconsistent with the notion that actual rents do not vary between individuals. It seems sensible to abandon the bid rent concept altogether.

Another problem concerns Williams and Senior's interpretation of the ω_j^n terms, which follows that of Herbert and Stevens. According to Wheaton (1974),

> Herbert and Stevens were both insightful and correct . . . [in interpreting these terms as] subsidies or surpluses which each household must receive to achieve location in a particular market.

However, as Wheaton demonstrated, the existence of non-zero ω_j^n terms is inconsistent with the existence of an equilibrium essentially because the *ex ante* assumptions about household income are inconsistent with the *ex post* conditions. Having $\omega_j^n = 0$ for all j and n is, of course, equivalent to removing the second set of constraints from the doubly constrained model. The implication of this is that the either/or (housing choice/job choice) interpretation of the doubly constrained spatial interaction model is untenable.

4.3 The employment location model

The Williams and Senior employment location interpretation of the doubly constrained gravity model takes the form

$$\max_{T_{ij}^{mn}} \quad \sum_{ijmn} \left[-(w_i^{mn} + c_{ij}) \, T_{ij}^{mn} - \frac{1}{\lambda^m} \, T_{ij}^{mn} \ln \frac{T_{ij}^{mn}}{D_i^m \, E_j^n} \right] \tag{5.9a}$$

subject to

$$\sum_{im} T_{ij}^{mn} = E_j^n \qquad \forall jn, \tag{5.9b}$$

$$\sum_{jn} T_{ij}^{mn} = D_i^m \qquad \forall im, \tag{5.9c}$$

$$T_{ij}^{mn} \geq 0 \qquad \forall ijmn, \tag{5.9d}$$

where $(w_i^{mn} + c_{ij})$ is interpreted as the bid wage 'by persons resident in zone i with job skills or qualifications m for jobs of type n in zone j', in which w_i^{mn} is said to be 'housing expenditure plus expenditure on other goods'.

This formulation suffers from the same problems as the residential location model. An employment choice model should generate an expression like equation (5.3) but the above problem implies that

$$T_{ij}^{mn} = \frac{D_i^m E_j^n \exp [\lambda^m (\omega_j^n - w_i^{mn} - c_{ij})]}{\sum\limits_{j'n'} E_{j'}^{n'} \exp [\lambda^m (\omega_{j'}^{n'} - w_i^{mn'} - c_{ij'})]} .$$

Both models need to be refined. Particular attention needs to be given to the interpretation of the constraint sets and the nature and size of the decision-making population.

5 SURPLUS MAXIMIZATION AND DISCRETE CHOICE EQUILIBRIUM

Consider first the question of the size of the population and the decisions its members are making. In the multinomial logit model, the presumption is that each individual chooses one and only one discrete alternative. In applying this model to the multidimensional problem of selecting a house (type and location) and/or job (type and location), it is necessary to regard the choice alternatives as composites or bundles.[2] It is also necessary to have the number of decision-makers equal to the number of available bundles. This does not entail an assumption that everyone is housed and/or employed since unemployment and homelessness can be taken to be employment and dwelling types. Assuming that there are D_i^m units of dwelling type m in location i and E_j^n units of employment type n in location j, then a condition for the application of the multinomial logit model to a combined housing-employment-journey choice is that

$$\sum_{im} D_i^m = \sum_{jn} E_j^n = K$$

where, as above, K is the total population of decision-makers.

This population may be subdivided into classes with different characteristics. For example, classes could be distinguished by assuming that each household is capable of one and only one type of employment. Thus, it could be assumed that, for $n = 1, \ldots, N$, class n has K_n members, where

$$K_n = \sum_j E_j^n \quad \text{and} \quad K = \sum_n K_n .$$

Alternatively, households might be classified by dwelling type m, such that

$$K_m = \sum_i D_i^m \quad \text{and} \quad K = \sum_m K_m .$$

For the time being, let us assume that the population is divided into H household classes ($h = 1, \ldots, H$) in a way which is independent of employment, housing, and locational characteristics. Defining x_h^0 to be the aggregate demand by members of class h for the continuous composite commodity, u_h^0 to be the associated utility term, T_{hij}^{mn} to be the number of members of class h choosing dwelling type m in location i and job type n in location j, u_{hij}^{mn} to be the associated utility term, and K_h to be the population of class h, the welfare of class h may be written as

$$u_h = u_h^0 x_h^0 + \sum_{ijmn} \left(u_{hij}^{mn} T_{hij}^{mn} - \frac{1}{\lambda_h} T_{hij}^{mn} \ln \frac{T_{hij}^{mn}}{K_h} \right)$$

where

$$\sum_{ijmn} T_{hij}^{mn} = K_h \quad \text{and} \quad T_{hij}^{mn} \geq 0 \quad \forall ijmn.$$

In addition to this welfare or aggregate utility function, it is possible to define the total expenditure of household-class h as

$$p^0 x_h^0 + \sum_{ijmn} (r_i^m + c_{ij} - w_j^n) T_{hij}^{mn},$$

where p^0 is the price of the composite commodity, r_i^m is the rent (per month, say) for a dwelling of type m in i, c_{ij} is the (monthly) cost of travel from i to j, and w_j^n is the wage (per month) for a job of type n in j.

Using these welfare and expenditure functions, two optimization problems can be formulated: one in which welfare is maximized subject to a budget constraint; the other in which expenditure is minimized subject to a welfare constraint. These two problems, in which the u_h^0, u_{hij}^{mn}, p^0, r_i^m, c_{ij}, and w_j^n terms are all parameters, yield solutions that are consistent with the corresponding problems for individual decision-makers (as discussed above). Certain reformulations of these two problems allow subsets of the above parameters to be converted into variables so that their values may be determined endogenously. This can be done within the welfare-maximizing and expenditure-minimizing frameworks. However, it is more fruitful to convert welfare into benefit and then combine it with cost (or expenditure) to produce a net-benefit or surplus maximization model.

5.1 Surplus or net-benefit maximization

The above expression for welfare, or aggregate utility, can be converted into a measure of benefit through the introduction of an appropriate multiplier, α_h, the precise nature of which will be discussed later. Once converted, cost terms can be subtracted to produce a net-benefit or surplus function. Surplus can be summed across household classes and this sum can be maximized subject to the probability restriction. The solution to the maximization problem takes the multinomial logit form. In addition to the maximand and the probability restriction, it is possible to introduce market-clearing conditions.[3] The Lagrange multipliers attached to these market-clearing conditions may be interpreted as the associated market prices. Thus, it is possible to formulate a surplus maximization problem for the combined choice of housing, employment, and journey-to-work in which rents and wages are endogenous. The problem takes the form

$$\max \sum_h \left\{ \alpha_h \left[u_h^0 x_h^0 + \sum_{ijmn} \left(u_{hij}^{mn} T_{hij}^{mn} - \frac{1}{\lambda_h} T_{hij}^{mn} \ln \frac{T_{hij}^{mn}}{K_h} \right) \right] - \sum_{ijmn} c_{ij} T_{hij}^{mn} - p^0 x_h^0 \right\}$$

subject to

$$\sum_{hjn} T_{ij}^{mn} \le D_i^m \qquad \forall im,$$

$$\sum_{him} T_{ij}^{mn} \ge E_j^n \qquad \forall jn,$$

$$\sum_{ijmn} T_{hij}^{mn} = K_h \qquad \forall h,$$

$$T_{hij}^{mn} \ge 0 \qquad \forall hijmn.$$

The first two sets of constraints in this problem are market-clearing conditions for the housing and job markets respectively. The third and fourth constitute the probability restriction. The c_{ij} terms are spatial interaction costs and p^0 is the price of the composite continuous commodity, as above. These terms could treated as endogenous variables by specifying market-clearing conditions for the transport and continuous-commodity markets (in which case they would appear as the associated Lagrange multipliers). However, to keep the model as close as possible to the work of Williams and Senior, they will be taken to be exogenous.[4]

The Lagrangian for the above problem may be written

$$L = \sum_h \left\{ \alpha_h \left[u_h^0 x_h^0 + \sum_{ijmn} \left(u_{hij}^{mn} T_{hij}^{mn} - \frac{1}{\lambda_h} T_{hij}^{mn} \ln \frac{T_{hij}^{mn}}{K_h} \right) \right] - \sum_{ijmn} c_{ij} T_{hij}^{mn} - p^0 x_h^0 \right\}$$

$$+ \sum_{im} r_i^m \left(D_i^m - \sum_{hjn} T_{hij}^{mn} \right) - \sum_{jn} w_j^n \left(E_j^n - \sum_{him} T_{hij}^{mn} \right) + \sum_h \eta_h \left(K_h - \sum_{ijmn} T_{hij}^{mn} \right)$$

so the Kuhn–Tucker conditions include the following expressions:

$$\frac{\partial L}{\partial T_{hij}^{mn}} = \alpha_h \left[u_{hij}^{mn} - \frac{1}{\lambda_h} \left(1 + \ln \frac{T_{hij}^{mn}}{K_h} \right) \right] - c_{ij} - r_i^m + w_j^n - \eta_h \le 0 \qquad \forall hijmn,$$

$$\frac{\partial L}{\partial T_{hij}^{mn}} T_{hij}^{mn} = \left\{ \left[u_{hij}^{mn} - \frac{1}{\lambda_h} \left(1 + \ln \frac{T_{hij}^{mn}}{K_h} \right) \right] - c_{ij} - r_i^m + w_j^n - \eta_h \right\} T_{hij}^{mn} = 0 \qquad \forall hijmn,$$

$$\frac{\partial L}{\partial x_h^0} = \alpha_h u_h^0 - p^0 \le 0 \ \forall h,$$

$$\frac{\partial L}{\partial x_h^0} x_h^0 = (\alpha_h u_h^0 - p^0) x_h^0 = 0 \ \forall h.$$

Using the first two of these expressions, it can be shown that

$$T_{hij}^{mn} = K_h \exp \left\{ \lambda_h \left[u_{hij}^{mn} + \left(w_j^n - r_i^m - c_{ij} - \eta_h \right) \Big/ \alpha_h \right] - 1 \right\} \ .$$

With the probability restriction, this expression implies that

$$T_{hij}^{mn} = \frac{K_h \exp \left\{ \lambda_h \left[u_{hij}^{mn} + \left(w_j^n - r_i^m - c_{ij} \right) \Big/ \alpha_h \right] \right\}}{\displaystyle\sum_{i'j'm'n'} \exp \left\{ \lambda_h \left[u_{hi'j'}^{m'n'} + \left(w_{j'}^{n'} - r_{i'}^{m'} - c_{i'j'} \right) \Big/ \alpha_h \right] \right\}} \ .$$

If it is assumed that the non-wage income[5] of each member of class h is larger than the price of each discrete commodity bundle for all h; i.e., that

$$w > r_i^m + c_{ij} - w_j^n \qquad \forall ijmn,$$

then the positivity of u_h^0 implies that $x_h^0 > 0$ for all h. For this result to hold, it must be (from the fourth of the Kuhn–Tucker conditions listed above) that

$$\alpha_h = p^0 / u_h^0 \qquad \forall n.$$

Thus, the surplus for household class h reduces to

$$\sum_{ijmn} \left(b_{hij}^{mn} T_{hij}^{mn} - \frac{p^0}{\lambda_h u_h^0} T_{hij}^{mn} \ln \frac{T_{hij}^{mn}}{K_h} \right) - \sum_{ijmn} c_{ij} T_{hij}^{mn}$$

and the above formula for T_{hij}^{mn} becomes

$$T_{hij}^{mn} = \frac{K_h \exp \left[\dfrac{\lambda_h u_h^0}{p^0} \left(b_{hij}^{mn} + w_j^n - r_i^m - c_{ij} \right) \right]}{\displaystyle\sum_{i'j'm'n'} \exp \left[\dfrac{\lambda_h u_h^0}{p^0} \left(b_{hi'j'}^{m'n'} + w_{j'}^{n'} - r_{i'}^{m'} - c_{i'j'} \right) \right]}$$

where the benefit term, b_{hij}^{mn}, is defined to be equal to $p^0 u_{hij}^{mn} / u_h^0$.

5.2 Dwelling choice

Now consider two variants of the above model based on different assumptions about the decision-making population and the choice that its members face. The first variant is a housing choice model. Here, it is assumed that the population is divided into groups identified by the type and location of their employment such that class jn has E_j^n members. The decision to be made is on the type and location of dwelling. The dwelling-choice surplus maximization problem takes the following form:

$$\max \sum_{jn} \left\{ \alpha_j^n \left[u_j^{n0} x_j^{n0} + \sum_{im} \left(u_{ji}^{nm} T_{ji}^{nm} - \frac{1}{\lambda_j^n} T_{ji}^{nm} \ln \frac{T_{ji}^{nm}}{E_j^n} \right) \right] - \sum_{im} c_{ij} T_{ji}^{nm} - p^0 x_j^{n0} \right\}$$

subject to the market-clearing condition,

$$\sum_{jn} T_{ji}^{nm} \leq H_i^m \qquad \forall im,$$

and the probability restriction,

$$\sum_{him} T_{ji}^{nm} = E_j^n \qquad \forall jn$$

$$T_{ji}^{nm} \geq 0 \qquad \forall ijmn.$$

With the contracted objective function, this becomes

$$\max \sum_{jn} \left[\left(b_{ji}^{nm} - c_{ij} \right) T_{ji}^{nm} - \frac{p^0}{\lambda_j^n u_j^{n0}} T_{ji}^{nm} \ln \frac{T_{ji}^{nm}}{E_j^n} \right] \tag{5.10a}$$

subject to

$$\sum_{jn} T_{ji}^{nm} \leq H_i^m \qquad \forall im, \tag{5.10b}$$

$$\sum_{im} T_{ji}^{nm} = E_j^n \qquad \forall jn, \tag{5.10c}$$

$$T_{ji}^{nm} \geq 0 \qquad \forall ijmn. \tag{5.10d}$$

This problem should be compared with problem (5.5). It generates the solution

$$T_{ji}^{nm} = \frac{E_j^n \exp\left[\dfrac{\lambda_j^n u_j^{n0}}{p^0}\left(b_{ji}^{nm} - r_i^m - c_{ij}\right)\right]}{\displaystyle\sum_{i'm'} \exp\left[\dfrac{\lambda_j^n u_j^{n0}}{p^0}\left(b_{ji'}^{n'm'} - r_{i'}^{m'} - c_{i'j}\right)\right]}$$

which is fully consistent with equation (5.2).

5.3 *Employment choice*

The second variant is the job-choice problem in which classes are identified by the type and location of their dwelling (or, to be consistent with Williams and Senior, their skills and home location) such that class *im* has D_i^m members. The employment-choice surplus maximization problem takes the form

$$\max \sum_{im} \left\{ \alpha_i^m \left[u_i^{m0} x_i^{m0} + \sum_{jn} \left(u_{ij}^{mn} T_{ij}^{mn} - \frac{1}{\lambda_i^m} T_{ij}^{mn} \ln \frac{T_{ij}^{mn}}{D_i^m} \right) \right] - \sum_{jn} c_{ij} T_{ij}^{mn} - p^0 x_i^{m0} \right\}$$

subject to the market-clearing condition,

$$\sum_{im} T_{ij}^{mn} \geq E_j^n \qquad \forall jn,$$

and the probability restriction,

$$\sum_{jn} T_{ij}^{mn} = D_i^m \qquad \forall im$$

$$T_{ij}^{mn} \geq 0 \qquad\qquad \forall ijmn,$$

which can be contracted to

$$\max \sum_{im} \left[\left(b_{ij}^{mn} - c_{ij} \right) T_{ij}^{mn} - \frac{p^0}{\lambda_i^m u_i^{m0}} T_{ij}^{mn} \ln \frac{T_{ij}^{mn}}{D_i^m} \right] \qquad (5.11a)$$

subject to

$$\sum_{im} T_{ij}^{mn} \geq E_j^n \qquad \forall jn, \qquad\qquad (5.11b)$$

$$\sum_{jn} T_{ij}^{mn} = D_i^m \qquad \forall im, \qquad\qquad (5.11c)$$

$$T_{ij}^{mn} \geq 0 \qquad\qquad \forall ijmn. \qquad\qquad (5.11d)$$

This problem should be compared with problem (5.9). It has the solution

$$T_{ij}^{mn} = \frac{D_i^m \exp\left[\dfrac{\lambda_i^m u_i^{m0}}{p^0}\left(b_{ji}^{nm} + w_j^n - c_{ij}\right)\right]}{\displaystyle\sum_{j'n'} \exp\left[\dfrac{\lambda_i^m u_i^{m0}}{p^0}\left(b_{ij'}^{mn'} + w_{j'}^{n'} - c_{ij'}\right)\right]}.$$

It is worth noting that problems (5.10) and (5.11) are not symmetrical, unlike problems (5.5) and (5.9), and they do not contain any bid-value terms. They are demonstrably consistent with discrete choice theory and the existence of market equilibria. Note also that the interpretations given to T_{ij}^{mn}, D_i^m, and E_j^n have subtle but important differences from those given in Williams and Senior.

6 CONCLUSION

The models described in section 5 are not full computable general equilibrium systems. In particular, they do not include income formation or production, although they could be developed to do so (see Macmillan, 1994). They do, however, go some way towards closing the gap between the computable general equilibrium literature and spatial interaction models based on discrete choice theory. To that extent, they bring a unification of the disparate parts of location theory and spatial interaction modelling closer together. Hopefully, that is something of which Peter Haggett would approve.

NOTES

1 For a simple introduction to CGE modelling see Dinwiddy and Teal (1988); for a formal proof of the existence of a general equilibrium in an economy with discrete commodities and dispersed preferences, see Macmillan (1994).
2 The multidimensionality of the problem could be retained by using the nested logit model; the models presented in this section can all be extended to the nested logit form.
3 For information on other possible additions, see Macmillan (1994).
4 Treating the price of the continuous commodity as endogenous creates an ancillary problem connected with the computation of the values of the α_h terms but this need not concern us here.
5 Note that the variable w_j^n represents wage income whilst w_h is non-wage income. The question of income formation and distribution is not considered here but is covered in the companion paper.

REFERENCES

Dinwiddy, C.L. & Teal, F.J. (1988). *The Two Sector General Equilibrium Model: a New Approach.* New York: St. Martin's Press/Oxford: Philip Allan.

Haggett, P. (1965). *Locational Analysis in Human Geography.* London: Edward Arnold.

Herbert, D.J. & Stevens, B.H. (1960). 'A model for the distribution of residential activity in urban areas.' *Journal of Regional Science*, 2, 21–36.

Macmillan, W. (1994). 'General economic equilibrium with dispersed preferences over discrete alternatives' (forthcoming).

Senior, M.L. & Wilson, A.G. (1974). 'Explorations and syntheses of linear programming and spatial interaction models of residential location.' *Geographical Analysis*, 6, 209–38.

Wheaton, W. (1974). 'Linear programming and locational equilibrium, the Herbert–Stevens model revisited.' *Journal of Urban Economics*, 1, 278–87.

Williams, H.C.W.L. & Senior, M.L. (1978). 'Accessibility, spatial interaction and the spatial benefit analysis of land-use transportation plans.' In A. Karlqvist, L. Lundqvist, F. Snickars and J.W. Weibull (eds), *Spatial Interaction Theory and Planning Models*. Amsterdam: North Holland.

Wilson, A.G. (1969). 'Developments of some elementary residential location models.' *Journal of Regional Science*, 9, 377–85.

Wilson, A.G., Coelho, J.D., Macgill, S.M., & Williams, H.C.W.L. (1981). *Optimization in Locational and Transport Analysis*. Chichester: John Wiley.

6

Britain at the Heart of Europe?

M.D.I. Chisholm

1 INTRODUCTION

The British Prime Minister desires Britain to be at the heart of Europe, to be central in the deliberations of the European Union (EU) and not peripheral to policy. The Euro-sceptics in Britain, on the other hand, believe that closer union with the countries across the Channel is undesirable, or even downright damaging to British interests. That debate continues even though the Bill to implement the Maastricht Treaty was finally ratified in 1993. The context for that debate has changed dramatically in recent years. From its inception in 1958 until the signature of the Maastricht Treaty in November 1991, the EU was perceived to be an economic powerhouse, propelling the member countries along the upward path of economic development. But, by the close of 1992, there were unmistakable signs of crisis in the EU, suggesting that the formulae which had given such rewards over a period of 30 years might have lost their potency, or that other economic forces had gained in relative significance.

For centuries, Britain has regarded itself as being apart from Europe, protected by a 35-kilometre moat and in any case turning its gaze to the far quarters of the globe. Accession to the EU in 1973 implied a fundamental reassessment of Britain's role in the world, recognition that the days of empire lie in the past and that the bonds of commerce and culture tie it to the European mainland. However, that reassessment has not been accepted wholeheartedly. At the most general level, some politicians and citizens dream of maintaining, even enhancing, the powers of Westminster, and work to limit the influence of 'alien' bureaucrats in Brussels. One component of these doubts about Europe is the fact that Britain is an island which lies geographically on the periphery of Europe. This geographical fact used to be regarded as an asset. Now, as the economies of the EU become progressively more interdependent, and as Britain's trade with these countries becomes of ever greater importance to its economy, the fact of being peripheral is viewed by some as a grave and growing handicap, such that moves to ever closer integration should be resisted.

In this essay, we will explore some aspects of this ongoing debate, focusing in particular on the following questions. Is it the case that ever closer economic union within the EU implies that 'peripheral' countries and regions will lose out as the more favoured 'central' ones gain a disproportionate share of new investment and new jobs? Or is it the case that these fears are misplaced? In asking these questions, we are looking at the 'permanent' factors associated with relative location, and we eschew the high drama of Britain's ignominious withdrawal from the European Exchange Rate Mechanism (ERM) in September 1992 or the minutiae of votes for and against the Maastricht Treaty in Denmark, Ireland, France, and Britain itself. An alternative formulation of these questions would be to ask whether the long-term weakness of Britain's economy is to be attributed to the fact that the EU is now the country's largest trade partner and that most of the country is remote from the 'central' region focused on the River Rhine.

If we may anticipate the conclusions to be drawn from the evidence that will be reviewed, the answer to these questions is unambiguously clear. If Britain does suffer from its remoteness from the core region of the EU, the disadvantage is trivial and of no consequence in explaining the performance of the British economy. Other factors, unrelated to relative location, must be examined both to explain Britain's past performance and what may be done to change things in the future.

1.1 The European Union

The EU came into existence in 1958. Fifteen years later, the original six members admitted Britain, Denmark, and Ireland; by 1986, Greece, Portugal, and Spain had also joined. Further expansion was in prospect following agreement at the Edinburgh summit in December 1992 to open discussions with Austria, Finland, Norway, and Sweden at the earliest opportunity; in the fullness of time, there is little doubt that others will wish to join, including possibly Hungary and the successor states in Czechoslovakia now that Soviet control of Eastern Europe has disintegrated. Clearly, 'Europe' is a changing concept, so that in discussing Britain's relationships with the mainland we are not dealing with a fixed and immutable political arrangement, implying that Britain's position relative to Europe is also in a state of flux.

When the EU initially came into existence, three important steps were taken with the aim of opening up trade between the member states. Tariffs on intra-EU trade were lowered and then abolished. Artificial freight rates which impeded intra-EU trade were eliminated. And the Common Agriculture Policy (CAP) was established, embodying, *inter alia*, the idea of a single price within the EU for the main agricultural products. By general agreement, the CAP has outlived such usefulness as it may ever have had, and some tentative steps have been taken to modify it. In the non-agricultural sector, the much-heralded Single European Market (SEM) came into existence at the beginning of 1993. The SEM builds on the initial liberalization of intra-EU trade in two main ways; by eliminating (or reducing) remaining barriers to trade, and by facilitating the mobility of the factors of production. Non-tariff barriers to trade include frontier documentation processes, national technical standards and government procurement policies; all of these and many others are supposed to have been removed under the SEM, though in practice numerous trade barriers still remain. As for the factors of production, capital movements had already been liberalized and the main feature of the SEM is the abolition of border controls on the movement of people. The final ratification of the Maastricht Treaty will take this process of economic integration somewhat further, with the concept of common citzenship and of a single currency. Even without the Maastricht Treaty, the EU countries had taken giant strides to open up the channels for the movement of goods, people and capital, on a scale that was hard to imagine in the early post-war years. These changes in the structure of the EU and its geographical extent imply substantial changes in the significance of relative location, and in particular of Britain's island position off the north-west shores of mainland Europe.

1.2 Britain on the periphery?

There is an influential strand of thinking which holds that a country, such as Britain, on the periphery of the EU suffers a substantial economic penalty. The argument goes as follows. When firms make their investment choices, they select a location which will maximize their profits. If other things are equal, they will wish to minimize the cost of access to their inputs – components, design contractors, professional services and so on – and at the same time minimize the cost of reaching customers. To minimize total transfer costs, a location which is 'central' in the economic space is to be preferred. A popular way of assessing 'centrality' is to use measures of economic potential (Clark, 1966; Clark, Wilson, and Bradley, 1969; Keeble, Owens, and Thompson, 1982, 1988). Economic potential shows the relative accessibility of each area to all other areas within the economic space. Calculated for the EU, economic potential is rather low in much of Britain, with only the south-eastern part of the country reaching a level comparable to the most accessible regions of mainland Europe. Britain as a whole is somewhat peripheral to the rest of the EU, and this peripherality is accentuated towards the south-west, the west and the north, being most evident in Cornwall, Wales, Northern Ireland, and Scotland.

The static problems posed by peripheral location are, so it is argued, compounded by two sets of dynamic processes. Of these, cumulative causation is the more familiar. Cumulative growth theorizing denies the spatially equilibrating process identified by neo-classical economists. Hirschman (1958) and Myrdal (1957) start by emphasizing the role of scale economies (both internal to the firm and, more important, externally). A region which gets a head start, for whatever reason, provides conditions in which scale economies can be obtained, which enhances the profits accruing to firms. This will attract further capital investment. At the same time, these more profitable firms located in a central area can pay higher wages than is possible in more peripheral locations, with the result that labour will migrate to the central area. The simultaneous migration of labour and capital in the same direction fosters cumulative growth in the more favoured areas and (relative) stagnation, even decline, in the more peripheral locations.

The theory of economic union draws attention to the trade-creating and trade-diverting effects of reducing import duties, and, *a fortiori*, any other impediments to trade, between a group of cooperating countries (Balassa, 1962, 1989; Scitovsky, 1958). Geographically, the main benefits to be derived from these trade effects will be along the internal frontiers, and especially in any area where a large number of frontiers is located. Within the EU, the region which most benefits from this effect is centred on Belgium. Although south-east England is immediately adjacent to this favoured area, the rest of the country is rather remote.

The proponents of this general line of reasoning argue that, whatever the overall gain for the EU, Britain stands to lose from the creation of the SEM – and also the opening of the Channel Tunnel – in either or both of two ways:

1 At the national level, Britain is perceived to be peripheral to the EU as a whole, and therefore likely to suffer the negative effects of cumulative growth processes and integration effects.
2 Within Britain, it is the South-east which will gain but at the expense of the more remote western and northern regions.

There is a substantial body of literature which takes it for granted that these centralization processes dominate the processes reshaping the geography of the EU. For example:

> With regard to peripherality, there can be little question that much of the 'North' of the UK suffers from its remoteness from London and the South East, so that a shift of the economic centre of gravity further towards the core of the community would exacerbate this phenomenon. Indeed, it is arguable that the UK as a whole is peripheral in community terms, even if not so obviously as countries like Greece or Ireland. The main disadvantages of peripherality stem from the higher costs of communications and of market access. Unless there are sufficiently lower factor costs in peripheral areas, it would be expected that such economic activities would tend to gravitate towards the core of the EC. (Begg, 1990, pp. 90–1)

Despite the caveat, the tenor of this paper is that centralization is to be expected, a view put rather more forcibly in another recent publication:

> The move to a Single European Market is expected to reallocate markets and redistribute production in favour of the most efficient and best situated firms. In addition to greater concentration of industry, it implies growing divergence at regional level. The gains from trade are expected to concentrate at the centre of the Community in the more prosperous regions: transient and long-term unemployment emerge at the periphery. (MacKay, 1992, p. 278)

Views such as these, concerning the impact of further integration, have become embedded in the conventional wisdom of the EU itself:

> Historical experience suggests, however, that in the absence of counter-vailing policies, the overall impact on peripheral regions could be negative. Transport costs and economies of scale would tend to favour a shift in economic activity away from less developed regions, especially if they were at the periphery of the Community, to the highly developed areas at its centre. (Committee for the Study of Economic and Monetary Union, 1989, p. 22)

If these perceptions are correct, then indeed there are grounds for concern in Britain about the effects of closer economic integration with the EU, a concern that would not be easily allayed by explicit policies of the EU to assist peripheral countries and/or regions.

2 THE CHANGING PATTERN OF BRITAIN'S TRADE

If the fears expressed in the previous section have a foundation in fact, then the changing orientation of Britain's external trade serves to confound them. Since the Second World War, there has been a steady shift in the geography of imports and exports, as is shown by table 6.1. In 1950, the six original members of the EU accounted for just over 10 per cent of our external trade; by 1990, the proportion had risen to over 40 per cent. At the same time, there was very little change in the relative importance of the other members of the EU, their share staying at around 10 per cent, while the rest of Western Europe has also seen only a small shift in relative importance. The mirror image of the rise of the EU has been the collapse of trade with non-European countries from about three-quarters of the total in 1950 to under two-fifths now. If one examines the annual data, it is clear that these trends have been remarkably continuous over the whole post-war period (Chisholm, 1992). Viewed in the light of the above data, the argument that there are significant advantages in proximity leads to the following conclusion. By shifting trade from distant trading partners to countries in Europe, and especially the EU6, Britain is economizing on expensive transfer costs. This should be beneficial for the national economy, since any disadvantage which arises from being peripheral to Europe is more than offset by the overall reduction in average length of haul on both imports and exports; the economy as a whole should have received a significant boost over the last four decades. The more serious is the problem of being peripheral to the EU the greater the overall gain to the British economy from this global reorientation of trade.

An alternative interpretation is that distance costs are not particularly important and that changes in the geographical pattern of trade are driven by other factors, which include product range and availability, price and quality. In which case, Britain's location relative to mainland Europe is not an issue of great importance.

Table 6.1   United Kingdom imports and exports (all commodities): percentage by value with main trade partners

		1950	1960	1970	1980	1990
EU 6						
	Imports	12.7	14.4	20.3	35.3	43.4
	Exports	11.2	15.4	21.7	35.2	41.3
EU 12						
	Imports	20.5	22.3	29.8	43.7	52.3
	Exports	20.0	23.0	32.7	45.8	53.0
Rest of Western Europe						
	Imports	6.3	9.2	12.0	12.0	12.5
	Exports	9.5	9.7	13.0	11.6	8.7
Rest of the world						
	Imports	73.2	68.5	58.2	44.3	35.2
	Exports	70.5	67.3	54.3	42.6	38.3

Source: Annual Abstract of Statistics

In the following sections, we will explore some aspects of these propositions, to see whether existing evidence can throw useful light on the question whether Britain's location may be expected to have an impact on its economic performance.

3 DISTANCE AND INTERNATIONAL TRADE

There is a very large literature, both theoretical and empirical, based on the proposition that the volume of interaction between two places is some positive function of their respective sizes and some negative function of the distance (transport cost) which separates them (for example, Batten, 1983; Batten and Boyce, 1986; Chisholm and O'Sullivan, 1973; Fotheringham and O'Kelly, 1989; Haynes and Fotheringham, 1984; Isard and Bramhall, 1960). By far the greatest amount of work in this field has been concerned with the travel choices of people (for work, shopping, and leisure), given the location of facilities, and the reciprocal problem of where to locate such facilities, given the origins of travellers. Relatively little work has been done on the spatial modelling of freight movements. For all kinds of spatial interaction model, practically all the work has been done at the national or subnational level; the number of international studies that has been published is very small indeed.

Linnemann's 1966 study remains the most comprehensive attempt to model international trade flows (cf. the 1976 study by Johnston). The main variables that he used to explain the volume of trade between pairs of countries were the GNP of the exporter and of the importer and the distance (in nautical miles) which separates them. He used data for 79 countries and obtained coefficients and levels of R^2 that compared with the earlier studies of Tinbergen and Pulliainen, both of whom employed data for smaller samples of countries (Linnemann, 1966, p. 84). Linnemann himself calibrates four equations, all in logarithms to the base *e*, two using all trade flows and two using only those flows that were equal to or greater than $50,000 (nominally $100,000), in each case computing the equations with their nominal or 'real' GNP data. All four equations yield similar results, though the importance of the distance variable was marginally greater using all trade flows rather than just those over $50,000. His data refer to the mean values for the three years 1958, 1959, and 1960.

Unfortunately, Linnemann does not provide sufficient raw data to calculate standardized partial regression coefficients and thereby to assess the relative importance of the GNP, distance and other variables (King, 1969, 139–41). However, it is possible to gauge the significance of the distance variable, albeit in a much cruder way. For this purpose, we will use the parameters estimated using all trade flows and nominal GNP values (Linnemann, 1966, pp. 82, 84). These are:

- GNP of export country   0.99
- GNP of import country   0.85
- Distance   −0.81
- Constant   0.13

The above parameters allow one to calculate what the volume of trade should be for any pair of countries assuming that different distances separate them. This shows the distance effect while GNP is held constant. By doing this calculation also for different sizes of country, the impact of country size can be measured holding distance constant. Table 6.2 presents the results. The United States had the largest GNP at $483 billion, with the United Kingdom second at $67 billion; Libya, with $0.09 billion, was the smallest economy in the study. If one compares the variation across the rows of table 6.2 with the column variation, it is immediately apparent that country size contributes about one thousand times more variation to trade flow than does the distance variable.

Table 6.2   Export volumes estimated from Linnemann's data ($ billion)

		Volume of exports at different nautical miles		
Exporter	Importer	100	1000	13,000
USA	UK	368.5	18.4	2.3
UK	USA	279.5	14.0	1.8
USA	Small economy[a]	10.3	0.5	0.06
Small economy[a]	USA	4.4	0.2	0.03
Small economy[a]	Small economy[a]	0.002	0.0001	0.00001

[a] GNP of $1 billion.

Source: Linnemann (1966, equation AC1)

These admittedly rather crude measurements from Linnemann's data indicate that the distance variable, although statistically significant, plays a limited role in the geographical patterns of international trade. This fact, which is not explicitly acknowledged by Linnemann, probably accounts for the difficulty which he had in making sense of the country-by-country variation in the distance exponent, noting, as he does, that: 'the individual standard errors of the estimates are so large that the differences [in the values of the distance exponent] are hardly significant' (Linnemann, 1966, p. 92). As a result, Linnemann approached the problem in a different way by standardizing trade flows between pairs of countries on the basis of their respective trade volumes, to generate an alternative measure of the effects of distance on trade patterns. Summarizing these findings, he says:

> The results are very interesting, as they quantify the significance of a 'good' or 'bad' geographical location for the relative importance of foreign trade in the economy. At opposite ends of the scale we find (a) the Netherlands and Belgium, as countries with an 'ideal' foreign trade location, and (b) Japan, Australia and New Zealand as badly situated countries with long distances to the major markets. On the basis of our findings we are able to say that the effort involved in realizing a certain volume of trade is about six times greater for the latter countries than for those mentioned under (a). *Admittedly, the meaning of the word 'effort' in this context is somewhat vague; it should be understood as referring to the overcoming of the natural obstacles to trade.*(Linnemann, 1966, p. 187, my italics)

This conclusion, while emphasizing the role of distance, fails to provide a useful measurement of the scale of the impact relative to other factors and in no way contradicts the conclusion we have already reached that Linnemann's evidence shows the impact of the distance variable in international trade to be rather small.

Linnemann (1969) returned to the problem of distance as a factor in international trade by first standardizing trade flows for the aggregate volume of imports and exports of trade partners and then taking the ratio of the expected volume of trade to the actual volume. He regressed these ratios, as the dependent variable, on the distance between pairwise trade partners. The regressions he obtained indicate that at a distance of between 1500 and 2500 kilometres the actual volume of trade would be twice the expected volume, whereas at distances under 30 kilometres there would be a hundredfold increase. These results are hard to reconcile with the 1966 study and also with further evidence from other authors, to which we now turn.

Lipsey and Weiss (1974) report the most thorough extant study of the structure of ocean freight charges, using data for imports to the United States for 76 SITC commodities which cover the range from raw materials to manufactures. They take as their dependent variable the import freight charged in US dollars per metric ton of cargo. The three main independent variables for which data were obtained were the unit value of the commodities, the volume of space occupied by one metric ton of each commodity and the distance over

Table 6.3 Ocean transport charges estimated from the data of Lipsey and Weiss ($ US per ton)

Maximum UV[a] and ST[b]		Minimum UV[a] and ST[b]	
Max. distance[c]	Min. distance[c]	Max. distance[c]	Min. distance[c]
649	374	2.1	1.2

[a] *UV* is the unit value, $ per metric ton: maximum 22,000, minimum 8.
[b] *ST* is the stowage factor, cubic feet per metric ton: maximum 206, minimum 9.
[c] Distance in nautical miles: maximum 9765, minimum 1906.

Source: Lipsey and Weiss (1974, equation 15)

which consignments travelled. Thus, the raw data are average figures for each commodity. The equations are calculated in logarithms and, although this is not specified in the text, these are to the base *e* and not to base 10.

Table 6.3 reports an exercise similar to that performed on the Linnemann data, taking the reported maximum and minimum figures. It is immediately apparent that the recorded freight charge is not quite doubled if the distance of shipment increases from 1906 nautical miles to 9765 (these are the minimum and maximum values reported). However, the nature of the consignment – its unit value and the number of cubic feet per metric ton – has a far greater impact on the freight cost, the ratio of lowest to highest charge being just over 1:300. The relative unimportance of distance is confirmed by the standardized partial regression coefficients. These are:

- Unit value   0.807
- Stowage factor   0.216
- Distance   0.090

  (I am indebted to Kavita Datta for calculating the standard deviations from the Lipsey and Weiss data used as a basis for calculating the partial regression coefficients.)

Thus, of the variance in freight rates explained by the regression equation, almost three-quarters is attributable to the unit value of the consignments, just under one-fifth to the stowage factor, and only 8.1 per cent to distance. However, the regression equation accounts for 80 per cent of the variance, so that the contribution of distance in explaining the total variation in freight rates is just 6.5 per cent (8.1×0.8). On this evidence, charges for international freight transfers by sea are little affected by length of haul, the main determinant being the unit value of consignments. It is little wonder, therefore, that the distance variable has a small impact on the volume of international trade.

An examination of Canadian exports throws some further light on the role of ocean transport costs. In this case, Bryan (1974) posed the following question: to what extent does the cost of liner freight affect the level of demand for Canadian exports in various markets? Data were compiled for 25 commodities, shipped to 22 countries which have direct access to oceanic traffic, the freight rate being calculated as a percentage of the f.o.b. price. Multiple regression techniques were used to estimate gravity models for each commodity. The results obtained showed quite clearly that demand for Canadian goods was affected by ocean freight rates only in the case of raw materials and bulky semi-processed goods:

> If these elasticities are correct, it can be inferred that Canada encounters particularly strong price competition in the overseas markets for lumber and newsprint. The fact that transport costs were not a significant explanatory variable for commodities such as wire and cable, copper tubing, construction machinery, aircraft engines and assembly, agricultural machinery, telephone apparatus, and card punching machinery probably suggests that factors like design, quality, tastes, guarantees, speed of delivery, and service conditions, are more important for these and similar commodities. The results may indicate that transport costs are more important for primary manufactures than secondary manufactures, the main reason being product differentiation. (Bryan, 1974, p. 651)

These Canadian findings have been confirmed by evidence for the export performance of the United States (Kravis and Lipsey, 1971). For the products covered in this study, average outbound freights were probably somewhat in excess of 10 per cent of the wholesale prices of the goods shipped. Yet evidence from a sample of 26 firms, which together accounted for about 2 per cent of American exports, showed that delivered price was not a very significant factor in competitiveness in overseas markets, except in the case of crude materials and chemical products (table 6.4). For most manufactures, non-price considerations dominated. A comparison of American exports of factory equipment with German imports of the same category showed that in only 7 per cent of cases was price the determining factor; product differentiation and service considerations accounted for 93 per cent of decisions. These results are consistent with more qualitative data for the United Kingdom relating to the choice made by domestic firms between suppliers located in the United Kingdom and abroad (Kravis and Lipsey, 1971, pp. 154–7) and more general measures of the competitiveness of British manufacturers (Chisholm, 1985).

These findings carry a clear implication. If price, including the costs of transport, plays a rather limited role in the competitiveness of products in world markets, it follows that spatial variations in international transport costs will have a small, even negligible, impact on trade patterns.

Finally, Balassa (1986) has examined the determinants of intra-industry trade in manufactures in the overseas transactions of the United States, using 167 industry categories traded with 38 countries. He hypothesized, *inter alia*, that the significance of intra-industry trade should be negatively associated with transport costs. Although the coefficient for the transport cost variable has the correct sign, it has a very low statistical significance, falling below the 10 per cent level when zero observations for intra-industry trade are included. The weakness of the association with distance costs serves to confirm the findings already reported.

Table 6.4   Relative importance of factors explaining US export success (%)

Factors underlying ability to export	Crude materials (SITC 2)	Chemicals (SITC 5)	Manufactures (SITC 6)	Machinery and transport equipment (SITC 7)	All products
Prices equal to or below foreign	43	56	18	14	28
Product more expensive but off-setting characteristics	42	30	66	70	57
Unique product: no close foreign substitute	6	5	10	14	10
Other	10	8	6	3	5
Total	100	100	100	100	100

Source: Kravis and Lipsey (1971, p. 153)

To conclude this section, two findings seen to be inescapable:

1 The impact of distance costs seems to have only a small and hard-to-detect impact on the geography of international trade.
2 The primary reason for this seems to be that non-price factors are the main determinants of competitiveness, so that spatial variations around an average freight cost of perhaps 10 per cent of f.o.b. price is not a major consideration.

In addition, though, the spatial variation in transport costs is much less than the distance variation, since a considerable part of international freight costs relates to the costs of handling at either end of the journey, these costs being invariant with distance.

4 SPATIAL VARIATION IN TRANSPORT COSTS, BRITAIN

In the previous section, we have noted that the costs of overcoming distance seem to play a rather limited role in shaping international trade. We now turn to the regional scale, to examine the evidence for Britain as to whether locational differences are a significant element in the spatial variation of costs for firms.

Direct evidence on the significance of transport costs may be obtained either *ex ante* or *ex post*. In the former case, the problem is posed in terms of the location choice facing a firm and how to assess what the costs would be in the available locations, given assumptions about the way the business would be organized. The alternative *ex post* approach ascertains what actual costs have been for existing firms in various locations. Fortunately, the two forms of study yield essentially the same results.

Tyler and Kitson (1987) develop an *ex ante* model for Great Britain, in which it is assumed that the spatial pattern of domestic demand is unaffected by the location choice made, and that there is a similar fixity in the spatial pattern of export traffic through the ports. They conclude that, given these assumptions, the optimum location to serve the domestic market is Birmingham, and that for firms serving both domestic and foreign markets, London is to be preferred. Comparing these low-cost locations with the remotest region of Scotland, they estimate that transport costs vary in a ratio of 1:3. However, a companion study of the profitability of firms shows that variation in transport costs of this relative magnitude is of little moment (Tyler, Moore, and Rhodes, 1988a, b).

Census data give the cost structure of individual industries and may be used to represent the structure of costs for a representative firm in each industry. Data were collected for the spatial variation in these cost items, to establish the geographical pattern of profitability. This procedure was applied to the Minimum List Industries in England. Up to a distance of 400 km from London (Cornwall), calculated profits *rise* with increasing distance from the metropolis, a finding which is directly opposite to the one which would be expected were transport costs to be the dominant factor. About one half of the geographical variation in profits is attributable to spatial differences in salary levels, and a further quarter arises from purchased industrial services. Transport cost variations are included in the residual category 'other', which in aggregate accounts for only 8 per cent of the geographical variation in gross profits:

> The contribution of the other costs [to higher profits] declines with distance from London and this reflects two opposing factors; the decline of costs for items like insurance payments and to some extent energy being [partially] offset by rising bought-in transport costs. (Tyler, Moore, and Rhodes, 1988a, p. 38)

On the assumption that there is no adjustment of marketing patterns in response to the location chosen, it is quite clear that although remote locations do suffer a transport cost disadvantage, this may be more than offset by compensating advantages. However, the assumption that marketing patterns are invariant with location is implausible, and firms may avoid some or all of the transport cost penalties assumed in *ex ante* models by adjusting their trading patterns. Chisholm (1987) re-examined the census of production data for Scotland and the United Kingdom, for the years 1963 and 1974. For manufacturing industry, total transport cost as a percentage of net output or gross value added was almost identical in Scotland and the United Kingdom in both years. This close similarity arises from the industry-by-industry variations in transport costs, and not from the mix of industries. Thus, at the main Order level, the industries of Scotland *ex post* reveal no transport cost disadvantage relative to the rest of the country.

The findings reported above appear to contradict a much-quoted sample survey of 515 firms in Northern Ireland, Scotland, and south-east England (PEIDA, 1984). This report draws a careful distinction between the *perception* that firms have regarding the relative advantages of locations, and the measurable *reality*. Of the numerous findings, the one that has received the most attention is the view held by firms that a peripheral location is disadvantageous. However, the reality, embodied in the measurable cost penalty, is quite small: measured transport costs as a proportion of gross value added in manufacturing for the sample firms was estimated to be:

- Northern Ireland   10.8 %
- Scotland   8.3 %
- South-east England   7.7 %

Given the problems of sample size and industrial composition, these differences are small and could readily be dwarfed by spatial variations in the components of the remaining 90 per cent of gross value added:

> The measured transport cost differences found – certainly between Scotland and South East England – do not seem capable of accounting for observed differences in regional economic performance. In Northern Ireland, the cost differential is more significant, though still, in itself, unlikely to account for the weakness of the region's economic performance. (PEIDA, 1984, p. 87)

Therefore, despite the commonly asserted view to the contrary, the PEIDA findings actually support the conclusions derived from the other work cited above and reinforce the earlier finding of Chisholm (1971, p. 242) that: 'inter-regional location makes very little difference to the total demands made upon the transport sector and consequently the consumption of real resources.'

The evidence cited above shows quite clearly that the measurable differences in transport costs within the United Kingdom are small or non-existent and, much more important, that such spatial variations as do exist are dwarfed by spatial variations in the cost of other factors. This conclusion casts considerable additional doubt on the utility of the centre–periphery model as applied to Britain and the rest of the EU.

5 DISTANCE AND EUROPEAN TRADE PATTERNS

The best-known study of the spatial structure of intra-European trade was published in 1956 by Beckerman. Unfortunately, he structured his analysis by standardizing trade flows for the size of the countries involved in pairwise flows and does not report the proportion of total trade which is thus accounted for. His spatial analysis is the analysis of residuals whose significance cannot be gauged. There are similar problems with other, more recent, studies (for example, Brams, 1966; Peschel, 1985; Prewo, 1974). But Yeates (1968) reports the results of a gravity model study of Italy's trade, with the impact of distance fully incorporated. His model includes interval-scaled data for the national income of the trade partner, its *per caput* income and the distance from Italy, as well as five dummy variables. Distance was taken as the square root of the distance along the arc of the great circle route connecting Rome with the capital of the trade partner. Equations were calculated for imports and exports in 1954 and 1965, and standardized partial regression coefficients are presented for each of the four equations.

These standardized coefficients show considerable variation between the import and export equations and also between the two years, which raises questions concerning the robustness of the findings. Of more immediate interest, though, is the relative importance of the distance variable. The standardized partial regression coefficients for distance account for between 2.8 per cent and 9.4 per cent of the variance in the trade flows, the mean value for the four equations being 5.6 per cent. This finding for Italy serves to confirm the evidence which we have already discussed.

It is clearly worth reconsidering the role of distance costs for the trade of European countries, and especially of the 12 members of the EU in 1994, to see whether any further light can be shed on the advantages and disadvantages of relative location. Suitable data on aggregate trade flows between the member states (intra-trade) have been compiled by the European Union for two years, spanning a considerable part of the post-war period. Full details of the analysis of these data are being published elsewhere (Altham, Chisholm, and Cliff, in preparation). In the present context, the key points to consider are the following. To formulate a gravity model, some measurement of the distance or transfer cost separating trade partners is needed. Cost data are exiguous and present several serious technical problems. On the other hand, the use of distance implies selecting a centroid in each country and assuming that all traffic originates and terminates at these centroids, a procedure that introduces increasing error as the size of countries increases and the closer together they are. Inevitably, therefore, gravity models using national data are subject to considerable specification errors. Furthermore, we have reason to believe that distance (transfer cost) plays a rather small part in the geography of international trade, whereas the size of an economy has a very big influence.

To overcome these difficulties, it is appropriate to turn the problem around and ask what proportion of the intra-EUR 12 trade can be accounted for by the size of country, and then to examine whether there is any spatial pattern in the residuals. For this purpose, it is possible to generate from the available data for 1958 and 1989 trade flow matrices in value terms for both imports and exports, and to determine the proportion of the observed trade flows which can be accounted for by the size of the trade partners measured by their respective trade volumes. In 1958, country size accounted for between 82 and 86 per cent of the volume of trade flows; in 1989, the proportion had risen somewhat, to 91–92 per cent. Adding in a distance variable (road distance between capital cities) improved the model performance by only 1–3 per cent. Residuals calculated from the model in which import data were used to predict the volume of exports yielded a very small number that were statistically significant. Ireland figured in 12 out of 16 cases pooled for the two years of the study. Quite clearly, distance plays a negligible part in determining the pattern of trade between the present members of the EU.

6 CONCLUSION

There can be no doubt that many observers accept the view that Britain suffers a significant disadvantage by virtue of its location on the periphery of Europe. However, when we examine the evidence relating to the movement of goods, where spatial interaction costs are likely to be higher than is the case for information and for personal travel, there appears to be little or no basis for the anxieties which have been aired regarding the ill effects of Britain's location. Indeed, it turns out that the costs of transferring most goods from one location to another are sufficiently small relative to all the other determinants of economic prosperity that we may discount the location of Britain relative to the rest of Europe. The implication of this conclusion is the following. If Britain's geographical position is really not a matter of great moment, then the prosperity of the country depends on factors which are internal and mutable, rather than factors which are external and unchangeable. It could be said, therefore, that Britain has nothing to fear but fear itself. More practically, there is no geographical reason why Britain cannot play a full part at the centre of the European stage.

REFERENCES

Altham, P.E.M., Chisholm, M., & Cliff, A.D. (1995). 'Distance and the pattern of international trade' (in preparation).

Balassa, B. (1962). *The Theory of Economic Integration*. London: Allen & Unwin.

Balassa, B. (1989). *Comparative Advantage, Trade Policy and Economic Development*. Hemel Hempstead: Harvester Wheatsheaf.

Balassa, B. (1986). 'The determinants of intra-industry specialization in United States trade.' *Oxford Economic Papers*, 38, 220–33.

Batten, D.F. (1983). *Spatial Analysis of Interacting Economies: the role of entropy and information theory in spatial input–output modelling*. Boston: Kluwer–Nijhoff.

Batten, D.F. & Boyce, D.E. (1986). 'Spatial interaction, transportation, and interregional commodity flow models.' In P. Nijkamp (ed.), *Handbook of Regional and Urban Economics*, 1, *Regional Economics*. Amsterdam: North Holland, 357–406.

Beckerman, W. (1956). 'Distance and the pattern of intra-European trade.' *Review of Economics and Statistics*, 38, 31–40.

Begg, I. (1990). 'The Single European Market and the UK regions.' In G. Cameron, B. Moore, D. Nicholls, J. Rhodes, and P. Tyler (eds), *Cambridge Regional Economic Review. The Outlook for the Regions and Countries of the United Kingdom in the 1990s*. Cambridge: Cambridge Economic Consultants and Department of Land Economy, 89–104.

Brams, S.J. (1966). 'Transaction flows in the international system.' *American Political Science Review*, 60, 880–98.

Bryan, I.A. (1974). 'The effect of ocean transport costs on the demand for some Canadian exports.' *Weltwirtschaftliches Archiv*, 110, 642–62.

Chisholm, M. (1971). 'Freight transport costs, industrial location and regional development.' In M. Chisholm and G. Manners (eds), *Spatial Policy Problems of the British Economy*. Cambridge: Cambridge University Press, 213–44.

Chisholm, M. (1985). 'De-industrialization and British regional policy.' *Regional Studies,* 19, 301–13.

Chisholm, M. (1987). 'Regional variations in transport costs in Britain, with special reference to Scotland.' *Transactions and Papers, Institute of British Geographers,* NS, 12, 303–14.

Chisholm, M. (1992). 'Britain, the European Community, and the centralisation of production: theory and evidence, freight movements.' *Environment and Planning A,* 24, 551–70.

Chisholm, M. & O'Sullivan, P. (1973). *Freight Flows and Spatial Aspects of the British Economy.* Cambridge: Cambridge University Press.

Clark, C. (1966). 'Industrial location and economic potential.' *Lloyds Bank Review,* October, 1–17.

Clark, C., Wilson, F., & Bradley, J. (1969). 'Industrial location and economic potential in Western Europe.' *Regional Studies,* 3, 197–212.

Committee for the Study of Economic and Monetary Union (1989). *Report on Economic and Monetary Union in the European Community.* Luxembourg: Office for Official Publications of the European Communities.

Fotheringham, A.S. & O'Kelly, M.E. (1989). *Spatial Interaction Models: formulations and applications.* Dordrecht: Kluwer.

Haynes, K.E. & Fotheringham, A.S. (1984). *Gravity and Spatial Interaction Models.* Beverly Hills: Sage Publications.

Hirschman, A.O. (1958). *The Strategy of Economic Development.* New Haven: Yale University Press.

Isard, W. & Bramhall, D.F. (1960). 'Gravity, potential and spatial interaction models.' In W. Isard et al., *Methods of Regional Analysis.* Cambridge, Mass.: MIT Press, 493–568.

Johnston, R.J. (1976). *The World Trading System. Some enquiries into its spatial structure.* London: Bell.

Keeble, D., Offord, J., & Walker, S. (1988). *Peripheral Regions in a Community of Twelve Member States.* Luxembourg: Office for Official Publications of the European Communities.

Keeble, D., Owens, P.L., & Thompson, C. (1982). 'Regional accessibility and economic potential in the European Community.' *Regional Studies,* 16, 419–31.

King, L.J. (1969). *Statistical Analysis in Geography.* Englewood Cliffs, NJ: Prentice-Hall International.

Kravis, I.B. & Lipsey, R.E. (1971). *Price Competitiveness in World Trade.* New York: National Bureau of Economic Research.

Linnemann, H. (1966). *An Econometric Study of International Trade Flows.* Amsterdam: North Holland.

Linnemann, H. (1969). 'Trade flows and geographical distance, or the importance of being neighbours.' In H.C. Bos (ed.), *Towards Balanced International Trade,* Amsterdam: North Holland, 111–28.

Lipsey, R.E. & Weiss, M.Y. (1974). 'The structure of ocean transport charges.' *Explorations in Economic Research,* 1, 162–93.

MacKay, R.R. (1992). '1992 and relations with the EEC.' In P. Townroe and R.L. Martin (eds), *Regional Development in the 1990s. The British Isles in Transition.* London: Jessica Kingsley, 278–87.

Myrdal, G. (1957). *Economic Theory and Under-Developed Regions.* London: Duckworth.

PEIDA (Planning and Economic Consultants). (1984). *Transport Costs in Peripheral Areas.* Edinburgh and Henley-on-Thames, mimeo.

Peschel, K. (1985). 'Spatial structures in international trade: an analysis of long term developments.' *Papers and Proceedings of the Regional Science Association,* 58, 97–111.

Prewo, W. (1974). *A Multinational Interindustry Gravity Trade Model for the European Common Market.* Baltimore, Maryland: unpublished doctoral dissertation, Johns Hopkins University.

Scitovsky, T. (1958). *Economic Theory and Western European Integration.* London: Allen & Unwin.

Tyler, P. & Kitson, M. (1987). 'Geographical variations in transport costs of manufacturing firms in Great Britain.' *Urban Studies,* 24, 61–73.

Tyler, P., Moore, B.C. & Rhodes, J. (1988a). *Geographical Variations in Costs and Productivity in England.* London: Her Majesty's Stationery Office.

Tyler, P., Moore, B.C., & Rhodes, J. (1988b). 'Geographical variations in industrial costs', *Scottish Journal of Political Economy,* 35, 22–50.

Yeates, M.H. (1968). *An Introduction to Quantitative Analysis in Economic Geography.* New York: McGraw-Hill.

7

Research and Rural Planning: from Howard Bracey to Discourse Analysis

P. Cloke

1 INTRODUCTION

In his 1990 book, *The Geographer's Art*, Peter Haggett presents a highly individualistic account of the imaginative stimulus and intellectual challenge that is geography. As I prepared to write this essay, I reread *The Geographer's Art*, perhaps hoping that Peter would have found the opportunity to touch on rural geographies, his chosen living place, and a fundamental characteristic of *his* county of Somerset. Rather than any direct reference to the rural, I stumbled across a number of indirect references which helped me to understand a little more about the man and the placing of his geographical imagination. I will briefly mention just two. First, he refers to Paul Tillich's *Systematic Theology* (1963) in which the author recalls that

> Nearly all the great memories and longings of my life are interwoven with landscapes, soil, weather, the fields of grain and the smell of the potato plant in autumn, the shapes of clouds, and with mud, flowers and woods. In all my later travels through Germany and southern and western Europe, the impression of the land remained strong. (p. 318)

Second, he describes Torsten Hägerstrand's work on the adoption of agricultural innovations by farmers in central Sweden and suggests that Hägerstrand's choice of these topics was influenced by his childhood experiences of rural places and environments

> The destination of family walks and solitary excursions were either hilltops with a wide prospect over the valley or some exceptionally large trees which had their own names . . . The whole of nature was not just nature as an undifferentiated environment . . . It was a room inhabited by personalities . . . For my memories of this world, images of touch and smell and sound come side by side with the visual pictures. (Hägerstrand, 1982, p. 335)

These and other references suggest that Peter's life has also been, and continues to be, an intertwining of geographical imagination, place-experience and environment-memory. He describes Hägerstrand as 'the geographer who particularly influenced my own research' (Haggett, 1990, p. 127) and it seems most likely that rural experiences, imaginations, and placed-senses are one of the sets of characteristics which bond these two great geographers together.

In this chapter I unashamedly focus on a lesser known element of Peter Haggett's work which concerns surveys of rural communities in Somerset. I describe this work both in terms of its own value and as a springboard for some thoughts on the changing philosophical and methodological relations between social science research and rural planning. In particular, the chapter centres upon three moments of change in these relations – first, briefly assessing the direct research inputs to planning achieved by Howard Bracey; second, the resistance to traditional research–planning relations which arose as part of the turn towards political economic approaches; and third, the struggle to include qualitative accounts of lay discourses of rural life and lifestyle in the considerations that are deemed appropriate for inclusion in discussions of rural planning and policy.

2   HOWARD BRACEY AND PETER HAGGETT

My first encounter with the work of Howard Bracey was in 1975 as a postgraduate student at Wye College in the University of London. The thesis which I was writing focused on the role of so-called 'key-settlements' in rural settlement planning and, on the advice of my supervisor, Robin Best, I was seeking out the conceptual foundations for this notion of the planned concentration of services, housing, and employment into selected rural centres. Almost inevitably this involved an understanding of how central place and growth centre theories had been used in the rural context and so, equally inexorably, I was drawn to the published work of H.E. Bracey:

> the principal early attempt to test the central-place model in rural environments was carried out by Bracey who undertook extensive and detailed surveys of Wiltshire and Somerset, and then tested his results in a wider investigation taking in the six counties of Somerset, Dorset, Wiltshire, Oxfordshire, Berkshire and Hampshire . . . the research found substantial support for the central-place model in the rural areas of southern England. (Cloke, 1983, p. 58)

Had I more sensitivity at that time towards detailed understandings of rural life and change I might well have followed up these readings of Bracey, and discovered some of the richness contained within these surveys which are given such scant mention above. It is unsurprising to me, however, that a man of both Somerset county and Somerset country, Peter Haggett, *did* appreciate the intrinsic value of Bracey's research and found time in his hectic and enormously productive career to undertake a 'rescue geography' in order to secure much of Bracey's work for posterity.

The story is told that the Bristol agricultural economist, and Haggett, the Bristol geographer, were in conversation after the sad occasion of the funeral of Frank Walker, a colleague of Peter's in the Geography Department. Bracey let slip that he was on the point of disposing of all of his old research papers and materials and Haggett, realizing the unique value and importance of this intended 'junk', persuaded him to allow an archive of Bracey's work to be established. Regrettably, Bracey's Wiltshire materials had not survived, but the Somerset papers were made available, much to Peter's delight. With the help of Michael Morgan, Peter then set about persuading the Social Science Research Council to fund a research project which would permit both a reanalysis of Bracey's original work in Somerset, and a repeat survey which would enable an analysis of change in Somerset villages between 1947 and 1980. Liz Mills was appointed as a full-time researcher on the project, and the findings are detailed in a series of working notes and working papers (Haggett, 1981; Haggett, Mills, and Morgan, 1982; Mills, 1981a, b, c; 1982a, b, c, d) and summarized in Liz Mills's PhD thesis (Mills, 1988).

The importance of Bracey's work to the geography and planning of rural areas is starkly illustrated in these publications. Not only was he a pioneer of central place concepts in the rural context, but he also established a place for social science researchers in the process of planning for rural settlements and rural communities. The first of these roles can be recognized in his published work (Bracey, 1951, 1952, 1953, 1956, 1962, 1970; Brush and Bracey, 1955) but the second is only fully recognizable in the Peter Haggett-inspired reworking of the raw materials archived from Bracey's research. It is crucial to appreciate the historical context in which Bracey's work was carried out. The radical post-war Town and Country Planning Act was passed in 1947, and one of its provisions was to require local authorities to prepare a Development Plan for the area under their jurisdiction (see Ambrose, 1986; Cullingworth, 1985). The Development Plan was to be founded on surveys of physical, economic, and social features of each county, which assessed both the existing potential and future requirements for growth and development. As Bracey (1952) himself noted:

> This is not another piece of bureaucratic interference, but a genuine recognition that for legislation to be effective, accurate detailed knowledge of the areas to be planned is essential. One of the most serious obstacles in this field is, indeed, the incompleteness of our present knowledge of places and people. This is particularly true of villages and small towns, whose individual populations may be small, but which together house six or seven million persons. (p. xvii)

Bracey's motives in this were clearly both beneficent and idealistic. He realized, for example, that 'the provision of rural services leaves much to be desired' (p. xviii) and that 'one of the major tasks of town and country planning is a general raising of rural standards' (ibid.). Moreover, he linked his own research role with this raising of standards:

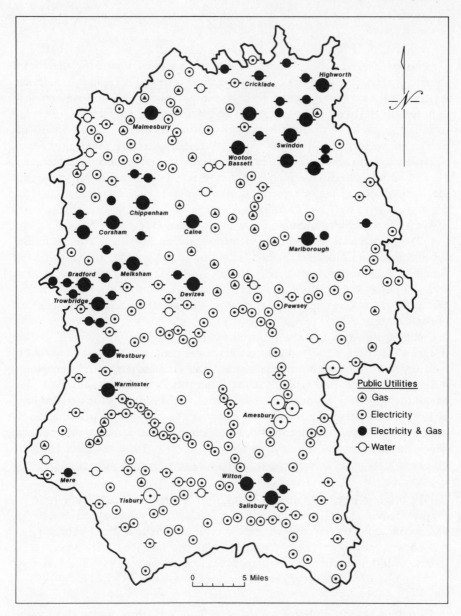

Figure 7.1   Distribution of public utility services in rural Wiltshire, 1950. Bracey's chapter
includes the following intriguing acknowledgement: 'The author's thanks are due to Professor
R.F.E.W. Peel, Head of the Department of Geography, University of Bristol, England, who
kindly redrew the map.' Peel was renowned as a cartographer and Bristol Geography
Department historians confirm that he would, indeed, have enjoyed this cartographic
collaboration with Bracey
(*Source*: Bracey, 1952, p. 81)

Improvements must clearly be preceded by some assessment of existing conditions (ibid.)

Between 1947 and 1951, therefore, Bracey undertook a range of surveys in the rural parts of the counties of Somerset and Wiltshire. His research methods included detailed questionnaire surveys, completed on a parish basis by local dignitaries – the headteacher, vicar, parish councillor or secretary of some local voluntary organization. These surveys covered the distribution and quality of public utility services, the spread of professional services and commercial activities, and the availability of a range of social and community organizations. He also undertook wide-ranging field surveys so that he could bring a personal local knowledge to an interpretation of findings from his respondents. His surveys yielded a wealth of detailed and localized information which, in the case of Wiltshire, is fully expounded in his book, *Social Provision in Rural Wiltshire* (1952). An indication of how he presented these findings is illustrated in figure 7.1 which shows Bracey's mapped distribution of public utility services in rural Wiltshire. At a time when contemporary analyses of the 'rural' are re-evaluating issues of power and light (see Thrift, 1994), historical distributions such as this may yet prove to be an invaluable inventory for understanding recent histories of rural change.

Bracey's Somerset surveys received far less published attention (but see Bracey 1953, 1956, 1962), and the materials rescued, analysed and archived by the Haggett/Mills/Morgan team are now available for a similarly detailed mapping out of rural services and facilities in that county. In fact, Bracey undertook two parish surveys in the county – the first in 1947, and a second more detailed one in 1950. These survey findings were reconstructed from the original question-naires by the Bristol research team, and then matched with the information which they constructed about the same rural areas in 1980. As Peter Haggett notes in his social science research abstract for the research project:

Our original intention was to follow Bracey's research design, using a questionnaire to selected individuals in each parish to collect up-to-date information. However, following close contact with the Rural Community Councils for Somerset and Avon, and with the statutory authorities, we have found that much of the material we require is already available, and that a questionnaire survey is only necessary in south Avon.

The resultant comparative information has, alas, thus far received little exposure in the rural geography and planning literatures, and the best source of the comparative analyses that were undertaken is to be found in Liz Mills's PhD thesis, *Changes in the Rural Spatial Economy of an English County (Somerset 1947–1980)*. Here we are given tantalizing glimpses of what can be gleaned from Bracey's data and its replications. Mills, for example, contrasts the distribution of professional services in 1950 and in 1980 (table 7.1), noting that 'in 1980 it was still the case that the most populous parishes and those with a substantial number of shops were most likely also to have professional services' (p. 165) and that

Table 7.1   Professional services in rural Somerset, 1950 and 1980

	1950			1980		
Parishes with:	*(No.)*	*(%)*	*N*[a]	*(No.)*	*(%)*	*N*
Bank	43	11.4	378	42	10.8	388
Building society				22	5.7	
Accountant	12	3.2		18	4.6	
Vet	17	4.5		16	4.1	386
Solicitor	21	5.6		23	5.9	389
Estate agent	17	4.5		29	7.5	389
Other professional service	127	33.6		34	8.7	391

[a] *N* = parishes reporting.

Source: Mills (1988, p. 162)

Table 7.2   Somerset parishes with transport facilities, 1950 and 1980

	1950			1980		
Parishes with:	*(No.)*	*(%)*	*N*[a]	*(No.)*	*(%)*	*N*
Regular bus service[b]	305	75.5	347	257	65.2	394
Coach hire				33	13.6	242
Car hire or taxi service	280	75.5	371	55	23.2	237
Special local transport arrangements[c]	55	15.1	363	140	45.9	305
Rail service within 5 miles	325	87.4	372			

[a] *N* = parishes reporting.
[b] Buses every weekday, 1947.
[c] Excludes trains, 1947.

Source: Mills (1988, p. 169)

although some rural parishes have lost professional services, there has been, if anything, a slight increase in the percentage of rural parishes supporting them, together with a broadening of the range of services available, *although it is now no longer usual for rural parishes to have their own undertakers*. (ibid.; my emphasis!)

Similar comparative analyses were undertaken on a range of other services, including transport facilities (table 7.2) where a very obvious decline is illustrated.

One of the major contributions of Bracey's original work was his use of these survey findings from 1947 and 1950 to conceptualize what he called the *English central village* (Bracey, 1962), defining it as 'the village with more shops and services than one would expect for its size which is operating services for

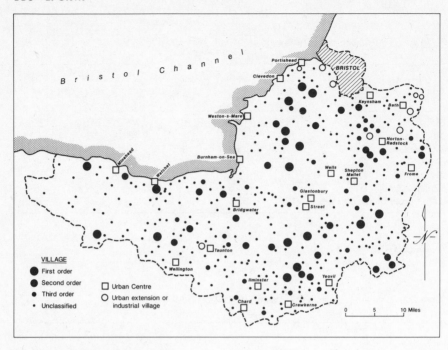

Figure 7.2   Central villages in Somerset
(*Source*: Bracey, 1962, p. 176)

neighbouring villages and hamlets' (p. 170). As shown in figure 7.2, he catego-
rized these central villages into first order (20 shops or more), second-order (10
to 19 shops) and third order (5 to 9 shops), and their spheres of influence were
defined according to the range and extent of mobile services based in the central
village but serving smaller villages in the rural hinterland.

Bracey's ideas were a formative influence on early rural settlement planning
policy. The existence of these seemingly 'natural' centres within settlement
hierarchies was incorporated into the policy decision which underpinned the
post-war development plans. Indeed, it is known that Bracey's specific findings
were used as a direct input to the Wiltshire County Council Plan (1953); and
it seems likely that this was also the case in Somerset, although the 1980
reanalysis throws some doubt on the extent to which this was so. This research
also had a much wider impact. In a review of Bracey-type studies and planning
in 1952, Lipman argued:

> For the physical planner the importance of studies of this kind is equally
> obvious; indeed, it is significant that much recent research in this field has
> been conducted as part of the survey's preliminary to planning. This holds
> good whether the task is to analyse the social structure of an area like a
> County or to plan the future layout of a town, in the light of the services
> it performs for the surrounding countryside. Analysis of the pattern of
> rural settlement and service centres provides the background to attempts

Table 7.3 Parish Deficit Indicator in relation to the 1964 rural settlement planning hierarchy in Somerset

| Settlement category | No. of parishes | Average parish population | | | Average parish deficit indicator | | | | | |
| | | | | | Unweighted | | | Weighted | | |
		1950	1980	% change	1950	1980	Shift	1950	1980	Shift
Town[a]	1	1972	2463	+25	1.5	0.0	−1.5	1.5	0.0	−1.5
Main/local centre	19	1805	2616	+45	3.5	2.0	−1.5	3.4	1.7	−1.7
Village[b]	107	1011	1376	+36	12.5	15.1	+2.6	11.5	11.8	+0.3
Village[c]	145	444	512	+15	26.6	33.6	+7.0	23.7	30.9	+7.2
Total[d]	378	626	827	+32	27.2	33.5	+6.3	16.6	17.0	+0.4

[a] Of secondary importance.
[b] First schedule.
[c] Second schedule.
[d] Includes 106 parishes for which no information was available.

Source: Mills (1988, p. 271)

to determine what should be the future distribution of rural population and the provision of social and educational facilities and other public services in rural areas. (pp. 212–13)

Therefore *at the time* it would seem that the research findings on central villages were recognized as important by local authority planners and administrators themselves. With the benefit of hindsight, my own analysis of key settlement policies also attributed enormous significance to the valorization of central village ideas in post-war rural settlement planning:

At the time of the Development Plans, planners perceived a logical progression from the identification of existing rural centres to the continuing support of these centres as the focus for investment in rural areas. In effect, many planners were attempting to build up certain key settlements into the ideal central-village model whereby additional service provision in one central location would benefit a wide rural hinterland. (Cloke, 1979, p. 42)

Bracey's work, then, was crucial both empirically and conceptually to the rural planning of his day and, by implication, to rural planning over much of the ensuing 40 years since the key settlement model (often under other names) has continued to take centre stage in the planning strategies employed in most areas of rural Britain. Peter Haggett, too, recognized an essential link between social science research (such as that done by the Bristol team) and planning in rural areas. In a progress report to the Social Science Research Council in 1980, he wrote:

In our own work, as Bracey did in his, we hope both to contribute to the planning process locally by our collection of detailed information not as yet available, and to add to the current debate in rural geography concerning the effects of various planning policies on changes in rural service provision.

And indeed, the material from the 1980 survey was used in the Avon Structure Plan. Here, we can detect both an idea of research as a most useful input to planning policy formation, and the notion of research as an evaluative tool aimed at understanding the impacts of existing planning policies. Haggett's rural stage, unlike Bracey's, has been subject to some 30 years of supposedly planned change, and therefore the policy process consists of iterative manoeuvres of policy-evaluation, policy-making and policy-implementation (see Barrett and Fudge, 1981), each of which is susceptible to the diffusion of research findings.

Much of the Bristol research team's work focused on the impacts of hierarchical planning in rural areas on levels of service provision. For example, they devised a Parish Deficit Indicator (Mills, 1988, p. 269) which reflected the number of key services which were missing in the Somerset study area in 1950 and 1980. The Indicator used a scale from zero (indicating a parish with no deficit) to 100 (indicating a parish where all of the key services were missing). This Indicator was then mapped out against the hierarchical designations given to rural settlements in the County Development Plan Review (Somerset County Council, 1964). As table 7.3 shows, the larger settlements ('towns') and the key rural centres ('main' and 'local' centres) experienced service gains, whereas in the smaller, non-selected villages ('first' and 'second schedule') there were further deficits of services between the two survey dates. As Mills suggests, however, 'in view of the way in which the presence of services in settlements has been used to identify these places as suitable for future growth, this is not entirely unexpected' (p. 306). As she also suggests, the patterns of population growth associated with counter-urbanization have more recently highlighted growth in small non-selected settlements, regardless of their status as declining service centres. In seeking to evaluate the policy position for Somerset's villages, she concludes:

national and urban policies have often had *unintended* consequences for rural areas in terms of support for counterurbanising forces. Local policies for rural settlements seem to have been more directive, though they too may have had unintended consequences for the places at the very base of the settlement hierarchy. While socio-economic change, encouraged by government policies, is continuing to underwrite non-metropolitan growth, on the ground the local authorities fight to contain it and to deal with the consequences, endeavouring to protect the countryside and to support those rural residents not sharing in the new rural affluence. (p. 309)

Howard Bracey, with his localized knowledge of rural places through field visits as well as remotely constructed data, and certainly Peter Haggett, resident of Chew Magna and *very* much in touch with the changes occurring in his beloved Somerset, would, I am sure, endorse the importance of recognizing these complexities. Social science researchers can provide important information inputs to the planning process, but that process itself is but one element of the 'ensemble of relations' (Schoenberger, 1989) which constitute the socio-spatial arena of regulatory change in contemporary times. Indeed, planning itself has been subjected to deregulatory tendencies and can no longer adequately be represented as a process which offers any kind of blueprint for the future. As planning has changed, so has the focus and role of social science research associated with planning. It is to these changing interconnections that I now turn.

3 POLICY IMPLEMENTATION AND THE ROLE OF THE STATE:
THE 'POLITICAL ECONOMIC TURN'

The foregoing account is not intended solely to highlight a lesser known aspect of Peter Haggett's work – although the reconstructions of Bracey's planning-related findings do deserve more attention. It also serves to indicate a phase during which social science research and rural planning practice were 'discourse compatible'. Bracey was presenting information to planners using concepts which were acceptable, data analyses which presented a familiar, clear, and non-threatening picture, and language which was equivalent to (and perhaps even formative of) that of local authority planners and administrators. In turn, the Haggett/Mills/Morgan study was similarly framed in such a way as to be directly relevant to local policy-makers. Although they made use of more sophisticated multivariate statistical procedures such as cluster analysis, their work was received as authoritative, legitimate, and useful. This will undoubtedly have been due in part to the personal standing of Peter Haggett, but it was also due to the acceptability of purpose, language, quantitative analysis, and general 'policy-relevance' which characterized their work.

In the remainder of this chapter, I want to discuss ways in which research by some geographers on rural planning has become discursively incompatible with the languages, analyses, and legitimacies of planning. What research directions have been taken over the last 15 years which have engendered this incompatibility, and why has it been important for researchers to seek out relations with planning that go beyond the information service and evaluation roles discussed above? Rather than attempting a glib history of all of the philosophical and practical twists and turns concerned, I want to focus on a few key moments which illustrate the critical moves which have taken rural planning research into analyses and positions which have become less compatible, acceptable and policy-relevant in the perceptions of most actors in rural policy processes. I should emphasize that by no means all researchers have gone along with these moves, and many continue to prefer a Bracey-type purpose and practice for their work. Others, however, have challenged the conventions of planning research, and it is on these moments of challenge that I will briefly focus here.

Perhaps the fundamental resistance to an uncomplicated interface between social science research and rural planning arose from the begging of simple but far-reaching questions about the nature of planning itself. As researchers began to realize that rural policies and promises are not matched by planning actions in the areas concerned, interest sharpened on the questions of policy-making and policy implementation. In a series of international essays on rural planning in the late 1980s (see Cloke, 1988; 1989), there were clear signs from an array of rural planning researchers in the 'developed' world that planning and policy practices had largely failed to regulate the market-based trends which would, planning or no planning, have exacerbated both social problems of polarization and disadvantage in rural areas and rural land use problems connected with landscape and wildlife conservation. For example, Hodge's (1988) evaluation of rural planning in Canada concluded that:

> Over the past four decades, there have been many planning efforts *directed* at rural areas in the name of economic development, conservation of resources, presenting scatteration, and so forth . . . the results of these directive actions range from fiasco to fleeting success. (p. 189)

Attention therefore began to turn to the often yawning divide between planning intentions and practices. Traditionally, this would have yielded analyses of an *implementation problem*, whereby somehow better techniques of implementation would be supported in order to compare the prospect of a planning response to the perceived needs of rural people. As an alternative, rural researchers began to explore the suggestion that suitable policies for rural areas were being precluded within the complex manoeuvres of the rural planning process. Not only could rural planning not deliver its objectives because there was no rational and sequential interconnection between policy and implementation, but also there appeared to be internal survival mechanisms within planning which repelled the adoption of socially progressive policies. Drawing on the work of implementation theorists in the United States (see, for example, Pressman and Wildavsky, 1973; and Van Meter and Van Horn, 1975) and later on the work of state theorists such as Clark and Dear (1984), Dunleavy (1980) and Saunders (1979), researchers began to delve both into the idea that the activities of planning are responsive to the underlying policy aims of the state agencies concerned, and into the related idea that these policy aims will be in some ways conditioned by the form and function of the state, of which planning and policy-making are but one part of the apparatus. Thus, it is argued, different views of the function of the state will offer different explanations for state intervention through planning and policy-making.

This political economic turn in the philosophical underpinning of rural policy research seems light years away from the work of Howard Bracey. However, although methodological and conceptual distance cannot be denied, there is a sense in which research into rural policy from a political economy perspective represents a logical progression from Bracey's goals. He bemoaned the 'incompleteness of our knowledge' about places and people, and wished to 'raise rural standards'. In attempting to answer questions of why rural planning and policy takes the form that it does, geographies of the rural state have sought to provide a knowledgeable rationale for the currency of spatial and social regulation, and the selective nature of 'gain' and 'improvement' in rural society. The suggestion that the state (and therefore its planning apparatus) acts to protect and reproduce existing social structures and existing social relations of production (Mandel, 1975), and that this protection and reproduction are selectively beneficial to specific powerful interests, offers a radical and often unpopular critical edge to studies of rural planning. It certainly begins to offer some theoretical pointers to what is and what is not possible within the planning process and therefore to the degree to which our expectations of planning and policy powers are too tough or misplaced.

To some, however, planning is a matter of very simple democratic process, only involving adjustment or regulation of market trends within the constraints of the need for profit for reinvestment, and within the dictates of majority requirements. An American planner, Catanese, argues this case with vigour:

> Planning is in the service of individuals in the community. When the planner disagrees with the majority of those individuals, he or she should leave that role. Some argue against this assertion and insist that the planner should be an agent of change, even if that means radical and revolutionary change. That means that the planner is charged with the responsibility for societal change. When the change is an attempt to reorder basic values, however, something is wrong in the concept of public service. The only way out is for someone else to do the planning . . . If the values of a community are so corrupt that constitutional rights or moral order are imperiled then the more appropriate change is through the political or legal process. Unless the planner is directly participating in those processes, he or she should not be trying to refuse the beliefs of the community. (Catanese, 1984, p. 39)

For me, at least, attitudes such as these serve to reinforce a sense of protection and reproduction of societal *status quo* in the planning process, and those who assume a basically pluralist set of power relations in rural (as in other) areas tend to ignore issues of social justice, uneven development, and the idea that planning and policy might be directed to specific, but not necessarily *majority*, needs. As Newby (1979) has pointed out in the British context:

> So far it has been the most privileged members of English rural society who have benefited most from the operation of the planning system in rural areas, while the poor and deprived have gained comparatively little. (p. 237)

Thus the political economic turn towards understanding rural planning and policy *in its state context* has seemed to open doors on new perspectives for rural planning research (see Cloke, 1987; Cloke and Little, 1990). It has offered insights into the constraints on local planning action (what was possible, what was not); the relations of planning (central–local, local–local, public–private sector, and so on); and the complex but very necessary idea of the power to be found in, and exerted through, planning action. In practical terms, this has meant that researchers have needed to use suitable research methods to gain an understanding of decision-making processes both within planning agencies and beyond in the boardrooms of private sector capital institutions. They have also had to find ways of accommodating the variability of local outcomes in society and space with the often seemingly deterministic expectations of political economic theory.

The response of planners to research from a political economic perspective was at once alienating and liberating. Alienation was prompted in many different ways. One important factor was that political economy approaches brought with them a specific language and narrative, which was often dismissed as mere 'jargon' by planning actors. I well remember proudly presenting one of my initial forays into these ideas (see Hanrahan and Cloke, 1983) to a group of senior planners in Norfolk County Council, and returning with my tail very much between my legs because of the huge gulf they perceived between these political economic writings and what was regarded as practical, relevant research. On the other hand, many rural planners in Britain have told me of their own very practical awareness of the constraints of planning an apparatus for wider state functions: the frustrations caused by policy implementation without power, leading to an enforced acceptance of market mechanisms and their resultant actions, whether in line with policy or not; and the working knowledge of a political 'art of the possible' beyond which the (often central state) constraints on planning action do not permit a 'response' to 'problems'.

By and large, however, political economic studies of rural planning have not been regarded as useful, relevant, or compatible with the needs of professional planning practitioners. It would perhaps be naïve to expect otherwise. The intention has not been to provide research material which can be easily slotted into particular practices of policy evaluation or new policy formulation. Rather, such studies have represented an evaluation of planning itself, providing knowledge about the structures which restrict or permit certain forms of action, the agency which manages such action, and the politics and power within state and locality which mediate change in localized society and space. This is not to say that research which builds upon these theoretical foundations cannot be of relevance to planning in a particular region or jurisdiction (see, for example, Pawson and Scott's 1992 work in New Zealand, the 1989 account by Day, Reese, and Murdoch of rural Wales, and Cloke and Little's study of the English county of Gloucestershire: Cloke and Little, 1987a, b). But it does suggest that the discursive interpretation of the nature and usefulness of planning apparatus in rural areas from a political economy perspective has taken a direction which has problematized direct liaison with the planning process. Planning professionals and planning politicians have often appreciated data on economic restructuring and social recomposition but, when it comes to political economic discourse on the role of the state, then that has generally been too sensitive an issue to embrace directly, and too far beyond the short-termism of most planning practices to be thought of as being politically applicable to the nitty-gritty of planning work. In this way, much of the research linked with the political economic turn has been discursively incompatible with rural planning practices.

4 PEOPLE AND PLANNING: THE (RE)TURN TO LAY DISCOURSE

My own engagement with political economic approaches, for the reasons outlined above, represented a disabling of my continuing wish to contribute directly to policy-related research. Previous work on key settlement policies and evaluations of rural policies in several different sectors had, it seemed, been compatible with the notions of relevance and acceptability as defined by practising planners. However, political economic notions of the state, and the hidden societal functions therein, were seen more often than not as too 'conspiratorial' or 'political' to be of any practical use. Political economy concepts of rural planning were criticized on other grounds also – they were reductionist, meta-theoretical, modernist and overemphasized structure rather than agency. I retained, however, a wish to be able to influence policy-makers over issues of injustice, powerlessness, prejudice and so on (see Cloke, 1994a).

The opportunity to reclaim this relational ground with planning and policy practice came with a research programme designed to study changing rural lifestyles in England which was co-sponsored by the Economic and Social Research Council, the Department of the Environment and the Rural Development Commission (Cloke, Milbourne, and Thomas, 1994). This research was to be based on household surveys in 12 case study areas in England, and the objective was to provide information on all aspects of rural life and lifestyle in order to inform policy-making for rural communities. Here, then, was an ideal opportunity to 'get back to basics' and to present geographical research data which would be 'relevant' to planning. I could even use political economic concepts of economic restructuring and social recomposition as background information for the study.

Two factors inhibited the ultimate policy-relevance of this work, however, and these point to much wider issues within social science research. First, the question of what is 'rural' about rural lifestyles led to some considerable discussion about the nature of rurality. I had become convinced (see Cloke and Goodwin, 1993) that rurality could no longer be represented as a single space, but rather as a multiplicity of social spaces (Mormont, 1990). In this light, rurality needs to be viewed as a social construct, reflecting and constituting a world of social, moral, and cultural values, and people's decisions about where to live and how to live will thus be influenced by the social construct(s) which indicate(s) that a place is rural. Contemporary rural geography, therefore, has become very interested in the way in which meanings of rurality are being constructed, negotiated, and experienced, and researchers are drawing on an increasingly wide body of text on rurality and idyll in pursuit of these interests (see Cloke and Milbourne, 1992; Crouch, 1992; Mingay, 1989a, b, c; B. Short, 1992; J. Short, 1991).

The second of these wider issues follows on from this idea of rurality as being socially constructed. What is happening here is an emphasis on deconstruction and difference drawn from recent discussions in post-modernism and post-structural thinking. Thus 'rural' as a macro-category is being deconstructed and, in its place, different discourses and representations of rurality are being investigated. Halfacree (1993) has shown how the need to understand social constructions of rurality has prompted academic discourses to be routed through lay discourses so that the voices of 'ordinary' people can both be heard and be used in academic and even policy debates.

One of the most important questions here concerns the purposes for which lay discourses are to be used in academic discourses. A recent debate in *Journal of Rural Studies* emphasizes some of the complexities involved. Philo (1992) addresses the issue of 'neglected rural geographies' and suggests that rural geography should be made more open to the 'circumstances *and* to the voices of "other" peoples in "other" places: a new geography determined to overcome the neglect to "other" which has characterized much geographical endeavour to date' (p. 199). In a response, Murdoch and Pratt (1993) argue that, to permit the voices of rural peoples to emerge from lay discourses, is insufficient *per se* as a reason to undertake rural studies of this genre. They insist that 'simply "giving voice" to "others" by no means guarantees that we will uncover the relations which lead to marginalisation or neglect. This raises a whole clutch of issues relating to difference, space and power in relation to the "rural"' (p. 422).

Philo's reply clarifies his position:

> [A]lthough I would add that in 'spirit' my own concern for injustice, exploitation and possible ways of improving conditions in the lives of rural 'others' is probably not so distant from the . . . one animating their approach to rural studies, . . . I am still . . . unhappy about the assertive modernist impulse present in Bauman (and thus in Murdoch and Pratt) which proceeds with such certainty, which still puts faith in the *a priori* theoretical specification of how the world and its injustices operate, and which heroically assures the duty of assessing from without the realities of 'other lives' against trancendental yardsticks of 'right'/'wrong' and 'good'/'bad' that may have little relevance for the people and places concerned. (Philo, 1993, p. 433)

And Murdoch and Pratt (1994) continue to disagree:

> Should we not attempt to reveal the ways of the 'powerful', exploring the means by which they make and sustain 'their' domination (perhaps in the hope that such knowledge could become a 'reservoir' to be drawn upon by oppositional actors)? Do we not also seek to influence the decisions of the 'powerful', such as policymakers in the hope that they might be persuaded to produce more effective and just interventions in the world?

These notions of socially constructed rurality and the need to include lay discourses of the rural in academic discourses led to a series of important methodological and interpretative decisions relating to the Rural Lifestyles research project. The need to study variations in the material opportunities available in different rural areas remained the same but, given the above considerations, it seemed essential that variations in material opportunities be understood in a context which acknowledges that opportunities are experienced in a variety of different ways by different people. This necessitated as full a use as possible of qualitative text gathered in the survey interviews in order that the people concerned were 'given a voice' in the reported findings. Inevitably, however, the power over which voices are heard, and over what they are heard to say, rests with the researchers, and so this methodological manoeuvre is not as emancipatory as it may at first appear. A second device, which acknowledged the importance of lay discourse, was an attempt to interpret survey information in categories and under headings which reflected people's own reporting of their own problems and significant issues, rather than just using preconceived notions on the part of the researchers about what their problems should be.

A full account of the findings of this research is available in Cloke, Milbourne, and Thomas (1994). However, the reason for using the Rural Lifestyles work as an example of the (re)turn to lay discourse in research relating to rural planning and policy is the response which the work received from the policy-making agencies which were its co-sponsors. In particular, specific points of criticism about the research highlight a mismatch between our attempts as researchers to route discussions of rural lifestyle through lay discourses, and the requirements of the policy discourses of the sponsors who sought to define the relevance, acceptability and validity of research from the policy perspective. Three major areas of our research were so criticized:

1 The use of qualitative text (so often labelled 'soft', 'unfactual' and 'subjective' – each term used pejoratively) proved to be a major stumbling block. Numbers were seen as factual and policy-relevant, whereas 'quotations' tended to be relevant only in so far as they were fully and clearly connected to the numbers.

2 There was strong resistance to the idea of using headings of analysis derived from the qualitative responses of our interviewees, rather than those already ingrained in policy discourses. Thus non-traditional ideas about rural life-status, social power, community conflict, cultural competence, non-formal work, and so on, were not regarded as suitably policy-relevant for the purposes of this research.

3 Particular policy discourses strongly represented particular ways of seeing the rural, and ways of doing the rural, which could not easily be deconstructed within the discourses themselves by the introduction of other conceptual or methodological ideas. This 'hard' information on self-defining policy areas (employment, housing, transport, and so on) was fine, whereas 'soft' information on policy-irrelevant areas such as rural people's own views of what their problems and non-problems were was not fine.

These criticisms starkly illustrate an interesting set of relations between academic discourses of the rural and other such discourses.

The Rural Lifestyles study suggests that the routing of academic discourses through lay discourses is likely to result in the introduction of more qualitative and experiential narratives of the different needs, experiences and lifestyles of rural people. Two important implications arise from this:

> First, such an approach will often clash with existing policy discourses which appear to require narratives of sameness – common needs, clearly defined spatial problems, clearly ordered needy social groups, a simply explained problematic and so on – and which are confused by narratives of difference, which tend to subvert the clarity of sectoral and spatial policy models. Secondly, such an approach, with its emphasis on different experiences, is vulnerable to a response based on the politics of individual responsibility. If rural need is so diverse and intangible, then why should the state intervene at all? If rural problems are so different, then why interfere with individual responsibility in the market-place? (Cloke, 1994b, p. 27)

In the latter case, a research programme which emphasizes the need for affordable housing, the need for jobs, the incidence of low income and poverty, and so on, and thereby in the view of its authors bears strong testimony to the need for continued collectivist action (including 'policy' and 'planning') by the state in order to address the inequalities of the market-place, can be subverted *because of its emphasis on difference* to the propaganda of individualist politics. By turning, and in a very real sense *re*turning, to issues of making people important in planning discussions, it is possible that we can provide ammunition for those who want to undermine and deregulate planning itself.

5 CONCLUSION

Have we, then, come full circle? Is it only by adopting a Bracey-like research posture, with all of the conceptual and methodological implications of that stance, that rural researchers can contribute to policy-making and planning decisions in rural areas? Were those who have argued that a theory-free rural geography and a quantitative empirical monopoly were the sole mechanisms for policy-relevance right all along? I believe not. Perhaps instead of arguing that geographers and other social scientists should get back to quantitative empirical basics, we should be arguing that planning should be redirected back to the basics of being able to respond to people's needs. If this appears simplistic, it is perhaps because I would strongly suggest that the use of socio-cultural concepts of representation and difference do not necessarily demand individualist responses. For example, we need to know a great deal more about the power vested in representation; and the differential experience of life in rural communities would seem to me to point towards new forms of bottom-up, community-led, integrated and sustainable development in rural areas.

Nevertheless, the problem remains that academic discourses routed through lay discourses tend to produce narratives which will be unacceptable to conventional policy discourses. The question is, then, as stated by Murdoch and Pratt above, whether we are attempting merely to provide a reservoir of knowledge to be made available to actors who are in opposition to the powerful and the dominant, or whether we are seeking to influence the decisions of powerful decision-makers in the hope of bringing about more effective and equitable policies. If it is this second goal which excites our geographical imaginations, then there will be a continuing need to liaise our normative and experiential findings far more closely than before, so as to bring together the critical understandings of how rural opportunities are structured and how these opportunities are experienced differently in relation to powerful social constructs of communities, natures, and environment. As these kinds of interconnections become more tightly entwined, so will our academic discourses come closer to meeting these grand but critical ambitions, and we can once again make progress in tackling the 'incompleteness of our present knowledge of places and people' in rural areas.

ACKNOWLEDGEMENT

I gratefully acknowledge the help of Liz Mills in checking the accuracy of some of the material in section 2.

REFERENCES

Ambrose, P. (1986). *Whatever Happened to Planning?* London: Methuen.
Barrett, S. & Fudge, C. (eds) (1981). *Policy and Action*. London: Methuen.
Bracey, H. (1951). 'Rural planning: an index of social provision.' *Journal of Agricultural Economics*, July.
Bracey, H. (1952). *Social Provision in Rural Wiltshire*. London: Methuen.
Bracey, H. (1953). 'Towns as rural service centre: an index of centrality with special references to Somerset.' *Transactions and Papers, Institute of British Geographers*, 19, 95–105.
Bracey, H. (1956). 'A rural component of centrality applied to six southern countries in the United Kingdom.' *Economic Geography*, 32, 38–50.
Bracey, H. (1962). 'English central villages: identification, distribution and functions'. In K. Norberg (ed.), *Proceedings of the IGU Symposium in Urban Geography*. Lund, Sweden, 1960: Department of Geography, Royal University of Lund.
Bracey, H. (1970). *People in the Countryside*. London: Routledge & Kegan Paul.
Brush, J. & Bracey, H. (1955). 'Rural service centres in southwestern Wisconsin and southern England.' *Geographical Review*, 45, 559–69.
Catanese, A. (1984). *The Politics of Planning and Development*. Beverly Hills, CA: Sage.
Clark, G. & Dear, M. (1984). *State Apparatus*. Boston: Allen & Unwin.
Cloke, P. (1979). *Key Settlements in Rural Areas*. London: Methuen.
Cloke, P. (1983). *An Introduction to Rural Settlement Planning*. London: Methuen.
Cloke, P. (ed.) (1987). *Rural Planning: Policy into Action?* London: Harper & Row.
Cloke, P. (ed.) (1988). *Policies and Plans for Rural People*. London: Unwin Hyman.
Cloke, P. (ed.) (1989). *Rural Land Use Planning in Development Nations*. London: Unwin Hyman.

Cloke, P. (1994a). '(En)culturing political economy: a life in the day of a rural geographer.' In P. Cloke, M. Doel, D. Matless, M. Phillips, & N. Thrift, *Writing the Rural: Five Cultural Geographies*. London: Paul Chapman Publishing.

Cloke, P. (1994b). 'Rural lifestyles: material opportunity, cultural experience, and how theory can undermine policy.' Unpublished paper presented to the Annual Meeting of the Association of American Geographers, San Francisco.

Cloke, P. & Goodwin, M. (1993). 'Rural change: structured coherence or unstructured incoherence?' *Terra*, 105, 166–174.

Cloke, P. & Little, J. (1987a). 'Rural policies in the Gloucestershire structure plan, I: a study of motives and mechanisms.' *Environment and Planning A*, 19, 959–81.

Cloke, P. & Little, J. (1987b). 'Rural policies in the Gloucestershire structure plan, II: implementation and the county–district relationship.' *Environment and Planning A*, 19, 1027–50.

Cloke, P. & Little, J. (1990). *The Rural State: Limits to Planning in Rural Society*. Oxford: Clarendon Press.

Cloke, P. & Milbourne, P. (1992). 'Deprivation and rural lifestyles in rural Wales, II.' *Journal of Rural Studies*, 8, 360–74.

Cloke, P., Milbourne, P., & Thomas, C. (1994). *Lifestyles in Rural England*. London: Rural Development Commission.

Crouch, D. (1992). 'Popular culture and what we make of the rural, with a case study of village allotments.' *Journal of Rural Studies*, 8, 229–40.

Cullingworth, B. (1985). *Town and Country Planning in Britain* (ninth edn). London: Routledge.

Day, G., Rees, G., & Murdoch, J. (1989). 'Social change, rural localities and the state: the restructuring of rural Wales.' *Journal of Rural Studies*, 5, 227–44.

Dunleavy, P. (1980). *Urban Political Analysis: the Politics of Collective Consumption*. London: Macmillan.

Hägerstrand, T. (1982). 'Diorama, path and project.' *Tijdschrift voor Economische en Sociale Geografie*, 73, 323–39.

Haggett, P. (1981) 'Note on Population Size Classes.' *Changes in the Rural Spatial Economy of an English County (Somerset 1947–80)*, working note 4, Department of Geography, University of Bristol.

Haggett, P. (1990). *The Geographer's Art*. Oxford: Blackwell.

Haggett, P., Mills, L., & Morgan, M. (1982). 'The Loss of Rural Services in Somerset and South Avon 1950–80: a Preliminary Analysis.' *Changes in the Rural Spatial Economy of an English County (Somerset 1947–80)*, working paper 3, Department of Geography, University of Bristol.

Halfacree, K. (1993). 'Locality and social representation: space, discourse, and alternative definitions of the rural.' *Journal of Rural Studies*, 9, 1–15.

Hanrahan, P. & Cloke, P. (1983). 'Towards a critical appraisal of rural settlement planning in England and Wales.' *Sociologia Ruralis*, 23, 109–29.

Hodge, G. (1988). 'Canada'. In P. Cloke (ed.), *Policies and Plans for Rural People*. London: Unwin Hyman.

Lipman, V. (1952). 'Town and country: the study of service centres and their areas of influence.' *Public Administration*, 30, 203–14.

Mandel, E. (1975). *Late Capitalism* (transl. edn). London: New Left Books.

Mills, L. (1981a). 'Report of Pilot Survey in South Avon April/May 1980.' *Changes in the Rural Spatial Economy of an English County (Somerset 1947–80)*, working note 2, Department of Geography, University of Bristol.

Mills, L. (1981b). 'Community Council for Somerset/Somerset County Planning Department Community Facilities Survey via *Thatch* Magazine 1979.' *Changes in the*

Rural Spatial Economy of an English County (Somerset 1947–80), working note 3, Department of Geography, University of Bristol.

Mills, L. (1981c). 'Selection of the Survey Parishes.' *Changes in the Rural Spatial Economy of an English County (Somerset 1947–80)*, working note 5, Department of Geography, University of Bristol.

Mills, L. (1982a). 'The Parishes of Somerset in 1950.' *Changes in the Rural Spatial Economy of an English County (Somerset 1947–80)*, research report, Department of Geography, University of Bristol.

Mills, L. (1982b). 'Mobile and Delivery Services in Somerset and South Avon 1950–80.' *Changes in the Rural Spatial Economy of an English County (Somerset 1947–80)*, working paper 1, Department of Geography, University of Bristol.

Mills, L. (1982c). 'Public Utility Services in Somerset and South Avon 1980, with 1950 Comparisons.' *Changes in the Rural Spatial Economy of a English County (Somerset 1947–80)*, working paper 2, Department of Geography, University of Bristol.

Mills, L. (1982d). 'Population Trends in the Study Area.' *Changes in the Rural Spatial Economy of an English County (Somerset 1947–80)*, working note 7, Department of Geography, University of Bristol.

Mills, L. (1988). *Changes in the Rural Spatial Economy of an English County (Somerset 1947–80)*. Unpublished PhD thesis, University of Bristol.

Mingay, G. (ed.) (1989a). *The Rural Idyll*. London: Routledge.

Mingay, G. (ed.) (1989b). *The Unquiet Countryside*. London: Routledge.

Mingay, G. (ed.). (1989c). *The Vanishing Countryman*. London: Routledge.

Mormont, M. (1990). 'What is rural? or, How to be rural: towards a sociology of the rural.' In T. Marsden, P. Lowe, & S. Whatmore (eds), *Rural Restructuring*. London: David Fulton.

Murdoch, J. & Pratt, A.C. (1993). 'Rural studies: modernism, postmodernism and the *post-rural*.' *Journal of Rural Studies*, 9, 411–28.

Murdoch, J. & Pratt, A.C. (1994). 'Rural studies of power and the power of rural studies: a reply to Philo'. *Journal of Rural Studies*, 10, 83–7.

Newby, H. (1979). *Green and Pleasant Land?* Harmondsworth: Penguin Books.

Pawson, E. and Scott, D. (1992). 'The regional consequences of economic restructuring: the West Coast, New Zealand (1984–1991).' *Journal of Rural Studies*, 8, 373–86.

Philo, C. (1992). 'Neglected rural geographies: a review.' *Journal of Rural Studies*, 8, 193–207.

Philo, C. (1993). 'Postmodern rural geography? A reply to Murdoch and Pratt.' *Journal of Rural Studies*, 9, 429–36.

Pressman, J. & Wildavsky, A. (1973). *Implementation*. Berkeley, CA: University of California Press.

Saunders, P. (1979). *Urban Politics: a Sociological Interpretation*. London: Hutchinson.

Schoenberger, E. (1989). 'Thinking about flexibility: a response to Gertler.' *Transactions, Institute of British Geographers*, NS 14, 98–108.

Short, B. (ed.) (1992). *The English Rural Community*. Cambridge: Cambridge University Press.

Short, J. (1991). *Imagined Country: Society, Culture and Environment*. London: Routledge.

Somerset County Council (1964). *County Development Plan: First Review*. Taunton: Somerset County Council.

Thrift, N. (1994). 'Inhuman geographies: landscape of speed, light and power.' In P. Cloke, M. Doel, D. Matless, M. Phillips, & N. Thrift, *Writing the Rural: Five Cultural Geographies*. London: Paul Chapman Publishing, pp. 191–248.

Tillich, P. (1963). *Systematic Theology* (vol. III). Chicago: University of Chicago Press.

Van Meter, D. & Van Horn, C. (1975). 'The policy implementation process: a conceptual framework.' *Administration and Society*, 6, 445–88.

Wiltshire County Council (1953). *County Development Plan*. Trowbridge: Wiltshire County Council.

PART III

Medical Geography

Plate III In all the miles travelled and original handwritten records about disease turned by Peter in his pursuit of understanding about the way in which infectious diseases spread from one geographical area to another, there have been many magic moments. But few can compare with a Saturday afternoon in 1979, shared with one of the editors, reconstructing the spread of the 1904 measles epidemic that affected north-west Iceland. This epidemic produced childhood mortality in a virgin soil population rarely recorded before or since, and started with a single case present at a Whitsuntide confirmation ceremony in an isolated parish church at Eyri. Our first view of the church was as we rounded a corner. Suddenly it was there, perched on a spit at the fjord edge, bathed in afternoon sunlight. The photograph of the church taken on that occasion by Peter is here superimposed on an aerial photograph of the fjord area affected by the resulting epidemic.

8

Estimating Epidemic Return Times

A.D. Cliff and J.K. Ord

For most of our professional careers, we have been lucky enough to work with Peter Haggett. We have been privileged to share his intellectual excitement as we have explored together a variety of issues in, initially, locational analysis and, later, in the application of ideas of spatial diffusion to the spread of human epidemic disease. As partners-in-crime in so many writing ventures, we would not embarrass Peter by spelling out here what we *really* think of him; he will know that, and others can use their imagination. Instead we turn immediately to the business in hand.

In the study of the geographical spread of epidemics, two topics have constantly intrigued Peter. The first is the ability (or otherwise) to forecast spread, and the second is the size of the so-called Bartlett thresholds for the persistence of infectious diseases in a community. With Peter, we have confronted these topics on many occasions – we wish we could say over a pint in a pub, but he still owes us that! So in this paper, we return again to these two villains. As we shall see, we obtain a somewhat different perspective on the forecasting problem by pushing the two topics together and developing a forecasting model for epidemic return times.

1.1 The need for forecasts

With the global eradication of smallpox in 1979, following a ten-year international Intensified Smallpox Eradication Programme articulated by the World Health Organization (WHO), attention has turned to other diseases to assess their potential as candidates for similar worldwide eradication. In a list of six diseases (the others are poliomyelitis, neo-natal tetanus, diphtheria, tuberculosis and pertussis), measles has been recognized as an illness which is theoretically capable of such elimination (Fenner, 1986; Henderson, 1976; Hinman et al., 1980). As figure 8.1 shows for the United States, the introduction of measles

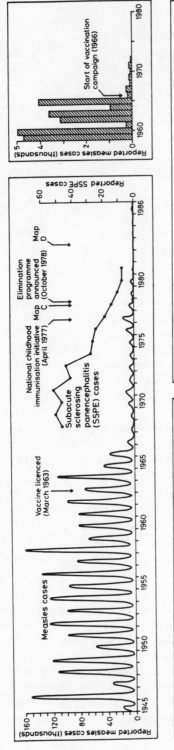

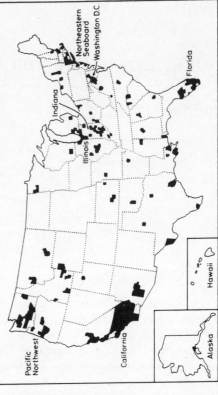

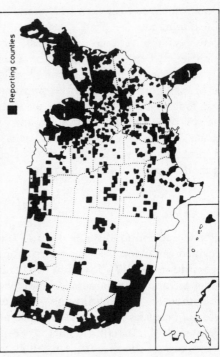

Figure 8.1 Incidence of measles morbidity in the United States. *Upper left*, reported cases, 1945–1986, and annual cases of subacute sclerosing panencephalitis (SSPE), 1968–1981. *Upper right*, reported cases in the Hawaiian Islands, 1959–81. *Lower left*, US counties reporting measles in 1978 and, *lower right*, in 1983. Since 1986, measles morbidity has risen sharply to several thousands of cases annually.

(Source: Cliff and Haggett, 1988, figure 4.9, pp. 164–5)

vaccination programmes in many developed countries since the licensing of vaccine in March 1963 has produced sharp falls in incidence, not only in the disease itself but also in the frequency of suspected associated long-term neurological complications such as subacute sclerosing panencephalitis (SSPE). But a gap has opened between the attack and death rates in the developed world and those in less developed countries, where they remain at a level typical of Europe or the United States in the nineteenth century. Mortality rates of 20–30 per cent are commonly reported in African countries; the latest United Nations figures suggest that measles still retains the position it has held since the Second World War in the top ten causes of death in the world as a whole, yielding nearly 2 million deaths annually.

It is the combination of easy reduction in disease incidence through vaccination and enormous pay-back in terms of years of potential life saved which appears to make measles such an attractive candidate for elimination. However, the United States experience suggests that maintaining immunization at 90–95 per cent of the childhood population is required to bring elimination within sight when blanket vaccination methods are employed (Senser, Dull and Langmuir, 1967). Such a figure is impossible to achieve without a high degree of political will, and economic and medical resources beyond the scope of many countries, especially in the developing world where death rates from the disease are highest.

The temporal and geographical patterns of measles incidence on a global scale do, however, have certain features which imply that, even though global eradication may be unlikely in the foreseeable future, vastly reduced levels of diseases incidence can be achieved over large sections of the globe, even with scarce resources, if we can forecast the time–space incidence of the disease and target medical assistance. Thus we need models to forecast the start of measles epidemics in time and space, with lead times of several weeks to organize vaccination of at-risk populations and to allow three weeks for immunity to build up following vaccination.

1.2 The nature of measles outbreaks

When plotted as a time series, the reported number of cases of measles, like that of most common infectious diseases propagated by person-to-person transmission, displays two common characteristics. First, most are recorded in intense epidemic phases which appear to recur at regular intervals. These epidemic episodes are separated by relatively quiet inter-epidemic periods when either a few or no cases of the disease occur. Second, the time gap between the epidemics appears to be a function of the population size of the community.

Figure 8.2 shows these features for four countries arranged in decreasing order of population size. The period covers 1945–70 and so is substantially prior to large-scale vaccination which began in the mid 1960s. The upper graph shows that, in the United States, with a population of 210 million in 1970, epidemic peaks arrived every year. In the United Kingdom, with a 1970 population of 56 million, peaks occurred every two years. Denmark, with a population of 5 million, had a more complex pattern with some evidence of a three-year cycle

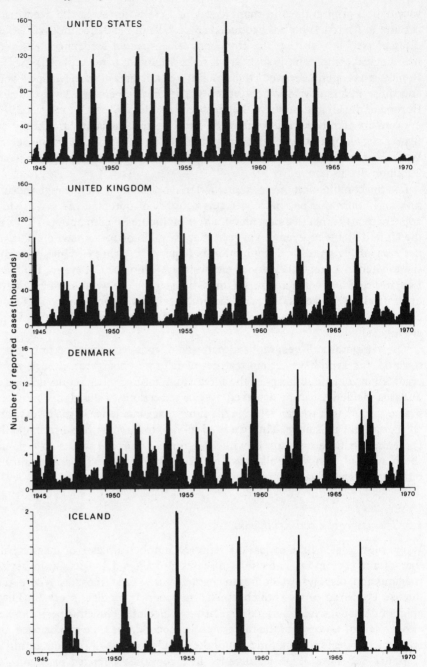

Figure 8.2   Reported cases of measles per month, 1945–1970, for four countries arranged in descending order of population size
(*Source*: Cliff, Haggett, Ord, and Versey, 1981, figure 3.1, p. 39)

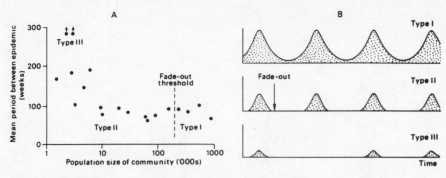

Figure 8.3 (A) Impact of population size of towns on the spacing of measles epidemics and (B) characteristic epidemic wave trains for town types I–III in (A)
(*Sources*: Bartlett, 1972; Cliff, Haggett, Ord, and Versey, figure 3.2, p. 40)

in the latter half of the period. Iceland (0.2 million) stands in contrast to the other countries in that only eight waves occurred in the 25-year period on an approximate four-year cycle, and no cases were reported in several years.

This relationship between community size and spacing of epidemics has been considered in important papers by Bartlett (1957, 1960, 1972). Using a sample of 19 English towns, Bartlett plotted the mean period between epidemics, in weeks, against population size (figures 8.3A and 8.3B). Like the international series shown in figure 8.2, the largest communities have an endemic pattern with periodic eruptions (Type I waves in diagram B), while cities below a certain size threshold have an epidemic pattern with fade-out (cf. Iceland). A distinction can be drawn between urban areas above about 10,000 people with a regular pattern of epidemics (Type II waves in diagram B) and those where occasional epidemics may be missed, giving a more irregular pattern (Type III waves in diagram B). Given the rates of reporting at the time of Bartlett's original study, the endemic/epidemic threshold for measles lay at a population size of around 250,000, a figure which has been confirmed on many occasions since; see Cliff and Haggett (1989a) for a recent review.

The issue of the size of the threshold is critical to our later work. Bartlett's figure was established before the advent of mass vaccination against measles, and it relates to total population rather than the true 'at risk' population. This would be reasonable before mass vaccination when most people contracted wild measles at some stage in their lives, and all individuals not exposed were at risk. However, work is needed to assess ways of determining a threshold concept appropriate to the era of mass vaccination. Similarly, the threshold may vary spatially as between the developing (high birth rate) and developed (low birth rate) nations. In addition, the degree of co-mingling between susceptibles and infectives is also critical, spatial scale-dependent, and equally difficult to determine.

Nevertheless, figures 8.2 and 8.3 carry important implications for attempts to eliminate or reduce measles incidence. First, the existence of an endemicity threshold implies that blanket vaccination is not necessary; instead, vaccination coverage need only ensure that the at-risk population is reduced below the

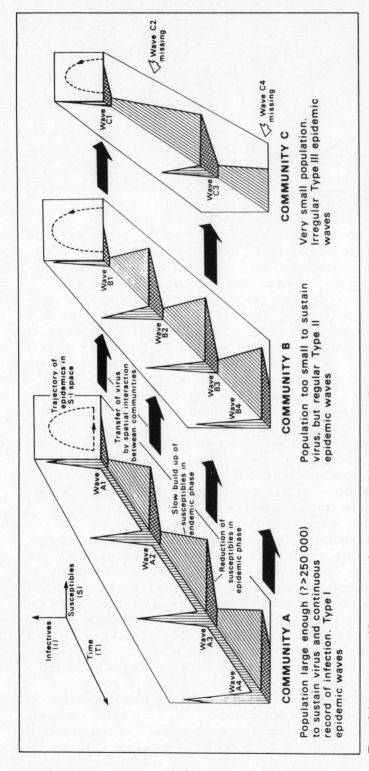

Figure 8.4 Implications of Bartlett model for the geographical persistence of measles in communities of different population sizes

(*Source*: Cliff and Haggett, 1988, figure 6.5A, p. 246)

endemicity threshold. The disease should then be naturally self-extinguishing because the chains of transmission whereby the virus is repeatedly passed from infective to susceptible will be broken. Second, once an area becomes measles-free, an epidemic can recur only if the virus is reintroduced from a geographical reservoir of infection elsewhere. Thus the generalized persistence of measles implies spatial transmission between regions as shown in figure 8.4. In large cities above the size threshold, like community **A**, a continuous trickle of cases is reported. These provide the reservoir of infection which sparks a major epidemic when the susceptible population, S, builds up to a critical level. Since clinical measles confers subsequent lifelong immunity to the disease, this build-up occurs only as children are born, lose their mother-conferred immunity and escape vaccination or the disease. Eventually the S population will increase sufficiently for an epidemic to occur. When this happens, the S population is diminished and the stock of infectives, I, increases as individuals are transferred by infection from the S to the I population. This generates the characteristic 'D'-shaped relationship over time between sizes of the S and I populations shown on the end plane of the block diagram.

When the total population of a community falls below the population size threshold, as in settlement types **B** and **C** of figure 8.4, measles epidemics recur only when the virus is reintroduced by the influx of infected individuals from reservoir areas (community **A** in figure 8.4). These movements are shown by the broad arrows. In such smaller communities, the S population is insufficient to maintain a continuous record of infection. The disease dies out and the S population grows in the absence of infection. Eventually the S population will become big enough to sustain an epidemic when an index case arrives. Given that the total population of the community is insufficient to renew by births the S population as rapidly as it is diminished by infection, the epidemic will eventually die out.

It is the repetition of this basic ·process which generates the successive epidemic waves witnessed in most communities. Of special significance is the way in which the continuous infection and characteristically regular Bartlett Type I epidemic waves of endemic communities break down, as population size diminishes, into first, discrete but regular Type II waves in community **B** and then, secondly, into discrete and irregularly spaced Type III waves in community **C**. Thus disease-free windows will automatically appear in both time and space whenever population totals are small and geographical densities are low.

The implication of the Bartlett model is that a mixture of *cordon-sanitaire* and vaccination procedures to bring the fade-out periods into phase over large geographical areas has the potential to eliminate the disease from substantial parts of the world. Different spatial intervention strategies are reviewed in Cliff and Haggett (1989b). Central to the proper articulation of such spatial strategies is an ability to forecast the space–time occurrence of epidemic outbreaks. When an epidemic is forecast, targeted vaccination can be used to reduce locally the susceptible population below the endemicity threshold in situations where, for whatever reason, maintenance of high levels of vaccination over time in the whole population is difficult. Griffiths (1973) has explored the consequences of increased vaccination rates and concluded that both the time between epidemics and the average age of attack would be increased. But, equally important, Griffiths showed that the chance of breaking the chains of infection would be dramatically enhanced.

However, the process is not quite as simple as the above discussion might imply. Susceptibles are normally concentrated among children and are replenished by births. But, as epidemics become less common, there will be a gradual 'greying' of the susceptible population. In addition to new births, S will also contain individuals who escaped vaccination for one reason or another (for example, the Amish of Pennsylvania), plus vaccine failures. The potential for such hidden susceptible cells to cause epidemics is illustrated by the campus outbreaks of measles in the United States in the 1980s (Amler et al., 1983; Bridgewater and Lotz, 1984; Centers for Disease Control, 1985; Frank et al., 1985; Narain et al., 1985) and in religious groups (Sutter et al., 1991). A similar situation is illustrated in figure 8.1 where the measles outbreaks along the southern border of the United States are a function in part of the influx of non-vaccinated immigrants, and this has thwarted attempts to eradicate the disease in the states bordering Mexico (Cliff and Haggett, 1988, pp. 102–7).

1.3 Aims

The purpose of this paper is to look again at ways of developing a model to predict the spatial occurrence of measles epidemics. Many approaches have been tried, and these are briefly reviewed in section 2. A full assessment appears in Cliff, Haggett, and Smallman-Raynor (1993, chs 14 and 15). The model limitations identified in section 2 suggest that, rather than attempt to develop a model that forecasts both the size and spacing of epidemic trains, we might focus upon the time interval between epidemics and develop a model for recurrence times (and places). This concept parallels the notion of return times used in the analysis of extreme natural events (Gumbel, 1958). Modelling return times may be more important for control purposes than estimating the size and case load of epidemics.

Thus, in section 3, a conventional *SIR* (susceptible, infective, removal) model is outlined as a lead-in to the development of a model to predict epidemic return times (section 4). Simulation results are given in section 5. The model is illustrated more fully in section 6 by an application to monthly measles incidence data for Iceland from 1945 to 1970. The paper is concluded in section 7.

2 EXISTING SPACE–TIME FORECASTING MODELS

Existing models used to forecast the space–time patterns of measles epidemics are of two main types. One class, which we shall call *process-based*, takes the stocks of susceptible, infected and removed individuals in a population, formalizes the various transitions that may occur between the population subgroups, and uses these as a basis for studying the size and spacing of epidemics. These include, for example, the Hamer–Soper model and the chain binomial. Reviews

Table 8.1 Characteristics of forecasting models with Icelandic measles data, 1945–1970

Model	Application format Single region	Multi-region	Main data inputs S	I	Temporal parameter structure Fixed	variable	Comments
SIR (Hamer–Soper)	To all medical districts		×	×	×		Good at forecasting epidemic recurrence years ahead; average to poor on estimating epidemic size
Chain binomial	Capital city		×	×	×	×	Initial one month lag effect; able to lock onto course of epidemic; reasonable estimates of epidemic size
		Northwest Iceland (n = 5)	×	×	×		Use of main town as epidemic lead indicator produces good estimates of epidemic starts in other medical districts; poor estimates of epidemic size
Auto regressive	Capital city			×	×		One month lag effect; always misses epidemic starts; reasonable estimates of epidemic size
	Capital city			×		×	Initial one month lag effect; adapts to changing phase characteristics; overestimates epidemic size
GLIM		Northwest Iceland (n = 5)	×	×	×		As fixed in time parameter chain binomial
Kalman filter	Capital city			×		×	Initial lag effect; locks on to epidemic course but over estimates epidemic size
Bayesian entropy	Capital city		×	×		×	Despite separate models for epidemic & no epidemic states, one month lag effect in predicting epidemic curve; probability forecasts of epidemic/no epidemic good; model switches states in correct month
Simultaneous equation		Multi-region chains	×	×			Areas studied as causal chains;phase characteristics guaranteed by formulation of model; non-registration of serial and data recording intervals limits forecasting use
Logit		Multi-region chains	×	×			Good probability forecasts of epidemic/no epidemic states; slow state switching

of the properties of these models appear in Mollison and Isham (1994). A second class, which we shall refer to as *time series methods*, employs the past history of the process in an area to predict the future within an autoregressive/moving average framework. Standard accounts of the aspatial structure of such models appear in Box and Jenkins (1970) and Chatfield (1980).

Geographical extensions of models in both classes are described and applied to Iceland measles and influenza data by Cliff, Haggett, Ord, and Versey (1981, chs 5 and 6), Cliff, Haggett, and Ord (1986, ch. 7) and Cliff, Haggett, and Smallman-Raynor (1993, chs 14 and 15). On the basis of these studies, table 8.1 summarizes the strengths and weaknesses of each approach. The table highlights two common failings. First, some models, especially the ARMA formulations, miss the start of epidemics. These models subsequently lock on to the epidemic curve and model its shape one month in arrears. Repeated failure to project the start of epidemics is unacceptable if control is desired. Other models, such as the Hamer–Soper, detect the start of epidemics more accurately but then produce highly inaccurate estimates of total cases. This is a drawback in control because amounts of vaccine and levels of health care provision cannot be successfully planned if ultimate size is unknown.

On the basis of table 8.1, several main conclusions can be reached:

1 No model produces accurate projections of both epidemic recurrence times and epidemic size. Generally, if a model is devised which will forecast recurrence acceptably, epidemic size is overestimated. To forecast inter-epidemic times accurately, it is generally necessary to tune the model to be sensitive to changes signalling the approach of an epidemic, with the result that it overshoots when the epidemic is in progress.

2 Models which are based only on the size of the infective population in previous time periods consistently fail to detect the approach of an epidemic. Instead, they provide reasonable estimates of cases reported, but lagged in time.

3 Models with parameters fixed through time have a tendency to smooth through epidemic highs and lows because they are unable to adapt to the changes between the build-up and fade-out phases. Time-varying parameter models are better at avoiding this problem.

4 Epidemic recurrences can be reasonably anticipated only by incorporating information on the size of the susceptible population and/or properly identifying the lead-lag structure among medical districts for disease transmission. Addition of spatial interaction information markedly improves our ability to forecast recurrences in lagging areas. Information on susceptible population levels also serves to prime a model to the possibility of a recurrence, as is made clear by the various threshold theorems (Kermack and McKendrick, 1927–39; Kendall, 1957). Models based on susceptible populations, but which are single- rather than multi-region, tend to miss the start of epidemics but rapidly lock on to the course of an epidemic thereafter. Models which are dominated by spatial transmission information at the expense of information on the level of the susceptible population in the reference region produce estimates of epidemic size

which reflect the course of the epidemic in the triggering regions rather than in the study region.

5 Stochastic process models enhance our understanding of disease transmission across geographical space and increase the chances of devising time series models appropriate to the task of forecasting.

These conclusions highlight the fact that naïve models produce poor results. However, table 8.1 indicates clearly the gains to be made for each extra element of complexity added to our models, namely:

1 Time-varying parameters to handle the non-stationary nature of within-epidemic structure, particularly the fundamentally different character of the build-up and fade-out phases of an epidemic.
2 Separate models for epidemic and inter-epidemic episodes to recognize the different characteristics of these periods.
3 Spatial lead-lag information to improve our ability to forecast epidemic recurrences and to understand the transmission of disease between areas.
4 Incorporation of data upon the susceptible population level to improve estimates both of epidemic size and likely recurrence intervals.

It is important to be able to identify the gains that arise by increasing model complexity. When the aim is forecasting, it is easy to specify sophisticated models which produce forecasts that are inferior to those generated by simple trend predictors. However, a proper underlying process-based model structure is required if we wish to understand the mechanisms of disease spread, when we wish to investigate, for example, the impact of changes in model inputs, or where intervention in the spread of a disease is contemplated.

In view of the weaknesses in the various models implied by our earlier discussion, an alternative modelling strategy for predicting epidemic return times is considered in the following sections. We focus upon recurrence intervals as of central importance in devising control strategies.

3 BASIC *SIR* MODEL

The return times model described in the next section is developed from the standard *SIR* model, and so we first outline its structure.

At any time t, we assume that the total population in the region can be divided into three classes: namely the susceptible population of size S_t, the infected population of size I_t, and the removed population of size R_t. The removed population consists of individuals who have contracted measles but who can no longer transmit it to others because of recovery, isolation on the appearance of overt symptoms (usually the rash), or death. Four types of transition are allowed:

1 A susceptible being infected by contact with an infective.
2 An infective being removed. For measles, we can assume that infection confers lifelong immunity to further attack.

Table 8.2   *SIR* model: transition types and rates

Type of transition	Transition rate
1 $S \to S - 1$; $I \to I+1$; $R \to R$	βIS
2 $S \to S$; $I \to I-1$; $R \to R+1$	μI
3 $S \to S+1$; $I \to I$; $R \to R$	ν
4 $S \to S$; $I \to I+1$; $R \to R$	ε

3   A susceptible 'birth'. This can arise either through a child growing up into the critical age range (that is, reaching about six months of age and escaping vaccination), or else through a susceptible entering the population by in-migration.

4   An infective entering the I population by in-migration. For simplicity, we assume that there is no out-migration.

Suppose that transition i occurs at the rate r_i ($i = 1, 2, 3, 4$); that is, in a small time interval (t, $t + \delta t$) the probability of transition i occurring is $r_i \delta t + o(\delta t)$, where $o(\delta t)$ means a term of smaller order than δt. All events are assumed to be independent and to depend only on the present state of the population. The probability density of the time between any pair of successive transitions is

$$r \exp(-rt), \tag{8.1}$$

where

$$r = \sum_{i=1}^{4} r_i \tag{8.2}$$

and the probability that the next transition is of type i is

$$r_i/r, \quad i = 1, 2, 3, 4. \tag{8.3}$$

We assume, in transitions 1–4, that the infection rate is proportional to the product, SI, that the removal rate is proportional to I, and that the birth- and immigration-rates are constant. We can thus prepare the table of transitions given in table 8.2.

The model was first put forward in its deterministic form by Hamer (1906) and was studied extensively by Soper (1929). Table 8.3 summarizes the general characteristics of the epidemic resulting from the deterministic model for various values of the total population and ρ, where ρ is defined as the *relative*

Table 8.3   Some characteristics of a general deterministic epidemic

Epidemic intensity	Ratio of total population to ρ	Infectious at central epoch (%)	Removals occurring before central epoch (%)
0.00	1.000	0.00	50.0
0.10	1.054	0.13	49.5
0.20	1.116	0.56	49.1
0.30	1.189	1.33	48.5
0.40	1.277	2.55	47.9
0.50	1.386	4.30	47.1
0.60	1.527	6.79	46.2
0.70	1.720	10.33	45.0
0.80	2.012	15.55	43.4
0.90	2.558	24.20	40.8
0.95	3.153	31.87	38.3
0.98	3.992	40.27	35.4

Source: Bailey (1957, table 4.1, p. 28)

removal rate, given by $\rho = \mu / \beta$. The main drawback of the deterministic model is that it leads to damping of successive epidemic waves. This is not observed in practice.

We therefore consider the more realistic stochastic formulation. Even this relatively simple model is surprisingly intractable analytically and, except in special cases such as $\nu = \varepsilon = 0$, it is best studied using Monte Carlo techniques. It is, however, possible to see intuitively how the model operates. An infective is isolated after an average period of $\frac{1}{\mu}$ days, and while (s)he is infectious (s)he causes new infections at the rate of βS per day. If we ignore the changes in S during this period, one infective infects an average number of $\beta S/\mu$ ($= \kappa$, say) susceptibles before (s)he is removed. From the theory of the simple birth and death process, we would expect that, when $\kappa \le 1$, a small epidemic would die out. However, when $\kappa > 1$, a small epidemic will spark off a major outbreak, although, of course, as the epidemic spreads, S will fall and $\beta S/\mu$ can become less than unity. Thus, the general pattern will be that the susceptible population will build up (transition type 3) to around the critical threshold population size $S = \mu/\beta$, when an epidemic will continue to spread until the susceptible population falls sufficiently for the epidemic phase to pass (cf. Kermack and McKendrick's Threshold Theorem (1927) and Kendall's (1957) development of the Pandemic Threshold Theorem). The cycle will then repeat itself. The parallels with the Bartlett model described are clear.

In large communities where measles is endemic, the period between epidemic peaks is of approximate length $\mu/\beta\nu$, the mean time for the birth of μ/β susceptibles. In smaller communities, where there is fade-out, the period is longer because, once the critical susceptible population size is reached, there is a delay until the disease is introduced again into the region from outside (see Bartlett, 1956).

4 EPIDEMIC RETURN TIMES

4.1 *Probability of extinction*

In his classic paper, Kendall (1948) developed an approximation to the probability of extinction of an epidemic by ignoring the depletion of the stock of susceptibles by infection. That is, the population of infectives may be modelled as a birth–death process with

$$\text{birth (infective) rate} : \beta(n + \nu t) \tag{8.4}$$

$$\text{death (removal) rate} : \mu, \tag{8.5}$$

where n denotes the number of susceptibles at time $t = 0$ and ν represents the (deterministic) rate of increase of susceptibles. Then, if the number of infectives at time $t = 0$ is x, Kendall showed that the probability of extinction is

$$P = [\mathcal{J}/(1 + \mathcal{J})]^x, \tag{8.6}$$

where

$$\mathcal{J} = \int_0^\infty \mu \exp\left[(\mu - \beta n)t - 0.5\beta\nu t^2\right]dt \tag{8.7}$$

$$= [1 - F(u)]/f(u), \tag{8.8}$$

where $f(u)$ and $F(u)$ denote the pdf and DF of the standard Normal distribution,

$$\mu = \gamma(w - 1), \quad \gamma = \mu(\beta\nu)^{(-1/2)}, \quad w = n\beta/\nu = n/\rho, \tag{8.9}$$

and ρ is the relative removal rate defined in section 3.

When $\nu = 0$ (that is, no addition of new susceptibles), this reduces to

$$P = (\rho/n)^x \quad \rho < n, \tag{8.10}$$

$$= 1, \quad \rho \geq n$$

indicative of the threshold effect with fadeout guaranteed when $n \leq \rho$ (cf. section 3). When $\nu > 0$, the sharp cutoff disappears but $\mathcal{J}$ will still increase rapidly as n exceeds ρ if γ is at all large.

4.2 *Time between epidemics*

If extinction occurs and the susceptibles are replenished at rate ν, the population will eventually exceed the threshold size and the introduction of infective(s) will trigger a new epidemic. As in section 3, the rate of introduction of new infectives is taken to be ε; we let $P(u)$ denote the probability of extinction when one new infective is introduced at time u. When the number of susceptibles is negligible at time $t = 0$, Bartlett (1956) showed that the probability that no epidemic occurs by time t is, approximately,

$$1 - G_t = \prod_{0 < u < t} [1 - \varepsilon\, du + \varepsilon\, P(u)du] \sim \exp(-\varepsilon\, Q_t) \tag{8.11}$$

where

$$Q_t = \int_0^t [1 - P(u)]\, du; \tag{8.12}$$

G_t denotes the DF for the time until the epidemic occurs. Using the approximation (8.10) with $x = 1$ yields

$$P(u) = \sigma/u, \quad u > \sigma$$

$$= 1, \quad u \le \sigma$$

where $\sigma = \rho/v = \mu/\beta v$, and (8.12) reduces to

$$Q_t = t - \sigma - \sigma\log(t/\sigma). \tag{8.13}$$

Finally, from (8.11)

$$G_t = 1 - T^{\Theta} \exp[-\Theta(T - 1)], \quad T > 1 \tag{8.14}$$

where $T = t/\sigma$ and $\Theta = \varepsilon\sigma$. From (8.14), the pdf for t is

$$\Theta\sigma^{-1}(T - 1)T^{\Theta-1} \exp[-\Theta(T - 1)], \quad t > \sigma. \tag{8.15}$$

The mode of (8.15) occurs at $T = 1 + \Theta^{\frac{1}{2}}$, which may be viewed as a point estimate of the time to the next epidemic. A $100(1 - 2\alpha)$ per cent prediction interval may be obtained by finding t_1 and t_2 such that

$$G_{t_1} = \alpha, \quad G_{t_2} = 1 - \alpha.$$

These equations are solved using recursions of the form

$$T_{j+1} = 1 + \Theta^{-1} \log\alpha^* + \log T_j \tag{8.16}$$

where $\alpha^* = \alpha$ or $1 - \alpha$ and $T_0 = 1$.

If the initial population at $t = 0$ is n_0, the approximation may still be used with

$$t^* = t + (n_0/v) \tag{8.17}$$

in place of t; this modification is particularly important in cases where an epidemic is small so that another epidemic may occur fairly quickly.

4.3 Spatial effects

The probabilities specified in (8.11) presuppose that the rate of introduction of new infectives is constant. This is not a problem while $P = 1$, but becomes critical when $P < 1$, since reintroduction is much more likely when $t > \sigma$ and the disease is present in neighbouring areas. A complete treatment of this problem would need a detailed spatio-temporal specification for ε; special cases may be of theoretical interest, but a general treatment seems intractable. Instead, we resort to an approximation as follows.

Since we are dealing with data aggregated over time, (8.11) and (8.12) yield

$$P[\text{first epidemic in } (t, t+1)] = H_t$$

$$= \exp(-t\, Q_t)[\exp(-\varepsilon Q_{t,\, t+1}) - 1], \tag{8.18}$$

where

$$Q_{t,\, t+1} = Q_{t+1} - Q_t.$$

As the time interval shrinks towards zero, (8.18) yields (8.15). In order to incorporate the impact of infectives in neighbouring areas, we write the exponent in the second term of (8.18) as

$$\varepsilon_t\, Q_{t,\, t+1} \tag{8.19}$$

where $\varepsilon_t = \varepsilon + \Sigma \alpha_j I_{jt}$, I_{jt} is the number of infectives in area j at time t, and α_j is a parameter measuring the impact of area j on the study area. That is, we build in a migratory component for the infectives similar to that used by Baroyan et al. (1969, 1971, 1977) in their geographical adaptation of the *SIR* model described in section 3; the $\{\alpha_j\}$ may include population and distance adjustments, as do the Russian models. The approximation in (8.19) means that we ignore previous migrations of infectives from neighbouring areas. Since the first migration after t that exceeds the threshold is likely to trigger an outbreak, this assumption is less drastic than it appears at first sight.

When we apply (8.19) to (8.18), using (8.14), we obtain

$$H_t = T^{\Theta} \exp[-\Theta(T-1)] \times$$

$$\times (\exp\{-\varepsilon_t[1 - \sigma \log\left(1 + \frac{1}{\sigma T}\right)]\} - 1). \tag{8.20}$$

As the time interval shrinks to zero, the last term in (8.20) reduces to

$$\varepsilon_t(1 - T^{-1})$$

in accordance with (8.15), apart from the new rate for infectives.

4.4 Estimation procedures

From equation (8.20), the model parameters to be estimated are Θ and σ. We may suppose that the available data relate to $k = 1, 2, \ldots, m$ regions and to $j = 1, 2, \ldots, \mathcal{J}_k$ epidemics in the kth region. We denote the j-th inter-epidemic time in region k by t_{kj}. Given the various rates of change and the initial stock of susceptibles at the end of the previous epidemic, we shall assume that the inter-epidemic times are conditionally independent. This seems reasonable for Iceland where its isolation and small population imply measles extinction between epidemics, and the initiation of new epidemics by the introduction of infection from overseas. For more closely connected communities, such an assumption is not warranted, although it would still be possible to justify the proposed estimators by the pseudo-likelihood argument (Besag, 1974).

4.4.1 Specification of rates

(1) *Infectives.* Initially we shall assume that

$$\beta_{kj} = \beta \text{ for all } k \text{ and } j. \tag{8.21}$$

(2) *Susceptibles.* The birth-rate for new susceptibles depends upon actual birth-rates and levels of immunization. We specify this birth-rate as

$$\nu_{kj} = (1 - \alpha_{kj})n_{kj} \tag{8.22}$$

where we define

n_{kj} average number of births/month in region k during period j
α_{kj} proportion of the population immunized in region k during period j.

Where monthly or even annual figures are available for births, the monthly rate is easily determined; on occasion, it will be necessary to use census figures for the (0–1) year or (0–5) year age groups. In the developed nations, total births will not vary substantially from one inter-epidemic period to another unless some intervals are extremely long compared with others, so that these figures will be reasonable first approximations. It will, however, need modification in developing countries with rapidly growing populations.

It is assumed that, once mother-conferred immunity has disappeared, no natural immunity occurs for measles (other than through infection), so that the immunization rate is zero prior to the introduction of vaccination programmes. When studying the incidence of measles after 1963, the date a measles vaccine was first licensed in the United States, due allowance must be made for vaccination coverage achieved when estimating the susceptible population.

(3) *Removals.* In the absence of any public health policy to isolate infectives, the removal rate for measles will be roughly constant across communities and epidemics. Such policies, if instituted, may be expected to vary in their impact across social groups and over time. As a first approximation, we take the removal rates to be

$$\mu_{kj} = \mu \text{ for all } k \text{ and } j. \tag{8.23}$$

(4) *Migrations.* The migration rate for infectives is more difficult to assess. For island communities such as Iceland where total fade out of infection between epidemics occurs, it seems reasonable to relate this to the number of visitors to k at the time of the j-th epidemic, V_{kj} say, taken from official records. We consider two possibilities:

(i) $\varepsilon_{kj} = \varepsilon$; $\qquad\qquad\qquad\qquad\qquad\qquad\qquad\qquad$ (8.24)

(ii) $\varepsilon_{kj} = \varepsilon V_{kj}$. $\qquad\qquad\qquad\qquad\qquad\qquad\qquad\qquad$ (8.25)

(5) *Model parameters.* Given the assumptions we have made above about infection, susceptible and removal rates, the parameters for the *j*-th epidemic in *k* are

$$\sigma_{kj} = \mu_{kj}/(\beta_{kj} v_{kj})$$

$$= \mu/[\beta n_{kj}(1 - \alpha_{kj})], \qquad\qquad\qquad (8.26)$$

and

$$\Theta_{kj} = \varepsilon V_{kj}^{\delta} \sigma_{kj}, \qquad\qquad\qquad\qquad\qquad (8.27)$$

where $\delta = 0$ or 1 depending on whether (8.24) or (8.25) is used. These may be rewritten as

$$\sigma_{kj} = \sigma C_{kj} \text{ and } \Theta_{kj} = \Theta D_{kj} \qquad\qquad\qquad (8.28)$$

where (C_{kj}, D_{kj}) are either known or are estimated from other sources. Maximum likelihood (ML) estimators for the parameters σ and Θ are given in the appendix to this chapter.

4.4.2 *Number of susceptibles.*

Since the population of susceptibles is continually changing through recruitment by births and depletion by infection and immunization, we need to specify the size of this population in a consistent manner. We define the following terms for each region, *k* :

N_{kj} number of susceptibles at start of period $j + 1$ (end of epidemic *j*);
E_{kj} number of reported cases during epidemic *j*;
A_{kj} effective reporting rate during epidemic *j*;
u_{kj} duration of *j*-th epidemic;
E_{kj}^* total number of cases actually occurring, allowing for under-reporting $(= E_{kj}/A_{kj})$.

The updating relationship is, as illustrated in figure 8.5,

$$N_{k,j+1} = N_{kj} + v_{kj}(t_{kj} + u_{kj}) - E_{kj}^*. \qquad\qquad\qquad (8.29)$$

Since the density function (8.15) is based upon a negligible number of susceptibles at the start of the cycle, we use the adjusted time intervals

$$t_{kj}^* = t_{kj} + N_{kj}/v_{kj}. \qquad\qquad\qquad\qquad (8.30)$$

Because the modal time between epidemics is given by $T = 1 + k^{(-1/2)}$, it follows from (8.29) and (8.30) that the modal time between epidemics will increase with α_{kj} as expected; by implication, the mean age at attack will also

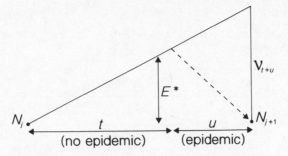

Figure 8.5   Updating relationship of equation (8.29).
The straight line decay during the epidemic is by way of
illustration only

increase since birth-rates are essentially independent of the level of infection
except in epidemics.

5   SIMULATION EXPERIMENTS

In order to evaluate the performance of the ML estimators, we ran a small
simulation study. We set $C_r, D_r = 1$ in all cases and took the total number of
inter-epidemic phases available to be $M = 20$ or $M = 50$. A total of $N = 500$ runs
were completed in each case for the following parameter settings:

$\sigma = 1$ and $\Theta = 0.1, 0.2, 0.5$; $M = 20, 50.$

Results are presented for σ and $\varphi = \Theta^{-1}$ and appear in table 8.4. For σ, there
is a slight upwards bias that increases with Θ, but it is not serious. The variability
of the estimates increases sharply with Θ; the 95 per cent confidence interval
increases in width when $M = 20$ from ± 0.10 at $\Theta = 0.1$ to ± 0.24. There is a
systematic upwards bias for φ (downwards for Θ) of about 30 per cent at
$M = 20$, reducing to about half of that at $M = 50$. The figures based upon
asymptotic variances are somewhat lower. On the basis of these results, it
appeared that reasonable estimates can be obtained from observational data,
and so we turn to an application to Icelandic measles data in the next section.

6   ICELANDIC STUDIES

6.1   *The north-west fjords*

As a first illustration, the model is applied to monthly reported measles
morbidity data covering those of the 16 post-1945 Icelandic waves, 1945–74,
that affected eight medical districts in the north-west fjords; see figure 8.6. The
selected districts all experienced four or more of these waves (time series graphs
in figure 8.6) in this period. We use $k = 1, 2, \ldots, 8$ to index the districts and j
$= 1, 2, \ldots, \mathcal{J}_k$ to reference the $\mathcal{J}$ epidemics in the k-th district. The inter-

Table 8.4 Results of simulation study using epidemic return times model: $N = 500$ replicates and $\sigma = 1$ in all cases

M[a]	φ	$\hat{\varphi}$			$\hat{\sigma}$		
		Mean	Variance		Mean	Variance ($\times 10^{-2}$)	
			Sample	Asymptotic[b]		Sample	Asymptotic[a]
	10	13.13	23.26	18.74	1.04	0.26	0.21
20	5	6.54	6.19	4.90	1.05	0.54	0.43
	2	2.66	1.19	0.90	1.07	1.52	1.09
	10	11.72	6.16	5.35	1.03	0.08	0.08
50	5	5.76	1.60	1.35	1.03	0.18	0.16
25	2	2.54	0.78	0.63	1.07	1.14	0.84

[a] Computer time for simulations increased markedly with both M and Θ. So, for $\Theta = 0.5$ ($\varphi = 2$), we finished up using $M = 25$ rather than $M = 50$.
[b] By the asymptotic variance, we mean the average value of the large sample variance computed from the likelihood equations.

epidemic times, $\{t_{kj}\}$, may be recorded as t_r, $r = 1, 2, \ldots, M$, $\Sigma \mathcal{J}_k = M$. The strategy employed was to pool the inter-epidemic times for the first $(\mathcal{J}-1)$ epidemics in the eight districts to estimate model parameters, and then to use these estimates to forecast the time in months to the $\mathcal{J}$-th epidemic in each district. This causes a slight bias since incomplete inter-epidemic phases (for example, at the beginning and end of the time period studied) should be treated as censored observations. However, numerical experiments suggested that this effect is relatively unimportant. Afer completion of data editing, we had available 34 observations for fitting and 8 for forecasting.

6.1.1 Model fitting. Observed inter-epidemic times were determined from the reported measles time series plotted in figure 8.6 using the rules outlined in Cliff, Haggett, Ord, and Versey (1981, pp. 106–11) for defining epidemics. Nothwithstanding these rules, in the course of identifying epidemics, outlier cases and gaps occurred in some medical districts during a particular wave. This was the result of local temporary fade-out, followed by the reintroduction of infection from another district during the course of a single national epidemic. For the purposes of model fitting, we identified the major epidemic in the medical district in question as 'the' epidemic for that wave. Obviously, other definitions are possible and would lead to slightly different results.

In specifying the rates of section 4.4.1, the assumptions outlined there were made for β, μ and ε. To fix ν_{kj}, the birth rate for new susceptibles, the demographic accounting model described in Cliff, Haggett, Ord, and Versey (1981, pp. 194–200) was used. When estimating the model parameters using (8.28), four variations were tried as follows:

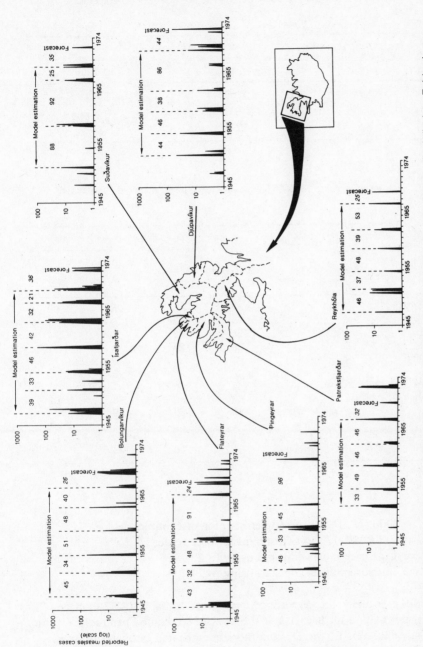

Figure 8.6 North-west fjords, Iceland, 1945–1974. Time series of reported measles cases in eight medical districts. Epidemics used for model calibration and forecasting in the epidemic return times model are marked. Inter-epidemic intervals (in months) in the calibration period are given in Roman lettering; intervals in the forecast period in italic

Table 8.5   North-west Iceland, 1945–1974: parameters of model for inter-epidemic waiting times

	Estimated value	
Parameter	Expectation	Variance
Θ	0.6404	0.0323
σ	12.2607	2.4533
$\mathrm{corr}(\hat{\Theta},\hat{\sigma})$	–0.792	

Table 8.6   North-west Iceland, 1945–1974: inter-epidemic times in the model estimation period

			Average inter-epidemic interval (months)		
				Model percentile	
District	No.of intervals		Observed	50	10	90
Bolungarvíkur	5		44	45	25	86
Djúpavíkur	4		54	33	16	71
Flateyrar	4		54	38	19	77
Ísafjarðar	6		36	24	9	59
Patreksfjarðar	4		44	33	16	70
Pingeyrar	3		42	46	25	87
Reykhóla	5		45	66	41	113
Suðavíkur	3		68	49	28	92
Total	34	Median	45	38	19	77
		Mean	47	42	22	81
		Minimum	21	24	9	58
		Maximum	92	70	44	116

1   $C_r = 1000/N_r$, $D_r = 1$, no adjustment for susceptibles.
2   $C_r = D_r = 1000/N_r$, no adjustment of susceptibles.
3   As 1, but susceptibles adjusted using (8.29);
4   As 2, but susceptibles adjusted using (8.29).

We found, eventually, that 2, setting $C_r = D_r = 1000/N_r$ in (8.32), where N_r is the total population of district k at the start of epidemic j produced as good results as calculating C_r and D_r from more complicated estimates of rates.

The maximum likelihood estimates obtained in the model fitting period are given in table 8.5. The estimates were then used with equation (8.16) to generate the percentage points of the distribution of inter-epidemic times for the districts. The results appear in table 8.6. We consider first the summary results at the end of the table. There is good correspondence between the observed median, mean

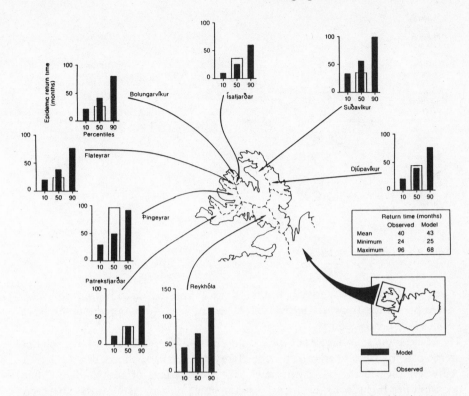

Figure 8.7 North-west fjords, Iceland, 1968–1974. Observed and projected epidemic return times in eight medical districts. Median, 10th and 90th percentage points are plotted

and minimum inter-epidemic times and the corresponding 50th percentile values; the median, mean, minimum and maximum are taken over the pooled set of inter-epidemic intervals for all eight districts. The approximate four-year cycle evident from the line graphs in figure 8.6 is modelled but underestimated. However, the observed maximum exceeds the estimated maximum at the 50th percentile as a result of the occasional missed epidemic in these small communities (leading to some very long inter-epidemic intervals as, for example, in Suðavíkur). But even these observed outliers are within the model values at the 90th percentile.

For individual districts in the main part of the table, correspondence between the observed and model 50th percentile values is weak (rank correlation between the 34 values is 0.24); however, as the table shows, the observed district means do lie within the upper and lower 10 per cent points of the model distribution. There is some evidence of a downwards bias in the estimated return times at the 50th percentile as compared with observed return times.

The estimated parameters were then used with demographic data for the last inter-epidemic interval in each medical district to generate *ex post* forecasts of the time gap between the penultimate and ultimate epidemics; these gaps are marked on the time series of figure 8.6. The results are plotted as bar graphs in figure 8.7. As in the calibration period, observed values again lie within the

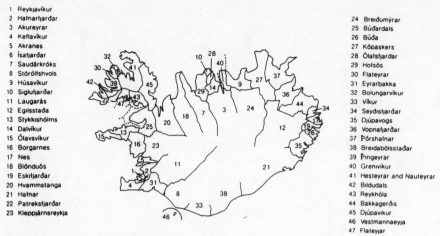

1 Reykjavíkur
2 Hafnarfjarðar
3 Akureyrar
4 Keflavíkur
5 Akranes
6 Ísafjarðar
7 Sauðárkróks
8 Stórólfshvols
9 Húsavíkur
10 Siglufjarðar
11 Laugarás
12 Egilsstaða
13 Stykkishólms
14 Dalvíkur
15 Ólavsvíkur
16 Borgarnes
17 Nes
18 Blönduós
19 Eskifjarðar
20 Hvammstanga
21 Hafnar
22 Patreksfjarðar
23 Kleppjárnsreykja

24 Breiðumýrar
25 Búðardals
26 Búða
27 Kópaskers
28 Ólafsfjarðar
29 Hofsós
30 Flateyrar
31 Eyrarbakka
32 Bolungarvíkur
33 Víkur
34 Seyðisfjarðar
35 Djúpavogs
36 Vopnafjarðar
37 Þórshafnar
38 Breiðabólsstaðar
39 Þingeyrar
40 Grenivíkur
41 Hesteyrar and Nauteyrar
42 Bíldudals
43 Reykhóla
44 Bakkagerðis
45 Djúpavíkur
46 Vestmannaeyja
47 Flateyjar

Figure 8.8   Location map for Icelandic medical districts

upper and lower 10 percent points of the estimated distribution, although correspondence between individual observed and 50th percentile forecast values is generally poor.

Goodness-of-fit statistics. Appropriate goodness-of-fit statistics for the model remain to be developed and tested. Here we have used the rank correlation between the observed return times and the median of the model. Other possibilities include, for example, residual sums of squares between observed return times and the model median, and the residual mean square.

6.2   Return times in the Icelandic central place hierarchy

In this subsection, the analysis of the previous subsection is extended to all the medical districts of Iceland. Figure 8.8 is a location map.

As noted in the introduction to section 6, 16 main epidemic waves have affected Iceland since 1945. Figure 8.9 illustrates the time taken on average for these waves to reach each of the districts; see Cliff, Haggett, and Ord (1986, pp. 173–7) for details. Nationally, the average time to epidemic arrival was 7.4 months but, as figure 8.9 shows, the average over the period varied from 1.5 months in Reykjavíkur (map A) to 17 months in the instance of the island community of Flatey (map D). Analysis described in Cliff, Haggett, and Ord (1986, pp. 173–4) suggests that measles spreads from one medical district to another in Iceland primarily through the central place hierarchy, so that settlements with larger populations are infected before those with smaller populations. This would be expected from the Bartlett model discussed in section 1.2. Thus initial introduction of measles into Reykjavíkur (map A) is followed by spread both locally in the Reykjavíkur region and on to other major population centres in other parts of Iceland (map B in figure 8.9). Further local infilling and spread to other population centres in a size-ordered sequence is shown in maps C and D of the diagram.

This known population size sequencing of average time to infection is

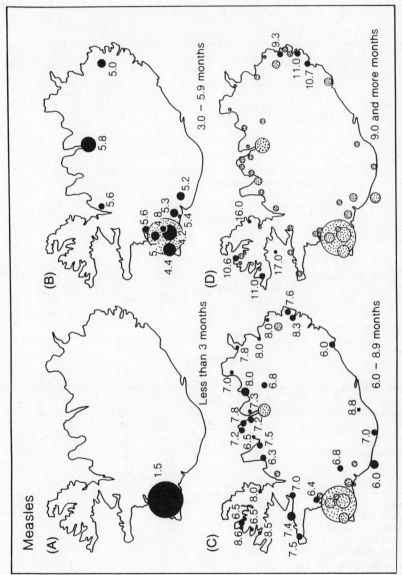

Figure 8.9 Average time in months taken for measles epidemics to reach each Icelandic medical district. Location names appear in figure 8.8 Circle sizes are proportional to the 1970 medical district populations. Districts reached on a given map are in solid black; districts reached on a previous map are stippled. (A) less than 3 months to infection; (B) 3–5 months; (C) 6–8 months; (D) 9 months or more

(*Source*: Cliff, Haggett, Ord, and Versey, 1981, figure 5.2, p. 96)

Table 8.7   Iceland, 1945–1974: parameter estimates of model for inter-epidemic waiting times applied to groups of settlements

Group[a]	Θ		σ		corr($\hat\Theta,\hat\sigma$)
	Expectation	Variance	Expectation	Variance	
1	1.7799	0.1588	33.2108	11.5140	–0.746
2	0.6183	0.0057	13.8862	0.5116	–0.691
3	0.4032	0.0126	9.5630	1.3653	–0.698

[a] Average time to infection from start of epidemics in Iceland as follows: Settlement group 1, 3–5 months; Group 2, 6–9 months; Group 3, over 9 months.

Table 8.8   Iceland, 1945–1974: observed and modelled inter-epidemic waiting times for groups of settlements, parameter estimation period

No. of intervals		Average inter-epidemic interval (months)			
			Model percentile		
		Observed	50	10	90
		Group 1 settlements			
	Median	42.0	31.3	14.5	67.2
45	Mean	41.2	36.1	18.2	73.2
	Minimum	21.0	20.7	7.1	53.0
	Maximum	80.0	61.4	37.6	105.6
		Group 2 settlements			
	Median	44.5	40.3	19.3	84.2
124	Mean	49.1	42.5	21.2	36.9
	Minimum	6.0	24.0	7.9	62.9
	Maximum	148.0	99.9	160.3	67.3
		Group 3 settlements			
	Median	44.0	40.0	18.6	85.7
25	Mean	47.2	39.3	18.0	34.6
	Minimum	12.0	32.1	12.9	75.1
	Maximum	124.0	45.9	22.9	93.4

Group 1 settlements:
  corr (observed), 50th percentile) = 0.16
  residual sum of squares = 2.38
Group 2 settlements:
  corr (observed), 50th percentile) = 0.25
  residual sum of squares = 1.16
Group 1 settlements:
  corr (observed), 50th percentile) = –0.07
  residual sum of squares = 1.22

exploited here in fitting the epidemic return time model. First, Reykjavíkur was dropped from the analysis. Almost half the total Icelandic population lives in this primate city, and the capital is some eight times larger than the next largest centre. It will, ultimately, require special treatment from a modelling viewpoint. The remaining districts illustrated in figure 8.9 are more similar in population size and range from some 15,000 (at mid-period in 1970) downwards.

The return times model was then applied to these remaining districts. The sets of settlements on maps (B)–(D) were treated separately both for model fitting and forecasting. We refer to the districts on map (B), which had an average time to infection of 3–5 months, as group 1; those on (C), 6–8 months, as group 2; and those on map (D), 9 months and over, as group 3. As in section 6.1, we took $C_r = D_r = 1000/N_r$ in equation (8.28), used the $\mathcal{J}-1$ inter-epidemic intervals from each district for parameter estimation, and then substituted the estimated parameter values into the model to forecast the waiting time to the $\mathcal{J}$-th epidemic in each district.

The values obtained for the model parameters appear in table 8.7. For Group 1 settlements, the estimation was based upon 45 inter-epidemic periods, for Group 2, 124 and for Group 3, 25 periods. The estimated values of both Θ and σ fall with the decline in settlement sizes from Group 1 to Group 3, as do the variances. Table 8.8 summarizes the correspondence between observed and modelled inter-epidemic waiting times for the epidemics used for parameter estimation. As judged by the rank correlations between the observed inter-epidemic periods, fit is poor. The correlations may imply that the model is sensitive to sample sizes, since the correlations reflect the number of inter-epidemic periods used for estimation; the highest correlation occurs for Group 2 (largest number of inter-epidemic periods) and the lowest for Group 3 (smallest number).

Despite the low correlations between the point estimates, the average 50th percentile point in table 8.8 from the model shows reasonable correspondence with the observed average for all groups of settlements. The rank order of observed and calculated means agrees exactly. As with the north-west Iceland example of section 6.1, the estimated 50th percentile is less than the observed – by 5.1, 6.6 and 7.9 months respectively for settlements in Groups 1, 2, and 3 respectively. Thus, on average, epidemic return times are underestimated by some six months, with the error increasing as settlement size decreases. While the consistent pattern of underestimation needs attention, anticipating epidemics is a fault in the right direction from the viewpoint of control. It is not that surprising that error should be worse with smaller settlements, since return times will be more variable and reflect the chance arrival of measles virus at times when the susceptible population has grown enough to sustain an epidemic.

Table 8.9 gives the point estimates of the time to the $\mathcal{J}$-th epidemic in each medical district, calculated using the parameter estimates in table 8.8. The correlation between observed and modelled 50th percentile points is high for the Group 1 settlements, and this falls monotonically for Groups 2 and 3. As with previous applications, the average 50th percentile of the model underestimates the observed mean. In the case of the Group 1 settlements, the observed

Table 8.9   Iceland: observed and *ex post* point forecasts of inter-epidemic waiting times for groups of settlements

		Inter-epidemic interval (months)		
			Model percentile	
District	Observed	50	10	90
Group 1 settlements				
Hafnarfjarðar	34	20.2	6.7	52.3
Akureyrar	36	21.0	7.2	53.5
Keflavíkur	34	22.5	8.2	55.4
Eyrarbakka	67	27.3	11.6	61.8
Akranes	34	29.9	13.5	65.3
Stórólfshvols	36	38.3	19.6	76.3
Egilsstaða	40	44.6	24.4	84.4
Hvammastanga	167	53.0	31.0	95.1
Kleppjárnsreykja	118	57.4	34.4	100.6
All Median	36	29.9	13.5	65.3
Mean	62.9	34.9	17.4	71.6
Minimum	34.0	20.2	6.7	52.3
Maximum	167.0	57.4	34.4	100.6
Group 3 settlements				
Patreksfjarðar	66	32.5	13.2	75.8
Búða	44	37.1	16.4	81.8
Djúpavíkur	44	38.5	17.5	84.7
Bolungarvíkur	26	40.4	18.8	86.1
Seyðisfjarðar	38	40.6	19.0	86.4
Djúpavogs	92	42.6	20.4	89.0
All Median	44	39.5	18.2	85.4
Mean	52	38.6	17.6	83.8
Minimum	26	32.5	13.2	75.8
Maximum	92	42.6	20.4	89.0

Group 1 settlements:
  corr (observed, 50th percentile) = 0.76
  residual sum of squares = 1.03
Group 3 settlements:
  corr (observed, 50th percentile) = 0.03
  residual sum of squares = 1.38

Table 8.9   *(continued)*

| | | Average inter-epidemic interval (months) | | |
| | | Model percentile | | |
District	Observed	50	10	90
		Group 2 settlements		
Vestmannæyja	24	24.4	8.1	63.1
Ísafjarðar	36	28.4	10.8	68.5
Sauðárkróks	68	29.2	11.4	69.6
Húsavíkur	38	30.2	12.1	70.9
Blönduós	46	31.3	12.9	72.4
Siglufjarðar	72	30.8	12.5	71.8
Laugarás	42	32.5	13.7	74.0
Stykkishólms	66	32.5	13.7	73.9
Dalvíkur	39	33.3	14.3	75.0
Ólafsvíkur	62	34.3	15.0	76.4
Borgarnes	66	35.3	15.7	77.7
Eskifjarðar	76	37.4	17.2	80.5
Hafnar	44	37.5	17.2	80.5
Breiðumyrar	37	39.8	19.0	83.7
Þórshafnar	41	41.4	20.1	85.7
Búðardals	36	42.8	21.2	87.5
Ólafsfjarðar	43	44.1	22.1	89.2
Hofsós	68	43.7	21.8	88.7
Flateyrar	24	43.9	21.9	88.8
Víkur	70	47.1	24.4	93.1
Vopnafjarðar	63	51.2	27.5	98.4
Kópaskers	123	54.6	30.1	102.7
Kirkjubæjar	47	56.8	31.8	105.6
Þingeyrar	96	56.5	31.6	105.2
Grenivíkur	38	60.0	34.3	109.6
Súðavíkur	35	63.9	37.3	114.5
Bíldudals	168	64.0	37.4	114.7
Reykhóla	25	78.4	48.9	132.8
Bakkagerðis	79	89.1	57.7	146.0
All Median	46	41.4	20.1	85.7
Mean	58	43.9	22.3	88.7
Minimum	24	24.4	8.1	63.1
Maximum	168	89.1	57.7	146.0

Group 2 settlements:
  corr(observed, 50th percentile) = 0.26
  residual sum of squares = 1.22

mean is badly inflated by the high values for Hvammastanga and Klep-pjárnsreykja. If these two districts are omitted, the revised observed mean is 40.1, much closer to the model value of 34.9. Both observed and model means reflect the general 3–5-year cycle of measles epidemics in Iceland evident from figure 8.2. In all but 8 of the districts listed in table 8.9, observed return times fall within the 10 and 90th percentage points.

6.3 Discussion

In fitting the model to the Icelandic measles epidemics, a number of heroic assumptions were made that arise directly from the Bartlett–Kendall models discussed in sections 1 and 4. The critical assumptions are:

1   The communities are small (not unreasonable for Iceland) and closed. Lack of closure was a problem and led, as noted, to difficulties in identifying the core epidemic in a given district in some instances.
2   The susceptible populations are zero after each epidemic, or at least can be adjusted using equation (8.29).
3   Simplifying assumptions about the specification of rates could be made. We assumed that the immunization rate was effectively zero in this pre-mass immunization time period up to 1970.
4   The number of visitors, V_{kj}, was proportional to n_{kj}.
5   Epidemics, and therefore inter-epidemic times, could be specified by the rules governing isolated case reports and epidemic duration specified in Cliff, Haggett, Ord, and Versey (1981, pp. 106–11).
6   No allowance has been made for seasonal effects.

All these assumptions will need modification in further developments of the model. It will also be important to link the model to intervention strategies; planned vaccination campaigns, for example, will feed back to affect epidemic return times.

7 CONCLUSION

This paper has outlined a model to estimate the return times of epidemics in a set of geographical areas, and the utility of the model for forecasting has been explored using Icelandic measles data for the period since 1945. Several problems have emerged. These include the closed communities assumed by the model which can never properly be met in practice, the sensitivity of the model to the definition of epidemic starts and ends, and the time dependence of ε, the migration rate for infectives. Nevertheless, despite these difficulties, the model is capable of further development, for example by adding seasonal components and strengthening the inter-regional basis. Estimation of return times will become increasingly critical as WHO's Expanded Programme of Immunization pins measles back into diminishing geographical areas of the world.

APPENDIX

Maximum likelihood estimation inter-epidemic spacing

Suppose we have $k = 1, 2, \ldots, m$ regions and $j = 1, 2, \ldots, \mathcal{J}_k$ epidemics in the k-th region. Denote k,j by the single subscript, r, where $r = 1, 2, \ldots, M$ and $\Sigma \mathcal{J}_k = M$. Equations (8.26) and (8.27) may then be rewritten as

$$\sigma_r = \sigma C_r \quad \text{and} \quad \Theta_r = \Theta D_r \tag{8.A1}$$

where (C_r, D_r) are known, or at least estimated, from other sources. Using (8.A1), the log-likelihood function becomes

$$L(\Theta, \sigma) = \text{constant} + M \log \Theta - \Sigma \, (\Theta D_r + 1) \log(\sigma C_r)$$

$$+ \Sigma \, (\Theta D_r - 1) \log t_r + \Sigma \log (t_r - \sigma C_r)$$

$$- (\Theta / \sigma) \, \Sigma \, D_r(t_r - \sigma C_r)/C_r, \tag{8.A2}$$

and the summations are over $r = 1, 2, \ldots, M$. Clearly,

$$\sigma < \min_r \, (t_r / C_r). \tag{8.A3}$$

Since the likelihood goes to zero as σ approaches this upper bound, some care is necessary in evaluating the estimates, as we note below.

The first derivatives of the log-likelihood function given in (8.A2) are as follows:

$$\frac{\partial L}{\partial \Theta} = \frac{M}{\Theta} + \Sigma \, D_r \log (t_r / \sigma C_r) - \Sigma \, D_r(t_r - \sigma C_r)/(\sigma C_r)$$

and

$$\frac{\partial L}{\partial \sigma} = \Theta \Sigma \, D_r t_r / (\sigma^2 C_r) - \Sigma \, C_r / (t_r - \sigma C_r) - \Sigma(\Theta D_r + 1)/\sigma.$$

The second derivatives are

$$\frac{\partial^2 L}{\partial \Theta^2} = - M \Theta^{-2},$$

$$\frac{\partial^2 L}{\partial \Theta \partial \sigma} = \Sigma \, D_r(t_r - \sigma C_r)/(\sigma^2 C_r),$$

$$\frac{\partial^2 L}{\partial \sigma^2} = \sigma^{-2} \, \Sigma(\Theta D_r + 1) - \Sigma C_r^2 \, (t_r - \sigma C_r)^{-2}$$

$$- 2 \Theta \Sigma D_r t_r / (\sigma^3 C_r) \, .$$

These expressions may be used to develop the usual Newton–Raphson procedures; however, the starting values must be chosen with care, since $\partial^2 L/\partial\sigma^2 \rightarrow -\infty$ as σ approaches the upper bound given in (8.A3). In general, it was found useful to start with a grid search and to switch to Newton–Raphson only when the neighbourhood of the solution was well identified.

REFERENCES

Amler, R.W., Kim-Farley, R.J., Orenstein, W.A., Doster, S.W., & Bart, K.J. (1983). 'Measles on campus.' *Journal of American College Health*, 32, 53–7.

Bailey, N.J.T. (1957). *The Mathematical Theory of Epidemics*. London: Griffin.

Baroyan, O.V., Genchikov, L.A., Rvachev, L.A., & Shashkov, V.A. (1969). 'An attempt at large-scale influenza epidemic modelling by means of a computer.' *Bulletin of the International Epidemiology Association*, 18, 22–31.

Baroyan, O.V., Rvachev, L.A., Basilevsky, U.V., Ermakov, V.V., Frank, K.D., Rvachev, M.A., & Shashkov, V.A. (1971). 'Computer modelling of influenza epidemics for the whole country (USSR).' *Advances in Applied Probability*, 3, 224–6.

Baroyan, O.V., Rvachev, L.A., & Ivannikov, Y.G. (1977). *Modelling and Prediction of Influenza Epidemics in the USSR* (in Russian). Moscow: N.F. Gamaleia Institute of Epidemiology and Microbiology.

Bartlett, M.S. (1956). 'Deterministic and stochastic models for recurrent epidemics.' *Proceedings of the Third Berkeley Symposium on Mathematical Statistics and Probability*, 4, 81–108.

Bartlett, M.S. (1957). 'Measles periodicity and community size.' *Journal of the Royal Statistical Society A*, 120, 48–70.

Bartlett, M.S. (1960). 'The critical community size for measles in the United States.' *Journal of the Royal Statistical Society A*, 123, 37–44.

Bartlett, M.S. (1972). 'Epidemics.' In J.M. Tanur (ed.), *Statistics: a Guide to the Unknown*. San Francisco: Holden-Day, 66–76.

Besag, J. (1974). 'Spatial interaction and the statistical analysis of lattice systems.' *Journal of the Royal Statistical Society B*, 36, 192–236.

Box, G.E.P. & Jenkins, G.M. (1970). *Time Series Analysis, Forecasting and Control*. San Francisco: Holden Day.

Bridgewater, S.C. & Lotz, D.I. (1984). 'Measles (rubeola): the control of an outbreak at a large university.' *Journal of American College Health*, 32, 201–4.

Centers for Disease Control (1985). 'Multiple measles outbreaks on college campuses – Ohio, Massachusetts, Illinois.' *Morbidity and Mortality Weekly Report*, 34, 129–30.

Chatfield, C. (1980). *The Analysis of Time Series: An Introduction* (2nd edn). London: Chapman & Hall.

Cliff, A.D. & Haggett, P. (1988). *Atlas of Disease Distributions: Analytic Approaches to Epidemiological Data*. Oxford: Blackwell Reference.

Cliff, A.D. & Haggett, P. (1989a). 'Epidemic control and critical community size: spatial aspects of eliminating communicable diseases in human populations.' In R.W. Thomas (ed.), *Spatial Epidemiology*. London: Pion, 93–110.

Cliff, A.D. & Haggett, P. (1989b). 'Spatial aspects of epidemic control.' *Progress in Human Geography*, 13, 313–47.

Cliff, A.D., Haggett, P., & Ord, J.K. (1986). *Spatial Aspects of Influenza Epidemics*. London: Pion.

Cliff, A.D., Haggett, P., Ord, J.K., & Versey, G.R. (1981). *Spatial Diffusion: an Historical Geography of Epidemics in an Island Community*. Cambridge: Cambridge University Press.

Cliff, A.D., Haggett, P., & Smallman-Raynor, M.R. (1993). *Measles: an historical geography of a major human viral disease from global expansion to local retreat, 1840–1990*. Oxford: Blackwell Reference.

Fenner, F. (1986). 'The eradication of infectious diseases.' *South African Medical Journal*, 66 (supplement), 35–9.

Frank, J.A., Orenstein, W.A., Bart, K.J., Bart, S.W., El-Tantawy, N., David, R.M., & Hinman, A.R. (1985). 'Major impediments to measles elimination.' *American Journal of Diseases of Children*, 139, 881–8.

Griffiths, D.A. (1973). 'The effect of measles vaccination on the incidence of measles in the community.' *Journal of the Royal Statistical Society A*, 136, 441–9.

Gumbel, E.J. (1958). 'Statistical theory of floods and droughts.' *Journal of the Institution of Water Engineers*, 12, 157–84.

Hamer, W.H. (1906). 'The Millroy lectures on epidemic disease in England. The evidence of variability and persistence of type.' *Lancet*, 1, 733–9.

Henderson, D.A. (1976). 'Smallpox-eradication and measles-control programmes in west and central Africa.' *Industry and Tropical Health*, 6, 112–20.

Hinman, A.R., Brandling-Bennett, A.D., Bernier, R.H., Kirby, C.D., & Eddins, D.L. (1980). 'Current features of measles in the United States: feasibility of measles elimination.' *Epidemiologic Reviews*, 2, 153–70.

Kendall, D.G. (1948). 'On the generalized 'birth-and-death' process.' *Annals of Mathematical Statistics*, 19, 1–15.

Kendall, D.G. (1957). 'La propagation d'une épidémie au d'un bruit dans une population limitée.' *Publications de l'Institute de Statistique de l'Université de Paris*, 6, 307–11.

Kermack, W.O. & McKendrick, A.G. (1927–39).'Contributions to the mathematical theory of epidemics.' *Proceedings of the Royal Society A*, 115, 700–21 (Part I, 1927); 138, 55–83 (Part II, 1932); 141, 94–122 (Part III, 1933); *Journal of Hygiene, Cambridge*, 37, 172–87 (Part IV); 39, 271–88 (Part V).

Mollison, D. & Isham, V. (eds) (1995). *Epidemic Modelling: Proceedings of the NATO Advanced Workshop, Isaac Newton Institute for Mathematical Sciences, Cambridge, January–June, 1993*. Cambridge: Cambridge University Press.

Narain, J.P., Farrell, J.B., Lofgren, J.P., & Gunn, R.A. (1985). 'Imported measles outbreak in a university.' *American Journal of Public Health*, 75, 397–8.

Senser, D.J., Dull, H.B., & Langmuir, A.D. (1967). 'Epidemiological basis for the eradication of measles.' *Public Health Reports*, 82, 253–6.

Soper, H.E. (1929). 'Interpretation of periodicity in disease prevalence.' *Journal of the Royal Statistical Society A*, 92, 34–73.

Sutter, R.W., Markowitz, S.E., Bennetch, J.M., Morris, W., Zell, E.R., & Preblud, S.R. (1991). 'Measles among the Amish: a comparative study in primary and secondary cases in households.' *Journal of Infectious Diseases*, 163, 12–16.

9

AIDS in Neighbourhoods of San Francisco: some Geographical Observations on the First Decade of a Local-Area Epidemic

M.R. Smallman-Raynor

1 INTRODUCTION

1.1 Background

Well over a decade has passed since the pioneering descriptions of the Acquired Immunodeficiency Syndrome (AIDS) in North America in 1981. In this period, the disease has emerged as a leading cause of morbidity and premature mortality in cities across the United States. By 1990, AIDS-related illnesses had out-stripped murder, suicide, cancer and accidents as the principal killer of young adult males in at least 64 major US cities, from Norfolk (Virginia) on the eastern seaboard to San Francisco on the Pacific coast, and from Seattle on the northern border with Canada to Baton Rouge in the deep south (Saunders et al., 1990; Selik, Chu, and Buehler, 1993). From these metropolitan reservoirs, the causative agent of AIDS, the Human Immunodeficiency Virus (HIV), has spread down the urban population size hierarchy to appear in increasingly smaller settlements and rural communities (Cohn et al., 1991; Shannon, Pyle, and Bashshur, 1991). Today, HIV is present in virtually every corner of the United States.

Despite this diffusion, however, major urban agglomerations remained the primary foci of the US HIV/AIDS epidemic throughout the first decade of disease surveillance. So, 85 per cent of the 213,641 US AIDS cases identified by February 1992 – representing some two-fifths of the global AIDS total reported to the World Health Organization – heralded from metropolitan areas with populations in excess of half a million (Centers for Disease Control, 1992a). In such areas, specialized lifestyles and, frequently, multiple deprivations have provided an environment ripe for the rapid propagation of HIV.

Notwithstanding this metropolitan focus, studies of the spatial patterns of AIDS in the neighbourhoods of US cities are rare. This remains so despite their obvious importance to the steering of outreach programmes (Aldrich et al., 1990), and to the development of high-resolution models for spatial forecasting

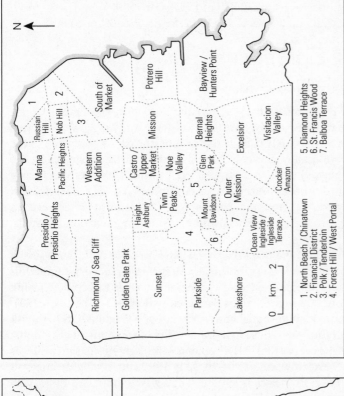

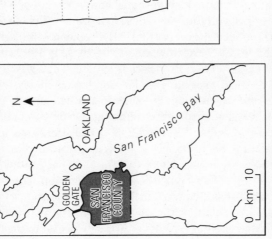

Figure 9.1 Locational map of San Francisco. *Left*, the city is located on the Pacific coast of California, some 3800 km west of New York City (*upper map*). It occupies an area of about 100 km^2 at the tip of a tongue of land which, with Marin Peninsula to the north of the Golden Gate Strait, separates San Francisco Bay from the Pacific Ocean (*lower map*). *Right*, neighbourhoods of San Francisco referred to in the text.

(*Source*: Smallman-Raynor, Cliff, and Haggett, 1992, figure 5.5A, p. 211)

(Shannon, Pyle, and Bashshur, 1991, pp. 133–4). The lacuna owes much to the confidential nature of US AIDS statistics; data are frequently stripped of all but the most rudimentary geographical markers so that maximal spatial detail and maximal socio-demographic and temporal detail are irreconcilable goals (see, for example, Gould, 1993, pp. 168–77). Rare exceptions to this rule do, however, exist. The city of San Francisco provides one such exception (Aldrich et al., 1990a; Smallman-Raynor, Cliff, and Haggett, 1992), and it is to an examination of the spatial patterns of AIDS in the neighbourhoods of this city that the paper is addressed.

1.2 San Francisco as an AIDS laboratory

San Francisco (1980 population approximately 700,000; see figure 9.1 for location) forms a natural laboratory for the local-level study of HIV-associated disease patterns. In terms of AIDS high-risk groups, the city is renowned as the homosexual (or, colloquially, the gay) capital of the world.[1] Historically, the roots of the city's gay culture can be traced back to the 1940s although, as a social movement, it flourished in the late 1960s and 1970s. The liberal social climate of these years spurred the homosexual community to achieve an unprecedented degree of social, political and economic organization (Castells, 1983).

Despite this high profile, the exact size of the San Francisco male homosexual community is unknown. Estimates for the late 1970s have placed the figure for the entire homosexual population (male and female) at close to 100,000, giving an overall density of 1000 homosexuals per square kilometre (Castells, 1983). This seemingly uniquely high spatial concentration of a single AIDS high-risk group, coupled with the apparent sexual promiscuity of some members (Shilts, 1987), has fuelled a homosexual AIDS epidemic in San Francisco which is unequalled in the Western world. Thus, by May 1992, the bodily defences of probably one in 40 San Franciscans had been so severely impaired by HIV as to place them at especial risk for developing life-threatening opportunistic infections and cancers; one in 60 residents had already succumbed to AIDS, while one in 83 had died of the condition (Hirozawa et al., 1992; San Francisco Department of Public Health AIDS Office, 1992). As a natural disaster, the human toll of the San Francisco AIDS epidemic already exceeds – by an order of magnitude – that associated with the 1906 earthquake.

The position of San Francisco amongst the metropolitan AIDS epidemics of the United States is illustrated in figure 9.2. Proportional circles plot AIDS rates per 100,000 population in each of the 93 largest (over 500,000 population) Standard Metropolitan Statistical Areas (SMSAs) to the end of October 1989. Each circle has been shaded according to the probability of that rate having occurred by chance.[2] In this manner, figure 9.2 affirms the zenithal position of San Francisco SMSA. Here, the cumulative AIDS rate of 427 per 100,000 was almost twice that of the second ranked SMSA, New York City. With a few notable exceptions (Fort Lauderdale, Jersey City, Miami, Newark, and San Juan), most other metropolitan AIDS rates fell well below the national average (123 per 100,000).

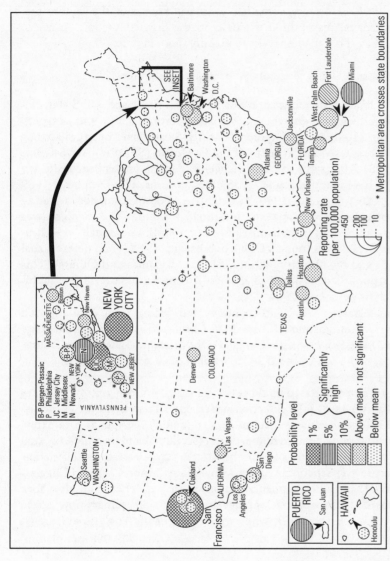

Figure 9.2 The US metropolitan AIDS epidemic. Proportional circles show cumulative AIDS incidence rates in the 93 largest (> 500,000 population) Standard Metropolitan Statistical Areas (SMSAs) to 31 October 1989. Circles have been shaded according to the probability of that incidence rate having occurred by chance. (*Source*: Smallman-Raynor, Cliff, and Haggett, 1992, figure 5.4C, p. 206)

1.3 Data sources and layout of chapter

Against such a background, it is not surprising that the San Francisco HIV/ AIDS epidemic should be one of the most intensely studied city-level epidemics in the world. Indeed, much of our medical understanding of HIV and AIDS rests with the scientific community of the Bay Area (Cohen, Sande, and Volberding, 1990). However, remarkably little is known of the factors that moulded the spatial distribution of AIDS in the districts of San Francisco during the 1980s. This chapter seeks to identify those factors.

1.3.1 Data sources. Use is made of two primary data sources:

1   *AIDS statistics.* The nature and quality of San Francisco AIDS statistics has been reviewed elsewhere (Smallman-Raynor, Cliff, and Haggett, 1992, pp. 210–13). In brief, reports of AIDS cases have been collated by the San Francisco Department of Public Health (SFDPH) AIDS Office since 1981. Using this source, Michael R. Aldrich and colleagues in the SFDPH have mapped crude AIDS cases, diagnosed by December 1989 and reported to March 1990, by neighbourhood of residence; a plan of these neighbourhoods appears in figure 9.1 (right). The mapping was carried out for three transmission categories (homosexual non-Intra-Venous Drug Users (non-IVDUs), homosexual IVDUs and heterosexual IVDUs) and by ethnicity (Whites, Blacks, Hispanics and Others). This dataset, published in Aldrich et al. (1990), forms the basis of all geographical analysis described below.
2   *Population statistics.* All socio-economic and demographic data analysed here have been abstracted from *1980 Census of Population and Housing: Census Tracts, San Francisco–Oakland Calif. Standard Metropolitan Statistical Area*, published by the US Department of Commerce (1983).

1.3.2 Layout of chapter. Based on these two statistical sources, section 2 defines the underlying waves of HIV infection which spread through San Francisco during the 1980s. Subsequent sections seek to identify the spatial parameters of these infection waves, first for homosexuals (section 3) and then heterosexual intravenous drug users (section 4). For the latter group, adequate spatial models of AIDS have proved particularly elusive (Smallman-Raynor, Cliff, and Haggett, 1992, pp. 222–4) and a new model, based on existing evidence from New York City, is proposed. This spatial model is developed into a preliminary time–space forecasting model in section 5, while the results of the analysis are drawn together in section 6.

2 PATTERNS IN TIME

2.1 Trends in AIDS

Despite the very high incidence of AIDS in San Francisco, the disease was a relatively late visitor to the city. So, while retrospective studies have dated the

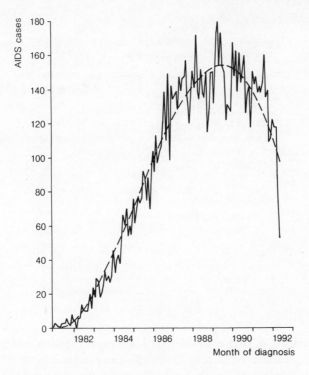

Figure 9.3 AIDS morbidity in San Francisco, January 1980 to May 1992. Full line plots AIDS cases by month of diagnosis. Broken line defines the underlying trend. (*Source*: data from San Francisco Department of Public Health AIDS Office 1992)

first AIDS cases in New York City to 1977 (Biggar, Nasca, and Burnett, 1988), the first case in San Francisco did not present until November 1980 (San Francisco Department of Public Health AIDS Office, 1992). The growth of the San Francisco AIDS epidemic from this ostensible start is charted in figure 9.3. The solid line trace plots AIDS incidence by month of diagnosis for the period from January 1981 to May 1992. The broken line trace, which is a cubic regression line fitted to the incidence curve by ordinary least squares, defines the underlying trend. This trendline is sigmoidal, and the two turning points separate the growth pattern into three distinct phases, namely: (a) an initial slow build-up in 1981–2, when the average monthly caseload did not exceed half a dozen; (b) the main growth phase, when the monthly incidence spiralled from an average of 26 cases in 1983 to 148 in 1989; and (c) an apparent decay phase which, subject to reporting delays, set in from 1990.

2.2 HIV levels

Given an estimated mean incubation period of ten years or more between primary infection with HIV and the development of AIDS (Costagliola et al., 1990), disease patterns are relict features of much earlier HIV spread processes.

Table 9.1   San Francisco, 31 May 1992:
cumulative AIDS cases by transmission category

Transmission category	AIDS cases (%)	
Adults (13 years and over)		
Homosexual non-IVDU	10,522	(84.6)
Homosexual IVDU	1,157	(9.3)
Heterosexual IVDU	435	(3.5)
Transfusion recipient	108	(0.9)
Heterosexual contact	88	(0.7)
Haemophiliac/ coagulation disorder	16	(0.1)
Other/unknown	78	(0.6)
Children		
All categories	33	(0.3)
Total	12,437	

Source: San Francisco Department of Public Health AIDS
Office (1992)

So, although the first San Francisco AIDS case dates to the winter of 1980, HIV is known to have been circulating in the city since at least 1978 (Hessol et al., 1989). From this beginning, the epidemic has remained firmly rooted in the male homosexual and IVDU populations. As table 9.1 shows, members of these transmission categories accounted for over 97 per cent of the 12,437 AIDS cases reported to the San Francisco AIDS Office by 31 May 1992 (San Francisco Department of Public Health AIDS Office, 1992).

An insight into the temporal dynamics of HIV in the homosexual and heterosexual IVDU communities is offered in figure 9.4. For an 11-year period from 1978, the upper graph shows the annual incidence (heavy line) and cumulative prevalence (bars) of HIV infection among 320 homosexual members of the Hepatitis B Vaccine Trial Cohort of the San Francisco City Clinic For Sexually Transmitted Diseases (Hessol et al., 1989). Similarly, the lower graph shows back-forecasted estimates of HIV incidence and prevalence in the city's heterosexual IVDU community (Aldrich, Mandel, and Newmeyer, 1990). Finally, for the city as a whole, table 9.2 lists the estimated size of the homosexual and heterosexual IVDU populations (column 2) and their average density per square kilometre (column 3).

In the context of essentially unimodal waves of the type depicted by the incidence curves in figure 9.4, Cliff, Haggett, and Ord (1986, pp. 198–201) have noted that the relative velocity of an epidemic wavefront can be estimated by the higher order moments of the frequency distribution of infections against time. Accordingly, columns 4 and 5 of table 9.2 list the sample Pearson measures of skewness (b_1) and kurtosis (b_2) for the incidence curves in figure 9.4. In addition, the standard deviations, s, of the incidence curves are indicated (column 6), as are the average times to infection ($\bar{t}$, in years) implied by the respective distributions (column 7). Computational details are given in Cliff,

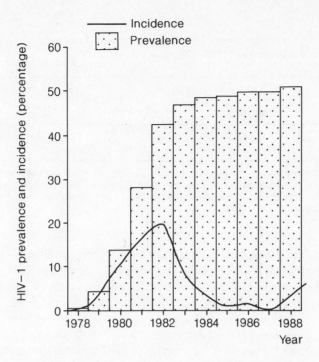

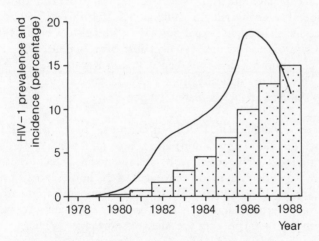

Figure 9.4 Annual incidence (line trace) and cumulative prevalence (bars) of HIV in two San Francisco transmission groups, 1978–1988. *Upper*, a cohort of 320 male homosexuals/bisexuals. *Lower*, back-forecasted estimates for heterosexual IVDUs. Note variation in the vertical scale of the two graphs.
(*Sources*: Smallman-Raynor, Cliff, and Haggett, 1992, figure 5.5B, p. 212) and Aldrich, Mandel, and Newmayer, 1990, table II, p. 346)

Table 9.2   Demographic parameters and measures of epidemic velocity for the spread of HIV in two San Francisco cohorts, 1978–1988

Group	Estimated size	Density (per km^2)	b_1	b_2	s	$\bar{t}$
			\multicolumn{4}{c}{HIV epidemic velocity[a]}			
Homosexuals	100,000[b]	1,000	1.82	5.59	1.89	4.82
Heterosexual IVDUs	13,000[c]	130	–0.07	2.65	2.01	8.34

[a] Estimates based on incidence curves plotted in figure 9.4. b_1: signed Pearson's skewness coefficient; b_2: Pearson's kurtosis coefficient; s: standard deviation; $\bar{t}$: average time (in years) to infection.
[b] Estimate for the entire homosexual (male and female) population (Castells, 1983).
[c] Back-forecast estimate for 1988 (Aldrich and Mandel, 1989).

Haggett, and Ord (1986, p. 198) but, assuming an 'average-velocity' wave to be Normally distributed, a 'high-velocity' wave typically displays positive skewness ($b_1 > 0$), leptokurtosis ($b_2 > 3$), a low standard deviation and a short average time to infection. A 'low-velocity' wave has the reverse characteristics.

High-velocity wave: homosexuals.   According to table 9.2, the spread of HIV in the large and dense homosexual community of San Francisco was characterized by a high-velocity wavefront which swept through the city in the early 1980s. The incidence curve for homosexuals (figure 9.4, upper) shows that HIV began to spread at an explosive rate from 1980, with almost 20 per cent (or one in five cohort members) seroconverting in 1982 alone. After this year, in accordance with evidence for changes in sexual practices (Winkelstein et al., 1987) and, possibly, virus saturation of the sexually most promiscuous elements of the homosexual community (Hethcote, Van Ark, and Karon, 1991a), the annual incidence of HIV fell dramatically; from 1985, the cumulative HIV prevalence rate began to stabilize at approximately 50 per cent.

Low-velocity wave: heterosexual IVDUs.   In contrast, the spread of HIV in the relatively small (*c.*13,000 population) and sparse (130 per km^2) heterosexual IVDU community was characterized by a slow-moving infection wave (table 9.2) whose mid-decade peak in incidence lagged the homosexual wavefront by some four years (figure 9.4, lower). By 1988, the estimated cumulative prevalence of HIV in heterosexual IVDUs had risen to 15 per cent. This should be compared with the 40–60 per cent prevalence reported for IVDUs in some east coast US cities during the mid–1980s (Dondero et al., 1991).

3 SPATIAL PATTERNS OF AIDS, I: HOMOSEXUALS

Male homosexuals dominate the AIDS statistics of San Francisco. As table 9.1 shows, males who had sex with males accounted for almost 94 per cent of the caseload by May 1992. However, for one in ten of these homosexual cases,

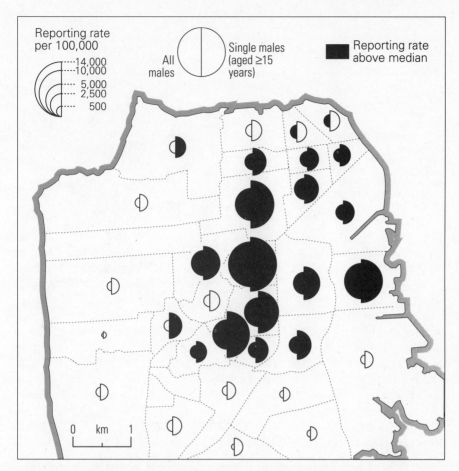

Figure 9.5   Homosexual AIDS incidence rates by district, San Francisco, 1980–1989. Rates are expressed per 100,000 males (left-hand semicircles) and per 100,000 single males aged ≥ 15 years (right-hand semicircles). Semi-circles have been shaded if rates exceeded the respective citywide medians. Districts are named in figure 9.1.
(*Source*: Smallman-Raynor, Cliff, and Haggett, 1992, figure 5.5F, p. 216)

possible exposure to HIV via intravenous drug use could not be ruled out. These cases, referred to in table 9.1 as homosexual IVDUs, are excluded from the discussion of the homosexual epidemic below, and the analysis is restricted to homosexuals for whom sexual exposure was the only reported risk factor (homosexual non-IVDUs).

3.1 Spatial patterns

Figure 9.5 plots the district-by-district incidence of AIDS for the 5858 homosexual cases reported to March 1990, and for whom a place of residence in San Francisco could be determined; districts are named in figure 9.1. To form this map, AIDS cases have been scaled in two ways.

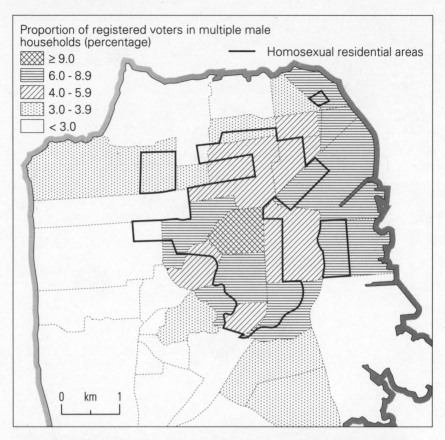

Figure 9.6   Districts of homosexual residence in San Francisco. *Left*, proportion of registered voters living in multiple male households in 1977. *Right*, proportion of adult males (aged 15 years and over) who were single (never married) in 1980. Heavy lines identify areas of homosexual residence according to a qualitative delimitation made by homosexual community informants in the late 1970s. Districts are named in figure 9.1. (*Source*: Smallman-Raynor, Cliff, and Haggett, 1992, figure 5.5G, p. 216)

Rate 1: Here, the AIDS total has been divided by the absolute size of the male population in each district to give a cumulative incidence rate per 100,000 males. The area of the left-hand semicircle associated with each district has been drawn proportional to this rate; the semicircle has been shaded if the district rate exceeded the citywide median (783 per 100,000 males).

Rate 2: Rate 1 does not adjust for age or for sexual preference. Some 80–90 per cent of San Francisco male homosexuals have never married (Moss et al., 1985). Thus, Rate 2 scales the AIDS total by the never-married adult male population in each district to give a cumulative AIDS incidence per 100,000 single males aged ≥ 15 years. This rate is represented by the right-hand semicircle associated with each district in figure 9.5. Again, semicircles have been shaded if the district rate exceeded the city-wide median (1.979 per 100,000 never married males aged ≥ 15 years).

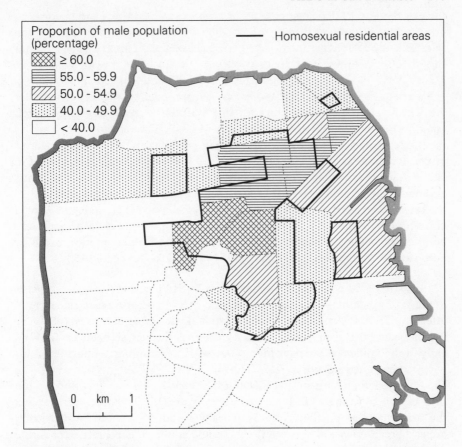

Figure 9.6 *continued*

For the city as a whole, these two measures yielded incidences of 1989 cases per 100,000 males (Rate 1) and 5040 cases per 100,000 single males aged ≥ 15 years (Rate 2). However, figure 9.5 reveals striking spatial variations in these incidences. The highest rates (denoted by the shaded semicircles) were found at the geographical heart of the city, and in neighbouring districts to the north and east. Disease rates peaked in Castro/Upper Market and Western Addition; see figure 9.1 for locations. There, Rates 1 and 2 exceeded 1 in 25 and 1 in 10 respectively. High incidence (1 in 50 for Rate 1 and 1 in 20 for Rate 2) was also recorded in five other central and eastern districts (Diamond Heights, Noe Valley, Haight Ashbury, Mission and Potrero Hill). In most other districts, Rates 1 and 2 fell well below their corresponding city averages.

3.2 Explanatory factors

3.2.1 Hypotheses. Two factors have been proposed to explain the distinctive disease pattern shown in figure 9.5:

(1) *The 'gay ghetto'.* As noted earlier, during the 1960s and 1970s, members of the homosexual community progressively colonized areas of the city such

that, by the late 1970s, distinct areas of homosexual residence had become an outstanding geographical expression of San Francisco's social organization (Castells, 1983). It may therefore be hypothesized that homosexual AIDS rates varied as some function of the distribution of areas of homosexual residence (Moss et al., 1983, 1985; Smallman-Raynor, Cliff, and Haggett, 1992).

Two frequently applied indices of homosexual residence are mapped in figure 9.6. The first (left map), based on Castells (1983), is the proportion of registered voters living in multiple male households in 1977. The second (right map) is the proportion of the adult ($\geq$ 15 years) male population that was single (never married) according to the 1980 US Census. Districts with high percentages of either measure are possible areas with a large number of homosexual residents, and both maps delimit, as areas of homosexual residence, the same districts in the central and north-eastern sectors of San Francisco. These patterns accord closely with the heavy line superimposed on each map. This represents the boundaries of the gay ghetto according to a qualitative delimitation made by homosexual community informants in the late 1970s (Castells, 1983).

(2) *Male age.* Epidemiological observations in San Francisco in the early years of the HIV epidemic successfully correlated age with an increased risk of HIV infection. Thus, observations on the Hepatitis B Vaccine Trial Cohort (cf. figure 9.4) indicated that young homosexuals were more likely to seroconvert for HIV early in the epidemic; younger men reported larger numbers of partners with whom they practised unsafe sex (Hessol et al., 1989). It may therefore be hypothesized that homosexual AIDS rates varied as some function of the distribution of young adult males shown in figure 9.7. This map, which plots the percentage proportion of adult males aged 20–44 years in each district, draws a precise division between northern and southern San Francisco. To the north, young adult males comprised 40 per cent or more of the male population; in central San Francisco, three contiguous districts (Castro/Upper Market, Haight Ashbury and Noe Valley) recorded rates in excess of 60 per cent. In contrast, to the south of the city, young adult males generally constituted less than 40 per cent of the male population.

3.2.2 Tests of hypotheses. Each factor (measures of the distribution of homosexual residence and young adult males) was used as explanatory (x) variables in a series of regression models in which homosexual AIDS case incidence rates (per 100,000 males; left-hand semi circles in figure 9.5) formed the dependent (y) variable. For the reasons outlined in Smallman-Raynor, Cliff, and Haggett (1992), the proportion of voters resident in multiple male households (figure 9.6, left map) was selected as the delimiter of homosexual residence in all regression models. Model fitting was by ordinary least squares using a stepwise algorithm; n, the sample size, was 34, the number of districts.

The critical regression results are summarized as model 1 in table 9.3. The order of entry (step 1 and step 2) of the independent variables is indicated. The regression coefficients are recorded, along with their t-statistics in parentheses. Finally, the coefficient of determination, R^2, and the F-ratio are also shown. Statistically significant t and F values are indicated by asterisks.

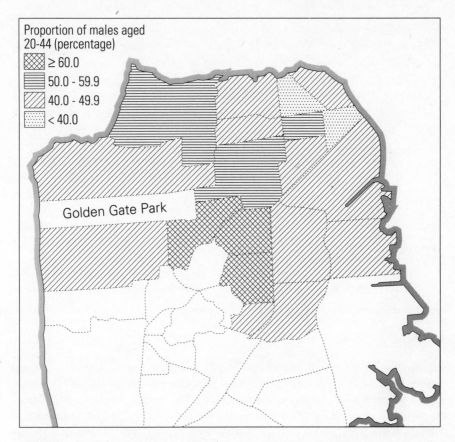

Figure 9.7 Distribution of young adult males in San Francisco. Districts are shaded according to the percentage proportion of adult males who were young (aged 20–44 years) in 1980. Districts are named in figure 9.1

Model 1 shows that, together, the two independent variables accounted for 69 per cent ($100R^2$) of the district-to-district variation in homosexual AIDS incidence rates. This was better than for either variable alone (about 50 per cent in each instance; see Smallman-Raynor, Cliff, and Haggett, 1992, pp. 217–22). The fact that the age variable (x_1) was entered first suggests that age, rather than homosexual residence (x_2), was the principal factor determining the geography of homosexual AIDS in the city over the study period.

3.3 Ethnic patterns

Models 2–6 in table 9.3 broaden the analysis to examine how far the homosexual residence and age factors account for the geographical variability in homosexual AIDS associated with different ethnic groups. To permit this extension, AIDS incidence rates per 100,000 ethnic-specific male population were estimated for each district of the city. For example, subject to the

Table 9.3 Regression results for tests of factors to explain the geographical patterns of homosexual AIDS in San Francisco

		Independent variable, slope coefficient, (t)		R^2 (F)
		Step		
Model	Ethnicity	1	2	
1	All	x_1, 88 (3.97**)	x_2, 422 (3.68**)	0.69 (31.63**)
2	White	x_2, 652 (3.21**)	x_1, 109 (2.76**)	0.58 (19.25**)
3[a]	White	x_2	728 (5.49**)	x_1, 70 (2.63**)
4	Hispanic	x_1, 78 (2.79**)		0.21 (4.80*)
5	Black	x_2, 458 (4.34**)		0.39 (18.85**)
6	Other	x_1, 18 (4.60**)		0.42 (11.19**)

* Significant at $p = 0.05$ level (one-tailed test); ** Significant at $p = 0.01$ level (one-tailed test).
[a] Omitting outlier of Western Addition.
x_1 = Proportion of males aged 20–44 years in each district; x_2 = proportion of registered voters resident in multiple male households.

Source: Smallman-Raynor, Cliff, and Haggett (1992, table 5.5.3, p. 220)

limitations of the available census data, AIDS rates among Whites were expressed per 100,000 White males. Similarly, among Blacks, AIDS rates were expressed per 100,000 Black males, and so on. These ethnic-specific AIDS rates formed the dependent (y) variables in models 2–6, while the independent variables x_1 (age) and x_2 (homosexual residence) were unchanged in the analysis.

(1) *Whites*. Regression models 2 and 3 in table 9.3 relate White homosexual AIDS incidence rates to the independent variables. Model 2 shows that these variables explained some 58 per cent of the district-to-district variability in the White AIDS epidemic, a value substantially below that observed for all ethnicities in model 1. A rather better result was obtained in model 3. Here, Western Addition, which served as an extreme outlier heavily influencing the parameters of model 2, was omitted. As table 9.3 shows, this modification increased the overall explanation to 73 per cent. In both models, the homosexual residence factor was entered in step 1 of the stepwise procedure indicating that, unlike the overall homosexual AIDS model (model 1), the most important predictor for the White epidemic was homosexual residence.

(2) *Other ethnicities*. A rather different picture emerged in models 4–6 for the remaining ethnicities. In each, only one predictor made a significant contribution and overall explanations were down. The only significant predictor for the Black epidemic (model 5) was homosexual residence which accounted for some 39 per cent of the variance in AIDS rates. In contrast, age was the only significant predictor in models 4 and 6; accounted variability in AIDS rates ranged from 21 per cent for Hispanics to 42 per cent for other ethnicities.

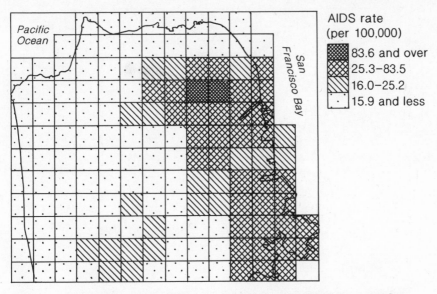

Figure 9.8   Heterosexual IVDU AIDS incidence rates (per 100,000 population) in San Francisco, 1980–1989

3.4 Summary

Early studies from San Francisco emphasized the role of the gay ghetto in determining the spatial parameters of the high speed HIV infection wave which swept through the homosexual community in the early 1980s (Moss et al., 1983, 1985). However, the transmission of HIV is effected by risky behaviour rather than risk group membership; the present analysis suggests that male age (as it related to increased sexual activity), rather than homosexual residence *per se*, was the principal factor shaping the distribution of homosexual AIDS in the city during the 1980s. Variations are, however, evident along ethnic lines.

4 SPATIAL PATTERNS OF AIDS, II: HETEROSEXUAL IVDUs

4.1 Introduction

It was noted in section 2 that, during the 1980s, HIV spread in the heterosexual IVDU population of San Francisco as a slow, low-level, infection wave. As such, the dynamics of HIV in this population differed fundamentally from the fast epidemic waves identified for IVDUs in New York and some other east coast cities (see, for example, Des Jarlais et al., 1989). This retarded spread of HIV in San Francisco has variously been attributed to: (a) the apparently low geographical concentration of heterosexual IVDUs (see table 9.2); (b) the limited practice of multiple and anonymous use of non-sterile injecting equipment at so-called 'shooting galleries'; and (c) the apparently low (but unquantified) levels of social interaction of homosexual and heterosexual IVDUs (Chaisson et al., 1987).

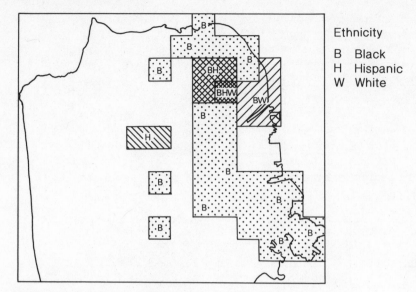

Figure 9.9 Ethnic-specific AIDS incidences for heterosexual IVDUs in San Francisco, 1980–1989. Cells with high rates (≥ 83.6 per 100,000) for each of three ethnic groups – Whites, W; Blacks, B; Hispanics, H – are shown

Nevertheless, despite these comments, and the relatively small number of heterosexual IVDUs in the San Francisco AIDS total (see table 9.1), heterosexual IVDU AIDS was the most rapidly developing epidemic in the city during the latter years of the 1980s (Smallman-Raynor, Cliff, and Haggett, 1992, p. 215). The apparently still low levels of HIV infection among the city's estimated 13,000 heterosexual IVDUs offer a chance for geographically directed intervention programmes (Aldrich and Mandel, 1989; Aldrich et al., 1990).

4.2 *Spatial patterns*

4.2.1 Standardization of areal units. Section 3 examined the spatial structure of the homosexual AIDS epidemic on the basis of natural city districts. A feel for the structure of the gay ghetto was maintained at the price of the disadvantages which accrue from the statistical analysis of irregular areal units (Haggett, Cliff, and Frey, 1977, pp. 348–52). In the present section, the neighbourhoods of San Francisco have been transformed to a regular grid system consisting of 147 cells of dimensions 0.72 km × 0.72 km. This system, which has been formed in the manner outlined by Cliff and Haggett (1988, pp. 18–19), serves automatically to standardize for the size of the data collecting units, thereby facilitating the correlation and regression analyses described below.

4.2.2 AIDS distribution. Figures 9.8 and 9.9 map cumulative AIDS rates per 100,000 population for heterosexual IVDUs in San Francisco to December 1989. figure 9.8 uses choropleth techniques to delimit the aggregate pattern, while figure 9.9 maps the distribution along ethnic lines. Full details are given in appendix 1 but, in figure 9.9, cells recording high AIDS rates (that is, ≥ 83.6 per 100,000) in Whites are identified by the letter W, Blacks by the letter B and Hispanics by the letter H; combinations of W, B and H mark cells in which high AIDS rates coincided for two or more ethnicities.

Figure 9.8 shows that the IVDU epidemic was concentrated in a north–south band in eastern San Francisco. Elsewhere, to the west and south of the city, low AIDS rates prevailed. As figure 9.9 shows, the Black epidemic followed this general pattern, with high AIDS rates concentrated along the eastside. In contrast, and with the exception of small pockets of disease activity in central San Francisco, the AIDS epidemics among White and Hispanic IVDUs were spatially restricted to the north-eastern sector of the city.

4.3 Explanatory factors

4.3.1 Hypotheses. On the basis of studies from New York City, two factors may be forwarded to explain the distribution of heterosexual IVDU AIDS shown in figures 9.8 and 9.9.

(1) *The poverty-led hypothesis.* This links HIV-related high-risk substance abuse to a breakdown in the physical and social fabric of a city district. In particular, Wallace (1991) has identified a statistically significant and positive association between the spatial distribution of AIDS in the Bronx, New York City, and an index termed the Poverty Index (*PI*). The *PI* is a composite measure of social status and poverty. A modified version of the index is given by

$$PI = (SES) \times (\text{per cent population below the poverty level}) \qquad (9.1)$$

As described in appendix 2, *SES* is formed as the rank of a geographical district on a city-wide measure of socio-economic status, while the percentage of the population below the poverty level is computed as a sample estimate under the 1980 census. Full details are given in appendix 2 but, following Sampson and Groves (1989), high *PI* scores identify relatively poor districts, and vice versa.

Prior to further discussion of the *PI*, a cautionary note must be sounded regarding its interpretation in the context of disease transmission. Any relationship between AIDS, poverty and social status is likely to be complex and multi-directional. As noted above, however, the *PI* has proved a useful descriptor of the spatial pattern of AIDS in parts of New York City. The index is examined here to test its more general applicability as a spatial descriptor of urban IVDU AIDS epidemics and, as discussed further below, to investigate its potential contribution in the construction of local-level space-time AIDS forecasting models.

Computation of the *PI* for San Francisco yields the choropleth map in figure 9.10. Here, the darkest shading categories identify the poorest areas (cells with high *PI* scores) while the lightest shading categories identify the richest areas (low *PI* scores). The map draws a rather precise division between the

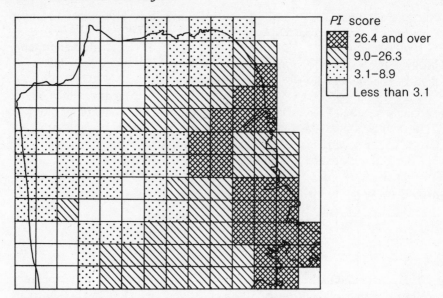

Figure 9.10   Distribution of poverty in San Francisco, 1980. Cells are shaded according to the Poverty Index (*PI*) defined in equation (9.1). Dark shading categories identify cells with high *PI* scores (relatively poor). Light shading categories identify cells with low *PI* scores (relatively prosperous)

impoverished districts to the east and south of the city, and the more prosperous areas to the north and west.

(2) *The homosexual IVDU hypothesis.* This proposes that homosexual IVDUs have served as a bridge for the spread of HIV from the core homosexual population to heterosexual IVDUs (Friedland et al., 1985). To assess this hypothesis for San Francisco, figure 9.11 maps cumulative AIDS rates (per 100,000 population) for homosexual IVDU to the end of December 1989. The highest AIDS rates (≥ 160 per 100,000) are identified in central and northern sectors of the city. These areas, which coincide with the principal districts of homosexual residence (cf. figure 9.6), are bounded by low AIDS incidence to the south and west of the city.

4.3.2 Tests of hypotheses. Each factor (*PI* and homosexual IVDU AIDS incidence) was used as explanatory (*x*) variables in a series of multiple regression models in which heterosexual IVDU AIDS rates formed the dependent (*y*) variable. Model fitting was by ordinary least squares using a stepwise algorithm; *n*, the sample size, was 147, the number of areal divisions defined in figure 9.8. Table 9.4, which summarizes the results, should be interpreted in the manner described for table 9.3 above.

Results. Model 1 shows that, together, the two independent variables accounted for some 65 per cent ($100R^2$) of the geographical variation in AIDS rates. This explanation increased to almost 80 per cent when four extreme outlying cells were omitted from analysis (model 2). Notice that this latter procedure resulted in the elimination of the homosexual IVDU variable (x_2) from the model. The

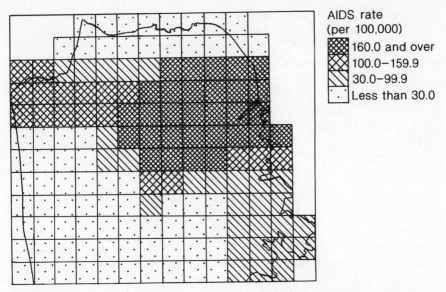

AIDS rate
(per 100,000)
▨ 160.0 and over
⊠ 100.0–159.9
◪ 30.0–99.9
⬚ Less than 30.0

Figure 9.11 Homosexual IVDU AIDS incidence rates (per 100,000 population) in San Francisco, 1980–1989

Table 9.4 Regression results for tests on factors to explain the geographical patterns of heterosexual IVDU AIDS in San Francisco

		Independent variable, slope coefficient, (t)		R^2 (F)
		Step		
Model	Ethnicity	1	2	
1	All	x_1, 1.63 (12.91**)	x_2, 0.05 (4.02**)	0.65 (128.8**)
2[a]	All	x_1, 1.80 (22.91**)		0.79 (260.6**)
3	White	x_2	0.12 (6.12**)	
4	Black	x_1, 3.01 (4.80**)		0.14 (13.56**)
5	Hispanic	x_2, 0.19 (7.87**)	x_1, −1.30 (−5.07**)	0.32 (33.56**)

** Significant at $p = 0.01$ level (one-tailed test).
[a] Four extreme outliers omitted.
x_1: Poverty Index (*PI*); x_2: homosexual IVDU AIDS rate per 100,000 population.

fact that the homosexual IVDU variable was entered second in model 1, and omitted from model 2, suggests that the *PI* was the single most important predictor of the spatial distribution of heterosexual IVDU AIDS during the study period.

Models 3–5 repeat the analysis, but this time with ethnic-specific heterosexual IVDU AIDS rates (expressed per 100,000 ethnic population) entered as the dependent (*y*) variables. The independent variables x_1 (*PI*) and x_2 (homosexual

IVDU AIDS incidence) were unchanged in the analysis. In each model, only one predictor displayed a significant and positive association with the dependent, and overall levels of explanation were reduced. The only significant predictor for the White epidemic (model 3) was the homosexual IVDU variable which accounted for some 21 per cent of the variance in AIDS rates. In contrast, *PI* was the only significant predictor for the Black epidemic (model 4), accounting for 14 per cent of the variance in AIDS rates (model 4). Finally, for Hispanics (model 5), both independent variables made a significant contribution to the model, but with a negative association identified between *PI* (entered in step 2) and AIDS incidence.

4.4 Summary

Cohort studies from the United States have consistently correlated HIV/AIDS in heterosexual IVDUs with race and low socio-economic status (see, for example, Guinan et al., 1984; Chaisson et al., 1987). Although these simple correlations may mask a highly complex nexus of urban decay, social trauma and disease transmission (Wallace, 1988), the relationships readily translate into intelligible and easily applicable geographical descriptions of AIDS in San Francisco IVDUs. As such, the present analysis suggests the more general applicability of Wallace's (1991) spatial model of AIDS in the Bronx.

5 SPACE–TIME MODELS

5.1 Epidemic models for San Francisco

Spatial descriptions of the San Francisco AIDS epidemic lead naturally to the question of the development of space–time models to predict the future course of AIDS in this, and other, cities. Such models have obvious practical utility in guiding the activities of AIDS outreach programmes, the planners of health care provision and others. In the context of San Francisco, the AIDS modelling literature already includes several sophisticated, but essentially aspatial, process-based models of the homosexual epidemic (Hethcote, Van Ark, and Karon, 1991; Hethcote, Van Ark, and Longini, 1991), while IVDUs have formed the subject of some back-forecasting approaches (Aldrich and Mandel, 1989; Aldrich, Mandel, and Newmeyer, 1990). Although the latter have proved particularly successful in short-term prediction (Newmeyer, 1991), their spatial calibration has been compromised by the lack of district-level HIV seroprevalence data (Aldrich and Mandel, 1989).

An alternative forecasting strategy, and one that builds naturally on the spatial models described in this paper, is the expansion method (Casetti, 1972; see also, Haggett, Cliff, and Frey, 1977, pp. 534–9). Theoretical and computational details of the expansion method are given in Casetti and Fan (1991, pp. 1591–99) but, in the application described below, the approach seeks to model temporal changes in the coefficients of spatial regression models of the type outlined in tables 9.3 and 9.4. By extrapolation, such models may then furnish a basis for short-term (of the order of 1–5 years) spatial forecasts.

In this final section, the expansion method is used to model the AIDS epidemic in the heterosexual IVDU population of San Francisco. This transmission category was selected on account of its expected numerical importance during the 1990s, and because of the relatively limited academic concern with this group to date (Aldrich and Mandel, 1989; Newmeyer, 1991). Before further discussion, however, the analysis is prefaced with a cautionary note regarding the temporal calibration of micro-scale AIDS models. As noted in section 1, owing to issues of patient confidentiality, maximal spatial detail forfeits maximal detail in other domains. So, in the instance of San Francisco, high-resolution spatial data are publicly available only on an annual basis from the mid-1980s. Given this severe constraint on temporal calibration, the model outlined below is to be considered illustrative of future work envisaged. The model should be recalibrated if, and when, adequate data become available.

5.2 The expansion method

5.2.1 Model selection.
In section 4, the spatial distribution of AIDS in the heterosexual IVDU population of San Francisco was described by a city-wide measure of socio-economic status termed the Poverty Index (PI). So, on the basis of regression models 1 and 2 in table 9.4, the following spatial model was specified:

$$R_i = a_o + a_1 P_i + e_i, i = 1, 2, \ldots, n, \tag{9.2}$$

where R_i denotes the heterosexual IVDU AIDS rate (per 100,000 population) in the i-th unit of an n-element spatial system, P_i denotes the Poverty Index, PI, a_0 and a_1 are parameters, and the $\{e_i\}$ are random disturbances.

When applied to the San Francisco data, ordinary least squares solutions of equation (2) for successive time periods, $t = 1, 2, \ldots, T$, revealed that the estimated parameters, $\{\hat{a}_0\}$ and $\{\hat{a}_1\}$, differed significantly from time period to time period. The expansion approach then proceeds by specifying a series of equations which describe this temporal variation in the relationship of AIDS rates to poverty. In the present analysis, $\{a_0\}$ and $\{a_1\}$ were expanded as cubics in time, thus

$$a_0 = y_{00} + y_{10} t + y_{20} t^2 + y_{30} t^3 + e_i, t = 1, 2, \ldots, T \tag{9.3}$$

and

$$a_1 = y_{01} + y_{11} t + y_{21} t^2 + y_{31} t^3 + e_i, t = 1, 2, \ldots, T. \tag{9.4}$$

Here, $\{y_{00}\}, \{y_{10}\}, \ldots, \{y_{31}\}$ are parameters to be estimated. Substitution of equations (9.3) and (9.4) into equation (9.2) yields the terminal expansion model

$$R_i = y_{00} + y_{10} t + y_{20} t^2 + y_{30} t^3 + y_{01} P_i + y_{11} P_i t \ldots y_{21} P_i t^2 + y_{31} P_i t^3 + e_i,$$
$$i = 1, 2, \ldots, n; t = 1, 2, \ldots, T. \tag{9.5}$$

The parameters in equation (9.5) may be obtained by ordinary least squares (OLS).

Table 9.5   Calibration of the terminal expansion model for heterosexual IVDU AIDS in San Francisco

Predictor	Regression coefficient (t-statistic)	R^2 (F-ratio)
Constant	10.79 (10.44*)	
Step 1: P_{it}^3	0.07 (15.21*)	
Step 2: t^3	−0.31 (−3.89*)	0.41 (136.2*)

* Significant at the $p = 0.01$ level (one-tailed test).

5.2.2 Model calibration. Equation (9.5) was fitted to annual AIDS data relating to 147 city divisions and reported to the San Francisco AIDS Office by March 1990. Time zero ($t = 0$) was scaled to 1986, the year preceding the ostensible start of a geographically widespread AIDS epidemic among heterosexual IVDUs (Aldrich et al., 1990). Model fitting was by OLS using stepwise multiple regression.

The critical regression results are summarized in table 9.5. The order of entry (step) of statistically non-zero predictors is indicated. The regression coefficients are recorded, along with their associated *t*-statistics in parentheses. The coefficient of determination, R^2, and the *F*-ratio are also given. Statistically significant *t* and *F* values at the $p = 0.01$ level (one-tailed test) are denoted by an asterisk. Only two predictors (P_{it}^3 and t^3) made a significant contribution to the stepwise regression (table 9.5), and a moderate overall fit was obtained ($R^2 = 0.41$; $F = 136.2$, $p = 0.001$). From table 9.5, the estimated terminal model may be written as

$$\hat{R}_i = 10.791 + 0.065P_{it}^{\,3} - 0.308t^3. \tag{9.6}$$

Finally, deriving $\hat{R}_i$ with respect to t yields the epidemic growth rate model

$$\delta R_i \,/\delta t = 0.195P_i t^2 - 0.924t^2. \tag{9.7}$$

5.2.3 Model application

(1) *Spatially aggregated predictions.* Equation (9.6) was first operationalized to generate city-level estimates of the cumulative incidence of heterosexual IVDU AIDS. The results are summarized in table 9.6. Column 2 lists the predictions for the calibration period (1987–9) and, by extrapolation, forecasts for the period 1990–2. It should be noted that column 2 relates to AIDS cases with known addresses in San Francisco; column 3 lists the cumulative number of reported AIDS cases with a known address to the end of 1989. Finally, for comparative purposes, columns 4 and 5 show back-forecast predictions of the cumulative incidence of heterosexual IVDU AIDS. These forecasts discount a fraction of cases (set at 0.25, the proportion to 1989) with no address.

Table 9.6 shows that predictions under the expansion model (column 2)

Table 9.6 Expansion predictions of the cumulative incidence of heterosexual IVDU AIDS in San Francisco, 1987–1992

	Cases		Back-forecasts	
Year	Predicted	Observed[a]	A[b]	B[c]
Calibration period				
1987	68	47	56	59
1988	86	89	95	104
1989	141	139	151	171
Forecasts				
1990	230		221	258
1991	387		306	360
1992	620		409	474

[a] Cases with known address in San Francisco (Aldrich et al., 1990).
[b] 1988 forecasts by Aldrich, Mandrel, and Newmeyer (1990).
[c] 1991 forecasts by Newmeyer and Aldrich (Aldrich, personal communication, 27 July 1992).

Back-forecasts have been discounted by an assumed 25 per cent for cases with no San Francisco address; see text for explanation.

accord closely with (a) reported cases to 1989 (column 3) and (b) corrected back-forecasts to 1991 (columns 4 and 5). This result is particularly encouraging given the good performance of back-forecasting models for San Francisco (Newmeyer, 1991). However, as table 9.6 shows, by 1992 the forecasts from the expansion and back-forecasting models departed markedly.

(2) *Spatially disaggregated predictions, 1989.* The spatial component of the expansion model is examined to its 1989 pattern in figure 9.12. Based on the grid system of 147 cells, the left-hand map shows AIDS cases correctly predicted by the model ($n = 100$) as judged by the San Francisco AIDS registry to March 1990. The central map shows AIDS cases incorrectly predicted by the model ($n = 41$), while the right hand map shows AIDS cases not predicted by the model ($n = 39$). The latter two distributions essentially define the spatial mis-allocation problem; the difference between the number of cases in the two distributions (that is, $41 - 39 = 2$ cases) is the level of model over-prediction observed to 1989 in table 9.6 ($141 - 139 = 2$ cases).

The left-hand map of figure 9.12 shows that the expansion model successfully predicted the spatial distribution of some two-thirds of the AIDS cases reported to 1989. Most of the remaining 41 cases predicted by the model were incorrectly allocated to central and southeastern districts of the city (map, centre), while the model failed to predict a tight cluster of cases to the northeast (map, right). This latter distribution largely corresponds with the four cells omitted as outliers from model 2 in table 9.4.

(3) *Epidemic growth rate, 1989.* The map in figure 9.13, which has been generated from equation (9.7), plots the rate of growth of the epidemic in heterosexual IVDUs to 1989. To form this map, cells with a growth rate in excess of 15 AIDS cases per 100,000 per annum (hatched) were defined as 'fast'.

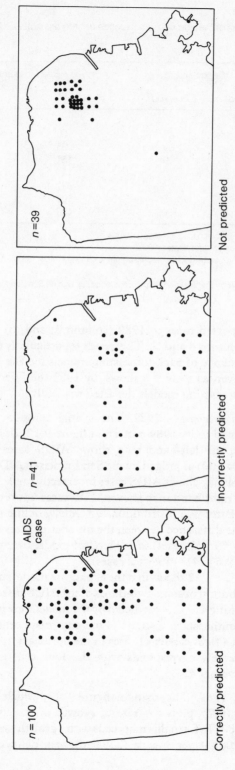

Figure 9.12 Heterosexual IVDU AIDS cases predicted by the estimated expansion model. *Left*, cases correctly predicted. *Centre*, cases incorrectly predicted. *Right*, cases not predicted

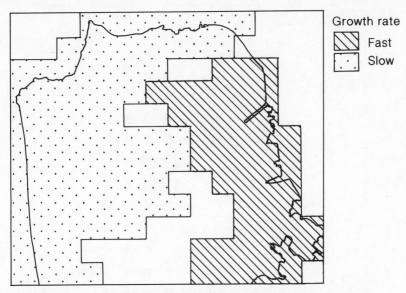

Figure 9.13 Estimated growth rate of the heterosexual IVDU AIDS epidemic in San Francisco, 1989. Growth rates are defined as fast (≥ 15 cases per 100,000 per annum) or slow (≤ 3 cases per 100,000 per annum)

Conversely, those with a growth rate below 3 AIDS cases per 100,000 per annum (stippled) were defined as 'slow'. In this manner, the map draws a division between the rapidly evolving epidemic to the east of the city, and the slowly evolving epidemic to the west.

Spatial forecasts, 1991. Spatially disaggregated forecasts of cumulative AIDS incidence to 1991 are shown in figure 9.14. At the time of writing, no data were available to test this distribution as an *ex post* forecast. However, recall from table 9.6 that, to 1991, the spatially aggregated predictions of the expansion model (387 cases) corresponded reasonably well with case levels predicted under back-forecasting approaches (306–360 cases).

In accordance with the estimated rates of epidemic development in figure 9.13, figure 9.14 shows a continued intensification of the heterosexual IVDU epidemic in a band along the eastside of San Francisco. The evolution of a secondary epidemic focus is identified to the south of the city, while epidemic development to the west is expected to remain minimal.

6 CONCLUSION

Spatial correlations of AIDS and urban structure undoubtedly mask many complex and multi-directional relationships. A critical remit of the epidemio-logical sciences is to unravel those relationships. In the interim, the simple spatial models described in this paper represent intelligible and easily applicable geographical descriptions of AIDS in San Francisco. For the purposes of AIDS

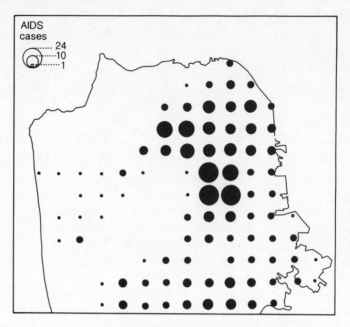

Figure 9.14 Cumulative heterosexual IVDU AIDS cases predicted by the estimated expansion model to December 1991

intervention, the models may provide a useful analytical foundation for other large urban centres where disease statistics are currently withheld from the public domain.

Much remains to be done, however, to develop the models into useful tools for spatial forecasting. First, for a given transmission category, the models do not readily commute between aggregate and ethnic-specific disease patterns. This may reflect data instabilities associated with relatively small AIDS counts for some ethnicities and transmission categories. Alternatively, it may suggest the presence of, as yet unidentified, ethnically determined factors which have influenced the distribution of AIDS (see, for example, Chaisson et al., 1989). Second, the forecasting model described in section 5 is a preliminary model calibrated on woefully inadequate serial data. Until high-resolution data – in both the spatial and temporal domains – enter the public realm, local-area forecasting models will remain little more than academic exercises.

The future outlook for San Francisco is not apocalytpic, but it is gloomy. Levels of HIV infection are already such that, in the absence of a cure, the city's AIDS epidemic will continue to spiral in the foreseeable future. With the recent change in the surveillance definition for AIDS in the USA (Centers for Disease Control, 1992b), new AIDS cases are expected to be diagnosed in San Francisco at a rate of 170 per month during the 1990s, with a cumulative total approaching 30,000 by the year 2000 (Hirozawa et al., 1992). The concomitant burden on the health services will be enormous; probably as many as 9,000 people will be living with AIDS in any one year, while the total annual costs of the disease may reach US$300 million (Hirozawa et al., 1992; Smallman-Raynor, Cliff, and

Haggett, 1992). Continued collaboration among geographers, medical scientists and outreach workers which leads to a clearer understanding of the distribution of the disease can only increase our chances of averting the worst excesses of the San Francisco AIDS epidemic.

APPENDIX 1

To produce figure 9.9, heterosexual IVDU AIDS incidences for each of three ethnic groups (Whites, Blacks and Hispanics) were first reduced to a rate per 100,000 ethnic-specific population. Cells with values at, or above, 83.6 per 100,000 (that is, cells falling in the highest choropleth category of figure 9.8) were then defined as having high AIDS rates. These high incidence cells are mapped in figure 9.9. Cells recording high rates in Whites are identified by the letter *W*, Blacks by the letter *B* and Hispanics by the letter *H*; combinations of *W*, *B* and *H* mark cells in which high AIDS rates coincided for two or more ethnicities.

APPENDIX 2

As described in Sampson and Groves (1989), *SES* in equation (9.1) is formed by reducing three indicators of social class (proportion of the population with college education; proportion in managerial/professional employment; proportion with very high incomes), measured across a set of geographical units, to standard Normal scores (*z*-scores). The three scores for each unit are then summed and ranked to give its *SES*; rank 1 denotes the highest socio-economic status, and so on. Finally, percentage of population below the poverty level is calculated as a sample estimate defined by the US Bureau of the Census. It follows from equation (9.1) that high *PI* scores identify relatively poor districts, while low scores identify relatively prosperous districts.

ACKNOWLEDGEMENT

I am grateful to Dr Michael R. Aldrich of the California AIDS Intervention Training Center, San Francisco, and Dr Rodrick Wallace of New York State Psychiatric Institute, New York City, for providing material cited in this paper.

NOTES

1 In this chapter, the term *homosexual* encompasses all males, including bisexuals, who reported sexual liaisons with other males. The term *intravenous drug user* is abbreviated to IVDU; sexual orientation is indicated where appropriate. Homosexuals with no history of intravenous drug use are referred to as *homosexual non-IVDU*. All references

to Human Immunodeficiency Virus (HIV) relate to Human Immunodeficiency Virus type 1.

2 Probabilities have been computed by reducing AIDS rates to standard Normal score form and comparing them to the Normal distribution; the three darkest shading categories denote significantly high incidence at the 1, 5 and 10 per cent levels in a one-tailed test. The two lighter shading categories flag whether non-significant incidence rates are above (stippled circles) or below (open circles) the average rate.

REFERENCES

Aldrich, M.R. & Mandel, J. (1989). 'Estimating intravenous drug user (IVDU) population from AIDS statistics in San Francisco.' *V International Conference on AIDS*, Montreal, Abstract TH.A.P.68.

Aldrich, M.R., Mandel, J., & Newmeyer, J.A. (1990). 'A spreadsheet for AIDS: estimating heterosexual injection drug user population size from AIDS statistics in San Francisco.' *Journal of Psychoactive Drugs*, 22, 343–9.

Aldrich, M.R., Payne, S.F., Little, S.M., Mandel, J., & Feldman, H.W. (1990). 'Classic epidemiological mapping of AIDS among San Francisco drug injectors, 1987–1989.' *VI International Conference on AIDS*, San Francisco, Abstract Th.C.705.

Biggar, R.J., Nasca, P., & Burnett, W.S. (1988). 'AIDS-related Kaposi's sarcoma in New York City in 1977.' *New England Journal of Medicine*, 318, 252.

Casetti, E. (1972). 'Generating models by the expansion method: applications to geographic research.' *Geographical Analysis*, 4, 81–91.

Casetti, E. & Fan, C.C. (1991). 'The spatial spread of the AIDS epidemic in Ohio: empirical analyses using the expansion method.' *Environment and Planning A*, 23, 1589–608.

Castells, M. (1983). *The City and the Grass Roots: a Cross-Cultural Theory of Urban Social Movements*. London: Edward Arnold.

Centers for Disease Control (1992a). *HIV/AIDS Surveillance: US AIDS Cases Reported Through February 1992*. Atlanta, Ga.: US Public Health Service.

Centers for Disease Control (1992b). '1993 revised classification system for HIV infection and expanded surveillance case definition for AIDS among adolescents and adults.' *Morbidity and Mortality Weekly Report*, 41 (RR–17), 1–19.

Chaisson, R.E., Bacchetti, P., Osmond, D., Brodie, B., Sande, M.A., & Moss, A.R. (1989). 'Cocaine use and HIV infection in intravenous drug users in San Francisco.' *Journal of the American Medical Association*, 261, 561–5.

Chaisson, R.E., Moss, A.R., Onishi, R., Osmond, D., & Carlson, J.R. (1987). 'Human immunodeficiency virus infection in heterosexual intravenous drug users in San Francisco.' *American Journal of Public Health*, 77, 169–72.

Cliff, A.D. & Haggett, P. (1988). *Atlas of Disease Distributions: Analytic Approaches to Epidemiological Data*. Oxford: Blackwell Reference.

Cliff, A.D., Haggett, P., & Ord, J.K. (1986). *Spatial Aspects of Influenza Epidemics*. London: Pion.

Cohen, P.T., Sande, M.A., & Volberding, P.A. (eds) (1990). *The AIDS Knowledge Base*. Massachusetts: Massachusetts Medical Society Publishing Group.

Cohn, S.E., van der Horst, C.M., Klein, J.D., & Weber, D.J. (1991). 'Migration of HIV-positive patients to North Carolina.' *VII International Conference on AIDS*, Florence, Abstract M.C.3219.

Costagliola, D., Laporte, A., Chevret, S., & Valleron, A.J. (1990). 'Incubation time for AIDS among homosexual and pediatric cases.' *VI International Conference on AIDS*, San Francisco, Abstract Th.C.661.

Des Jarlais, D.C., Friedman, S.R., Novick, D.M., Sotheran, J.L., Thomas, P., Yancovitz, S.R., Mildvan, D., Weber, J., Kreek, M.J., Maslansky, R., Bartelme, S., Spira, T., & Marmor, M. (1989). 'HIV-1 infection among intravenous drug users in Manhattan, New York City, from 1977 through 1987.' *Journal of the American Medical Association*, 261, 1008–12.

Dondero, T.J., Allen, D.M., McCray, E., Gwinn, M., Conway, G.A., Onorato, I.M., & Selik, R.M. (1991). 'Injected drug abuse: the driving force for much of the U.S. HIV epidemic.' *VII International Conference on AIDS*, Florence, Abstract W.C.3356.

Friedland, G.H., Harris, C., Butkus-Small, C., Shine, D., Moll, B., Darrow, W., & Klein, R.S. (1985). 'Intravenous drug abusers and the acquired immunodeficiency syndrome (AIDS): demographic, drug use, and needle sharing patterns.' *Archives of Internal Medicine*, 145, 1413–7.

Gould, P. (1993). *The Slow Plague: A Geography of the AIDS Pandemic*. Cambridge, Mass: Blackwell.

Guinan, M.E., Thomas, P.A., Pinsky, P.F., Goodrich, J.T., Selik, R.M., Jaffe, H.W., Haverkos, H.W., Noble, G., & Curran, J.W. (1984). 'Heterosexual and homosexual patients with the acquired immunodeficiency syndrome. A comparison of surveillance, interview and laboratory data.' *Annals of Internal Medicine*, 100, 213–18.

Haggett, P., Cliff, A.D., & Frey, A. (1977). *Locational Analysis in Human Geography* (2nd edn). London: Edward Arnold.

Hessol, N.A., Lifson, A.R., O'Malley, P.M., Doll, L.S., Jaffe, H.W., & Rutherford, G.W. (1989). 'Prevalence, incidence, and progression of human immunodeficiency virus infection in homosexual and bisexual men in hepatitis B vaccine trials, 1978–1988.' *American Journal of Epidemiology*, 130, 1167–75.

Hethcote, H.W., Van Ark, J.W., & Karon, J.M. (1991). 'A simulation model of AIDS in San Francisco: II. Simulations, therapy and sensitivity analysis.' *Mathematical Biosciences*, 106, 223–47.

Hethcote, H.W., Van Ark, J., & Longini, I.R. (1991). 'A simulation model of AIDS in San Francisco: I. Model formulation and parameter estimation.' *Mathematical Biosciences*, 106, 203–22.

Hirozawa, A.M., Lemp, G.F., Canabarro, G.M., Hessol, N.A., & Katz, M.H. (1992). 'Projections of the AIDS epidemic in San Francisco through 1997: impact of the new AIDS case definition.' *VIII International Conference on AIDS/III STD World Congress*, Amsterdam, Abstract PoC 4467.

Moss, A.R., Bacchetti, P., Gorman, M., Dritz, S., Abrams, D.I., Volberding, P., & Ziegler, J. (1983). 'AIDS in the "gay" areas of San Francisco.' *Lancet*, I, 923–4.

Moss, A.R., Bacchetti, P., Osmond, D., Dritz, S., Abrams, D., Conant, M., Volberding, P., & Ziegler, J. (1985). 'Incidence of the acquired immunodeficiency syndrome in San Francisco, 1980–83.' *Journal of Infectious Diseases*, 152, 152–61.

Newmeyer, J. (1991). 'The Aldrich model: a 1988 prediction hits within 1% of target.' *MidCity Numbers*, 4/9, 1–2.

Sampson, R. & Groves, W.B. (1989). 'Community structure and crime: testing social disorganization theory.' *American Journal of Sociology*, 94, 774–802.

San Francisco Department of Public Health AIDS Office (1992). *AIDS Reported Cases: From 7/81 to 05/31/92*. San Francisco, Ca.: Department of Public Health.

Saunders, L.D., Rutherford, G.W., Lemp, G.F., & Barnhart, J.L. (1990). 'Impact of AIDS on mortality in San Francisco, 1979–1986.' *Journal of Acquired Immune Deficiency Syndromes*, 3, 921–4.

Selik, R.M., Chu, S.Y., & Buehler, J.W. (1993). 'HIV infection as leading cause of death among young adults in US cities and states.' *Journal of the American Medical Association*, 269, 2991–4.

Shannon, G.W., Pyle, G.F., & Bashshur, R. (1991). *The Geography of AIDS*. New York: The Guilford Press.

Shilts, R. (1987). *And the Band Played On: Politics, People and the AIDS Epidemic*. London: Penguin.

Smallman-Raynor, M.R., Cliff, A.D., & Haggett, P. (1992). *Atlas of AIDS*. Oxford: Blackwell Reference.

US Department of Commerce, Bureau of the Census (1983). *1980 Census of Population and Housing: Census Tracts, San Francisco–Oakland Calif. Standard Metropolitan Statistical Area*. Washington: Department of Commerce.

Wallace, R. (1988). 'A synergism of plagues: 'planned shrinkage,' contagious housing destruction, and AIDS in the Bronx.' *Environmental Research*, 47, 1–33.

Wallace, R. (1991). *Urban Decay and AIDS in New York City: Public Policy and Disease Ecology*. New York City: R. Wallace, New York State Psychiatric Institute, Office of Mental Health.

Winkelstein, W., Samual, M., Padian, N.S., Wiley, J.A., Lang, W., Anderson, R.E., & Levy, J.A. (1987). 'The San Francisco men's health study: III. reduction in human immunodeficiency virus transmission among homosexual/bisexual men 1982–86.' *American Journal of Public Health*, 77, 685–9.

10

Spatial Point Process Modelling of Cancer Data within a Geographical Information Systems Framework

A.C. Gatrell

1 INTRODUCTION

The treatment of some geographical phenomena as a set of points distributed in space has a long and rich tradition, as the updated edition of Haggett's magisterial synthesis suggests (Haggett, Cliff, and Frey, 1977). Within human geography such phenomena have included settlements, retail stores and the locations of innovation adopters. The present work has three broad aims. First, to show how to extend the class of methods traditionally used by geographers to explore and model point patterns. Second, to show how such methods can be used to shed light on epidemiological data: specifically, the geographical distribution of two cancers (those of the larynx and prostate) within relatively small areas of Britain. A third aim is to show how the methods outlined can be embedded within the framework of a Geographical Information System (GIS). As is argued elsewhere (Gatrell and Rowlingson, 1993), spatial analysis within GIS environments is a little primitive, though research at a number of institutions is rectifying this deficiency.

Traditionally, research in the field of 'spatial' or 'geographical' epidemiology has relied on the aggregation of patient-based data (either mortality or morbidity) to a set of areal units; in Britain these are usually health districts or, at a smaller scale, electoral wards (see Lovett and Gatrell, 1988, Gatrell, 1986, for examples). More refined work has led to substantial improvements on this mapping, using empirical Bayes estimates of disease rates (Clayton and Kaldor, 1987). Other research, especially that concerned with assessing possible links between the incidence of childhood leukaemias and proximity to nuclear installations (see Hills and Alexander, 1989, for a review), has defined circular zones around such point sources and estimated relative risks within distance bands.

All such approaches suffer from the modifiable areal unit problem (Openshaw, 1984; see also Wrigley in chapter 4 of this volume). In other words, the areas used, whether irregular polygonal regions or annuli around point sources, are essentially arbitrarily defined and the results obtained are specific to the configuration of areal units used in those studies. With this problem in mind, might it not be possible to use instead spatially-referenced data on the individuals themselves? This is the approach adopted here.

Following such a strategy assumes that individual data are available. Although in Britain individual patient addresses are not, in general, made available to researchers, it is possible to get access to postcoded data. Unit postcodes (for example, LA2 8LD) relate, on average, to about 16 households. There are some 1.7 million unit postcodes in the country and a computer file (the Central Postcode Directory, or CPD) relates each of these to an Ordnance Survey grid reference. In England and Wales these have a resolution of 100 metres (10 metres in Scotland). Further details, and an evaluation of the CPD, are available in Gatrell, Dunn, and Boyle (1991). Thus, given a set of postcoded data, such as cases of cancer from a Cancer Registry, grid references can be obtained and the data mapped and analysed as a point pattern.

2 SPATIAL POINT PROCESS MODELLING

It is useful to distinguish between exploratory methods, for instance those which seek to detect clustering in disease data, from more confirmatory approaches that, for example, attempt to model the raised incidence of rare diseases around suspected point or linear sources of pollution. What tools are available to help us understand the distribution of disease data when treated as a set of points?

In the statistical analysis of point processes (Diggle, 1983) we can distinguish between 'first-order' and 'second-order' descriptions of the data. A first-order measure is the intensity function $\lambda(x)$, representing the mean number of points per unit area in the neighbourhood of location x. If the point process is stationary and intensity does not vary with location then λ is a constant. In general, however, because population is distributed heterogeneously in space λ will vary with location.

A second-order measure is the so-called K-function, $K(s)$, where s denotes distance. This is interpreted as the expected number of further points within distance s of an arbitrarily chosen point, scaled by the expected number of points in any subregion. For a stationary Poisson process, $K(s) = \pi s^2$, but although this serves as a useful benchmark against which to assess departures from randomness it is of little value in spatial epidemiology because complete spatial randomness is not a useful null model for population distribution.

It is more useful, in spatial epidemiology, to envisage bivariate point processes, in which we have two qualitatively different types of point. We can think of these as a set of disease 'cases' and a set of 'controls', either healthy individuals or those perhaps suffering from some other illness. We can then consider intensity functions for each set separately and, of more relevance in what follows, two different K functions, one for cases, the other for controls. For example, and using the subscript 1 to denote cases, $K_{11}(s)$ is the expected number of cases within a distance s of an arbitrarily chosen case, scaled by the intensity of cases. Now, if we combine the sets of cases and controls and imagine randomly labelling each point in turn as a case or control, we would expect the two K-functions to be identical. Alternatively, if there is any evidence of clustering of cases with respect to controls we would expect the two functions to be different. We estimate the K-function for cases as follows (that for controls is similarly defined):

$$\hat{K}_{11}(s) = |A| \{n_1(n_1 - 1)\}^{-1} \sum_{i=1}^{n_1} \sum_{j=1}^{n_1} w_{ij} I(d_{ij} \leq s) \tag{10.1}$$

where $|A|$ denotes the size of region, n_1 is the number of cases and $I(\cdot)$ takes the value 1 if $d_{ij} \leq s$, 0 otherwise. The $\{w_{ij}\}$ are a set of weights for correcting edge effects; w_{ij}^{-1} is the proportion, contained in area A, of the circumference of a disc centred on location i, of radius d_{ij}.

A test for spatial clustering (Diggle and Chetwynd, 1991) is then based on:

$$\hat{D}(s) = \hat{K}_{11}(s) - \hat{K}_{22}(s) \tag{10.2}$$

and a test statistic is given as:

$$D = \sum_{j=1}^{m} \hat{D}(s_j) / \sqrt{[\text{var}\{\hat{D}(s_j)\}]} \tag{10.3}$$

where s_j $(j = 1, \ldots, m)$ is the set of inter-point distances thought to be of epidemiological relevance and $\text{var}\{\hat{D}(s_j)\}$ is the set of variances of $\hat{D}(s_j)$ under the random labelling of cases and controls. In order to assess the significance of D, we may use Monte Carlo simulation, ranking the observed value of D amongst values of D obtained by randomly permuting the cases and controls. If, out of say 99 simulations, the observed D ranks within the first five values we can say that there is significant clustering at the 0.05 probability level.

We now consider some confirmatory analysis, where we wish to test the hypothesis that there is raised incidence of a disease in the vicinity of a suspected point source of pollution. A full treatment is available in Diggle (1990). Let $x = (x_1, x_2)$ denote location and consider a model of the following form:

$$\lambda(x) = \rho \lambda_0(x) f(x; \alpha, \beta) \tag{10.4}$$

where $\lambda(x)$ is an intensity function describing the disease of interest, $\lambda_0(x)$ is the intensity function for the population at risk, ρ is a scaling parameter, and $f(\cdot)$ describes the way in which incidence is hypothesized to vary with distance from the point source. A suitable functional form for $f(\cdot)$ is:

$$f(x; \alpha, \beta) = 1 + \alpha \, e^{-\beta d^2} \tag{10.5}$$

where d is distance from the point source and α and β are parameters to be estimated. Clearly, interest centres on these parameters (an intercept and 'distance decay' term, respectively), since, if they are not significantly different from zero, then disease intensity simply equals the intensity of background population distribution, scaled by ρ. This represents the null hypothesis of no distance decay effect. If α and β are significantly different from zero the alternative hypothesis of an association with the possible point source of pollution is accepted.

Estimates of ρ, α and β are generated by maximum likelihood methods, details of which are given in Diggle (1990). The log-likelihood is evaluated for the null model (when $\alpha = \beta = 0$) and compared with the maximum value. The main problem in fitting the model, however, is to determine a suitable description of the population at risk. There are a variety of possibilities. One is to use data on healthy controls. Another is to use data on another disease, one not thought to be linked to the point source in question. This option is used in the empirical work on cancer of the larynx, described below. A third option is to use a random sample of postcodes within the study area, but to bias the selection of these according to the age structure of the population. This kind of 'microsimulation' approach is discussed below and used in the work on prostate cancer.

Once the population at risk has been defined as a set of point data the model outlined above requires methods that will convert this into an intensity function. This is done using 'kernel estimation', a technique for estimating a continuous surface from data at discrete locations (Silverman, 1986).

3 MODELLING IN A GIS ENVIRONMENT

Having outlined some possible analytical methods for dealing with point patterns in an epidemiological context we now consider the extent to which they may be embedded within a GIS framework. Currently, few GISs offer much capability for spatial analysis, and even fewer for the kind of point process modelling that we wish to conduct here. As Goodchild, Haining, and Wise (1992) observe, we need to decide what approach we wish to pursue. We could, for instance, develop free-standing spatial analysis software or, at the other extreme, seek a complete integration of spatial statistical analysis into a proprietary GIS. Alternatively, we can develop a 'loose coupling' between a statistical package and a GIS, with data imported to and exported from either of the components in a reasonably seamless way. Or, we might have a 'close coupling', seeking either to embed a limited set of statistical functions within the GIS or to add some GIS tools into an analytical package.

Work at Lancaster University has explored both the 'coupling' options. Within the proprietary GIS ARC/INFO we have implemented both the exploratory K-function estimation and the confirmatory raised incidence model (Gatrell and Rowlingson, 1993). Each of these is embodied in external FORTRAN code, but within these programs calls are made to ARC/INFO routines and point and polygon coverages are thereby accessed. New ARC/INFO commands are created using the ARC Macro Language, with parameters corresponding to particular coverage names required to run the spatial analysis functions. Examples are given below for both larynx and prostate cancers.

A 'close coupling' has been developed within the framework of the statistical programming language *S*-Plus (Rowlingson and Diggle, 1993). This language has a series of built-in functions but also permits users to develop their own code for performing analysis and to have this included as a set of new functions. For example, Rowlingson and Diggle have added a suite of point process tools into S-Plus, including those for the second-order analysis of point data and density estimation. Display facilities within this environment are excellent. Although the system is not a 'fully-blown' GIS it does allow digital boundaries to be displayed and used for functions such as point-in-polygon searches.

4 THE GEOGRAPHY OF CANCER

There is a long tradition of mapping and analysing geographical variations in cancer incidence, at all spatial scales (see Howe, 1986, for example). Both geographers and epidemiologists have sought to examine associations between the distributions of some cancers and environmental factors. The present paper looks at two cancers in particular, examining the evidence concerning certain risk factors as a context for subsequent empirical work that seeks to model possible links to air pollution.

4.1 Cancer of the larynx: risk factors

Laryngeal carcinoma (ICD code 161) is relatively uncommon, the highest reported incidences being about 12.5 per 100,000 males in Turin, Italy, and 7.8 per 100,000 males in Poland. The disease shows a very marked sex bias, with about seven cases among males for every female case recorded (Kleinsasser, 1988).

The consensus in the epidemiological literature is that the main risk factors implicated in cancer of the larynx are exposure to cigarette smoke and alcohol (Rothman et al., 1980; Burch et al., 1981; Guénel et al., 1988; Kleinsasser, 1988). Work by Guénel et al. (1988) suggests that the effect of these factors is synergistic; in other words, the risk of developing the cancer multiplies when both alcohol and tobacco are consumed in excess.

4.1.1 Occupational environment. Lynch et al. (1979) found raised incidence of laryngeal cancer among those manufacturing isopropyl alcohol, high concentrations of diethyl sulphate being implicated as the carcinogen. The risk of the cancer appeared elevated among barbers, leather workers, painters and some chemical workers in Buffalo, with the inhalation of (unspecified) toxic fumes considered as a possible risk factor (Viadana, Bross, and Hoten, 1976).

Asbestos fibres are thought to be a causative factor, although there are likely to be confounding variables, such as smoking, involved in aetiology (Stell and McGill, 1975). Some studies (Freifeld, 1977; Burch et al., 1981) have controlled for smoking and conclude that exposure to asbestos is indeed a risk factor. Burch et al. (1981) also suggested elevated risks for those who had worked in foundries and metal processing.

4.1.2 Products of incomplete combustion. Particular attention is focused on these substances because of the hypothesis tested below. In the most thorough available review of risk factors Kleinsasser (1988) refers to the role of polycyclic aromatic hydrocarbons (PAHs). These are known carcinogens, whose presence in tar from cigarettes is the likely explanation for the role of tobacco in carcinogenesis. As by-products of combustion PAHs are produced in several industrial processes. Interestingly, a plausible biochemical explanation of the possible association between PAHs and laryngeal cancer has emerged. PAHs are activated in cells by an enzyme called aryl hydrocarbon hydroxylase, thereby causing damage to DNA. Evidence exists (Trell et al., 1976) that the 'inducibility' of this enzyme is substantially raised in patients with laryngeal carcinoma.

4.2 Cancer of the prostate: risk factors

There appears to be a quite substantial global variation in the incidence of this cancer (ICD code 185), with age-adjusted death rates ranging from about 25 per 100,000 in the US, to under 5 per 100,000 in Japan (Wynder, Mabuchi, and Whitmore, 1971). The incidence among Japanese immigrants to the US is considerably higher than in Japan. This suggests that an environmental factor may be implicated in disease aetiology. Some research, based on a case-control study (Armenian et al., 1975), suggests that there may be hormonal factors involved in increasing this cancer risk.

Since the spatial modelling that follows has access to very limited data on individuals, and since it attempts to explore and to model spatial variation in incidence (particularly in relation to possible point sources of pollution) comments on disease aetiology concentrate on two hypothesized risk factors: cadmium exposure and radiation.

4.2.1 Cadmium exposure. Cadmium is widely distributed in nature and is released into the environment by the smelting and refining of lead and zinc ores, by the recovery of scrap metals, by the combustion of coal and oil, and by the disposal of sewage sludge (Gloag, 1981). A critical exposure pathway (Gloag, 1981; Kazantzis, 1990) is via the transfer from soil to crops. A well-known instance of this was the presence of very high levels of cadmium in soils in the village of Shipham in Somerset (the site of an old zinc mine), leading to high concentrations in locally grown leafy vegetables. Interestingly, the old local authority of Axbridge, within whose boundaries Shipham lay, had, between 1968 and 1978, an elevated risk of prostatic cancer (Gardner, Winter, and Barker, 1983).

Kipling and Waterhouse (1967) were the first to suggest that there might be an association between cadmium exposure and prostatic cancer. They looked at occupational exposure to cadmium in a plant manufacturing cadmium-nickel batteries and found four cases of prostatic cancer where fewer than one was expected. Winkelstein and Kantor (1969) followed this with a geographical study in Erie County, New York State, finding that raised mortality from prostatic cancer was associated with higher levels of suspended particulate matter in ambient air. However, cadmium levels were not measured directly.

In a further geographical study, Bako et al. (1982) examined the association between cadmium concentrations in water supplies and the incidence of prostatic cancer in Alberta. Incidence of prostatic cancer was significantly elevated in the city of Medicine Hat; here, local residents drew water from the South Saskatchewan River, fed by tributaries that transport wastes from upstream industry and that drain irrigated land. These waters had high cadmium concentrations. Incidence of the cancer was much lower in those areas that had less contaminated water supplies. In a similar study, Garcia-Sanchez and others (1992) suggested evidence of a link between excess cadmium in local soils and stream sediments and the incidence of prostate cancer in part of Spain. However, few details are given and their observation (p. 224) that 'it is currently accepted that there is a relationship between cadmium and this disease' cannot be accepted unequivocally.

Although lacking data on exposure to cadmium, or geographical variations in cadmium concentrations, Blair and Fraumeni (1978) reported elevated risks of prostatic cancer in US counties with metal-using industries (such as primary metals, fabricated metal products, and machinery). Some counties in the North Central and North-eastern states display clustering of elevated rates.

The literature on links between those occupationally exposed to cadmium and prostatic cancer is contradictory. Lemen et al. (1976) found a small excess of the cancer in American smelter workers, but criticisms have been levelled at this research for an inadequate control for exposure to risk factors such as cigarette consumption and exposure to arsenic. Elinder et al. (1985) combined data from six separate studies and confirmed a link between cadmium exposure and prostatic cancer. However, an extensive cohort study (summarized in Kazantzis, 1990), investigating several thousand British workers exposed to cadmium, detected no increased risk of carcinoma of the prostate; interestingly, there did appear to be an increased risk of lung and stomach cancer. Kazantzis concludes that it 'appears exceedingly unlikely that cadmium, at least under current exposure conditions, would give rise to an increased risk of prostatic cancer' (Kazantzis, 1990, p. 132).

4.2.2 Radiation. There have been several recent speculations concerning links between radiation exposure and prostate cancer. Examining death certificates of those who had worked at the Sellafield nuclear reprocessing plant in Cumbria, Smith and Douglas (1986) found 19 deaths from the cancer, compared with 15.8 expected; however, this was not statistically significant. For those employed at the Atomic Energy Authority plants at Harwell, Dounreay, and Winfrith there was convincing evidence that mortality from prostate cancer is significantly related to cumulative radiation exposure; this was irrespective of whether no latent period, or a lag of 15 years, was assumed (Beral et al., 1985).

Henshaw and his colleagues (1990) have reported some aggregate geographical correlations among 15 countries (and, separately, for Canadian provinces) between various cancers and exposure to radon and radon daughters (such as polonium). Such cancers included acute myeloid leukaemia, kidney and skin, but not lung or stomach. Subsequently (Eatough and Henshaw, 1990), they analysed data on prostate cancer and found a high correlation between radon exposure and this cancer, both for the same set of countries and within the UK. They reasoned that alpha-emitting particles may lodge in the prostate. They further suggested that the possibility of such particles lodging in the male reproductive organs could be one mechanism whereby cancers are induced in the children of radiation workers.

5 SPATIAL MODELLING OF CANCER DATA

We now consider the fitting of a spatial model to data on incidence of both cancers, as outlined in section 2. In both cases data have been drawn from Cancer Registries and postcodes converted to grid references.

5.1 Spatial modelling of larynx cancer

The empirical work described here arose as a result of exploratory mapping of various cancers in the vicinity of a former industrial waste incinerator. This operated between 1972 and 1980 at a site about 2 kilometres south-west of the small town of Coppull in Lancashire. It was used for the disposal of a wide range of wastes, both liquids (mainly oils and solvents) and solids.

No visual evidence of 'clustering' appeared, with the exception of a suspicious aggregation of cancers of the larynx in Coppull, downwind of the incinerator. The spatial model outlined in section 2 was developed by Diggle (1990) and applied by Diggle, Gatrell, and Lovett (1990) to test whether there was locally raised incidence.

As noted in section 2 the model to be fitted requires data on the distribution of 'background population'. Initially (Diggle, Gatrell, and Lovett, 1990), we took data on the distribution of a much commoner cancer, that of the lung, to represent this, since there is some support in the literature for using other cancers as controls (Smith, Pearce, and Callas, 1988).

We have fitted the model within an ARC/INFO environment, as described in Gatrell and Rowlingson (1993). This environment allows any location of interest to be selected as a putative point source (in a manner similar to Openshaw's Geographical Analysis Machine: Openshaw et al., 1987). Here, we fit the model using a location not far from the site of the former incinerator. The GIS allows us to display the cases and controls and, in a separate window, to list model outputs (figure 10.1).

The null model gives a log-likelihood of -447.55, while the maximum log-likelihood is -439.55, with parameter estimates $\hat{\alpha} = 14.15$ and $\hat{\beta} = 0.76$. Twice the difference between the two likelihoods gives a statistic that is distributed as chi-square; this is significant at the 0.05 level and we may reject the null hypothesis of no association between intensity of cancer of the larynx and proximity to the incinerator. Additional work (Gatrell and Dunn, 1993) addressed criticisms over the choice of lung cancers as controls by using stomach cancers as an alternative set of controls. The conclusions remained the same.

One improvement to the selection of controls is to avoid using other cancers.

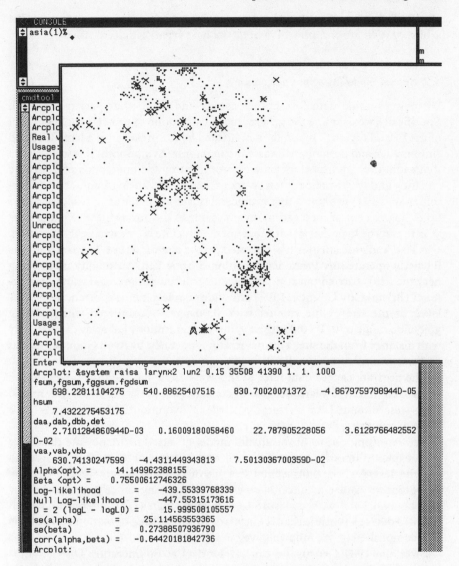

Figure 10.1 Modelling raised incidence of larynx cancer in part of Lancashire within an ARC/INFO environment

The modelling approach requires other point data, and this appears to rule out the use of Census data. However, some progress can be made here using a microsimulation approach, as shown in an examination of cancer of the prostate. At a rather crude level, we might use the set of all postcodes in the study area in order to define controls. When we do this and repeat the model-fitting exercise we again find our conclusions unchanged.

Of course, none of this means that cancer of the larynx is caused by proximity to the incinerator. However, it does establish an hypothesis that bears more rigorous scrutiny around other sites. This has now been attempted (Elliott et al., 1992), but by using the same set of techniques (such as imposing circles of arbitrary radii around sites of interest) as have been criticized earlier.

5.2 Spatial modelling of prostate cancer

We now examine data for another cancer and in another part of England. Specifically, we examine the geographical distribution of prostate cancer in part of the Bristol region. This study is motivated by the presence of a large lead and zinc smelter and a municipal waste incinerator in Avonmouth. It is well known that cadmium is released into the environment by the operations of both zinc smelting and waste incineration. Work at the Warren Spring Laboratory (Clayton et al., 1991) estimates that municipal waste incineration is responsible for up to 23 per cent of total cadmium emissions to the atmosphere. We therefore seek to test the hypothesis that cancer of the prostate is elevated near these sites.

A lead and zinc smelter has operated on the site for about 75 years and was formerly operated by Pasminco Smelting Europe Ltd. Air quality monitoring near the site is carried out regularly by the local Environmental Health Department (Bristol City Council, 1991) and cadmium levels are reported. In 1990–1 levels at the site of the smelter were 0.06 $\mu g/m^3$ (compared with a WHO guideline range of $0.01–0.02$ $\mu g/m^3$), but concentrations fell away dramatically with distance from the site. The incinerator is operated by Avon County Council and was commissioned in 1972.

The prostate cancer data refer to the years 1979–89. We look only at those cases aged under 75 years, because of concerns about diagnosis in older males. Data were obtained for a region centred on Avonmouth; this generated 167 cases of prostate cancer.

Before setting out to fit the spatial model of raised incidence the data have been explored in order to see if there is any evidence of clustering. In order to use the test described in section 2 a set of controls is required. It may be inappropriate to use a cancer such as that of the lung, since lung cancer may also be associated with exposure to cadmium. Instead, an attempt has been made to devise a sensible set of controls drawn from the population at risk. This is accomplished in the following way.

From the 1981 Census, we can extract data at Enumeration District (ED) level on the distribution of the male population by five-year age groups (45–49, 50–54, . . . , 70–74). We also extract centroids of EDs in order that we may construct pseudo-ED boundaries; in general, boundaries of EDs used in the 1981 Census were not digitized, so Thiessen polygons (Haggett, Cliff, and Frey, 1977, p. 436) have been used instead (figure 10.2). Applying region-wide data on the incidence of prostate cancer by age group we can determine a 'weighted' population for each ED:

$$Y_i = \sum_j w_j P_{ij} \tag{10.6}$$

where P_{ij} is the male population in age group j in the i-th ED, w_j is the incidence rate for prostate cancer among males in age group j, and Y_i is the weighted

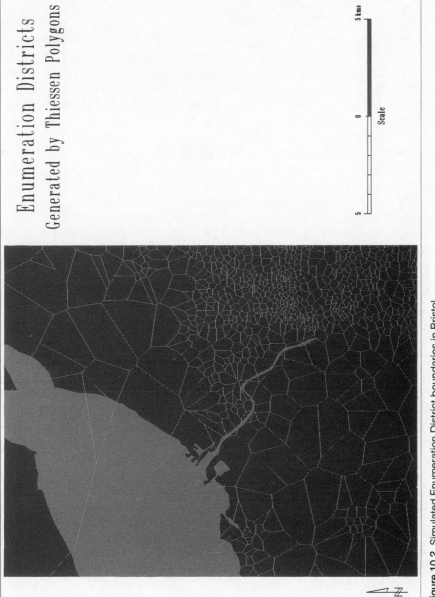

Enumeration Districts
Generated by Thiessen Polygons

Scale

5   0   5 kms

Figure 10.2 Simulated Enumeration District boundaries in Bristol

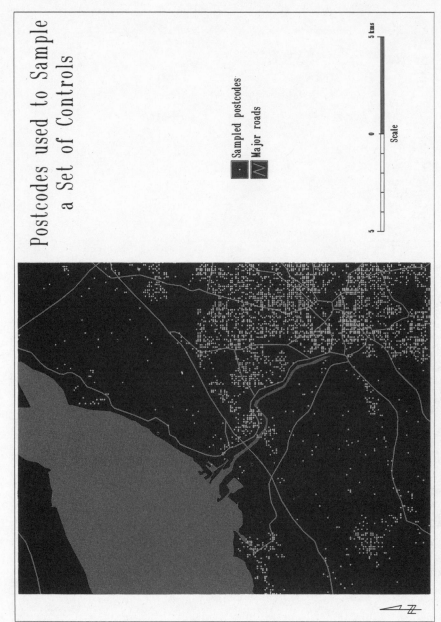

Postcodes used to Sample a Set of Controls

Sampled postcodes
Major roads

Scale

5   0   5 kms

Figure 10.3 Grid references of unit postcodes in Bristol

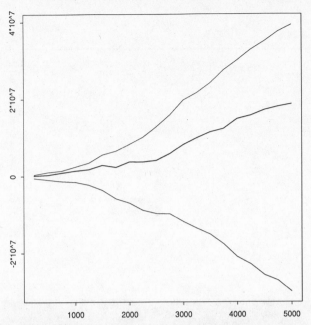

D-function and envelope from 99 Random Labellings

Figure 10.4   A test for the existence of spatial clustering of prostate cancers

population in the i-th ED. We may then use these weighted populations as a sampling frame and draw a random number that corresponds to a particular ED. For instance if $Y_i = 2Y_k$, where k represents another ED, then i is twice as likely to be chosen as k.

Having selected a particular ED as the location of a potential 'control' we need some way of assigning it to a postcode. This has been done by selecting, at random, postcodes that lie within the pseudo-ED boundaries. The set of all candidate postcodes is shown in figure 10.3. We have chosen $3n = 501$ controls, where n is the number of cases of prostate cancer.

We are now in a position to obtain estimates of the K-functions and hence an estimate of $D(s)$ as outlined earlier. Results (figure 10.4) indicate that there is no evidence of clustering of the prostate cancers with respect to controls, since the difference, $\hat{D}(s)$, between the two K-functions lies well within the upper and lower confidence bounds.

We now proceed to fit the raised incidence model, using as a location of interest the smelter (the incinerator occupies a location very close to the smelter, within one kilometre, and it makes little sense to separate the locations as possible independent influences on disease incidence). We hypothesize that intensity of prostate cancer is a function of background population (as measured now by the 'control' postcodes) and proximity to the point source.

Visual evidence, a simple comparison of the prostate cancers and controls

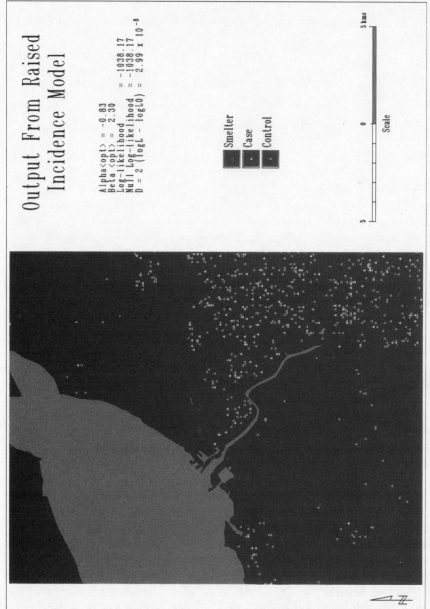

Figure 10.5 Modelling raised incidence of prostate cancer in Bristol

(shown together in figure 10.5), suggests that the hypothesis is unlikely to be upheld and the statistical modelling (also reported in figure 10.5) confirms this. The null log-likelihood and the maximized log-likelihood are identical. We conclude that there is no evidence that the combined point source (smelter and incinerator) has had any effect on, or association with, the geographical incidence of prostate cancer.

6 CONCLUSIONS

There are a number of ways in which this analytical framework can be extended, as well as a number of limitations that need addressing.

It should be clear that spatial epidemiological modelling is now possible within a GIS environment. Although such modelling does not require such an environment it would seem that a GIS framework is a natural setting and permits the ready assessment of the existence, or otherwise, of clustering, as well as the evaluation of locations thought to be putative sources of environmental contamination. It should be appreciated, however, that the main advantage of a GIS is the ability to integrate disparate data sets and to model associations between such data sets. For example, work needs to be undertaken on modelling associations between points (such as road traffic accidents) located on a network rather than in the plane.

There is scope for refining the modelling of raised incidence. This could take a number of forms. First, the model needs to be expanded to allow for additional covariates. This assumes, of course, that such data are available, but these might include data on smoking or alcohol consumption in the case of laryngeal cancer, for example. Further, we need to develop the model to allow for multiple point sources of pollution. In the case of the prostate cancer study it made no sense to treat the smelter and incinerator as independent influences; but in areas with concentrations of heavy industry we might wish to extend the model in this way; related work by Diggle and Rowlingson (personal communication) is pursuing this.

The major problem with all current geographical epidemiological modelling is the naivety of assumptions concerning exposure. There are several aspects to this. First, areas of risk are not circular in shape, nor does risk necessarily decrease monotonically with distance from the putative source. We know from studies of atmospheric pollution dispersion that pollutants do not disperse isotropically. Dispersion models can be used to predict likely spatial patterns, using information on stack heights, wind speed and direction, and so on. Research by Kingham (1992) has shown how to take the output from such models and put it into a GIS framework in order to define areas of risk.

Secondly, data on cases (and controls) give residential addresses and these fixed locations are used in the modelling. However, we know full well that people do not stay rooted to their home; they may have quite complicated 'activity spaces', based on journeys to work, school, shops, recreational destinations, and so on. The next stage in such modelling is surely to try to build in these other 'exposure opportunities' in order to develop more realistic representations of exposure.

Thirdly, we need some way of taking into account the effects of latency periods. As Elliott et al. (1992) have noted, we need to incorporate a lag period between first exposure to a possible carcinogen and manifestation of the disease. For instance, if we assume a lag of 10 years then only those cases registered at least 10 years after a suspected pollution source became operational would be used in the analysis. This is straightforward to do, but what lag period we use is clearly a matter for debate.

Related to this is the effect of migration. Virtually all current geographical epidemiology has failed to address this question; certainly, it has yet to be explored in a GIS context. We detected raised incidence of cancer of the larynx around an old industrial waste incinerator. Yet no information was available on past residential histories. Had one or more of the cases moved into the area in recent years, having been exposed to pollutants in another part of the country? Had some been exposed to carcinogens from the incinerator, only to move to another part of the country and to appear in another Regional Cancer Registry?

Finally, thought needs to be given to the philosophy underlying such modelling. The approach taken in the larynx cancer example was to derive an hypothesis from the data. The 'positive' result for that cancer does no more than establish an hypothesis for others to test elsewhere (as done by Elliott et al, 1992). The approach taken in the prostate cancer example was to begin with an hypothesis, based on existing literature. The hypothesis was not confirmed. The author takes the view that the deductive testing of hypotheses is more fruitful and scientifically sound than an inductive search for relationships within a GIS framework by overlaying multiple data sets. Regardless of the modelling philosophy, however, there seems plenty of scope for small-scale epidemiological investigations using the tools suggested here.

ACKNOWLEDGEMENTS

This work would have been impossible without help and advice from the following colleagues at Lancaster University: Professor Peter Diggle (Department of Mathematics), Mr Barry Rowlingson and Mrs Isobel Naumann (North West Regional Research Laboratory) and Dr Robin Flowerdew (Department of Geography). Dr Christine Dunn (Department of Geography, University of Durham) and Dr Andrew Lovett (School of Environmental Sciences, University of East Anglia) helped with some of the work on cancer of the larynx. The work on cancer of the prostate was facilitated by generous help from Dr Kieran Morgan (Director of Public Health, Bristol and District Health Authority), Dr Derek Pheby (Director, Cancer Epidemiology Unit, University of Bristol) and Mr Paul Cooper (Assistant Chief Environmental Health Officer, Bristol City Council). Data on cancer of the larynx were supplied by the North West Regional Cancer Registry. The Economic and Social Research Council are also thanked for financial support (grant R000232547).

REFERENCES

Armenian, H.K., Lilienfield, A.M., Diamond, E.L., & Bross, I.D.J. (1975). 'Epidemiologic characteristics of patients with prostatic neoplasms.' *American Journal of Epidemiology*, 102, 47–54.

Bako, G., Smith, E.S.O., Hanson, J., & Dewar, R. (1982). 'The geographical distribution of high cadmium concentrations in the environment and prostate cancer in Alberta.' *Canadian Journal of Public Health*, 73, 92–4.

Beral, V., Inskip, H., Fraser, P., Booth, M., Coleman, D., & Rose, G. (1985). 'Mortality of employees of the United Kingdom Atomic Energy Authority 1946–1979.' *British Medical Journal*, 291, 440–7.

Blair, A. & Fraumeni, J.F. (1978). 'Geographic patterns of prostate cancer in the United States.' *Journal of the National Cancer Institute*, 61, 1379–84.

Bristol City Council, (1991). Air quality in Bristol, 1990–1991, Report of the Chief Environmental Health Officer.

Burch, J.D., Howe, G.R., Miler, A.B., & Semenciw, R. (1981). 'Tobacco, alcohol, asbestos and nickel in the etiology of cancer of the larynx: a case-control study.' *Journal of the National Cancer Institute*, 67, 1219–24.

Clayton, D. & Kaldor, J. (1987). 'Empirical Bayes estimates of age-standardised relative risks for use in disease mapping.' *Biometrics*, 43, 671–81.

Clayton, P., Coleman, P., Leonard, A., Loader, A., Marlowe, I., Mitchell, D., Richardson, S., & Scott, D. (1991). 'Review of municipal solid waste incineration in the UK'. Warren Spring Laboratory, LR 776, Stevenage, Herts.

Diggle, P.J. (1983). *Statistical Analysis of Spatial Point Patterns*. London: Academic Press.

Diggle, P.J. (1990). 'A point process modelling approach to raised incidence of a rare phenomenon in the vicinity of a pre-specified point.' *Journal of the Royal Statistical Society A*, 153, 349–62.

Diggle, P.J. & Chetwynd, A.G. (1991). 'Second-order analysis of spatial clustering for inhomogeneous populations.' *Biometrics*, 47, 1155–63.

Diggle, P.J., Gatrell, A.C., & Lovett, A.A. (1990). 'Modelling the prevalence of cancer of the larynx in part of Lancashire: a new methodology for spatial epidemiology.' In R.W. Thomas (ed.), *Spatial Epidemiology*. London: Pion, 35–47.

Eatough, J.P. & Henshaw, D.L. (1990). 'Radon and prostate cancer.' *The Lancet*, May 26, 1292.

Elinder, C.G., Kjellstrom, T., Hogstedt, C., Andersson, K., & Spang, G. (1985). 'Cancer mortality of cadmium workers.' *British Journal of Industrial Medicine*, 42, 651–5.

Elliott, P., Hills, M., Beresford, J., Kleinschmidt, I., Jolley, D., Pattenden, L., Rodrigues, L., Westlake, A., & Rose, G. (1992). 'Incidence of cancer of the larynx and lung near incinerators of waste solvents and oils in Great Britain.' *The Lancet*, 339, 854–7.

Freifeld, S. (1977). 'Asbestos exposure and laryngeal carcinoma.' *Journal of the American Medical Association*, 238, 1280.

Garcia-Sanchez, A., Antona, J.F., & Urrutia, M. (1992). 'Geochemical prospection of cadmium in a high incidence area of prostate cancer, Sierra de Gata, Salamanca, Spain.' *Science of the Total Environment*, 116, 243–51.

Gardner, M.J., Winter, P.D., & Barker, D.J.P. (1983). *Atlas of Cancer Mortality in England and Wales 1968–1978*. Chichester: Wiley.

Gatrell, A.C. (1986). 'Immunisation aginst whooping cough in Salford: a spatial analysis.' *Social Science and Medicine*, 23, 1027–32.

Gatrell, A.C., Dunn, C.E., & Boyle, P.J. (1991). 'The relative utility of the Central Postcode Directory and Pinpoint Address Code in applications of Geographical Information Systems.' *Environment and Planning A*, 23, 1447–58.

Gatrell, A.C. & Dunn, C.E. (1993). 'GIS and spatial epidemiology: modelling the possible association between cancer of the larynx and incineration in North-West England.' In M. de Lepper, H.J. Scholten, & R.M. Stern (eds), *The Added Value of Geographical Information Systems in Public and Environmental Health*. Dordrecht: Kluwer Academic Publishers.

Gatrell, A.C. & Rowlingson, B.S. (1993). 'Statistical spatial analysis in a Geographical Information Systems framework.' In A.S. Fotheringham and P. Rogerson (eds), *Spatial Analysis and GIS*. London: Taylor & Francis.

Gloag, D. (1981). 'Contamination of food: mycotoxins and metals.' *British Medical Journal*, 282, 879–82.

Goodchild, M.F., Haining, R., & Wise, S. (1992). 'Integrating GIS and spatial data analysis: problems and possibilities.' *International Journal of Geographical Information Systems*, 6, 407–23.

Guénel, P., Chastang, J-F., Luce, D., Leclerc, A. & Brugere, J. (1988). 'A study of the interaction of alcohol drinking and tobacco smoking among French cases of laryngeal cancer.' *Journal of Epidemiology and Community Health*, 42, 350–4.

Haggett, P., Cliff, A.D., & Frey, A.E. (1977). *Locational Analysis in Human Geography*, vol. 2, *Locational Methods*. London: Edward Arnold.

Henshaw, D.L., Eatough, J.P., & Richardson, R.B. (1990). 'Radon as a causative factor in induction of myeloid leukaemia and other cancers'. *The Lancet*, April 28, 1008–12.

Hills, M. & Alexander, F.E. (1989). 'Statistical methods used in assessing the risk of disease near a source of possible environmental pollution: a review.' *Journal of the Royal Statistical Society A*, 152, 353–63.

Howe, G.M. (1986). *Global Geocancerology: A World Geography of Human Cancers*. Edinburgh: Churchill-Livingstone.

Kazantzis, G. (1990). 'The mutagenic and carcinogenic effects of cadmium: an update.' In J. Rose (ed.), *Environmental Health: The Impact of Pollutants*. London: Gordon & Breach, 117–34.

Kingham, S. (1992). 'The use of Geographical Information Systems in assessing links between air pollution and respiratory health.' Paper presented to the Institute of British Geographers Annual Conference, University College, Swansea, January.

Kipling, M.D. & Waterhouse, J.A. (1967). 'Cadmium and prostatic carcinoma.' *The Lancet*, i, 730–1.

Kleinsasser, O. (1988). *Tumours of the Larynx and Hypopharynx*. New York: Thienne Medical Publications.

Lemen, R.A., Lee, J.S., Wagoner, J.K., & Blejer, H.P. (1976). 'Cancer mortality among cadmium production workers.' *Annals*, New York Academy of Sciences, 271, 273–79.

Lovett, A.A. & Gatrell, A.C. (1988). 'The geography of spina bifida in England and Wales.' *Transactions, Institute of British Geographers*, NS 13, 288–302.

Lynch, J., Hanis, N.M., Bird, M.G., Murray, K.J., & Walsh, J.P. (1979). 'An association of upper respiratory cancer with exposure to diethyl sulphate.' *Journal of Occupational Medicine*, 21, 333–41.

Openshaw, S. (1984). *The Modifiable Areal Unit Problem*. Norwich: Geo Books.

Openshaw, S., Charlton, M., Wymer, C., & Craft, A.W. (1987). 'A Mark 1 Geographical Analysis Machine for the automated analysis of point data sets.' *International Journal of Geographical Information Systems*, 1, 335–58.

Rothman, K.J., Cann, C.I., Flanders, D., & Fried, M.P. (1980). 'Epidemiology of laryngeal cancer.' *Epidemiologic Reviews*, 2, 195–209.

Rowlingson, B.S. & Diggle, P.J. (1993). 'SPLANCS: spatial point pattern analysis code in S-Plus.' *Computers and Geosciences*, 19, 627–55.

Silverman, B.W. (1986). *Density Estimation for Statistics and Data Analysis*. London: Chapman & Hall.

Smith, A.H., Pearce, N.E., & Callas, P.W. (1988). 'Cancer case-control studies with other cancers as controls.' *International Journal of Epidemiology*, 17, 298–306.

Smith, P.G. & Douglas, A.J. (1986). 'Mortality of workers at the Sellafield plant of British Nuclear Fuels.' *British Medical Journal*, 293, 845–52.

Stell, P.M. & McGill, T. (1975). 'Exposure to asbestos and laryngeal carcinoma.' *Jounal of Laryngology*, 89, 513–17.

Trell, E., Korsgaard, R., Hood, B., Kitzing, P., Norr, G., & Simonss, B.G. (1976). 'Aryl hydrocarbon hydroxylase inducibility and laryngeal carcinoma.' *The Lancet*, July 17, 140.

Viadana, E., Bross, I.D.J., & Hoten, L. (1976). 'Cancer experience of men exposed to inhalation of chemicals or to combustion products.' *Journal of Occupational Medicine*, 18, 787–92.

Winkelstein, W. & Kantor, S. (1969). 'Prostatic cancer: relationship to suspended air pollution.' *American Journal of Public Health*, 59, 1134–8.

Wynder, E.L., Mabuchi, K., & Whitmore, W.F. (1971). 'Epidemiology of cancer of the prostate.' *Cancer*, 28, 344–60.

PART IV

Pacific Studies

Plate IV The Pacific region has many Haggettian attractions and has consequently received numerous airborne visits from him, the most recent not unconnected with the Australian base of his (medical) offspring and first grandchildren. In earlier times, of course, contact between Britain and Australia was by sea, with vessels bringing a mixture of short-term migrants (such as touring English cricket teams) and longer term colonists. Peter's study of the influence of shipping services upon the spatial diffusion of disease to and within the Pacific region has proved remarkably fruitful for his research. HMS *Dido* (pictured above) provides an example. Its party of Fijian royal dignitaries brought back home diseases acquired during an official visit to New South Wales in 1875. The ship's captain was more concerned with those ills contracted in the bright lights of Sydney, but he would have been better advised to focus, like Peter, on the measles virus which, once disembarked in the capital of Fiji, tragically spread to kill nearly 20 per cent of the island's population in the next five months.

11

The Shape of Tele-Cost Worlds: the Pacific Islands Case

R.G. Ward

1 INTRODUCTION

Our shrinking world, the global village, telecommuting, and even 'the end of geography' (O'Brien, 1990; Brunn and Leinbach, 1991), are all phrases which imply a world in which distance becomes less relevant to our social, economic, and political intercourse. In the last two decades satellites and fibre optic cables have greatly reduced the distance-related component in the cost structure of telecommunications. One can envisage that within two decades telephone calls between any two places on earth could be made at the same cost as a local call. It might seem that by the metric of tele-costs, distance might be eliminated as a factor in location analysis in human geography. However, even 'distance neutral' innovations do not diffuse instantly or uniformly over space. Neither are prices always set on the sole basis of operating costs. Service providers may cross-subsidize for social or political reasons, and constraints of demand exceeding system capacity at different times can lead to rationing by price on a daily or hourly cycle thus creating diurnal variations in price and 'cost-distances'. The tele-cost distance from London to New York changed four times per day in 1991 through three tariff steps reflecting the changing diurnal pressure of calls and in particular time slots when offices are open on both sides of the Atlantic.

In 1980, while on holiday in Austria, Peter Haggett noted the different spatial structures created by the packet boats on the Wolfgangsee (Haggett, 1990, pp. 47–52). In 1991, while visiting Pacific Island countries in the course of a consultancy review of the University of the South Pacific, I was struck by the different spatial structures created by variations in international telephone charges.

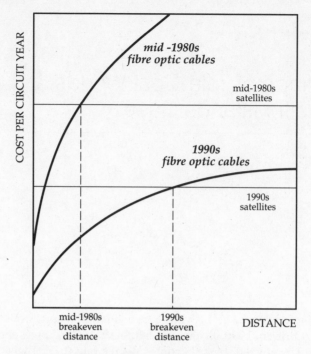

Figure 11.1　The changing relationship between telecommunication cost and distance for fibre optic cables and communication satellites
(*Source*: after Langdale, 1991, p. 197)

2 DISTANCE, COSTS AND TARIFFS

In most countries the tariff structures for long-distance calls, including international calls, have some positive relationship with distance. With wire and cable systems the capital cost of providing the service is quite closely related to distance, but with satellites distance between earth stations becomes virtually neutral in cost terms. Figure 11.1 shows the relationship between telecommunication cost and distance for satellites and fibre optic cables for the mid-1980s and the 1990s (Langdale, 1991, p. 197). Fibre optic cables obviously have a distance-related component in their capital cost but the cost per voice circuit has fallen dramatically with the rapid increase in circuit capacity per cable. The cost per voice path in the Hawaii 1 cable, which had 91 circuits and went into service in 1957, was $US378,022. The fibre optic cable TPC-4 linking USA and Japan, which opened in 1992, has a capacity of 75,600 voice paths at a cost per path of $US5500 (Staple, 1991, p. 60). Such high capacity spreads the distance-related component over so many circuits that it forms a very small element in the cost of any call.

Capacity across the North Atlantic and North Pacific now far exceeds demand. In the former case utilization of trans-Atlantic circuits was about

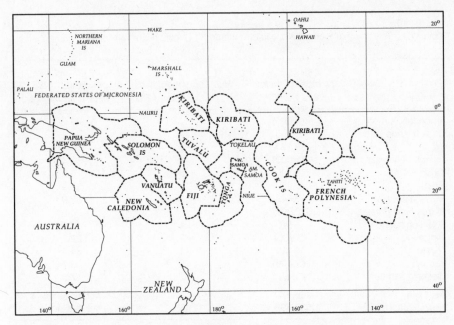

Figure 11.2 The South Pacific. The Exclusive Economic Zones of the sample South Pacific countries are shown. Disputed areas of EEZs are excluded

one-third of the capacity in the mid-1980s (Staple and Mullins, 1989, p. 109). Given the continued growth in capacity (Ergas and Paterson, 1991, p. 42), it is unlikely that the decline in real costs to the consumer which has occurred in many high-traffic areas will be reversed, and the tendency for the distance-related component of costs to fall will also continue. With excess circuit capacity, increasing competition as monopolies are abolished, and computer accounting systems which can readily record traffic by time slot, some service providers now offer tariffs in off-peak periods with very low distance gradients. For example, Telecom Australia offers weekend calls of up to 5 minutes duration to anywhere in the country (that is, for distances up to 3500 km) for no more than $A1.00 (*c.* US$0.70). It is these technological and organizational trends which make the idea of 'the end of geography', meaning the elimination of distance as a constraint to human interaction, superficially plausible.

In less developed and more isolated parts of the world the situation is very different and the effects of distance combine with other constraints to hold considerable though not absolute sway. Although the central governments and leading businesses in capital cities in such places may have reasonable telecommunication links to other countries, it will be many years before smaller centres and rural areas with low telecommunication traffic have services to match those of their capital cities. In 1988 half the world's population did not live within two hours walking distance of a telephone (Butler, 1988). Spatial differences in accessibility within developing countries will persist for many years.

Table 11.1   Telecommunications access and usage for Pacific Island groups

Country	Number of main lines, 1/1/90 [a]	Number of main lines per 100 people	Estimated total usage per capita, 1985 (Million paid minutes)
American Samoa	(5,000)	13	47.8
Cook Islands	2,600	12	45.1
Fiji	39,174	5	5.0
French Polynesia	(35,000)	18	52.4
Kiribati	(1,100)	2	0.4
Nauru	(1,200)	15	35.9
New Caledonia	26,643	17	53.9
Papua New Guinea	(32,000)	1	4.3
Solomon Islands	3,341	1	18.0
Tonga	(3,400)	3	22.3
Tuvalu	120	1	34.4
Vanuatu	(2,400)	2	55.7
Western Samoa	(5,400)	3	7.9
Australia	7,786,889	46	not available
New Zealand	1,537,395	46	not available

[a] Figures in brackets are estimates.

Sources: Columns 1 and 2 from Siemens (1991, p. 10); Tuvalu, number of telephones installed mid-1980s (Lewis and Mukaida, 1991, p. 235). Column 3 from Karunaratne (1984, p. 28)

3   THE SOUTH PACIFIC ISLANDS

Cliff and Haggett (1985, pp. 14–5) have noted that islands, because they exhibit some of the characteristics of closed systems, can offer 'a natural laboratory for geographical studies' and that different islands can be used 'as cameos of the colonial history of the area under different European powers'. Archipelagos, and especially those consisting of small islands, present extreme cases where the internal contrast in communication access between core and periphery is particularly marked. They may also exhibit characteristics in their international telecommunication services which reflect aspects of geographical, political, social, and economic distance. The South Pacific Island countries provide a useful case study of the differences in the cost of telecommunication access stemming from different tariff (tele-cost) structures. Their 'tele-cost worlds' have quite different shapes which reflect distance, technical features, political or social policies, and historical ties.

The island countries of the South Pacific (figure 11.2) are all small in population, land area, and size of monetary economy, and several major and middle-level powers have played colonial roles. Most of the Pacific Island states are archipelagic with extensive exclusive economic zones (EEZs). For example, Kiribati has a population of 70,000, a total land area of 684 square kilometres, and its 33 islands are spread across an east-west distance of 3600 km within an EEZ of 4,430,000 square kilometres. Inevitably telecommunication traffic densities are low in such countries where levels of monetary economy are low. There are few opportunities for economies of scale in international traffic and the cost of providing good telecommunication links for outer islands is high. Such inter-island links are often dependent on High Frequency (HF) radio and do not offer adequate access to modern information services such as computer data transfer or on-line data bases which require the higher quality of fibre optic or satellite services. Microwave systems are used where islands are close together. The majority of rural populations in the South Pacific Islands have no direct access to telecommunications at all (table 11.1). International and urban traffic makes up an unusually high proportion of total telephone usage (Karunaratne, 1984, pp. 28–9). This is due in part to the limited rural services but also because of the open, aid-dependent, and strongly import-oriented nature of the urban economies. Thus 'international calls from the Pacific Islands to overseas destinations have an economic parallel with calls made within a developed country between a small rural community and the urban capital city' (Davey, 1984, p. 19). As a result, as Davey points out (1984, p. 19), priority was given to international links in telecommunication planning through the 1970s and early 1980s.

Until the mid-1960s all South Pacific Island states were dependent upon HF radio systems for their international telecommunications. In 1964 Fiji's central location led to it becoming the shore-based repeater site for the coaxial COMPAC cable linking Canada, Hawaii, and New Zealand and in 1967 Papua New Guinea benefited in the same way from the laying of the SEACOM coaxial cable between Australia and South-east Asia. With the introduction of communication satellites, these were the only two independent South Pacific Island countries with sufficient traffic to meet INTELSAT requirements for servicing with the large Standard A earth stations in use in the early 1970s (Davey, 1984, p. 16). They are still the only South Pacific Island members and shareholders of INTELSAT (INTELSAT, 1992, pp. 32–6) although as French overseas territories, New Caledonia and French Polynesia had early earth stations for satellite links. In 1976 agreement was reached within INTELSAT to allow lower traffic countries to link to its system with smaller Standard B earth stations. This opened a route for small, low-traffic countries to use satellite systems for international links and by the mid-1980s all the Pacific Island states with populations of over 30,000 had earth stations. Smaller countries still used upgraded HF radio systems (Davey, 1984, pp. 19–22). In the late 1980s the Australian OTC International and the South Pacific Forum designed the Pacific Area Cooperative Telecommunications (PACT) analogue network to assist smaller countries to link with the global satellite systems. The analogue system will be enhanced by a digital version in 1994. Using a Demand Assigned Multiple Access (DAMA) system the smaller countries can link with satellite systems but pay only for actual satellite time used rather than having full time access and being required to pay for unused time. A Sydney switching station funded by Australian Government aid is the hub which provides a regional service linking a number of countries to a block of shared satellite capacity. Following this agreement satellite earth stations were installed in smaller countries such as Tuvalu and Niue while the installation of a PACT-related earth station on Aitutaki, in the Cook Islands, indicates the beginning of a process which could see the extensive use of satellites for inter-island telecommunications within the island countries (Butters, 1990).

Table 11.1 provides figures on the number, density, and use of telephones in the South Pacific. The figures for the number of lines for Australia and New Zealand are given to provide comparison with developed countries in the same general region but the source used for the last column does not include data for these countries. These are also the countries with which most of the South Pacific Island states have the heaviest telephone traffic.

The trend in a number of developed countries for government-owned telecommunication monopolies to be privatized and for other operators to be allowed to enter the market has not been followed for internal services in most Pacific Islands countries, although the expectation that government instrumentalities should operate profitably is spreading. In Vanuatu both internal and international services are now operated by Telecom Vanuatu in which Cable and Wireless, France Cables et Radio and the Vanuatu Government are shareholders, while in the Solomon Islands the Government and Cable and Wireless are shareholders in Solomon Telekom. The small size of the telecommunication sector makes it unlikely that any of the internal systems will have competing service providers in the foreseeable future.

The private sector is more involved in international traffic. For example, Cable and Wireless operates the service in Tonga and owns 49 per cent of Fintel, with the Fiji Government holding 51 per cent. The Australian Telstar Corporation, successor to OTC, operates in several countries. Nevertheless, for international calls, each island country is dependent on a single mode (except Fiji and Papua New Guinea) and a single 'Heavy Carrier', which owns the cable, satellite, or HF radio facilities, to provide the link to the systems operating in other countries. This is the 'old service paradigm' (Staple, 1992, pp. 32–3) and in the Pacific Islands there is little sign of the emergence of 'Light Carriers' or international value added networks (IVAN). The former provide 'international service by reselling, rerouting, repackaging or reprogramming the offerings of Heavy Carriers' and are 'primarily software based' and 'may not own a single trans-oceanic cable or satellite circuit' (Staple, 1992, pp. 32–3). The latter lease private lines from the Heavy Carriers and then sell services. Both are indicative of important emerging trends in the global industry (Staple, 1992) but these and other software-based developments which have begun to offer competition in the heavy traffic areas of North America and Western Europe are unlikely to penetrate the low traffic Pacific Islands area for some years.

Although the Pacific is now crossed by a number of fibre optic cables, most of these cross the North Pacific to link the United States and Canada with Japan, or Hawaii with the United States mainland. The TPC-5 cable links Hawaii and Japan through Guam and will be linked to Australia through the PacRimWest cable scheduled for completion in 1994. Guam could become a node for fibre optic cables linking North America and South-east Asia, but given low traffic volumes it is unlikely that the fibre optic network will be extended to other Pacific Island states in the short- or medium-term future. Similarly the commissioning of the PacRimEast fibre optic cable between New Zealand and

Hawaii in 1993 will make about 37,500 trans-Pacific voice circuits available for Australia (through the Tasman 2 link) and New Zealand, but it by-passes all the South Pacific Island countries en route. Just as the majority of new generation high-capacity jet aircraft on trans-Pacific routes now overfly the islands with their low traffic-generating capacity (Ward, 1989, p. 24), so the latest telecommunication technology with its high capacity and low cost potential by-passes the island states.

Apart from the Fiji and Papua New Guinea shareholding in INTELSAT, the first direct involvement of Pacific Island interests in ownership of international telecommunications cables or satellites came with the establishment of TONGASAT, owned partly by Princess Salote Pilolevu Tuita, daughter of King Taufa'ahau Tupou IV, and American interests. TONGASAT combined with two American companies to finance and manage up to six satellites to be placed in geostationary orbit slots allocated to Tonga by the International Telecommunications Union. The first of Tonga's satellites was purchased from Russia to be moved into one of Tonga's slots, and this has led to the first major international clash over rights to satellite parking slots. Tonga claims that an Indonesian satellite is illegally occupying one of its slots. TONGASAT and its partners will lease access to its satellites' transponders on the international market, but Princess Pilolevu has stated that she hopes the satellites will also be used to provide better inter-island communications within the country (Fonua, 1993, pp. 26–7).

As elsewhere, the financial regime operating in telecommunications between the Pacific Islands and the rest of the world is one in which the carriers providing the international link are paid at a wholesale rate (the 'accounting rate'). The two carriers concerned in the link between two countries will settle their accounts on the basis of the net traffic balances over the settlement period. Where the links between national systems must be made through a third country or carrier there may be further charges and participants in the settlement. The telephone caller is charged a retail rate by the service provider in the country where the call originates (Staple, 1992, p. 36). This retail rate includes a component to cover the accounting rate, but different national service providers can have different pricing policies for economic, political or social objectives. Thus even if all Pacific Island countries were charged the same accounting rates by the Heavy Carriers, one might still expect significant differences in the retail tariffs of different countries. Some countries may give preference through low charges to calls to one or more selected countries for political reasons, or because of the monopoly position of certain Heavy Carriers and the particular links they provide. In the case of the French territories the routing of some calls through Paris may influence rates. Other countries may offer preferential rates because of the heavier traffic which might arise, as in the case between the Cook Islands and New Zealand, from economic ties and the presence in one country of a large expatriate population from the other. Yet others may charge relatively high international tariffs across the board because the market will bear them, and the proceeds can then be used to cross-subsidize the cost of providing an internal service for areas of low monetary income and low telephone traffic.

Table 11.2   Cost of three-minute IDD call between countries at standard daytime rates, 1990–early 1991, in US$

From / To	Cl	Fiji	FP	Ki	NC	PNG	Sl	To	Tu	Va	WS	Aust	Fr	Ja	NZ	UK	USA
Cook I		5.29	5.29	5.29	5.29	5.29	5.29	5.29	5.29	5.29	5.29	5.29	9.35	9.35	3.70	9.35	9.35
Fiji	3.29		3.50	3.29	3.50	3.29	3.29	3.29	na	3.50	3.29	3.29	5.55	5.55	3.29	5.55	5.55
F Polynesia	14.85	14.85		na	7.95	14.85	14.85	14.85	na	7.95	14.85	12.73	15.91	24.39	12.73	21.21	24.39
Kiribati	6.50	6.50	6.50		6.50	6.50	6.50	6.50	6.50	6.50	6.50	6.50	9.28	9.28	6.50	9.28	9.28
N Caledonia	13.85	13.85	7.79	na		11.70	11.70	13.85	na	7.79	11.70	11.70	15.61	17.53	11.70	19.91	23.36
Papua N G	5.67	5.67	5.67	5.67	5.67		5.67	5.67	5.67	5.67	5.67	5.67	11.33	11.33	5.67	7.55	11.33
Solomon I	5.30	4.12	5.30	5.30	5.30	4.12		5.30	5.30	5.30	5.30	3.82	8.53	8.53	4.12	8.53	8.53
Tonga	3.47	3.47	3.47	3.47	3.47	3.47	3.47		3.47	3.47	3.47	3.47	6.95	6.95	3.47	6.95	6.95
Tuvalu	5.80	4.64	5.80	5.80	5.80	5.80	5.80	5.80		5.80	5.80	3.48	9.28	9.28	9.28	9.28	9.28
Vanuatu	7.96	5.24	7.96	7.96	5.24	7.96	7.96	7.96	7.96		7.96	5.24	10.29	10.29	5.24	10.29	13.02
W Samoa	3.86	3.86	3.86	3.86	3.86	3.86	3.86	3.86	3.86	3.86		3.86	5.14	5.14	3.86	5.14	5.14
Australia	3.71	3.71	3.71	3.71	3.71	3.02	3.02	4.87	na	3.71	3.71		3.71	4.87	3.02	3.71	3.71
France	12.80	12.80	7.53	na	7.53	12.80	12.80	12.80	na	12.80	12.80	11.17		11.17	11.17	2.63	5.47
Japan	6.27	6.27	6.27	6.27	6.27	6.27	6.27	6.27	na	6.27	6.27	6.27	7.88		6.27	7.88	5.20
N Zealand	2.79	2.79	2.79	2.79	2.79	2.79	2.79	2.79	2.79	2.79	2.79	2.79	5.40	5.40		5.40	5.40
UK	8.21	8.21	8.21	8.21	8.21	8.21	8.21	8.21	8.21	8.21	8.21	5.84	2.66	8.21	5.84		4.11
USA	5.77	5.77	5.49	5.77	5.77	5.77	5.77	5.72	5.77	5.77	5.72	4.66	5.27	4.14	5.53	4.08	

na: IDD Service not available.

Sources: Published rates for each country. UK – British Telecom; USA – Hawaiian Tel; Japan – KDD

Few of the island countries have sufficient pressure on available circuits to make it worthwhile offering off-peak rates to shed load from periods of high demand and, of the South Pacific Island countries whose rates are shown in table 11.2, only French Polynesia, New Caledonia and Vanuatu offer off-peak discount rates. The use of basic technology may also limit the capacity to have sophisticated systems monitoring diurnal changes in load in association with automatic accounting systems. Thus relative to countries such as UK and USA, most island countries have quite simple tariff structures for both internal long-distance and international calls. Nevertheless, there are significant differences between countries in the international tariffs they charge their customers for calls to a particular country, in the general level of basic tariff, and in the choice of countries which they place in any one charge zone. Thus, the tele-cost map of the world as measured from every island country is unique. It is the shape of these tele-cost worlds to which we now turn.

Table 11.2 provides a matrix of the charges in $US which applied in late 1990 or early 1991 for a three-minute call at standard daytime rates made through international direct dialling (IDD). In a few cases tariffs show that IDD service was not available to a particular country at that time. Figures 11.3 to 11.6 illustrate diagrammatically the shape of the tele-cost worlds of a selection of South Pacific Island countries. The same sample of destination countries is used in each diagram. In each tele-cost diagram the length of the ray from source country to destination country is proportional to the great circle distance between the capitals. For example from Nuku'alofa, Tonga, to Paris is 16,955 kilometres, and to Honiara, Solomon Islands, 3010 km. The bar on or beyond the end of each ray represents the cost-distance for a call from the source country to the destination using as scale the cost per thousand kilometres to one of the most distant countries, usually that with the highest tariff rate. Thus each of the tele-cost diagrams has a different cost-distance scale related to the source country's highest tariff step to any of the sample countries. The index country is marked by an asterisk and a heavier ray in the diagrams. In the Tonga case the rate of US$6.95 for a three-minute IDD call to France gives a cost per thousand kilometres of US$0.41, and as all countries outside the South Pacific region (which for these purposes includes Australia and New Zealand) are charged this rate, they are located at the same cost-distance from Tonga as is France (16,955 km.). With a tariff of US$3.47 for a three-minute IDD call, all the South Pacific destinations are located 8463 km from Tonga in terms of cost-distance relative to the scale of cost of calls to France. It is not surprising, given that the 'terminal cost' component of calls now makes up a large proportion of the total cost, that the prices charged for calls to nearby countries are much higher per thousand kilometres than those to distant countries. Only for some Franco-phone destinations from French Polynesia and New Caledonia (figure 11.6) is this not generally the case and no doubt this is a result of a tariff designed in part to facilitate links within the Franco-phone world.

Two countries, Kiribati and Tonga (figure 11.3), have simple two-tier tariff systems with no change in charges during the day or at weekends. The lower rate is charged for calls to other South Pacific states, including Australia and New Zealand, but in the case of Kiribati excluding United States territories, and the higher rate to all other countries. Although this paper focuses on the costs of IDD calls, it is of interest to note that for calls placed through the operator, as would be the case for most calls from outer islands, Tonga has a three-tier tariff in which calls to Western Europe, Canada, USA, Japan, Hong Kong and Macao are charged a middle rate between those for the South Pacific and the rest of the world. Although the tele-cost worlds for the two countries have the same two-step shape, the cost-distance relativities are different. From Kiribati it costs 87 per cent more to call another South Pacific country than from Tonga whereas the differential for calls to the rest of the world is only 33 per cent. Estimated international telecommunications demand for 1985 for Tonga was 72 times that of Kiribati (Karunaratne, 1984, p. 29) and this reflects both the higher level of activity in the monetary economy in the former and the large proportion of Tongans living in New Zealand and the United States. About 30 per cent of Tongans live overseas (Ward, 1989) and close social and economic links are maintained by families. The higher tariffs charged by Kiribati for international calls may also reflect greater cross-subsidy of income from international calls to the radio telephone system linking the country's widely scattered atolls.

The Cook Islands, Fiji, and Papua New Guinea (figure 11.4), have tele-cost worlds with three cost-distance steps. The Cook Islands has close constitutional, citizenship and economic ties with New Zealand where almost two-thirds of all

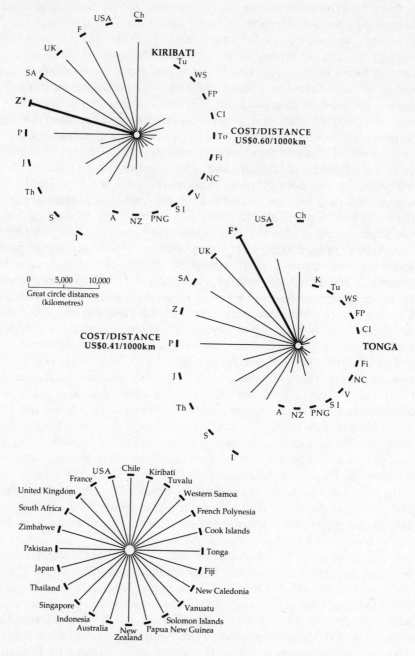

Figure 11.3   Relationships between distance and cost of international direct dialled telephone calls for selected South Pacific Island countries: Kiribati and Tonga

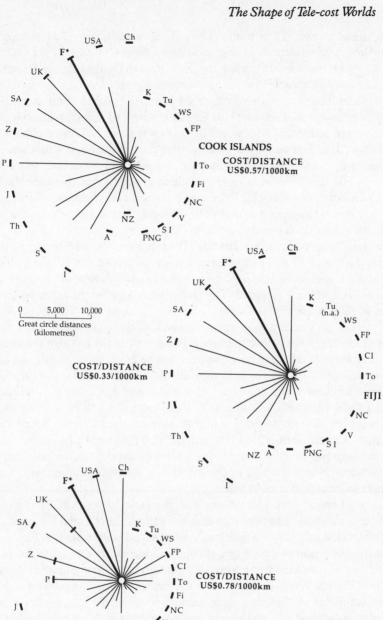

Figure 11.4   Relationships between distance and cost of international direct dialled telephone calls for selected South Pacific Island countries: Cook Islands, Fiji and Papua New Guinea

Cook Islanders live. Thus traffic is heavily skewed to New Zealand and the special low tariff reflects these close ties. Papua New Guinea exhibits a different pattern in that it has a uniform low rate for all South Pacific countries, including Australia with which it has the strongest economic ties, but then groups the rest of the world into two zones, of which the cheaper consists of the countries of the Commonwealth of Nations plus China. In terms of cost-distance this places neighbouring Indonesia 50 per cent further away than the United Kingdom or Zimbabwe, and France 50 per cent further than the United Kingdom. Fiji's tele-cost world provides a third pattern in which the American and French South Pacific territories and Vanuatu, which is partly Franco-phone and formerly administered jointly by France and United Kingdom, are slightly more distant in cost terms than the Anglo-phone South Pacific. But beyond the South Pacific all the world is equidistant from Fiji in tele-cost terms.

The third group, Solomon Islands, Tuvalu, Vanuatu, and Western Samoa (figures 11.5 and 11.6) has four-step worlds, with Vanuatu offering off-peak rates at night and on Sundays for calls to the nearby Melanesian countries and to Australia and New Zealand. This gives a five-step world at these off-peak times. Within this structure Europe, Hongkong, Japan, and Taiwan are significantly closer to Vanuatu than are Indonesia, Malaysia or the United States. Tuvalu has three tiers within the South Pacific with calls to Australia and Fiji, the countries with which it has closest economic or aid links, having the lowest two rates. As from Tuvalu, the Solomon Islands rates the world outside the South Pacific as equidistant in tele-cost terms but it also has three tiers within the South Pacific with calls to Australia cheaper than those to New Zealand, Fiji, or Papua New Guinea, which are in turn cheaper than to other South Pacific countries. Western Samoa has a low rate (US$1.93) to nearby American Samoa, a second-step rate for the Pacific Islands, New Zealand, and Australia, but then like Vanuatu divides the rest of the world into two tiers though with a quite different pattern to that of Vanuatu.

The two French territories of New Caledonia and French Polynesia (figure 11.6) have the most complex tele-cost worlds, and those which demonstrate most clearly the role of socio-political, historical and technical links. Figure 11.7 shows the relocation of the sample of countries used in table 11.2 which occurs when tele-cost distance from New Caledonia replaces geographical distance. The two French territories also have the highest cost regimes of the South Pacific countries studied and their rates to most of the Anglo-phone island countries are at least double those of other countries in the region (table 11.2). French Polynesia and New Caledonia have tariffs with 10 and 13 steps respectively, and both offer off-peak rates to France and some French territories. The lowest rate tier applies to the other Franco-phone Pacific Island countries, including Vanuatu. Calls to Australia and New Zealand, and in the case of New Caledonia to some island countries, are charged at a lower rate (which is not distance-related) than are calls to the other island countries. Calls to the Pacific Island countries or territories linked to the United States (for example, American Samoa, Guam and the former members of the United States administered Trust Territory of Micronesia) are charged the highest or second highest rates. A call from New Caledonia to Western Samoa costs US$11.70 compared with

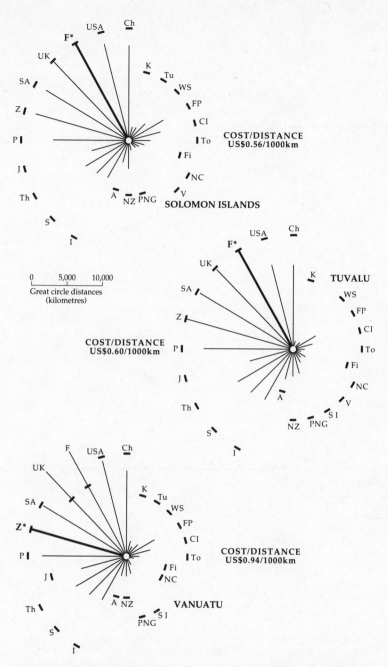

Figure 11.5   Relationships between distance and cost of international direct dialled telephone calls for selected South Pacific Island countries: Solomon Islands, Tuvalu, and Vanuatu

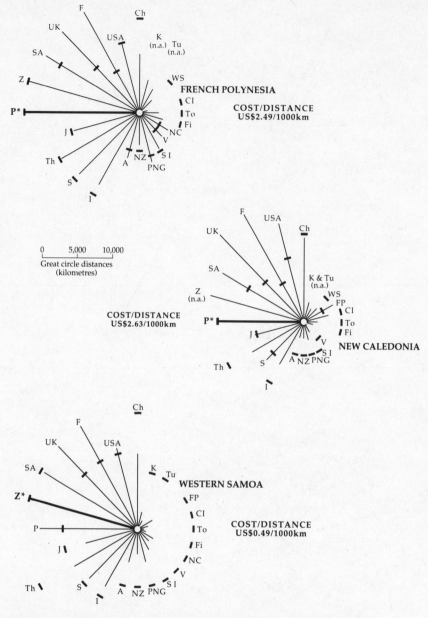

Figure 11.6   Relationships between distance and cost of international direct dialled telephone calls for selected South Pacific Island countries: Western Samoa, French Polynesia, and New Caledonia

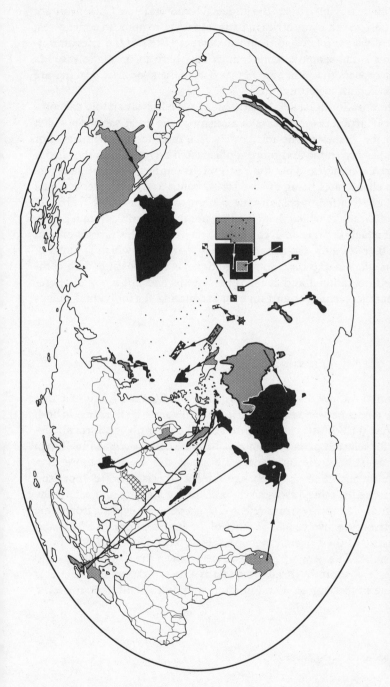

Figure 11.7 Relocation of sample countries in the tele-cost world of New Caledonia. The shaded area shows the geographical location of the sample countries with black areas placing the country at its tele-cost distance from New Caledonia, located by a star. Pakistan, the index country (see figure 11.6) is cross-hatched

US$25.07 to the nearby islands of American Samoa. Calls to France and Francophone countries in Africa, the Indian Ocean and the Caribbean are cheaper than those to other countries in their respective regions. In some cases, the rate differentials are related to technical characteristics of the telecommunication systems – for example, connections may have to be made through France – but it appears that other factors such as political or historical ties are also taken into account in setting tariffs.

Even though most South Pacific Island states have relatively simple telecommunication tariff structures their case demonstrates the great variation which exists between the shapes of the tele-cost worlds of different countries. For countries with heavier traffic and more sophisticated technologies, the shapes can be much more complex. That for British Telecom has nine standard rate steps and with cheap rates being offered for all bands and peak rates charged for two, a total of 20 different cost-distances are possible. Hawaiian Tel has 32 standard rates, for each of which there is an economy rate during certain hours, and for four of which there is an even cheaper night rate. This gives a total of 68 different IDD rates and cost-distances. Such complexity, which is tuned to demand and its diurnal and directional variations, is only possible with computer-controlled operational and accounting systems and not in small operations where manual exchanges and manual accounting for individual calls is still done.

4 RECIPROCAL TELE-COST DISTANCES

It is evident from the above discussion, table 11.2, and figures 11.3 to 11.6 that the tele-cost distances between two countries are unlikely to be the same in both directions. Figure 11.8 illustrates the differences between the reciprocal tele-cost distances for selected pairs of countries. In some cases, such as Fiji–Tonga or Cook Islands–Tuvalu, the differences are small and are little more than artifacts of the inconsistency of exchange rates as measures of comparison between currencies. In other cases the differences are striking and reflect the technical, political, or subsidy issues referred to above. As is evident from table 11.2, the extreme cases involve one or other of the Francophone Pacific Island territories because of their overall higher levels of tariff compared with other Pacific Island states. The geographical distance between the Cook Islands and French Polynesia is short by Pacific standards but the directional tele-cost difference is one of the largest. The Fiji–French Polynesia differential is even greater.

5 IMPLICATIONS AND CONCLUSIONS

Table 11.2 and figure 11.8 highlight the absolute differences which exist between countries in the prices they charge for telecommunication services. In the Pacific Islands, as elsewhere, tele-costs are a small component of overall costs for most businesses and the differences would have significant impact on

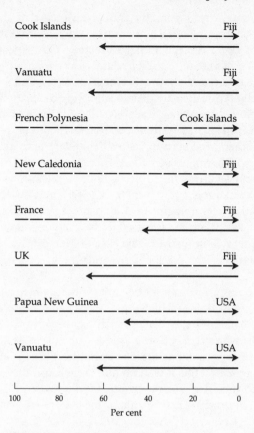

Figure 11.8   Reciprocal tele-cost distances
between pairs of countries

the relative cost structure of only those industries with a very high dependence on international telecommunications. Nevertheless, Langdale suggests that in the case of Japan its relatively low share (15 per cent) of the international telecommunication traffic sourced in the Asia–Pacific region is in part due to 'the high prices charged by KDD' limiting demand (Langdale, 1989, p. 215). Given that several South Pacific Island states have higher rates than Japan's KDD (table 11.2), it is possible that the current rates could become a constraint for businesses dependent on heavy use of international telephones or electronic information transfer. As yet there are few such industries in the South Pacific Island region but for regional organizations, such as the University of the South Pacific, telecommunication costs can be significant and price differences do impact on the relative costs of operating an extension centre in, for example, Kiribati compared with the Cook Islands.

As the economies of these countries are increasingly integrated into regional and world economies, there may be more opportunities for activities which exploit niche markets and rely on such factors as time-zone location and differential telephone rates. One business in Hawaii exploits the time-zone and offers to originate conference calls for businesses located in mainland USA wishing to link with, say, Japan. By taking advantage of the off-peak rates available in Hawaii at times when higher rates apply in either mainland USA or Japan, a business opportunity has been created. This type of activity could increase. The fact that the South Pacific Island countries are strategically located in terms of their time zones between North America and East Asia offers a potential advantage for some activities in which good telecommunications and low communication costs can be essential. Already Vanuatu and Cook Islands have tax haven industries and aspire to become financial centres. Off-shore data processing is another telecommunication-dependent activity which might be considered and which might benefit from time-zone and tele-cost location advantages as well as from the lower labour costs in the island countries compared with the major economies of the Pacific rim. With the rapid development of information technologies one can expect some South Pacific Island countries to consider becoming involved in the changing international division of labour within service industries. The case of North American airline reservation systems based in the Caribbean islands might be a model (Jussawalla, 1992, p. 32).

As the use of telecommunications becomes more sophisticated in the region, and if the differentials in rates which are demonstrated in table 11.2 and figure 11.8 persist, one can envisage greater use of techniques which take advantage of the lower rates when the option exists. Automatic call-back arrangements within or between organizations are one example. There is also scope for the private sector to by-pass official systems and larger business or regional organisations might do this. An existing example is the use of PEACESAT by the University of the South Pacific for some forms of communications between its extension centres (Lewis and Mukaida, 1991).

Now that almost all capital centres in the region are linked to the rest of the world through satellite ground stations, the next stage for telecommunication development within the region is the extension of high-quality links to the outer islands of the widely spread archipelagos. Although not considered in this chapter, the examination of tele-cost differentials can be extended to include internal tele-costs. At present the internal systems of several of the South Pacific Island countries use lower quality technology than their external links and the upgrading of internal systems to international standards is a major priority. The technical investment needed will be heavy. Karunaratne (1984) has suggested that a dedicated and regionally managed multi-beam satellite could provide the system needed but to extend the service throughout the archipelagos will require a multitude of earth stations, many of which would serve very small populations.

Despite falling capital costs per circuit, and increasing capacity of satellites and fibre optic cables, geography and distance will shape the development of the Pacific Islands for many years. Perhaps competition in the telecommunications field will reshape the tele-cost worlds of the islands but it is unlikely that distance will be eliminated as an important factor constraining development. Langdale (1982, pp. 283–4) has pointed out that the 'shift of industrialized countries into the information economy is likely to reinforce the existing level of information inequality among individuals and groups', and that greater competition and the concentration of access to new telecommunication services in heavy traffic areas 'are likely to exacerbate the already significant differentials between the information rich and information poor' (1982, p. 293). The spatial inequalities demonstrated in this chapter are likely to be reinforced with the shift to information economies, at least until the diffusion of new technology is much more spatially uniform and faster than has been the case in recent decades. For the South Pacific Islands this would require the expansion of high-quality links provided by satellite or fibre optic cables at a cost which would make them economic for low traffic and widely spaced islands. The South Pacific Island states are likely to remain on or beyond the fringe of the tele-cost worlds of the cores of the information economy in USA, Japan, and Western Europe, just as these areas are likely to remain on the fringes of the tele-cost worlds of the island states.

ACKNOWLEDGEMENTS

I am most grateful for the help of the following people in the preparation of this chapter: Ms E. Kingdon for assistance with data collection and analysis; Ms R. Grau and the Cartography Unit, Research School of Pacific Studies, for preparing the diagrams; to Dr D. Lamberton for advice; to staff of the University of the South Pacific Centres in the Cook Islands, Kiribati and Tuvalu for obtaining the rate schedules for these countries; and to Mr G. Fitzmaurice, Librarian, International Institute of Communications, London, for assistance in the Institute's library. Deficiencies in the paper are my responsibility.

REFERENCES

Brunn, S.D. & Leinbach, T.R. (eds) (1991). *Collapsing Space and Time: Geographical Aspects of Communication and Information*. London: Harper Collins.

Butler, R.E. (1988). 'Deregulation in the 1990s.' *Newsletter*, International Telecommunications Union, 8 March 1988.

Butters, J. (1990). 'OTC: Good neighbours in the South Pacific.' *Pacific Panorama*, 15, 42–4.

Cliff, A.D. & Haggett, P. (1985). *The Spread of Measles in Fiji and the Pacific*, Department of Human Geography Publication, HG/18, Canberra: Australian National University.

Davey, G.J. (1984). 'Telecommunications development in the South Pacific region.' In C.C. Kissling (ed.), *Transport and Communications for Pacific Microstates*. Suva: Institute of Pacific Studies, University of the South Pacific, 15–24.

Ergas, H. & Paterson, P. (1991). 'International telecommunication settlement arrangements.' *Telecommunications Policy*, 15, 29–48.

Fonua, M. (1993). 'Satellite business launches Tonga into the space age.' *Matangi Tonga*, May–June, 26–7.

Haggett, P. (1990). *The Geographer's Art*. Oxford: Basil Blackwell.

INTELSAT 1992 *Annual Report 1991–92*.

Jussawalla, M. (1992). 'Telecom and Southeast-Asian division of labor.' *Transnational Data and Communications Report*, 15, 31–7.

Karunaratne, N.D. (1984). 'Telecommunications infrastructure and economic development of the Pacific Island nations.' In C.C. Kissling (ed.), *Transport and Communications for Pacific Microstates*. Suva: Institute of Pacific Studies, University of the South Pacific, 25–47.

Kissling, C.C. (ed.) (1984). *Transport and Communications for Pacific Microstates*. Suva: Institute of Pacific Studies, University of the South Pacific.

Langdale, J.V. (1982). 'Competition in telecommunications.' *Telecommunications Policy*, 6, 283–99.

Langdale, J.V. (1989). 'International telecommunications and trade in services.' *Telecommunications Policy*, 13, 203–22.

Langdale, J.V. (1991). 'Telecommunications and international transaction services.' In S.D. Brunn and T.R. Leinbach (eds), *Collapsing Space and Time; Geographical Aspects of Communication and Information*. London: Harper Collins, 193–214.

Lewis, N.D. & Mukaida, L.V.D. (1991). 'Telecommunications in the Pacific Region: the PEACESAT experiment.' In S.D. Brunn, T.R. Leinbach (eds), *Collapsing Space and Time: Geographical Aspects of Communication and Information*. London: Harper Collins, 232–51.

O'Brien, R. (1990). 'The end of geography? The impact of technology and capital flows.' *The AMEX Bank Review*, 17, 2–5.

Siemens. (1991). *International Telecom Statistics 1991*. Munich: Siemens.

Staple, G.C. (ed.) (1991). *The Global Telecommunications Traffic Report – 1991*. London: International Institute of Communications.

Staple, G.C. (1992). 'Winning the global telecoms market: the old service paradigm and the next one.' *Telegeography 1992*, London: International Institute of Communications, 32–53.

Staple, G.C. & Mullins, M. (1989). 'Telecom traffic statistics – MITT in matter.' *Telecommuncations Policy*, 13, 105–28.

Ward, R.G. (1989). 'Earth's empty quarter? The Pacific Islands in the Pacific century.' *Geographical Journal*, 155, 235–46.

12

Off the Sheep's Back? Two Decades of Change in New Zealand

P.C. Forer

To live off the sheep's back: traditional saying
1. literal: to subsist on income from sheep
2. figurative: to live in a comfortable manner (see also *high on the hog*)

1 INTRODUCTION

The invitation to contribute to the Pacific Studies section of this volume
resurrected a project conceived on a migrant boat to New Zealand in 1974: a
look at national change and regional response in my then new country. It is an
appropriate theme, especially given Peter Haggett's interest in New Zealand,
his teaching of this theme while an Erskine Fellow at Canterbury in 1979 and
the legacy of his work on regional response models with Bassett, Cliff, and
Davies (Cliff et al., 1975), a precursor to later Pacific epidemiology (Cliff and
Haggett 1985, 1988).

Yet this chapter is not what I envisaged in 1974: this was an application of
quantitative models to unemployment, as a measure of economic activity, with
an eye for the lead–lag or amplification of trends. When New Zealand's economy
was stable enough for such models, unemployment was too low to provide a
reliable economic indicator. Subsequently, rising unemployment reflected
structural changes too strong for such models of tranquil times. In the end, this
chapter emerged as a broad perspective on the interaction of global ideologies,
national politics and regional economies over twenty years, and the transformation of a society. It is the story of the desire of New Zealand to elaborate its
economy and attain economic growth: to move off the sheep's back in terms of
produce but stay on it in terms of outcomes. To be sure, there remains a concern
with national trends and regional responses, abetted by lead–lags and amplify-
ing filters. The descriptive tools are simply less precise.

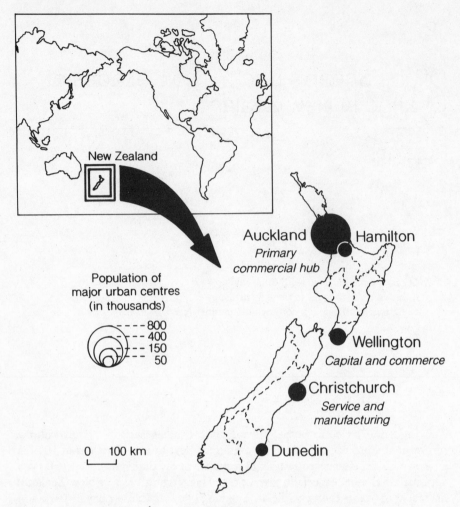

Figure 12.1 New Zealand's peripherality, regions and principal urban areas, 1991

2 AN INTERESTING FALL FROM GRACE?

Our story begins in 1973, with an island nation of 3 million people set deep in the Pacific margin, blessed by a remarkable scenic and agricultural wealth and with, by most international yardsticks, a prosperous, egalitarian and tolerant society. The year 1973 climaxed a period of golden weather for the New Zealand economy which saw Auckland, the largest employment area in the country (with 320,000 workers) experiencing 54 consecutive weeks from 2 November 1973 without a single person being registered as unemployed. Yet, even then, New Zealand faced an imminent repositioning in response to both the growing influence of transnational capital and the emergence of trading blocs to which it was peripheral.

The chapter ends, or rather pauses, the day after the 1993 General Election.

In 1993, registered unemployment averaged in excess of 200,000, of which 57,000 were in Auckland,[1] and New Zealand enjoyed the world's 27th highest per capita income (in 1973 it ranked fifth). Yet, for all the drama of those figures, the tale is one of adaptation to changing and adverse circumstances rather than abject decline. Many other OECD countries, with variations in severity and timing, have caught the same groundswell of the same global processes.

This national flux, and its regional flows-on, are made internationally interesting for four reasons. First is the nation's insular nature. New Zealand appears from a distance the perfect, isolated space-economy for academic observation. Second, its size, social cohesion and relative development level make it capable of well articulated, and sometimes very rapid, national adjustments to change. Third, the extreme and ossified levels of government involvement in the economy in the early 1970s form a distinct benchmark. This involvement ranged from draconian foreign exchange control to massive protection for local manufacturers. Apart from an involvement in regional policy, which was both limited and late (Johnston, R.J., 1973; Johnston, W., 1973), government influence was ubiquitously pervasive (Gould, 1982). Fourth, subsequent policy change has been profound, especially in the area of economic restructuring. It is fashionable, and in many ways correct, to date this change from the advent of the Fourth Labour Government in 1984, and indeed one theme of this chapter is the combination of vulnerability and stability evinced by New Zealand during the following decade. In truth, though, New Zealand has been undergoing three, partly simultaneous, economic restructurings whose genesis stems from the events of the early 1970s. These are a restructuring of trade, a restructuring of the economic base and a restructuring of the rules of economic life. One has been successful, one has not, and the jury is out on the third. All three have combined in the later 1980s to implement a restructuring of the national way of life. Each economic restructuring has stemmed from a national policy priority, and each has affected the regions of New Zealand through different mechanisms.

3 RESTRUCTURE FROM WHAT?

In retrospect, we can see that the early 1970s represented the last years of an epoch of relative stability and prosperity (Lane and Hamer, 1973), dating back to New Zealand's emergence from the 1930s depression. In this era of guaranteed primary markets, tariff protection and import substitution, their change characterized mild growth rather than structural shifts. This reflected an economy largely insulated from direct impacts from outside events: shielded by policies put in place from the 1930s for precisely that purpose. A *laissez-faire* amplifier of recession, followed by government intervention (Simpson, 1990), had sought specifically to stabilize future responses, a requirement which a solid UK-oriented trading pattern after World War II delivered. Even in 1972, trade with Britain accounted for 30 per cent of total trade and people, if not capital, flowed with little regulation between the two nations.

Within this protected environment, a space-economy had emerged with both high levels of protection and a unique regional structure in which the traditional four main centres of Auckland, Christchurch, Dunedin, and Wellington (figure 12.1), retained a considerable and surprising degree of equality in terms of traditional indicators such as employment, house prices, and economic control and structure (Johnston and Rimmer, 1967). Government intervention, such as national wage awards, produced a bland economic landscape accentuated in all regions by the consistent demand for labour associated with a strong immigration policy. In spite of labour shortage, a social orientation of life underpinned a two-day weekend. The same ethos ensured significant social welfare expenditure, supported by high levels of direct, voluntary community involvement. Whilst racist attitudes were latent rather than absent, Maori and Pakeha coexisted equably. Regional structural change in these times reflected the slowing pace of new agricultural land development, and the ornate intricacies of a largely protected manufacturing sector. Within this structure, the main regional responses to national change were driven by changes in primary commodity export prices, reflected in agricultural regions by their specific reliance on either sheep or cattle products. Based on what were then weekly statistics, a flurry of seminar papers (inspired by Peter Haggett's visit to Canterbury) suggested delicate patterns of amplification, lead and lag associated with the main economic downturns of 1968 and 1972 which could be traced to a classic case of transmission of cycles through inter-industry linkages (Mein, 1979; Williams, 1979; Burney, 1980).

All in all the New Zealand economy in the early 1970s seemed comfortable, stable and very British. R.J. Johnston's (1973) description of it as a 'small but prosperous ex-colony' provided a neat epithet. New Zealanders were worried about relatively trivial variations in regional indicators (McCracken, 1977) but, as an antipodean European outlier, the tyranny of distance seemed in abeyance except in so far as it permitted a more prosperous, equitable and personal society than that enjoyed in Britain.

3.1 Restructuring of trade

In the early 1970s, in one 12-month period that was surely New Zealand's *annus horribilis*, two events combined to precipitate radical changes and to reassert that dormant tyranny of distance: these were British entry to the EEC and the 1974 oil price shock. More significant was Britain's EEC commitment which foretold the inevitable dislocation of a symbiotic trading relationship that had made New Zealand a functional extension of rural England. Despite this forewarning, figure 12.2 indicates how, even in 1973, after several years anticipating the EEC decision, trade still remained channelled by primary product flows and high levels of 'imperial' tariff preference (see Robinson, 1993). There still persisted a narrow commodity range, and key industries remained chained by habit to a single dominant market.

New Zealand needed both geographical and constitutional diversification of its trade, and began ever more urgently to seek out new niches in a less friendly and increasingly less regulated global trading environment. Although the terms of trade (bottom line) have proved unhelpful, the geographical diversification

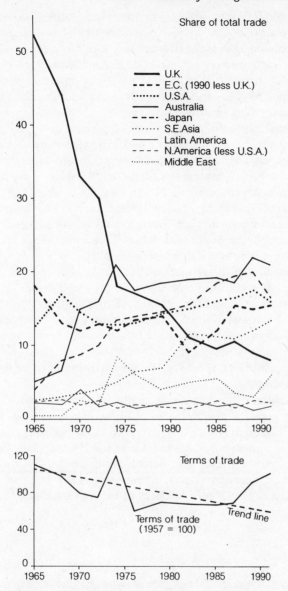

Share of total trade

- —— U.K.
- ---- E.C. (1990 less U.K.)
- ········ U.S.A.
- —— Australia
- – – – Japan
- ·········· S.E.Asia
- —— Latin America
- – – – N.America (less U.S.A.)
- ············ Middle East

Terms of trade

Terms of trade
(1957 = 100)

Trend line

Figure 12.2 Trade partnership restructuring: total share percentage and terms of trade between New Zealand and major trading areas for selected years, 1965–1992
(*Sources*: data in *New Zealand Official Year Book* 1966–93, and Crocombe, Enright and Porter, 1991)

of traditional products into markets in South-east Asia, the Middle East (Harris, 1982) and the former Communist bloc since 1973 have been impressive, especially when seen against the background of growing commodity dumping in world trade. Furthermore, trade with the United States, long New Zealand's second source of influence in economic and social matters (Grey, 1984), has prospered in spite of occasional bouts of protectionism and the deep disagreements on nuclear policy since 1984.

The differential impacts of this restructured national trade on New Zealand's regions was arguably small prior to the mid 1980s, given the careful recrafting of protective tariffs that accompanied bilateral negotiation of new trading opportunities. In the longer term some regions able to locate and support good export markets have prospered, as McDermott Associates (1983) forecast in respect of Australia. Inevitably, external influences, economic and social, have input increasingly directly into regions through diversified trade. Regions, such as the sheep areas in the South Island, have found themselves enmeshed with fluctuating wider patterns of politico-economic crises in Russia, China or Iran. Overall, the window of direct market concern for industry and workers has become widened, with inevitable impacts on social habits and outlooks. Whether in terms of migration policies, H'lal slaughtermen or restaurants diverse trade has brought diluted Anglocentrism. Using a simple cartographic representation (figure 12.3), we can see how these changes have brought New Zealand firmly back into the Pacific. In terms of both economic goals and a broadening of cultural perspectives, the restructuring of trade is a somewhat unheralded success.

This geographical diversification naturally reflects some parallel diversification of traded goods into new areas of niche manufacturing, services and tourism. With declining real travel costs, tourism in particular has permeated many provincial areas of New Zealand (Forer and Pearce, 1984; Pearce, 1990). However, to strengthen trade significantly by diversification implies a more diversified domestic economy but, as Robinson (1993) has shown, this featured to only a limited degree as a component of early geographical diversification. The next section discusses why.

3.2 Restructuring the economic base

The foreshadowed trade disengagement with Britain threatened both the volume and the terms of trade of the agricultural export sector, and intensified debate on possible means of diversifying the economy. However, this debate was accelerated and focused in a particular direction by the impact of the 1974 oil price crisis. With high energy use per capita and few onshore hydrocarbon resources, oil prices in the 6 months after Yom Kippur effectively negated 20 per cent of New Zealand's total exports at one stroke. A natural response was to couple a desire for diversification with energy-related initiatives.

So emerged one of two distinct policy directions of the period from 1975 to 1984. The dominant direction was large scale and interventionist: New Zealand would capitalize on its non-oil-based energy resources (principally hydro-electric power and the Maui natural gas field) to reduce its own oil dependence, to attract and develop energy-intensive basic industry, and to promote large-scale, globally competitive indigenous petrochemical production which would, in turn, generate downstream diversification and growth. Under the rubric of 'Think Big' the government oversaw investment in major energy and primary processing works totalling $NZ6.8 bn in nine years.

The second, and minor, direction was broader based, aimed at encouraging diversification through freer trade over and above that achieved by bilateral negotiations. This was articulated through policy which involved a gradual dismantling of trade barriers, particularly related to major protected manufacturing industries. It also involved the realization of Closer Economic Relations (CER) with Australia, the one obvious avenue for a full free trade agreement capable of providing a stable enhancement of 'domestic' market size (Bollard and McCormack, 1985).

The thrust of these policies during the period from 1975 to 1984 was an attempt to cope with fundamentally changed world circumstances within a basically unchanged economic regime – borrowing internationally to sustain and boost primary output, often through subsidy, while simultaneously seeking to develop globally competitive manufacturing by government intervention. Not surprisingly, this failed, aided and abetted by an international return to cheap oil prices. Most 'Think Big' projects failed to meet elementary goals on return on investment, and none produced the promised downstream generation of diversified economic activity. Furthermore, they reduced resources for promoting growth elsewhere in the economy, much of which remained stubbornly dependent on protection of 'Think Big' contracts. For example, agricultural subsidies increased production, but at an enormous cost in subsidies and drastic distortion in agricultural land prices and land use patterns.

Despite debt-funded intervention, unemployment climbed inexorably during this period (in line with the national debt), while belief in a significantly better trading environment for New Zealand slowly withered. By the first years of the 1980s, it was apparent that the hope for an easy transition to acceptable growth levels was ill-founded. Concern was increasingly registered that the protected manufacturing and trading sector was compromising the emergence of an efficient export base, and that the reversal of protectionism evidenced from the 1976 budget onward was too slow.

In spite of gratifying growth in manufacturing exports, the basic thrust of 'Think Big' had been misplaced. Its domestic impacts were clearly written on a few critical regional economies, particularly that of Taranaki (figure 12.4), but these were short-term impacts running against a tide of general decline that was only superficially moderated by subsidy-induced rural growth. Crucially, major elements of economic structure and the basic patterns of social service and lifestyle remained largely unaltered from the early 1970s. As reviewed in Franklin (1978, 1985) so, too, did the fundamental economic realities, which in time reasserted themselves on the space-economy, but not before a third and more violent restructuring happened.

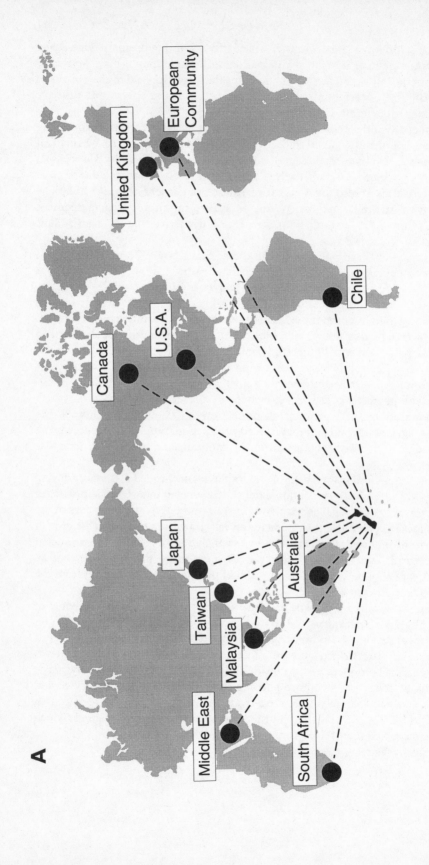

A

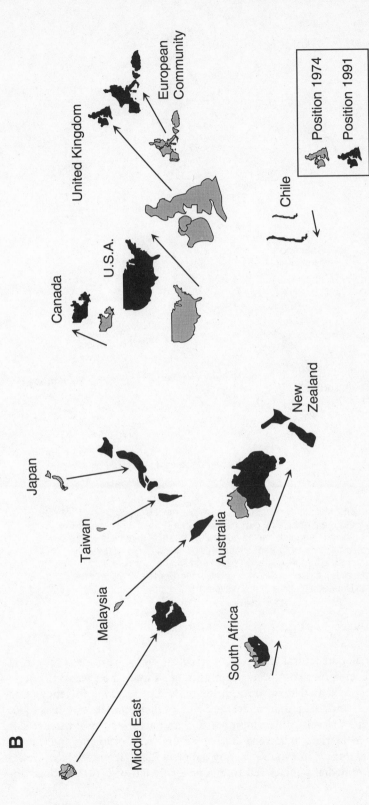

B

Middle East

Malaysia

Japan

Taiwan

South Africa

Australia

New Zealand

Canada

U.S.A.

United Kingdom

European Community

Chile

Position 1974

Position 1991

Figure 12.3 The changing trade space of New Zealand. (A) Sample regions. (B) Shifts of sample regions in effective trade space, 1974–91. Trade share is proportional to area of the trading unit for both years. For 1991, trading units are located as per their location in (A). The 1974 position is shown as a relative position which reflects the growth or decline in trade relative to 1991. The overall pattern of substantial growth of trade with countries of the Pacific Rim at the expense of Europe, especially the United Kingdom, and North America is clear

(*Source*: data in *New Zealand Yearbook*, 1975 and 1992)

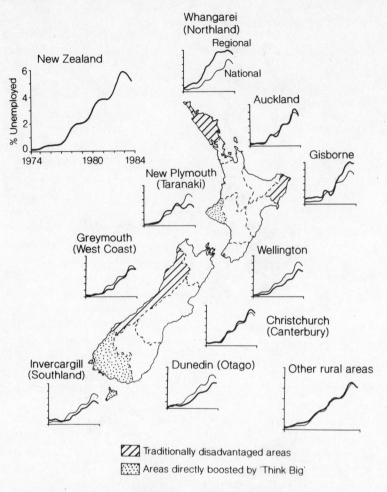

Figure 12.4 Unemployment curves for employment districts, 1974–1981. Heavy investment reduced unemployment rates in 'Think Big' regions like New Plymouth (Taranaki), but the general picture is of unremitting upwards climb. Figures are for employment districts (regional names in parentheses), appropriately aggregated and allowing for boundary changes over the period. Boundaries shown are for Regional Councils (*Source*: Department of Labour statistics, 1974–81)

4 RESTRUCTURING THE ECONOMIC ENVIRONMENT

After 1984, major structural changes occurred through government reform of the economic environment rather than through direct intervention. These reforms were predicated on a critique of both the quality (efficiency) and structural mix, and held that deficiencies in both stemmed not just from traditional factors (levels of development of manufacturing, local market size and distance to market) but from a range of deficiencies in the operational environment identified internationally by the New Right. Ironically, the implementation of remedial policies fell to a supposedly left-of-centre Labour administration. This administration, faced by over-extended credit, and auto-phagic subsidies, commenced a searing restructuring of the operational environment in which both national and regional economies were set. This initiative, a surprise to many and a betrayal to its union supporters, was subsequently maintained by a resurgent National Party, which took office in 1990 on an equally deceptive manifesto.

The restructuring entailed a long-overdue policy shift in the controversial and still hotly contested direction of deregulation of the economy (cf. Douglas, 1980; Novitz and Wilmott, 1992). In line with international thinking, typified by the agendas of Thatcher and Reagan, the economic critique focused on inadequate internal competition and the existence of protected markets. These are likely co-occurrences in a small economy, and New Zealand's domestic economy evinced low levels of competition due to import restrictions and the inevitable fact that many scale-efficient enterprises were locally monopolistic. As described in Crocombe, Enright, and Porter (1991), the obvious policy responses in a small nation context implied greater internationalization of ownership. The problem seemed quite clear and was later elaborated by links to arguments on the inadequate integration of technology for growth – another international fashion in economic critique, and one again likely to typify a small economy (particularly one with low investment in research and development). As with Reagonomics itself, these arguments were imported, with a time lag, from a currently popular overseas doctrine.

Reform, when it came, arrived largely by political ambush. The analyses described above did not form the material of substantive inter-party debate prior to the 1984 General Election, although the merits of a closer and less controlled integration with the world economy had long enjoyed academic attention (cf. Franklin, 1985). Neither political party in 1984 proposed drastic deregulation in its manifesto. Yet change did come. But the critical arguments for reform paid scant heed to New Zealand's unique nature. This was also true of the consequent policy prescriptions, reflected as they were in greater accountability, fiscal responsibility and government disinvestment from service provision, as well as competition and greater involvement of the market. These typical New Right responses are considered in Green (1986) and will not be rehearsed further here. However, three things invite comment in New Zealand's case.

The first is the nature of the society on which the impact fell, still, even in 1984, a notably personal and caring society – virtues encouraged by perceived isolation, small size and shared problems. New Zealand's welfare state was no spendthrift monolith. It was laced with user charges and community-help schemes to augment its service provision. The nation's local government and government of many services, such as hospital boards and ports, were deeply democratic, albeit with a comatose tinge. An egalitarian ethos appeared entrenched, and was even confirmed by the choice of a Labour government in 1984.

The second is the manoeuvrability of New Zealand society and economy. Small, dependent economies are often characterized as 'coat-tail economies' (Holland, 1976). Notwithstanding the limitations imposed by its economic structure, New Zealand does not suit this epithet. The surf-board economy might be a more active and appropriate metaphor. Because of size, social cohesion, high levels of education and few powerful checks or balances to Cabinet power, New Zealand was capable of what can be viewed as either remarkable dirigibility or frightening instability, depending upon one's view of the nature of change. A prime legacy of the period since 1984 has been a shocked and increasingly articulated popular domestic recognition of this.

The third aspect, reflecting this manoeuvrability, is the speed and depth of the changes undertaken in just nine years. New Zealand has been an amplifier of the international ideological trend. Within days of the 1984 election, the New Zealand dollar was soft-floated and foreign exchange freed: overnight the purchase of British pounds or Japanese yen became an over-the-counter trans-action rather than a tightly quota-ed negotiation over several weeks. Within months, government departments were dismantled (of the 13 main ones in 1984, only five survived in vaguely similar form), major state assets were sold to pay off (or in reality to maintain) debt levels, charges were levied for government services, and considerable protection was removed from manufac-turing. Within a few years, in Labour's second term, a new structure for school administration was being formed (NZTRE, 1988), asset sales mounted to $NZ6.7 bn, major state assets were privatized or corporatized, school manage-ment was localized and local government totally redrawn. Corporatization of many services removed public scrutiny and accountability in favour of closeted financial controls. With a change of government in 1990, this was extended to further asset sales, including railways in 1993, and some initial corporatization of health services. From being a bemused watcher of Thatcherism and Reagonomics in the late 1970s, New Zealand outstripped these pioneers for change.

Unlike the lesser restructurings described in section 3, these changes exerted major influences beyond the mere economy. They precipitated dynamic re-gional, social and finally political change. Britton, Le Heron, and Pawson (1992) have suggested that the 1990s will see both the emergence of new geographies of production and consumption, and the steady reshaping under global pressure of the territorial organization of social life. Already, regional change has seen distinct patterns of impact in several phases; social change has been more nationally consistent and more forceful, driven by economic pressures and resulting in an era of political restructuring which is only just beginning.

4.1 Restructuring the regions

The interlinked restructurings of trade, economic structure and economic environment have certainly produced symptomatic short-term perturbations and long-term adjustments in the space economy since 1974, but the latter half of this period evinces a different magnitude of change. In many countries, the structural adjustments of the last two decades have seen an increasing concentration of wealth into core industrial or service regions rather than in specific cities and, in a less dramatic way, shifts from rural to urban regions. New Zealand exhibits an atypical response, which is elaborated below and

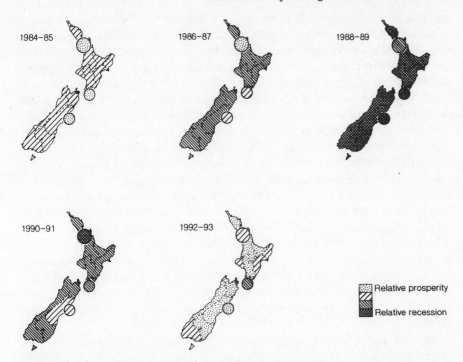

Figure 12.5 Impacts of deregulation in the New Zealand regional system, 1984–1993. Regional economic climate is indicated relative to the normal status of that area. Thus Auckland in 1990–1 enjoyed better absolute indicators than Northland, but poor ones relative to its normal economic position
(*Sources*: data in Ministry of Works and Development, 1986; Treasury, 1991; Departments of Labour and Statistics)

summarized in figure 12.5. Essentially the story since 1984 is a violent perturbation consequent upon financial deregulation, followed by a reassertion of New Zealand's natural trading strengths reflected through regional structure. Perhaps, on reflection, it is, too, a concentration on its core: it is just that the core is atypically rural.

In the decade from 1965, to recap, regional fluctuations in the economy tended to be driven, above all else, by commodity prices acting through the dominant agricultural mode in an area. The impact of dairy booms or wool busts could be traced through the farm gate into support service spending and eventually to the provincial centres. Most New Zealanders were urbanites, living in an egalitarian if policy-crafted urban hierarchy. Most of the policies from the mid-1970s sustained this urban structure, with a limited but persistent bleeding of control and employment into the most vital area around Auckland. The gradual pains of change were spread widely through the regions, with spatially concentrated short-term benefits of construction, often in marginal electorates. The critical transmission pulses were government policies.

The post-1984 period is both more complex and more breakneck in speed. To understand it fully we need to comprehend the interplay between four strands of impact: rationalization of production, expansion of agricultural services, restructuring of agricultural equity, and reorientation to exporting. The impact of immediate reform measures (devaluation and removing agricultural subsidies) was both to spur demand for manufactured goods due to enhanced price competition (the devaluation against some currencies was 37 per cent in the first three months), and to cause a catastrophic decline in farm prices to levels where the cost of land equated to its true production potential. In the short term, manufacturing had a growth spurt and unemployment declined, especially in areas such as Auckland, while many farmers acquired negative equity. As the dollar marginally rebounded, and the impact of the annihilation of equity in the rural sector cut in, the manufacturing boom proved relatively short-lived, and a significant rural recession commenced. Bolstered by drought and low commodity prices, this was to bite for the best part of seven years. It was deepened by a strong rise in interest rates (briefly to a 23 per cent base level), which began to place increasing strains on all business activity.

In spite of this, recession in the main urban centres in the North Island was tempered. Relative house prices and wage levels in the two main centres continued stretching away from other regions, indicative of their prosperity. Two factors underpinned this: the growth of financial services and information sector jobs, and the regional rationalization of domestic manufacturing and services.

Finance and other information sector jobs were already congregating into Wellington and Auckland (Parrott and Forer, 1986; Forer and Parrott, 1992). After deregulation, New Zealand's location in the global time zones permitted growth in areas such as currency exchange by plugging into patterns of international trading. A mood of optimism and change further supercharged the financial sector, carrying the New Zealand stock exchange from 1720 to 3840 points in 30 months, buoyed by the symbol of success in the America's Cup in Perth. Many of the key companies in this naively adopted boom were investment shells, whose trading combined with a massive public entry to the stock market to send stocks to quite unsustainable levels. Not unique to New Zealand, this accentuated boom was registered on the landscape by a spate of speculative office building which transformed the major city centres. In ink, it was shown by an over-extended stock market, and a prolonged, deep crash when Black Thursday came in 1987.

New financial services represented the superimposition of new functions focused on Auckland and Wellington. A less glamorous, but possibly longer standing, factor in Auckland's relative economic health was a parallel organizational restructuring that was reallocating resources in both the public and private sectors. In the private (and the increasing public corporatized) sector, the emphasis on open markets forced firms to maximize efficiency. In spatial terms, this usually reflected in concentration of domestic production and activity – typically into the Auckland region. Broadcasting, agribusiness, retailing – the list is long and influential, but can be sampled in Britton, Le Heron, and Pawson (1992). Uncompetitive industries simply ceased to exist, and these typically were the protected and import substitution industries of the larger centres. In this, Wellington's manufacturing base was especially hard hit, as were components of Auckland's. However, competitive or vital industries frequently retrenched into the Auckland region, providing a palliative. Major provincial centres, and second order national ones such as Dunedin and Christchurch, saw jobs and control migrate North. In the public sector, the same forces were afoot, typically adding a particular twist in low-density rural areas where social cross-subsidies were significant (for example, in the provision of work in postal services and forestry).

Until 1987, this change reflected a familiar stereotype: a concentration of wealth into an increasingly hierarchical regional structure. However, in the 1990s, this pattern has shown some diminution in terms of wealth, if not of control. Interestingly, this is in many ways not a new geography, but a return to an old one. Corporate and housing values retrenched after 1987, wasting large amounts of urban equity, a trend accelerated by further pressures from high interest rates. In the overheated property markets of Wellington and Auckland in particular, substantial drops in property prices occurred, shifting negative equity into the urban scene.

In contrast, helped by improved dairy and meat prices, the agricultural sector began to recover its vigour in the early 1990s and is now largely financially restructured. Its growing health, and optimism over GATT's Uruguay round, has powered a provincial revival. In all regions, agriculture and other sectors have become internationally competitive, helped by liberal trading which allows direct importing of low-cost products for producer needs. In provincial centres, the surviving economic activity had become increasingly tied to the regional market or to export.

During the 1990s, evidence began to be cited that sustainable, export-led growth was coming, consequent on reform. The economically most successful region in 1993, Canterbury, potentially endorses this view. Avoiding the over-heating of the urban economy from 1984 to 1987, but forced by circumstances to adopt an export orientation to survive, its economic platform in the 1990s has been well placed and has performed well (Treasury, 1991). What may be starting to emerge is a national economy of regions, which are globally competitive, resource-based and tied to international trade. Whether this is a triumph of enterprise with a stable and viable future or a blind eye to history will remain unclear for some time yet. There is, however, more than a hint of *déjà vu* in the air.

4.2 *Restructuring society*

Sense of place is an imprecise concept, but one bound up in society as well as buildings. Physical New Zealand, outside city centres and a few suburban excesses, does not dramatically testify to two decades of change. More tourists and newer cars (largely second-hand Japanese imports) are the most visible signs. In terms of society, the change is more dramatic, quite remarkable, but hard to quantify. Anecdotal comparisons may exemplify. According to an apocryphal American tourist, New Zealand's 1970s charm was that it was just like the States in the 1950s. Visiting the United Kingdom from New Zealand in the 1970s endorsed this view. The UK's was an arguably less personal, more commercial and more pressured society, an observation that went beyond simple comparisons of scale. In the UK, one felt a sense of movement to a future, albeit problematic, in which New Zealand lagged. It lagged in the adoption of many services and in the availability of new technologies, often by 12 to 24 months. It lagged in attitude – for example, by having the legally enforced two-day weekend. It lagged in not having confronted widespread poverty: welfare support minimized extremes and, even for the poor, many amenities were available. All this mirrored no real imposed ideology so much as a deeply, almost passionately, held consensus on the importance of social justice and equality.

Under the National government of 1975–84, the social ideas that under-pinned this situation retained priority over radical change. From 1984 onwards, reform without consultation became the norm, a reform predicated with little regard to economic and social equity concerns. Saturday, and then Sunday, trading were embraced. The Employment Contracts Act emasculated the unions and opened the door for major changes in pay and conditions. Signifi-cant stand-down periods for benefits were introduced, and benefits were themselves cut. State housing moved to market rentals for its houses. Tertiary education became a charge item, and parents became liable to child support in this respect until offspring attained the age of 25. Record matching for benefit fraud extended even to legislation that required doctors and priests to reveal the confidences of their patients and penitents (an excess currently under review). In areas such as health and education, sponsorship and competition saw what Pearson and Thornes (1983) forshadowed in *Eclipse of Equality*. As with value added tax in the UK, a shift from progressive income and corporate tax to consumer taxation in a Goods and Services Tax has placed revenue generation on a wider population while, in certain ways, disenfranchising them from benefits. An enthusiasm driven solely by economic considerations has reached into every facet of society, threatening to create an underclass and promoting a corporate culture where, for the first time, status symbols such as BMW cars are revered.

This catalogue is not unique to New Zealand and, in terms of targeting assistance and producing sounder management, it is not without positive components. However, the pace and depth of change once again demand mention. The United Kingdom comparison now seems like a visit to the past, and Thatcherism a mild purgative. To see *The Economist* (1988, 1992) lauding government accounting in New Zealand and its flexible labour laws still invokes a certain feeling of surrealism, but this passes when one encounters the reality of the relative levels of costs, services and infrastructure on offer in each country.

Clearly much has been gained and lost. It is plain that social and economic goals, certainly in the short term, have proved incompatible. Domestic debate, even academic, on the implications of the priorities chosen to date is value-rid-den and bedevilled by statistics that are customized to arguments or confounded by redefinition. It is, in fact, the case that so much has been reformed that baseline comparisons are virtually impossible (real levels of national debt, for instance, are highly controversial). What is undeniably interesting, however, is the facility with which change has taken place, given the immense pain involved. There is no geography of riots, and little civil disobedience. In spite of a rise in youth unemployment and the reduction in living standards of the poor – estimated to be 18 per cent by the New Zealand Planning Council (1990), compared with a 10 per cent *rise* for the rich – there has so far been no dramatic manifestation of social unrest.

The question, then, remains of how much people actually supported or endorsed change and restructured their own aspirations in line with it. For all the rhetorical debate, observation suggests that there has been an ongoing ambivalence to restructuring, the best indicator of which may be the record of general elections. In 1993, whether exhausted by duplicity or keen to moderate further amplifications of change, New Zealand restructured its politics.

4.3 Restructuring politics

Political geographers have reviewed the pattern of voting in New Zealand since the 1975 election, tracing a shift between the two dominant parties, Labour and National, as either a shifting preference for the respectively left or right wing, or as aversion therapy, driven by the desire to keep or move one party out (McRobie, 1989; Catt and Roberts, 1992; Holland, 1992). Traditionally, National has held power on a provincial mandate augmented by a broad range of prosperous urban seats. This held after 1974 and, as confidence gradually eroded, so marginal support engendered by 'Think Big' and the endorsement of a 1981 South African rugby tour proved crucial in maintaining power.

In 1984, the increasing personal manipulation of the economy by the then Prime Minister precipitated a new party of the Right (the New Zealand Party, NZP), splitting the vote and ensuring a Labour victory. This victory derived from a predominantly urban and Auckland base, and produced a young Cabinet with very few members with provincial loyalty. This Cabinet was tailored for reform, which it did. In 1987, in spite of three years energetic and potentially alienating reform, Labour retained power, keeping most of its traditional vote and gaining many of the votes from the now self-destructed NZP. It also maintained internal coherence in the face of mounting tension between the right faction, who had commandeered policy directions, and a sizeable minority representing traditional support.

By 1990, continuing radical change and unresolvable fractionalism fractured Labour and decimated support. Yet the electorate voted not for an abandonment of change (in the form of third party options), but for a shift from a disintegrating team to a party perceived as offering a similar but more gentle path forward: a resurgent National. The result was the largest majority in New Zealand's history. Enough people would seem to have endorsed enough of the change to sanction the limits of restructuring to that time.

National, in its turn, retrospectively decided on rapid change, on a harder line, which moved corporatization and the principle that the user pays further into the sensitive health and education areas. At a time when real benefits of change were still insubstantial and optimism consequently cowed, this decision was unwise. It exceeded National's mandate, violated the limits of public indifference and led to widespread disillusionment with politics and to a growing demand for a reform of the electoral system to curb the power of

Cabinet. By 1993, the electorate had identified both a need for control of radical change and the tool to achieve it. This was through electoral reform, spawned by Labour's Royal Commission, to consider proportional representation (New Zealand Royal Commission, 1986). The tool was to be the Mixed Member Proportional (MMP) system, in which half the members of parliament are constituency derived, with the other half ensuring appropriate representation for any party with over 5 per cent of the vote. To its credit, National, unlike Labour, actually honoured a pledge to hold a referendum on the issue of proportional representation. Thus in the General Election of 6 November, 1993, the vote was held, 52 per cent voting for MMP, and National retaining power by one seat.

Because of the consensus nature of MMP, this act is almost certainly the final curtain on radical economic restructuring, and the start of a political one potentially as radical. It will reduce the power of small intra-party groups to force accelerated change, and will enhance their power, and the power of other small parties, to stop change under certain coalition conditions. It will probably draw the high water mark of free-market reform in New Zealand, leaving education and health only marginally corporatized and leaving room for reversing some of the more severe benefit cuts. The more proactive and exposed economy, and the greater diversity of wealth, remain the legacy of change.

One can see these events almost as a feedback loop, with economic change precipitating social stress and, after evaluation, a political response. New Zealanders have been characterized as the 'passionless people' by McLauchlan (1976). Perhaps the evidence here is more for a national pragmatism, an acceptance of change and a desire for equity. In many ways, these two themes are written into the socio-economic history of the last two decades, and the electoral referendum result is the corporate consensus in how to reconcile the two more appropriately. It says something, as well, about controlling ideological amplification.

5 CONCLUSION

For New Zealand, greater integration into the world economy is an inevitable outcome of seeking higher economic growth while embracing doctrines of competition. Global intrusion is a significant concern for New Zealanders, and it is held by many to be at peak levels, even if epochs such as the early colonization waves and the 1930s recession suggest otherwise. Others argue that New Zealand is perhaps more truly free than at any time in its history. This contention will endure, as will the one of getting New Zealand off the sheep's back. In terms of short-term outcomes, New Zealanders have been rudely removed therefrom. They now generally work far harder for less in order to achieve their material goals. In terms of product diversity, New Zealand has achieved satisfyingly more export range. Two positive answers, and yet a deeper concern remains. In the new and challenging niche New Zealand occupies, agriculture and rural-based activities are positioning themselves as bases for provincial, export-led growth. Primary production from the heartlands is re-emerging as a key future hope, augmented by effective manufacturing. The successful conclusion of the Uruguay round has underpinned a satisfaction with what is, in many respects, a helical reversion to an earlier geography of trade based upon an agricultural growth engine. In this climate of opinion, the need to part company with the sheep's back, and other primary portions, has moved significantly down the agenda. History will tell for how long.

NOTES

1 Over the period in question, the reporting units for employment statistics have varied, especially in Auckland. These figures refer to those employment districts that are predominantly composed of land that lay historically within the original Auckland employment district.

REFERENCES

Bollard, A. & McCormack, D. (1985). *Closer Economic Relations*. Wellington: New Zealand Institute of Economic Research, Research Paper 30.

Britton, S., Le Heron, R., & Pawson, E. (eds) (1992). *Changing Places in New Zealand: a Geography of Restructuring*. Christchurch: New Zealand Geographical Society.

Burney, J. (1980). 'Unemployment and Long Term Permanent Migration.' Unpublished Seminar Paper, Department of Geography, University of Canterbury.

Catt, H. & Roberts, N. (1992). *Voter's Choice: Electoral Change in New Zealand?* Palmerstone North: Dunmore Press.

Cliff, A.D. & Haggett P. (1985). *The Spread of Measles in Fiji and the Pacific: Spatial Components in the Transmission of Epidemic Waves Through Island Communities*. Canberra: Research School of Pacific Studies, Australian National University, Department of Human Geography Publication Number HG/18.

Cliff, A.D. & Haggett, P. (1988). *Atlas of Disease Distributions: Analytic Approaches to Epidemiological Data*. Oxford: Blackwell Reference.

Cliff, A.D., Haggett, P., Ord, J.K., Bassett, K.A., & Davies, R.B. (1975). *Elements of Spatial Structure*. Cambridge: Cambridge University Press.

Crocombe, G., Enright, M., & Porter, M. (1991). *Upgrading New Zealand's Competitive Advantage*. Auckland: Oxford University Press.

Douglas, R. (1980). *There's Got To Be a Better Way: a Practical ABC to Solving New Zealand's Major Problems*. Wellington: Fourth Estate Books.

Forer, P.C. & Parrott, N. (1992). 'On the edge of the global village: New Zealand and the emerging information society.' In S. Brunn & T. Leinbach (eds), *Information, Communications: a Geographic Perspective*. London: Allen & Unwin, 302–24.

Forer, P.C. & Pearce, D. (1984). 'Spatial patterns of package tourism in New Zealand.' *New Zealand Geographer*, 40, 34–42.

Franklin, H. (1978). *Trade, Growth and Anxiety: New Zealand beyond the Welfare State*. Auckland: Methuen.

Franklin, H. (1985). *Cul de Sac: the Question of New Zealand's Future*. Wellington: Port Nicholson Press.

Gould, J.D. (1982). *The Rake's Progress? the New Zealand Economy since 1945*. Auckland: Hodder & Stoughton.

Green, D. (1986). *The New Right: the Counter-Revolution in Political, Economic and Social Thought.* Brighton: Wheatsheaf.

Grey, A. (1984). 'North American influences in the development of New Zealand's landscapes: 1800 to 1935.' *New Zealand Geographer,* 40, 66–77.

Harris, W.W. (1982). 'Middle East politics and New Zealand exports.' *New Zealand Geographer,* 38, 86–89.

Holland, M. (1992). *Electoral Behaviour in New Zealand.* Oxford Readings in New Zealand Politics, 1. Auckland: Oxford University Press.

Holland, S. (1976). *The Regional Problem.* London: Macmillan.

Johnston, R.J. (1973). 'Regional development in a small but prosperous ex-colony.' *Regional Studies,* 5, 321–31.

Johnston, R.J. & Rimmer, P.J. (1967). 'Commercial leadership in New Zealand.' *New Zealand Geographer,* 23, 188–93.

Johnston, W.B. (1973). 'The debate on regional planning and development in New Zealand.' *New Zealand Geographer,* 29, 188–93.

Lane, P. & Hamer, P. (1973). *Decade of Change: Economic Growth and Prospects in New Zealand, 1960–1970.* Wellington: Reed Educational.

McCracken, K. (1977). 'Social well-being within the New Zealand urban system.' *Proceedings,* Ninth New Zealand Geographical Society Conference, Dunedin. Christchurch: New Zealand Geographical Society.

McDermott Associates (1983). 'Regional implications of Closer Economic Relations with Australia: a Preliminary Report.' Wellington: Ministry of Works and Development/McDermott Associates.

McLauchlan, G. (1976). *The Passionless People.* Auckland: Cassell.

McRobie, A. (1989). *New Zealand Electoral Atlas.* Wellington: Government Printer.

Mein, B. (1979). 'Regional Variations in the Impact of Price Increases and Supply Limitations in Petroleum Products and Imports to New Zealand.' Unpublished Seminar Paper, Department of Geography, University of Canterbury.

Ministry of Works and Development (1986). *Mid Year Development Review.* Wellington: Ministry of Works and Development.

New Zealand Department of Statistics. *New Zealand Official Yearbook.* Annually. Wellington: New Zealand Department of Statistics.

New Zealand Planning Council (1990). *Who Gets What? the Distribution of Income and Wealth in New Zealand.* Wellington: Income Distribution Group.

New Zealand Royal Commission on the Electoral System (1986). *Report of the Royal Commission on the Electoral System: Towards a Better Democracy.* Wellington: Government Printer.

Novitz, D. & Wilmott, B. (1992). *New Zealand in Crisis.* Wellington: Government Printer.

NZTRE (1988). *Administering for Excellence: Effective Administration in Education.* Wellington: Taskforce to Review Education Administration.

Parrott, N. & Forer, P.C. (1986). 'The information sector in New Zealand, 1971–81.' *New Zealand Geographer,* 42, 25–30.

Pearce, D.J. (1990). 'Tourism, the regions and restructuring in New Zealand.' *Journal of Tourism Studies,* 1, 33–42.

Pearson, D. & Thornes, D. (1983). *Eclipse of Equality: Social Stratification in New Zealand.* Studies in Society, 17. London: Allen & Unwin.

Robinson, G. (1993). 'Trading strategies for New Zealand: the GATT, CER and trade liberalisation.' *New Zealand Geographer,* 49, 13–22.

Simpson, T. (1990). *The Sugarbag Years* (2nd edn). Auckland: Penguin Books.

The Economist (1988). 'Learning to Fly: Four Page Supplement on New Zealand's Reforms.' *The Economist,* 21 November 1988, 24–28.

The Economist (1992). 'Lessons from the Kiwis.' *The Economist*, AP, 3 October 1992, 64.

Treasury (1991). 'Regional Indicators.' Wellington: Ministerial Report T91/5108.

Williams, A.G. (1979). 'Leads and Lags in New Zealand: National Impacts on Regional Unemployment.' Unpublished Seminar Paper, Department of Geography, University of Canterbury.

13

Land Tenures, Property Rights, and Multiple Land Use: Issues for American and Antipodean Rangelands

J.H. Holmes

1 RANGELAND TENURES: UNRESOLVED ISSUES

1.1 Contemporary debates on property rights

Australia, New Zealand and the United States are three Western nations with important tracts of rangelands devoted primarily to extensive livestock grazing, and held under restricted tenures such as leases, licences and grazing permits. The extent of lands under limited title for grazing purposes is shown in table 13.1 and figure 13.1. In Australia, pastoral lease tenures embrace more than half the national lands and comprise 76.4 per cent of land held for private use. While vast in extent, these lands are of exceptionally low productivity. In New Zealand, only the 'High Country', on the drier eastern flanks of the Southern Alps, remains under pastoral lease tenures. Though small in area, these lands are of high scenic, biological, recreational and watershed value, and have a prominent place within the psyche of the nation. In the United States, rangeland grazing tenures are not readily delineated, but primarily involve lands with grazing permits under the administration of the National Forest Service (NFS) within the Department of Agriculture, and the Bureau of Land Management (BLM) within the Department of the Interior. See figure 13.2 for the location of NFS and BLM lands.

All of these nations are experiencing widening public debate about the future use, management and ownership of these rangelands, generated primarily by the rapid expansion of non-pastoral uses, interests and values, which have demolished the former pastoral hegemony. Central to this debate is the question of property rights, as expressed primarily in land tenures but also in land regulations, which determine the balance between the private and the public domains. A related question focuses on the appropriate governmental mechanisms to satisfy the various interests while serving wider public goals.

From the time of the initial wave of settlement, by squatters, runholders and ranchers, the allocation of property rights has remained an issue awaiting

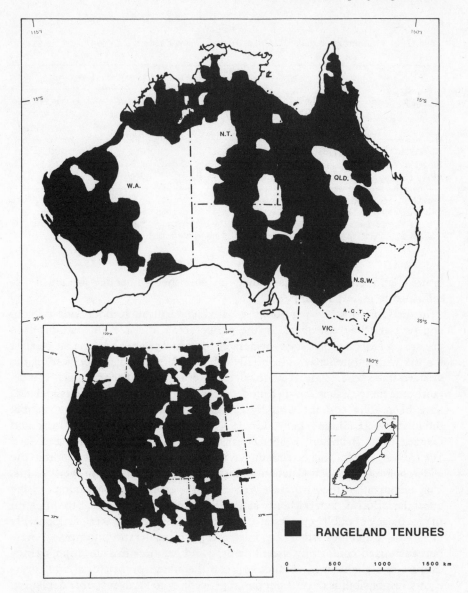

Figure 13.1 Rangeland tenures in Australia, New Zealand and the United States at identical map scales. These tenures are shown in more detail in subsequent maps (*Sources*: see figures 13.2–4)

further resolution. *De jure* public proprietary rights have been retained by limiting the opportunities to obtain freehold title and by relying on restricted titles, such as leases, licences and grazing permits. For many decades, following the loss of momentum towards further closer settlement and property subdivision, these basic tenure arrangements have been rarely questioned, but lately this quiescence has been disturbed, raising major issues concerning whether

Table 13.1   Area under rangeland tenures: Australia, New Zealand and the United States

Country	Total area (km²)	Area under rangeland tenures		
		km²	Percent of national area	As percent of Australian rangeland area
Australia	7,686,850	4,043,300	52.6	100.0
New Zealand	268,103	28,235	10.5	0.7
United States	7,982,000[a]	1,271,827[b]	15.9[a]	31.5

[a] Area of the conterminous United States only (48 states).
[b] Comprises land held by the National Forest Service (564,150 km²) and the Bureau of Land Management (707,677 km²) in the 11 western states (California, Oregon, Washington, Idaho, Nevada, Utah, Arizona, New Mexico, Colorado, Wyoming, Montana). Not all of this land is available to grazing.

limited land tenure systems should be abolished, amended or drastically reformed to meet current needs.

In the United States the public debate has been much more wide-ranging and probing than elsewhere. In the public arena, the issue of public versus private (or federal versus state) ownership of the rangelands became the catalyst for the widely publicized and briefly influential 'sagebrush rebellion' in the western states where federal landownership remains significant. Equally importantly, the policy issues arising from federal ownership of forests and rangelands have been fully and thoughtfully canvassed in a succession of substantial publications (Culhane, 1981; Libecap, 1981; Clawson, 1983; Francis and Ganzel, 1984; Brubaker, 1984; Dysart and Clawson, 1986; Fairfax and Yale, 1987; Foss, 1987). This discussion has also been closely interwoven within the wider, ongoing intellectual debate about appropriate regimes of property rights. The privatization theorists have seized upon perceived imperfections in the administration of federal lands as evidence to support general theories on the inefficacy of public ownership of resources, finding instances of supposedly inevitable outcomes such as: misdirected bureaucratic incentives, over-bureaucratized conformity, asset hoarding and resource misallocation, agency capture and clientelism, conflict between the state's proprietorial and sovereignty responsibilities, and a supposed propensity towards resource depletion. See, for example, Libecap (1981), and also the *Cato Journal*, the intellectual forum for private property theorists, which devoted an early issue (2, 1, 1981) to federal landownership issues (see also 2, 3, 1982). In response, the major critics of the privatization theorists have referred to the evidence on desirable outcomes from the public administration of federal forests and rangelands and the pitfalls from untrammelled privatization (Bromley, 1991).

By comparison, in Australia, debate on property rights and on the institutional basis for the use and management of rangelands has been desultory and subdued, and has usually been ancillary to the various public reviews of pastoral land tenures, undertaken over the last fifteen years, all of which have been very limited in scope. Australia lacks the critical mass of intellectual activity to mount a substantive, ongoing debate on property rights, comparable to that in the United States. In any case, as discussed later, land use competition is more subdued within Australia's rangelands, and multiple-use goals can often be reconciled with pastoralism's continued recognition as the 'highest and best use'. Also of critical importance are the much more substantial property rights attached to Australian pastoral leases compared with America's seasonal grazing permits, thus offering less scope for public intervention.

By contrast with Australia, the pastoral High Country of New Zealand's South Island has come increasingly under pressure from the growth of multiple resource demands, and from the localized diversity in resource values. However, proposals for restructuring property rights are constrained by the entrenched rights of pastoral lessees. Proposals for renegotiating property rights have involved complex trade-offs between public and private interests, leading governments increasingly towards a reliance on regulatory powers rather than on the state's residual proprietorial rights.

1.2 Antipodean and American models of rangeland ownership and administration

The historical record reveals a close parallelism in certain critical elements of frontier settlement in Britain's New World colonies. Regardless of timing, or of economic, political, or religious ideologies, or of the relative emphasis on large landholders (with or without slave or convict labour) or on smallholders, efforts were made to restrain settlement within defined bounds and to deny or, subsequently, to restrict severely the property rights of settlers seeking to occupy 'empty' lands beyond these bounds. This restraint on property rights is in sharp contrast to the frontier settlement philosophy, for example, of Spanish governments who privatized initially the exploitation of native peoples under the *encomienda* system which was readily translated in swift privatization of large land tracts under the *hacienda* system (Grindle, 1986, pp. 25–9). Even with settlement policies which permitted larger landholdings, as with the initial Wakefield colonization schemes, there was no comparable free, untrammelled award of property rights to vast areas. The current retention of *de jure* public ownership of the rangelands of the United States, Australia and New Zealand is the outcome of this shared heritage of restraint in land privatization. This has enabled governments to pursue land-related policies through proprietorial ('landlord') powers as well as sovereignty powers. However, there have been markedly different outcomes between the Antipodes and the United States, largely attributable to sharply differing degrees of success in the rate of expansion of the agricultural frontier, but also assisted by localized land resource differentials within America's rangelands.

Land settlement in nineteenth-century Australia and New Zealand was marked by recurring failure in intensive agricultural colonization, paralleled by unrivalled success in widespread but flimsy pastoral occupation of vast rangelands. Only after an extended period of dogged resistance did colonial governments and their London masters agree to give full legal recognition to squatter occupation, and then only on insecure, short-term, low-rental leases and licences. The landmark decision for New South Wales was contained in an Imperial Order-in-Council in 1847 which provided the basis for more secure pastoral occupancy through Crown leasehold tenures. A parallel tenure was granted in New Zealand in 1851. For a while, pastoralism continued to be regarded as a temporary expedient until the agricultural frontier caught up. However, the long hiatus and the runaway success of pastoralism forced further adaptation and elaboration of leasehold tenures as public policy instruments, rather than unwanted expedients (Heathcote, 1965, 1987; Powell, 1970; Williams, 1975). Limited-term leasehold tenures lent themselves to the articulation and implementation of flexible land settlement policies, with provisions being developed for lease termination and full or partial resumption, and with covenants being included in pursuit of minimum levels of stocking, of capital investment and of residency. Further adaptations were subsequently needed to ensure security in investment, including longer-term leases with provisions for 'roll-overs' well ahead of expiry dates. With the halting of the closer settlement frontier at the limits to agriculture, the acceptance of pastoralism as the pre-eminent use of the remaining rangelands and the loss of any well-defined public policy goal to match the previous goal of closer settlement, the system of property rights and land administration became entrenched with strong elements of clientelism mixed with bureaucratic conformism. The influence of the leaseholders was heightened by their role as the dominant, indeed sole, interest group and by their absolute reliance upon the lands held under lease as their year-round grazing resource. In this respect they differed significantly from the seasonal use of public lands available to American ranchers. Clientelism and the lack of other competing interests has allowed an entrenchment of the property rights of lessees and a diminution in the remaining proprietorial powers of the state in the Antipodean model.

While the western rangelands of the United States could also have been allocated under a system of low-rent, large-area, whole-property, year-round leasehold tenures, this mode of land tenure did not eventuate. The reasons are fairly clear. Unlike Australia, almost all vacant land was held by the federal government, not the states. Also, unlike Australia and New Zealand, American land legislation was not forced to adapt to a dominant mode of initial widespread pastoral occupance of its frontier lands. The remorseless expansion of the agricultural frontier across the productive interior encouraged Congress to maintain steadfast support for its Homestead Acts, by which land was freeholded into blocks of 160 acres or less. So successful were these policies that Congress was able to ignore the realities of low productivity in the western rangelands where a series of non-legislated adaptations occurred, including pre-emptive acquisition of strategic land parcels, corruption in land transactions and unregulated open access to federal rangelands; this led to 'range wars' and range mismanagement.

Between 1899 and 1927, 17 bills in Congress designed to alleviate rangeland problems all died in the committee stage. Only through strenuous pressure and threats from the Roosevelt administration did Congress finally adopt the Taylor Grazing Act of 1934 which 'changed the emphasis of federal land policy from disposal of lands to bureaucratic administration of them' (Libecap, 1981, p. 3).

Within the Department of the Interior, ' . . . the establishment of the Division of Grazing ended the non-management of the public domain, although it would be many years before the division's successor, the BLM, began to effectively manage the public domain' (Culhane, 1981, p. 84).

The Taylor Act has been of critical importance in shaping the subsequent management and use of the western rangelands, most importantly in its award of a very restricted set of grazing rights to ranchers, and largely attaching these rights to adjacent freeholded land. This provided legal recognition to the existing sharp bifurcation of property rights within the single grazing enterprise, with full freehold rights on the 'home ranch' and restricted, amendable, seasonal grazing permits on the public domain. While these outcomes were achieved belatedly, after an inordinately prolonged failure to recognize the mismatch between land legislation and land tenure requirements, nevertheless in broad outline it represented a reasonable satisfactory award of property rights in relation to land resources. Figure 13.2 reveals a mosaic of land tenures, reflecting localized productivity gradients between well-watered, well-grassed, arable, irrigable valley bottoms offering year-round grazing on the one hand, and the adjacent open range, comprising land of low productivity, usually suited only to limited seasonal grazing. Not surprisingly, the seemingly chaotic 'land grabs' of the homesteading era had effectively differentiated between these two major land classes, leaving most ranchers with a secure year-round production unit, and with varying degrees of reliance on their rangeland grazing permits. Over time this reliance was generally reduced, with more intensive use of the productive freehold lands.

In contrast to the prolonged period of non-intervention on vacant federal lands now administered by BLM were the strongly managerial policies pursued on NFS lands under a progressivist philosophy emphasizing managed, sustainable, multiple use, including controlled grazing under annual permits. This management model was subsequently applied to BLM lands.

2 CONTEMPORARY CHALLENGES AND RESPONSES

2.1 The American model: no longer an ugly duckling?

The American model, with its sharp bifurcation of property rights within the one pastoral enterprise, is thus an accident of history, emerging from the long period of obstructionism and legislative neglect within Congress. As a means of allocating property rights for modern pastoral enterprises, it is dysfunctional, though less so than during the period of unregulated open access. The evidence is clear that, if pastoralism had remained the only significant broadacres use of the lands now administered by the BLM, most of these lands would now have been available for freeholding by the grazing permittees. In its early years, following the 1934 enactment, the newly created Grazing Service was almost totally dominated by the livestock associations, and the movement towards freeholding, an outcome implicit in the Taylor Act, was gathering momentum.

However, strong counter-influences have emerged which have led to mark-

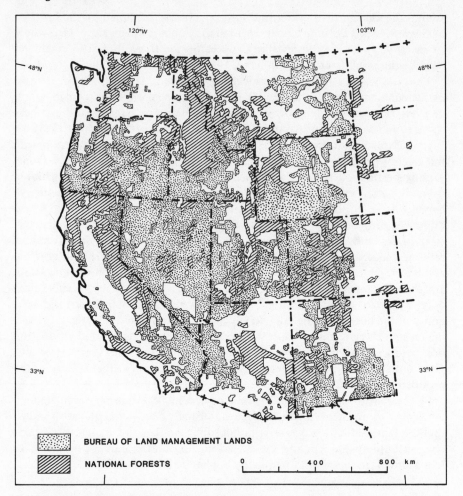

Figure 13.2 Federal lands administered by the Bureau of Land Management and the National Forest Service in the western United States
(*Source*: National Geographic, 1982. *Map of America's Federal Lands*. Washington, DC: National Geographic Society)

edly different outcomes, limiting the property rights of ranchers and expanding the powers and responsibilities of the BLM. Since mid-century, there has been a marked growth of interest in BLM lands, matching the prior interest in NFS lands, by powerful conservation and recreation lobbies. Their causes have been advantaged by the continued status of BLM lands as public domain, open to public use with only limited, seemingly insecure, rights held by the ranching interests.

The vast extent and enhanced, multiple uses of lands in the public domain have led to a transformation in actual and perceived values of these lands which now loom large in national and local debates on desired uses, on access, and on basic questions of property rights. With the growth of multiple constituencies, the main responsible federal agency has been transformed from a clientelist role dominated by one single interest group towards a more powerful, informed, professional role responsible for land management and land use planning. Within the Department of the Interior, in 1946, the Division of Grazing was disbanded and replaced by the Bureau of Land Management, with wider responsibilities in administering the public domain.

These widening responsibilities were recognized in the interim 1964 Classification and Multiple Use Act and in the organic 1976 Federal Land Policy and Management Act (FLPMA) which provided the BLM with a statutory mission to engage in comprehensive, long-term planning towards sustainable, multiple use of the public domain. Multiple Use Advisory Councils were established to counterbalance the Grazing Advisory Boards (Culhane, 1981, p. 95). The BLM has since followed the US Forest Service model in seeking to utilize independent, objective methods of land capability assessment and land use planning towards achieving its statutory obligations. However, as with other government agencies responsible for management of natural resources, it has been forced to be increasingly sensitive to conflicting pressures exercised by vocal, influential interest groups and must also respond to other federal legislation concerning environmental policy, public consultation, and accountability.

The complexity of BLM's task is indicated in its legislative mandate as spelt out in FLMPA Congress decided against a mandate that the agency identify 'the highest and best use' by which other uses were permitted only to the extent compatible with the best use. In the Act, no method was proposed to resolve the difficulties of establishing a preference order.

> Land use planning is a central component of FLPMA. The Bureau is charged with preparing a continuous inventory of the public lands and their resources, including recreational and scenic values. Land use plans are to be developed with public participation, by notice and comment rulemaking. Federal landuse planning, moreover, is to be coordinated where possible with state and local land use plans. Tension is thus built into the planning process. On the one hand, FLPMA calls for rational, scentific landuse planning, by experts; on the other hand, it assigns an important role to public participation, thus adding an inherently political dimension to the planning process. (Francis, 1984, p. 156)

As pointed out by many American commentators, this represents a significant switch in the *rationale* for multiple use, away from the 'progressivist' doctrine, espoused by Gifford Pinchot and initially applied to the NFS early this century, founded upon an assumed impartial, scientific approach to land use planning, and towards an alternative doctrine, described as 'interest-group liberalism', which assumes that the public interest is central to the determination of use, and that this is best achieved through accountable public procedures. While this mode of decision-making is placing greater emphasis to public processes over 'objective' scientific enquiry, the primary goal still remains multiple land use. Indeed 'interest-group liberalism' generally reinforces the concept of multiple use, already entrenched by the 'progressivists'.

More recently, some leading commentators, favouring retention of federal ownership, have nevertheless recognized that ' . . . multiple use has been used like a commercial advertising slogan . . . [which] . . . may have been oversold' (Foss, 1987, p. xx). In his comprehensive review of current issues, Clawson (1983, pp. 200–16) has argued in favour of long-term leasing of federal lands, where a primary use could be identified, in order to ' . . . harness the self-interests of the lessee to the social goals of the national government as landowner' (p. 204).

Foss has also supported the designation of primary use for appropriate management units, with greater tenure security for primary users, emphasizing that this could well prove an acceptable alternative to land privatization (Foss, 1987, p. xx).

In further support of long-term leasing, Nelson has presented proposals which can be interpreted as a partial switch from the American to the Antipodean model, particularly with its emphasis on limited tenure security, mechanisms for resumption, and attention to performance standards:

> Probably the best case for long-term leasing can be made for public grazing lands. The productivity of many grazing lands is so low that significant public management expenses cannot be justified. At present public management costs far exceed any revenues received by the government. The ranchers who use the lands know them well and are well equipped to make investment and management decisions. If ranchers are provided a secure long-term tenure, they will have the necessary incentive to maintain the lands in good condition . . . . Long-term grazing leases would also have to include performance standards for the achievement of non-grazing outputs on the lands. It would also be important to provide a readily available mechanism for abandoning grazing and conversion to higher value uses that might emerge. (Nelson, 1984, p. 292)

Nelson's proposal, and his rationale, could have been directly taken from the Antipodean model of pastoral leases, particularly in its earlier phase involving 'performance standards'and limited security, with mechanisms for partial resumption, and compensation only for improvements.

2.2 Possible convergence, with selective adaptations from the two models?

These lease proposals are only one of many indicators of emerging partial convergence in the American and Antipodean rangelands, not only in goals and policies for the management and use of these lands, but also in public institutions by which policies will be appraised, adopted, and implemented. Elements from these two models can be critically examined and selectively applied in emerging contexts, with the added advantage of insights gleaned from practical experience.

With its extreme restrictions on property rights and continued reliance upon proprietary control rather than sovereignty powers, together with the development of a strongly professionalized but consultative approach towards land use planning, the American model appears to have greatest relevance in contexts involving the complexities of multiple use where also a multiplicity of constituencies have recognized roles in decision-making and in final use. The American model also is of value where there is marked local variability in resource values, requiring parallel variability in uses and in property rights. However, there are inevitable tensions within this model, which seem designed to elicit and heighten conflict calling for exceptionally efficacious mechanisms for conflict avoidance and resolution.

In its pristine form, during the period of flux in rangeland occupance, the Antipodean model was exemplary in enabling land to be allocated to its 'highest and best use' where this use was likely to prove only temporary, and likely to be succeeded by new forms of 'best' use. With its retention of ultimate proprietary control, the leasehold system was also an excellent mechanism for allocating rights to engage in the 'best' use while ensuring these rights also carry specified responsibilities or 'performance standards' tied to public goals. Formerly these were goals of development whereas more recently these have been translated to goals of sustainable use or preservation of valued natural assets. However, there is a persistent tension between the lessee's demand for expanded rights and greater security of tenure, and the land administrator's responsibilities to enforce constraints. In the absence of any countervailing public interest, there is a strong propensity to agency capture and extension of property rights, barely differentiated from freehold, thus destroying the rationale for the institutional structure.

Referring to these two models, an appraisal can now be made of current, prospective and desirable directions in land tenure and land administration in Australia and New Zealand.

2.3 Australia: tinkering with the Antipodean model?

As recently as 1970, land use options for Australia's rangelands were simple, limited and founded upon self-evident truths. Pastoralism was the pre-eminent use, given absolute priority to occupy all suitable lands, and capable of being displaced only by a few 'higher' (that is, yielding higher returns) forms of land use, notably agriculture, either irrigated or dryland, and mining. The modest localized land demands of these two alternative uses posed little challenge to pastoralism's sway over Australia's arid and semi-arid rangelands. Land legislation was framed to accommodate and encourage these perceived land use options, with covenants on minimum stocking rates and required capital improvements, and with provisions for tenure conversion towards 'higher' forms of land use. Although five separate legislatures were involved in pastoral lease tenures, namely New South Wales, Queensland, South Australia, Western Australia, and Northern Territory, there were strong common elements in philosophy, legislation and administration of leased lands, as shown in figure 13.3.

Only over the last two decades has this simple model of pastoral land use and land management been subject to questioning, but the questions have rapidly proliferated. So also have the alternative land use options, obviously challenging the pastoralists' domain, particularly on marginal lands where pastoralism's hold is tenuous. Significant new forms of alternative land use include: restora-

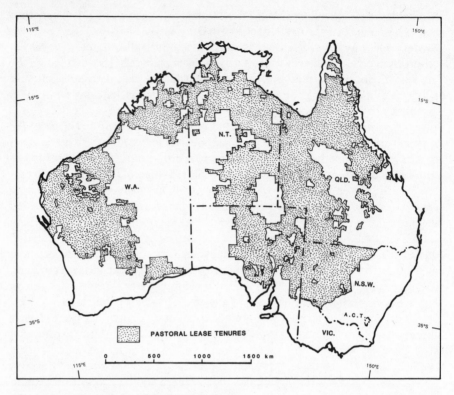

Figure 13.3   Australian pastoral leasehold lands
(*Source*: Commonwealth of Australia, Australian Surveying and Land Information Group, 1993. *Map of Australian Land Tenure*. Canberra: Government Printer)

tion of Aboriginal land rights, whether including pastoralism or not; nature preservation; wide-ranging recreation and mineral exploration; water catchments; defence and quarantine; locally focused but widely scattered intensification of land use, for tourism, mining, agriculture, urban, defence and other activities; and a growing incidence of land held for speculative purposes.

Pastoralism's case as the 'highest' form of land use has not been helped by growing public concern about such outcomes as: land degradation; loss of habitat and of native species; over-subdivision into non-viable holdings, with consequent low incomes and increased demands for public assistance; and the mounting cross-subsidies needed to support enhanced services, such as roads, telephones and electricity.

2.3.1 The modest momentum towards reform. Strangely, in spite of the rapid growth in interest constituencies devoted to Australia's rangelands, these interests have had only a modest impact in reshaping land use and land management policies and almost no impact on the institutional framework of property rights and land administration. It is true that there has been a succession of public inquiries into pastoral land administration in the four states and one territory with vast rangelands under pastoral leases (New South Wales, Queensland,

South Australia, Western Australia, and the Northern Territory). In all cases, these inquiries have endorsed and helped to formalize the gradual shift away from earlier goals of development and closer settlement towards current concerns about sustainable land use, and that lease covenants are now almost all rewritten towards these ends. Some attention has usually (but not always) been given to traditional Aboriginal rights, and to the need to resolve clouded issues of public access within pastoral leases. However, the public input into these inquiries from groups other than pastoralists has been very limited and low-key, and terms of reference, submissions, public hearings and recommendations have always been dominated by the concerns of the pastoral lessees and the administrators, with the notable exception of South Australia and, to a lesser extent, New South Wales. This is in marked contrast to the United States and, to a certain extent, New Zealand, where other interest groups would have used these inquiries as the catalyst for powerful campaigns in pursuit of highly focused goals, which would have markedly influenced the outcomes.

The low-profile approach to pastoral tenure reform and the modest outcomes, involving only modest 'tinkering' with the system, are not readily explained in terms either of a general public apathy in Australia towards involvement in major policy issues or of a general unconcern about the future of Australia's rangelands. The argument that Australians are apathetic to public policy issues relating to resources can readily be demolished. By any yardstick of international comparison, Australia has an exceptional record in environment/resource activism and public concern, paralleled by governmental action.

Why has there been no catalyst to generate a more wide-ranging public debate upon institutional reform of rangelands tenures and land administration? The explanation can be pursued at two levels, one relating to the processes of interest-group politics, and the second based on the geography of Australia's rangelands. Interest-group politics thrives where there are sharply focused test cases which acquire importance far beyond their immediate outcomes, by revising norms about processes and expected future outcomes. These test cases become trials of strength between contending interests, forcing governments to redirect their policies and procedures, according to the outcomes.

In Australia's rangelands, test cases which have captured national attention have related to issues such as mining (Coronation Hill, Roxby Downs and others) or to Aboriginal land claims (Wattie Creek, Noonkanbah, Maralinga, and so on), and have not focused on pastoral land tenures or issues of multiple land use. These latter issues have, so far, been the source of only minor, localized conflict, not capable of generating any momentum towards fundamental shifts in processes or policies.

An additional part of the explanation lies in the decision context, which is fragmented into five separate state/territory-based administrations, with little basis for national-level intervention through such mechanisms as export licences, corporation powers or World Heritage listings. Conservation groups, who usually act as the triggers in interest-group political processes, have been unable to find an effective national mechanism by which to pursue reform of pastoral tenures and land administration, although adopting a high public profile on issues of biodiversity, sustainable use and multiple use (Messer and Mosley, 1982; Cameron and Elix, 1991).

This leads to the more basic level of explanation, tied to the geography of Australia's rangelands, which are notable for their vast area (almost six times the area of BLM lands in the western states), their remoteness and distance from any major population centres, their low productivity, their sparse settlement and their apparent capacity to accommodate almost all current interests and values without leading to any highly contentious conflict over resource allocation.

2.3.2 The case for leasehold tenure. The crux of the matter is this. Notwithstanding the rapid recent growth in other interests and values, over most of Australia's rangelands grazing commands continued recognition as the 'highest and best use'. Providing it can mend its ways and satisfy national concerns about ecological sustainability it will be able to continue its role as the dominant land use. Save in various special situations, other competing land uses will have to be tailored to meet the requirements of grazing. In this context, the Antipodean model of leasehold tenure is appropriate, at least in theory, though there are obvious grounds for concern that there has been a persistent shift towards *de facto* award of additional property rights to lessees to an extent where the value of the leasehold system may be negated (Holmes, 1991).

The case for continued use of the pastoral leasehold system in preference to freehold over most of the pastoral lands rests on six considerations:

1   Because of the extensive nature of pastoralism, the large size of individual properties and the low levels of private investment in *landesque* capital, there is a weaker theoretical argument in support of a 'full' rights of private property than in areas of smaller holdings and higher intensity of private investment.

2   Also, compared with more intensively farmed lands, there is a stronger need for public intervention to preserve ecological values, not only because of the continued reliance of pastoralism on (altered) natural ecosystems but also because of the fragility of these ecosystems and the difficulties and prohibitive costs of rangeland rehabilitation.

3   The large size of properties often requires public involvement in property planning to accommodate non-pastoral uses and values. These individual prescriptions can best be achieved using leasehold covenants.

4   To a greater extent than in intensively farmed areas, there is a need to retain state powers to convert parcels of land to other uses, both public and private, more readily achieved through leasehold provisions than with freehold.

5   The limitation of the lessee's rights essentially to use of pastoral resources acts as an important constraint on both endemic and epidemic forms of land speculation which is otherwise readily fostered in a context of large properties with low entry costs, low holding costs, and prospects for windfall profits from local land monopolies (Holmes, 1990a).

6   The retention of leasehold, rather than freehold tenures, has a useful influence on the perceptions of all parties concerning property rights and responsibilities.

These arguments, which are an expansion of those presented in Young (1984), closely parallel those of the resource economists concerned to place constraints on property rights where an unacceptable level of 'market failure' may occur through existing or potential negative externalities disproportionate to the modest economic benefits accruing to the pastoral enterprise (Randall, 1983; Bromley, 1991).

2.3.3 Prospective future scenarios for Australia's rangelands. Because of the size and diversity of Australia's rangelands and the differing land administration tradition of the five governments involved, it would be simplistic to propose a uniform set of institutional processes or policy outcomes for these lands. Quite apart from the differing emphases in public priorities between, say, South Australia and the Northern Territory, a useful starting point is to examine the geographical contexts within which land use change is occurring. Our growing knowledge of rangeland ecosystems and productivity levels can be of considerable help in this task. The most critical basis for land tenure differentiation lies in the broad zonal gradients in land productivity and land resilience which can readily be identified, even though these two attributes are only imperfectly connected. This gradient is roughly parallelled by other zonal gradients including:

- diminishing livestock densities and income per unit area;
- lower land values and capital inputs;
- a lower relative importance of pastoralism vis-à-vis other uses, if only because of the diminishing value of pastoralism;
- further enhancement of environmental compared with economic values, partly from ecological fragility and partly from higher wilderness/habitat values;
- greater attractiveness of the land for certain other purposes, including recreation, conservation and, in some areas, Aboriginal use;
- accordingly, a strengthening of the accumulated public and outside private interests relative to the private interest residing with the landholder, and a parallel increase in the ratio of potential negative externalities to internal benefits.

This model of geographically differentiated land tenure systems is founded upon two major zonal pastoral productivity gradients, the first being associated with increasing aridity, proceeding towards the desert margins, and the second with lower pastoral productivity in the higher rainfall northern savanna zone. These zonal models provide only an approximation of localized diversity in pastoral productivity, but, even within this diversity, there generally persists an inverse relationship between pastoral value and the value of the land for other purposes, most notably recreation and preservation. This fortunate inverse relationship provides a very useful basis for differentiation of recommended land use and related land tenure, with the more secure pastoral tenure on the more productive land, unless there are strong competing values to be taken into account.

There are critical transitions within this overall pastoral gradient to suggest three distinctive zones in land occupancy and resource use, each meriting a distinctive approach to institutional processes (property rights and related public institutions) and to outcomes. These three zones are: the more closely settled inner pastoral margin; the zone of manageable pastoral lands; and the outer marginal zone. Differences in pastoral productivity are the prime basis for zonal differentiation. However, the influences of relative accessibility and regional infrastructure are also important. In addition, the historical outcome of closer settlement policies helps to distinguish between the first two zones.

The *inner pastoral margin* is a broad zone of shrublands, grasslands and woodlands in the interiors of Queensland and New South Wales where pastoral productivity combined with accessibility have sustained closer settlement schemes. Within this zone, there is a strong case for secure tenure and selective land development, such as the clearing of vegetation and extensive dryland cropping limited by requirements for sustainable use and the preservation of valued ecosystems. This would entail secure long-term or perpetual leases with permits for any additional development.

In Queensland, there is a patchwork of freeholding leases across this zone. Here it would be sensible to facilitate further freeholding in the pursuit of 'normalization'. Of course this means the end of land tenure administration as the major land policy mechanism. In such a freehold system, policy implementation would be dependent on land use zoning and permits for clearing and cultivation to meet goals of preservation and sustainable use. Most of the leases in the east of the New South Wales Western Division are also in the closer settlement zone. The existing system of licences and permits for clearing and cultivation should be retained with a review of conditions to cover emerging concerns for conservation and preservation. While there are some leases in South Australia, Western Australia, and the Northern Territory that are sufficiently productive, there are not enough to justify a separate tenure.

The *manageable pastoral zone* includes most of the pastoral land in all states except Queensland. Pastoralism is a stable activity here and mainly relies on natural sources of feed. Investment is directed towards water supply, fences and yards for the purposes of efficient herd management. Long-term or perpetual leases (without freeholding options) would be a suitable form of tenure with individual covenants relating to sustainable land use, the preservation of valued ecosystems and limited public access.

The *outer marginal zone* is an area of such low pastoral potential and limited carrying capacity that the capital investment needed for herd control is not economically sustainable. Instead, lessees rely on selective 'harvesting' of widely scattered herds of mostly unbranded, semi-feral cattle. The zone takes in land on the desert margins and the extensive belt of inferior tall-grass savannas in Cape York Peninsula, the Gulf of Carpentaria, and the Kimberley.

Within the outer marginal zone, the pastoral interest is so modest that the property rights attached to standard pastoral leases are not justified. Flexible, shorter-term tenures are more appropriate. There should be more opportunities to accommodate non-pastoral activities, including public access and Aboriginal use. These can either be incorporated in conjunction with 'pastoral activities' or as alternative uses. While multiple use should be facilitated by flexible tenure, it must be recognized that the inaccessibility of these lands severely limits the scope for generating income from alternative uses. Consequently, a modified form of open access resource use may be justified in some contexts, particularly for recreational resources. There are enough marginal leases in Queensland, the Northern Territory, Western Australia and, possibly, South Australia, to justify the recognition of a distinctive form of restricted pastoral leasehold tenure with limited occupancy rights.

Paralleling this threefold zonal differentiation in property rights would be a differentiation in public agencies engaged in land use and management. At the inner margin, the role of distinctive land administration agencies has progressively diminished and the case for 'normalization' of land-related public agencies is very strong. However, in the main zone of manageable pastoral lands, the continuing proprietorial responsibilities of the state do require a form of land administration, which needs to be more publicly accountable and responsive to pressure of multiple interest groups than has traditionally been the case. In the outer zone, because of the limited role of private investment, the significance of Aboriginal and conservation values, the growing importance of tourism and the fluidity in land use, there is a special need to engage in comprehensive, flexible regional land use and development planning, using the processes and policy directions now being developed in the most marginal lands of northern Canada and Alaska. The case for such an approach to Australia's marginal pastoral lands has recently been made elsewhere (Holmes, 1992). Already this need is being recognized in the preparation of regional land use and development strategies for the Gulf District, the Kimberley, and Cape York Peninsula (Holmes, 1990b).

Quite apart from these broad zonal scenarios, there is also a need for special tenure provisions either for individual leases or for a defined group of (usually) contiguous leases, where there are particularly strong pressures to accommodate a mix of pastoral and non-pastoral values. This has been recognized in South Australia, with the creation of a distinctive regional reserve tenure, with some regional reserves being created from pastoral leases, entailing detailed agreements on the appropriate mix of pastoral, conservation, tourism, mining and any other values. There could well be a case for applying the same mechanism to a group of leases, for example, in the northern Flinders Ranges where a regionally based set of multiple land use needs may best be treated on a coordinated basis. A similar purpose is proposed in the Northern Territory Gulf Strategy through the reclassification of the most marginal pastoral leases as multi-purpose crown leases.

Only in these exceptional, highly localized contexts is there a need to identify and delineate within-property variability in resources, to formally recognize a parallel differentiation in property rights and responsibilities, as in the American model, and as has emerged in New Zealand. Australian pastoral holdings generally do not lend themselves to such distinctive demarcations, save in some marginal lands, notably between manageable and unmanageable grazing lands (Holmes, 1990b).

It must also be recognized that policy emphases will differ appreciably from state to state, according to the relative balance of interest groups within the state. Already one striking difference is emerging, with South Australia becoming much more strongly concerned with issues of conservation and recreation than the other states. South Australia has led the way in establishing a comprehensive system of rangeland monitoring, linked to a coherent enforceable set of procedures to ensure sustainable grazing practices. It is also the only state to adopt a systematic procedure for determining rights of public access within pastoral leases. This is a logical outcome of the Wakefield colonization legacy, and also of the balance of interest groups in that state, arising from the dominance of the metropolitan population, the very small number and limited political influence of pastoralists, and the greater accessibility and importance of pastoral lands for both conservation and recreation to urban South Australians than to urban populations in any other state.

A closer understanding of the geographical diversity of Australia's rangelands should lead to a clear recognition of a parallel need for diversity in rangeland administrative processes and in land use and land management outcomes. Within this diversity, the most appropriate mechanism for the main pastoral lands will be a reformed version of the Antipodean model of leasehold tenure, utilizing the attributes of the lease system which have been already described. However, in areas where pastoralism is no longer pre-eminent, other forms of property rights and public administration will be more appropriate. Nevertheless, the historic entrenchment of property rights makes the adoption of the reformed American model an unrealistic strategy.

2.4 New Zealand: partial switch to the reformed American model?

This comparative appraisal suggests that, in the potential six-way transfer of ideas among the three countries, the greatest practical benefits are likely to be gained by New Zealand's selective borrowing from the American model; not the traditional model of rangeland non-tenure but the more constructive elements of the reformed model catering for multiple land use demands and for local sharp variability in resource values. This is a logical outcome of certain underlying similarities in resource values between the American rangelands and tussock grasslands of the South Island High Country, embracing the pastoral leasehold lands shown in figure 13.4. These similarities were obscured during the prolonged phase of pastoral dominance of the High Country, only to emerge in recent decades.

However, the reshaping of rangeland institutions towards the American model has been a hesitant, imperfect process, primarily because property rights held by pastoral lessees are so substantial that the central element of the American model – the concept of the 'public domain' – is no longer attainable over most of the High Country. Following an extended relatively unsuccessful

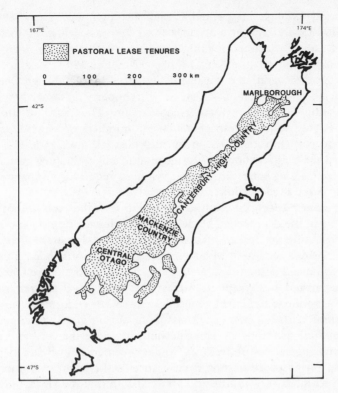

Figure 13.4 New Zealand pastoral lands
(*Source*: Blake et al., 1983)

period of complex, fragmented *ad hoc* negotiations in restructuring property rights, New Zealand governments have recently sought a radical solution, involving the abolition of any distinctive administrative arrangements or land tenures for the rangelands. This thrust is consistent with the so-called 'New Zealand experiment' directed towards a radically reduced governmental role throughout the nation's economy and society. This was initiated by the Labour government from 1984 to 1990 and subsequently expanded by the successor National Party government from 1990 to 1993.

The last half-century has been characterized by periods of crisis and uncertainty in governmental policies affecting the South Island High Country. Amid the sharp directional shifts and contradictions in proposed and accepted policy directions, three distinct major phases can be discerned, the first being the entrenchment of the Antipodean model of distinctive property rights and administrative institutions, the second being partial adoption of elements of the American model, and the third being the current push towards freeholding the productive rangelands and normalization of government functions.

2.4.1 Entrenchment of the Antipodean model of pastoral lease tenures. Over the first century of European settlement, from the 1840s to the 1940s, the dominance of pastoralism was unchallenged over the tussock grasslands of the South Island

High Country though not granted legislative recognition. 'The celebrated but belated 1948 Land Act articulated a place for pastoralism in the land use spectrum, on land classified as suited only to pastoral purposes, not to farming' (O'Connor, Lockhead, and Kerr, 1986, p. 100). The 1948 Act was the first to give legislative recognition to the distinctive character of the High Country and to entrench certain limitations on the present property rights of runholders and on any residual rights to convert to freehold tenure. The Land Settlement Board was empowered to place restrictions on the numbers of livestock carried, in addition to earlier restrictions on burning tussock grassland. The Act also formalized the classification and delineation of High Country pastoral lands, thereby recognizing their distinctive attributes, requiring a separate form of regionally based land administration.

In this latter respect, the Act was consistent with the evolution of both the American and the Antipodean models, in institutionalizing a separatist administrative structure for the rangelands. The 1948 Act also strengthened certain tenure provisions consistent with a reformed Antipodean model. Tenure security was enhanced and consolidated into a single pastoral lease tenure with a 33-year term and with perpetual rights of renewal. Also the removal of the freeholding option is consistent with twentieth-century reforms in most Australian pastoral tenures, in recognition of the accumulated evidence on the unsuitability of the lands to intensification. In 1948, the case for continued residual state ownership of the High Country seemed overwhelming, given the evidence on widespread pasture deterioration, soil erosion, rabbit infestation, declining productivity, and the accepted wisdom that the High Country was unsuited to aerial topdressing, oversowing, or any other method of pasture improvement.

2.4.2 Partial adoption of the American model. It is an irony of history that this entrenchment of pastoral tenures occurred just as the High Country was on the threshold of entry into a phase of comprehensive resource reappraisal, involving both intensification and diversification of land use. Diversification is associated with the sharp escalation in multiple land use values of the High Country, particularly of the unimproved rangelands of moderate to low pastoral value. Blake et al. point out that

> the area has come under increasing pressure for alternative uses – hydro-electric development, forestry, recreation and tourism, nature conservation and, in places, mining . . . Rising personal affluence, increased leisure time, improvements in roading and transport, have all contributed to an upsurge in recreation and tourism. Traditional High Country recreational activities such as tramping, hunting and fishing remain important . . . New recreational activities such as trail-bike riding, off-road vehicle use, canoeing and hang-gliding have become important . . . the High Country has become a place for family recreational activity . . . nowhere more important than in the spectacular growth of skiing . . . now in excess of a dozen [skifields] on land that is or was part of a run. (Blake et al., 1983, pp. 50–1)

The authors also highlight increased public attention to preservation of a diverse array of habitats as well as landscape values, and the critical importance of watershed management and erosion control.

In response to these new values, the former Department of Lands and Survey and the semi-autonomous Land Settlement Board promulgated a set of Crown land policies for leasehold land, governing such matters as: management principles and plans, wilderness, research, wetlands, rural landscape, tree planting, exploration, prospecting, mining, public recreation, commercial recreation and education, as well as revised High Country policies on soil disturbance, stock limitations, diversification (of livestock), land retirement, burning, noxious plants, wild animals, nature conservation, access and skiing, including ski-field development, heli-skiing, ski-planes, ski-touring and off-season use. However, unless linked to a coherent regional land use strategy, and tied to specified land use zonings, the reserve powers held by the state under leasehold tenures are inadequate instruments for guiding land use change. Unfortunately, the opportunity for operational linkage between regulatory and proprietary powers was not realized, and the tenure system remained a relatively ineffectual mechanism, save only in setting standards where major changes in use were proposed. This is not surprising, given the strong clientelist relationship between runholders and land administrators, founded on the continued belief in pastoralism as the dominant use, and the legal interpretations focusing on the rights of lessees. Much more influential in reshaping land use on individual runs was the recently disbanded National Water and Soil Conservation Authority and its local catchment boards, which actively negotiated management plans with more than half of all High Country runholders, by which runholders traded away rights to graze the least productive and most fragile Class VIII and the most highly eroded of the Class VII lands in return for financial assistance with control fencing and with pasture development to compensate for any loss of grazing capacity (Kerr and Douglas, 1983). While agreements were voluntary, nevertheless they had a significant impact in providing a formally recognized set of gradients in the type and intensity of land use on many runs. In the detailed land classifications, in their use of agreed criteria to allocate lands to appropriate uses, and in the resultant management plans, these agreements represent a distinct move towards the American progressivist philosophy of sustainable, multiple use of the range.

Paralleling this diversification in resource values has been a strong trend towards intensification of pastoral use, based on broad-scale methods of pasture improvement, aerial baiting of rabbits, improved fencing and enhanced mobility, leading to better flock control, increased carrying capacity, higher yields per sheep, improved livestock quality and reproduction, and reduced mortality. Initial capital came from the 1951 wool boom, but thereafter investment was aided by productivity gains and, more importantly, by the proliferation of government support programmes. These began in the 1960s with tax incentives and fertilizer subsidies. The 1970s brought the livestock incentive scheme, land development encouragement loans, catchment board conservation, farm plan subsidies, and supplementary minimum prices for stock. In response to these programmes, High Country runs achieved productivity gains greater than did other forms of livestock farming.

Pastoral intensification further accentuated the sharp productivity gradients within individual runs. In 1983, it was reported that, on average, 12 per cent of the area of runs had been oversown and topdressed and that these areas provided 55 per cent of livestock feeding (O'Connor, 1983). Thus, New Zealand's High Country runs were becoming functionally more differentiated with three broad classes of lands: first, the conservation and retirement lands transferred to public ownership or management; second, the remaining extensively grazed natural rangelands, in pastoral lease; and, third, various classes of 'improved' pasturelands, either held in lease or freehold, but, following a legislative amendment in 1965, capable of being reclassified and transferred to renewable lease with an entitlement to freehold. The productive grazing lands were moving towards elements of the bifurcated American model, both in resource use and property rights differentials.

However, the American model was not achievable, partly because of differences in the resource use context, but more importantly because of differences in land tenures. Concerning the resource context, New Zealand's less favoured marketing situation, with its cost-minimizing imperative, ensured that low-cost, broad-scale methods of production enhancement involving strips of favoured mid-altitude lands were preferred over more costly intensification confined to valley floors (O'Connor, personal communication).

An even greater impediment to adoption of the American model has been the historical transfer of substantial property rights to lessees. This acts as a severe constraint on government initiatives, particularly if these initiatives are not based upon a comprehensive, long-term strategy for the High Country. Inevitably, any proposals which impinge on property rights have proved difficult to pursue, generating extreme uncertainty about specific outcomes not only among run holders but also among increasingly vocal interest-groups.

Having experienced mounting frustration, from the demise of successive initiatives, it is not surprising that the government is showing a growing inclination to rid itself of the costs and complexities of its residual proprietorial role in the High Country.

2.4.3 The retreat of central government: moves towards privatization and normalization. The first vehicle intended to be used in this retreat was the 1981 Clayton Committee of Inquiry which, consistent with the stated wishes of the National Party government, proposed conversion of pastoral leases to a new renewable lease tenure, at higher rentals, but with opportunities and incentives for lessees to convert to freehold title. The committee also recommended that a new designation, multiple use land, should apply to those areas of high recreational, ecological and conservation value.

The report of the Committee caused widespread concern. Runholders were unhappy that their concerns about rental had not been met; that they were being pushed towards freeholding; that they faced loss of unspecified areas of their runs; and if legal rights of access to multiple use country were granted, that they would lose the control over access which they considered vital for proper management. Recreationists considered the provision made for access inadequate and considered intensification would interfere with their values. Nature conservationists viewed the Committee's vision of multiple use land as woefully inadequate. Soil conservators feared loss of control over land use practices. Many members of the general public reacted against freeholding of mountain lands which they felt to be their birthright, although in fact they have no legal rights of access under the existing tenure. (Blake et al., 1983, p. 3)

Given the concerted opposition, it was not surprising that the Clayton Committee's recommendations were not adopted, and that the Land Settlement Board subsequently undertook its own review, leading to a recommendation that the existing form of pastoral lease tenure be retained, but that a gradualist approach to freeholding be adopted by which suitable land could be reclassified and thus made eligible for freeholding, *within* individual runs. However, since 1984, proposals for tenure reform have been overtaken by the radical rewriting of the political agenda, involving a drastic shift from highly interventionist policies towards disengagement of government from a wide range of activities.

There are four major consequential effects upon land use, resource management, and property rights in the High Country. Firstly, and most obviously, is the pursuit of land privatization through the award of freehold title. Secondly, has been the complete removal of all governmental assistance, so that many intensive farming practices are no longer economically sustainable. This has accelerated a management crisis in the High Country, with land degradation and sharp declines in productivity and land values, epitomized by uncontrollable infestation of rabbits and hawkweeds (*hieracium ssp.*) (New Zealand Parliamentary Commissioner, 1991). Thirdly, many national government functions are being either privatized or corporatized, with land administration being transferred to a government-owned corporation, Landcorp, thereby separating administration from policy formulation, and perhaps unintentionally creating a policy vacuum at national level with regard to the future of the High Country. Fourthly, and linked to the third point, is the devolution of almost all resource management responsibilities to newly created regional councils. These councils will engage in wide-ranging, comprehensive planning and management in relation to all major resource matters within their regions, including land and water resources. Since the High Country rangelands are divided among three regions, Otago, Canterbury, and Nelson–Marlborough, there is a possibility that decisions in relation to the High Country will reflect local rather than national concerns.

Major proposed changes to the administration of Crown Lands were incorporated into the 1988 draft Land Management Bill, designed to recognize multiple values and uses in the High Country and particularly to differentiate lands according to their primary use. Consistent with certain earlier proposals, the Act would have required all Crown lands to be placed into three categories: Category A being land of sufficient conservation value to be retained by the Crown and administered usually under the Conservation Act; Category B being land which had highly significant conservation as well as production values, also to be retained by the Crown but available for lease; and Category C being all other land, with most presumably to be available for freeholding. As could be expected, the uncertainties surrounding these proposals, and particularly those concerning the methods and outcomes of categorization, aroused a storm of opposition. The strongest protest came from the runholders, who argued that their exclusive right to pasture could not be abridged without their consent, even for conservation purposes, that proposals for within-property stock limitations were also in breach of contract and that devolution to regional councils would lead to inconsistencies. Most importantly, the runholders adopted a strongly clientelist position, reasserting the special relationship between lessors and lessee, pointing out that pastoral leases may be 'Crown' land but not 'public' land and that, in any process of renegotiation of land uses and property rights, public input should be restricted to the initial phase, leaving the detailed negotiations to the two parties directly affected (Ensor, 1989).

Confronted with a political hornets' nest, the government failed to present a final bill to parliament and the matter was passed on to the incoming National Party government in 1990. The new minister, impatient for a speedy, simple solution, and backed by Treasury's urgings to prune administrative costs, revived an earlier proposal for a supposedly simple demarcation into two categories, namely conservation lands retained by the Crown and production (or commercial) lands, to be freeholded, thereby terminating any proprietorial role for the state on High Country grazing lands and transferring any administrative costs into the devolved regulatory and planning functions of the regional councils.

The government's case is founded on the belief that certain broad principles are applicable in all contexts, including the High Country. One principle is that shared responsibility is diminished responsibility. In applying this principle, a clear distinction is made between two different approaches to the regulation of land use within zones, namely

> either (a) allow within specified performance standards all activities unless expressly forbidden, or (b) forbid all activities unless expressly allowed.
> (Lincoln College, 1989, p. 8)

The current governmental view is that the former approach is applicable to all commercial land and the latter to conservation land. Such a demarcation would eliminate the Antipodean leasehold model, founded on the view that there is a category of commercial land on which activities are forbidden unless expressly allowed.

Paradoxically, the government's proposal to enhance property rights of runholders coincides with a period of severe economic and environmental stress, when runholders are least equipped to respond effectively to major institutional changes, particularly if such changes involve increased short-term or long-term costs. One major difficulty in the proposed subdivision of runs into conservation and production lands will be the allocation of the severely degraded lands, infested with rabbits and hawkweeds, where costs of pest control far exceed any economic return. Should these be classed as conservation lands or as production lands?

By mid-1992, little progress had been made on this proposed radical restructuring of rangeland property rights. The demarcation into commercial and conservation lands was generating problems particularly in areas with multiple values, notably grazing, conservation, preservation, and recreation, while the minister was also conceding that the High Country might well require a distinctive tenure, to be described as 'pastoral freehold', which would presumably differ only modestly from the existing lease tenure. In any case, and perhaps to the relief of the government, the issue of land reallocation and reform of property rights in the High Country has now been deferred, until Maori land claims have been fully resolved according to Waitangi Treaty principles.

2.4.4 The future? In the High Country, property rights and resource regulations will remain in a state of flux for some time to come. The task of designing an appropriate regime of rights and responsibilities is enormously complicated by the pre-existing structures, ill-suited to current needs. Any effective restructuring of property rights will need to be linked with a realistic, carefully designed, long-term 'grand strategy' for land use and resource management of the High Country. This will require a steady, persistent political will, sustained by a high level of public support. It will also need a high level of acquiescence by runholders, founded upon a reasonable mix of incentives and disincentives. In order to ensure operational success, such a comprehensive package of change would need to be 'trialled' in one or two limited areas.

Given the complex mosaic of lands included within most runs, involving increased differentiation in uses and values, it is inevitable that some differentiation in property rights within existing runs will be required. This has been increasingly recognized by all parties. Currently, a central issue is whether two or three basic forms of land tenure should be given legal recognition. Given that there still remain very large tracts of extensive rangelands of low productive capacity, but of some grazing value, and that it is not in the public interest to have all these lands retired from grazing, there is a parallel ongoing case to award an appropriate limited form of property right to those engaged primarily in this form of grazing. Whether this form of right is best achieved through the leasehold land tenure mechanism or by some form of strict land zoning is a matter for political decision. However, under either of these regimes, the appropriate planning principle is to forbid all activities unless expressly allowed.

3 CONCLUSION

Comparisons among the three Western nations with significant tracts of extensive rangelands can yield valuable insights into the differing pathways along which their rangeland systems of property rights and public agencies have evolved. More importantly, these studies can provide a basis for appraising current directions in reshaping institutional processes and policy outcomes.

In the United States, notwithstanding the comprehensive, multi-pronged campaigns for privatization of resources, normalization of public institutions, and localization of decision processes, the institutional structure of the federally owned public domain remains firmly entrenched. The case for continued public ownership, as a national responsibility, has been greatly strengthened by the recognition of multiple uses and values, backed by an expanding array of powerful interest constituencies, actively engaged in shaping land use outcomes. In an arena of shifting alliances, no single interest group can achieve ascendancy, and the role of federal agencies has been enhanced. However, decision processes have shifted away from supposedly objective, scientific procedures, based upon a progressivist philosophy, towards more politicized, participatory methods, founded on a philosophy of interest-group liberalism.

In Australia and New Zealand, a comparable direct, powerful public involvement in reshaping land use and resource values is not feasible, for two related reasons. Firstly, and most notably over most of Australia's rangelands, pastoralism retains public recognition as the 'highest and best use'. Secondly, and more decisively, pastoralism has already achieved *de jure* recognition of its primacy, through the award of secure property rights within leasehold tenures. This ensures an entrenched clientelist role between lessees and land administrators, and greatly reduces the legal standing of other interest groups. Nevertheless, the residual property rights, retained by the state, do provide a useful basis for some institutional restructuring to accommodate emerging multiple values. In Australia, such restructuring needs to be based on a recognition of the broad zonal differentiation of pastoral versus non-pastoral values, suggesting a parallel differentiation in rangeland institutions, with a reformed Antipodean model of leasehold tenures being used in the core pastoral zone, but with markedly different institutions at the inner and outer margins. Policies and institutions are being reshaped in a piecemeal and slipshod fashion in response to these increasingly obvious zonal differences, but there has been no attempt, to date, to develop a systematic land administration philosophy, responsive to these differing contexts.

In New Zealand, the increasing diversity and local variability in resource values is generating pressures for a comparable diversification in land use and property rights, with pastoral leasehold being confined to those lands where extensive grazing remains the dominant use. Attempts at negotiating new regimes of property rights and public institutions have been squeezed between the growing demands of major interest groups and the entrenched status of pastoral runholders. While various piecemeal responses are available to the New Zealand government, there appear to be two basic alternative pathways leading to a resolution of current dilemmas. One of these, currently being proposed, is the privatization of property rights over all production lands, the normalization of administrative and regulatory institutions and, optionally, the localization of responsibilities within regional councils. The alternative is to continue to recognize the distinctive resource attributes of the rangelands and the consequential need for a distinctive regime of property rights for these lands, involving identification and delineation of freehold, leasehold, and public lands, entailing a steady, purposeful renegotiation of property rights and resource use.

ACKNOWLEDGEMENTS

I am particularly indebted to Chris Kerr and Kevin O'Connor for the insights they have generously provided on the New Zealand context and to Mike Young and Laurie Knight for similar comments on Australian tenures. Travel funds were provided from Australian Research Grant Number A79030262 and from University of Queensland research funds.

REFERENCES

Cato Journal, 2, No. 1, 1981.

Cato Journal, 2, No. 3, 1982.

Blake, H. et al. (1983). *Pastoral High Country Proposed Tenure Changes and the Public Interest – A Case Study*. University of Canterbury and Lincoln College, Christchurch: Lincoln Papers in Resource Management No. 11.

Bromley, D.W. (1991). *Environment and Economy: Property Rights and Public Policy*. Oxford: Blackwell.

Brubaker, S. (ed.) (1984). *Rethinking the Federal Lands*. Washington, DC: Resources for the Future.

Cameron, J.I. & Elix J. (1991). *Recovering Ground: A Case Study Approach to Ecologically Sustainable Rural Land Management*. Melbourne: Australian Conservation Foundation.

Clawson, M. (1983). *The Federal Lands Revisited*. Washington, DC: Resources for the Future.

Culhane, P.J. (1981). *Public Land Politics: Interest Group Influence on the Forest Service and the Bureau of Land Management*. Washington, DC: Resources for the Future.

Dysart, B.C. & Clawson, M. (eds) (1986). *Managing Public Lands in the Public Interest*. New York: Praeger, Environmental Regeneration Series.

Ensor, H. (1989). *Submission to Minister of Lands*. Methven: High Country Committee of Federated Farmers.

Fairfax, S.K. & Yale C.E. (1987). *Federal Lands: A Guide to Planning, Management, and the State Revenues*. Washington, DC: Island Press.

Foss, P.O. (ed.). (1987). *Federal Lands Policy*. New York: Greenwood Press, Contributions in Political Science, Number 162.

Francis, J.G. (1984). 'Realizing public purposes without public ownership: a study for reducing intergovernmental conflict in public land regulation.' In J.G. Francis and R. Ganzel (eds), *Western Public Lands: The Management of Natural Resources in a Time of Declining Federalism*. New Jersey: Rowman & Allanheld, 149–172.

Francis, J.G. & Ganzel, R. (eds) (1984). *Western Public Lands: The Management of Natural Resources in a Time of Declining Federalism*. New Jersey: Rowman & Allanhead.

Grindle, M.S. (1986). *State and Countryside Development Policy and Agrarian Politics in Latin America*. Baltimore, MD: Johns Hopkins University Press.

Heathcote, R.L. (1965). *Back of Bourke*. Melbourne: Melbourne University Press.

Heathcote, R.L. (1987). 'Pastoral Australia.' In D.N. Jeans (ed.), *Australia: a Geography*, vol. II, *Space and Society*. Sydney: Sydney University Press, 259–300.

Holmes, J.H. (1990a). 'Land speculation and lease tenure.' In *A Conservation Strategy for Cape York Peninsula, Draft for Discussion*. Brisbane: Wildlife Preservation Society of Queensland, 202–13.

Holmes, J.H. (1990b). 'Ricardo revisited: submarginal land and non-viable cattle enterprises in the Northern Territory Gulf District.' *Journal of Rural Studies*, 6, 45–65.

Holmes, J.H. (1991). 'Land tenures in the Australian pastoral zone: a critical appraisal.' In I. Moffat and A. Webb (eds), *North Australian Research: Some Past Themes and New Directions*. Darwin: North Australian Research Unit, 41–59.

Holmes, J.H. (1992). *Strategic Regional Planning on the Northern Frontiers*. Darwin: North Australian Research Unit, Discussion Paper No. 4.

Kerr, I.G.C. & Douglas, M.H. (1983). 'The economics of soil and water conservation plans for High Country properties 1962–1982.' *Tussock Grasslands and Mountain Lands Review*, 42, 95–110.

Libecap, G.D. (1981). *Locking Up the Range: Federal Land Controls and Grazing*. Cambridge, Mass.: Ballinger, Pacific Studies in Public Policy.

Lincoln College (1989). *Resource Management Law Reform*. Submission prepared by Tussock Grasslands and Mountain Lands Institute, Lincoln College.

Messer, J. & Mosley, G. (eds) (1982). *What Future for Australia's Arid Lands?* Hawthorn: Proceedings of the National Arid Lands Conference, Australian Conservation Foundation.

Nelson, R.H. (1984). 'Ideology and public land policy – the current crisis.' In Brubaker, S. (ed.), *Rethinking the Federal Lands*. Washington: Resources for the Future, 275–97.

New Zealand Parliamentary Commissioner for the Environment (1991). *Sustainable Land Use for the Dry Tussock Grasslands in the South Island*. Wellington.

O'Connor, K.F. (1983). 'Land use in the Hill and High Country.' In R.D. Bedford & A.P. Sturman (eds), *Canterbury at the Crossroads*. Christchurch: New Zealand Geographical Society Special Publication, Miscellaneous Series, No. 8.

O'Connor, K.F., Lockhead, L., & Kerr, I.G.C. (1986). 'Administrative and managerial responses to changes in economic and ecological conditions in New Zealand tussock grasslands.' In P.J. Joss, P.W. Lynch, & O.B. Williams (eds), *Rangelands: A Resource Under Siege*. Canberra: Australian Academy of Science.

Powell, J.M. (1970). *The Public Lands of Australia Felix*. Melbourne: Oxford University Press.

Randall, A. (1983). 'The problem of market failure.' *Natural Resources Journal*, 23, 131–49.

Williams, M. (1975). 'More and smaller is better: Australian rural settlement, 1788–1914.' In J.M. Powell & M. Williams, *Australian Space, Australian Time*. Melbourne: Oxford University Press, 61–103.

Young, M.D. (1984). 'Rangeland administration.' In G.N. Harrington, A.D. Wilson, & M.D. Young (eds), *Management of Australian Rangelands*. Melbourne: CSIRO.

PART V

Geography and Higher Education

Plate V   Peter Haggett's involvement with higher education has not been confined to his contributions as a teacher and researcher. That third of the academic's trinity of tasks – administration – has exercised and displayed his skills at all tiers in the central place hierarchy of the university sector: from low-order functions as Head of Department at Bristol, through the progressively higher tiers of Deanship of Social Sciences, Pro-Vice-Chancellor and Vice-Chancellor, to the highest order membership of the University Grants Committee and a plethora of other roles in national academic planning in the UK and beyond. But universities are also part of broader environmental systems, as the following three chapters show, whether nationally or on a local scale, just as Bristol University Geography Department and other buildings illustrated above physically intermingle with the fabric and economy of the surrounding city.

14

UK Public Policy and the Emergent Geography of Higher Education

A.G. Hoare

1 INTRODUCTION

This chapter attempts to sketch something of the recently emergent geography of Higher Education (HE) in the UK, a geography driven by public policy in a variety of ways. As such it represents a geography that Peter Haggett has worked *in* rather than *on*. First I review briefly the form this policy has taken (see also Allington, 1990; Johnes and Taylor, 1990; Burnett, 1992 for fuller accounts), before following through four interrelated components of this emergent geography – those of its size, internal structure, interaction/ mobility, and system health. Many of these changes can be traced back to national government policy initiatives, especially those since 1979. However, specifying the precise linkage at every twist and turn is far from straightforward: sometimes the effects are subtle and indirect, sometimes they pull in different directions and often they are mediated by other sets of decision-makers. The geographical reference scale I adopt to follow through these complex interactions will mostly be national, but sometimes more localized, with examples drawn unashamedly from Peter's university home for most of his academic career.

2 POLICY CHANGES

Figure 14.1 attempts to summarize the complex of influences upon British HE. Some derive from national governmental action, but other higher and lower tiers of the polity hierarchy are also relevant, as are the independent role of students (actual and potential) and the private business section. Furthermore, figure 14.1 distinguishes between national government policy as directed squarely at the university sector, and as affecting it indirectly. The latter is well

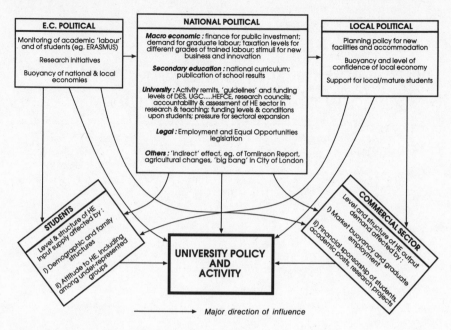

E.C. POLITICAL

Monitoring of academic 'labour' and of students (eg. ERASMUS)

Research initiatives

Buoyancy of national & local economies

NATIONAL POLITICAL

Macro economic : finance for public investment; demand for graduate labour; taxation levels for different grades of trained labour; stimuli for new business and innovation

Secondary education : national curriculum; publication of school results

University : Activity remits, 'guidelines' and funding levels of DES, UGC.....HEFCE, research councils; accountability & assessment of HE sector in research & teaching; funding levels & conditions upon students; pressure for sectoral expansion

Legal : Employment and Equal Opportunities legislation

Others : 'indirect' effect, eg. of Tomlinson Report, agricultural changes, 'big bang' in City of London

LOCAL POLITICAL

Planning policy for new facilities and accommodation

Buoyancy and level of confidence of local economy

Support for local/mature students

STUDENTS

Level & structure of HE Input supply affected by :

i) Demographic and family structures

ii) Attitude to HE, including among under-represented groups

COMMERCIAL SECTOR

Level and structure of HE output demand affected by :

i) Market buoyancy and graduate employment

ii) Financial sponsorship of students, academic posts, research projects

UNIVERSITY POLICY AND ACTIVITY

→ *Major direction of influence*

Figure 14.1   The major influences in British Higher Education

illustrated by the Tomlinson Report (Tomlinson, 1992) since its recommended transfer of much hospital care of patients to the provinces from London raises very serious questions for the continued viability of university teaching hospitals in the capital. But the emphasis in this chapter is rather with the former, and here the rationale behind Thatcherian and subsequent HE policy, as in other sectors, has been to rein back state financial commitments, to secure value for money returns on the residue and inject more competition and enterprise into the system. More particularly, three policy strands can be identified:

1   Reduced real-money funding for the level of HE activity expected both from the institutions (HEIs) and their students. Universities have been forced thereby to seek other funding sources and to consider more closely the type of institution each needs to be to maximize income in such impecunious times (see section 3.2).

2   Greater assessment of differential university performance, largely through the intermediary role of the University Grants Committee (UGC) and its successors. These, from the universities' perspective, have become less the benign intermediaries between HE and state that the UGC once was, and more the means for *dirigiste* Whitehall policy implementation. Research and teaching have become increasingly eased apart in these assessments which helps signal to those within and without the HE system where the strengths of each university might lie. And as components in the formulae whereby most bread-and-butter government funding is determined, they also affect the increasingly sharp differential funding levels among those universities (Hoare, 1981; 1986).

3 System expansion, to raise the UK from the foot of the First World international league table of *pro rata* HE penetration (see Richardson, 1981; Sultan and Sultan, 1990). Given 1 above this, the intention of the 1990 White Paper, *Higher Education: a New Framework*, could only come about through the reduction in funding per student taught. This in turn has led to incessant complaints from the universities over expansion damaging both teaching quality and research output, and thereby the nation's distinctive and internationally respected HE system. Even so, system expansion not only occurred, but even outpaced the government's own upward planned trajectory, causing it to call a (temporary ?) halt to further HE growth in late 1992.

3 THE GEOGRAPHY OF HIGHER EDUCATION

3.1 Expansion

National Scale. Despite its absorbing a far smaller percentage of school-leavers than in many other countries, Britain's HE sector is still much larger than it was. In the academic year 1955–6, when Peter Haggett began his academic career, the UK boasted 24 separate universities,[1] which produced some 17,250 graduating First-degree students that same year. By 1990–1 there were 46 producing over 77,000 equivalent graduates and the soon-to-be-university polytechnics graduated a further 40,000 First-degree students. Such growth has occurred through an increasing diversity of *mechanisms*, which find close parallels more widely in economic geography (see table 14.1), while *temporally* the experience over four decades has been one of gradual expansion interspersed with growth spurts.

The first of these occurred in the halcyon sixties when government commitment to HE was matched by commensurate funding. To newly founded HEIs, established by the UGC on its own initiative, was added the impetus of the government-instituted Robbins Report (1963a), which envisaged a further 260 per cent increase in full-time university students by 1980/81. In total, 9 green-field campuses (e.g. York, Sussex, Lancaster, and Essex) were founded in the decade and 10 former Colleges of Technology, such as Salford, Bradford, Aston, Surrey and Bath, attained university status.[2] The second growth spurt brought a tranche of 39 'new' universities in 1992 as the Further and Higher Education Act abolished the so-called binary divide between universities and (former) polytechnics, as foreshadowed in the 1990 White Paper.

What of the geography of this expansion? First, the effect of system growth upon the hierarchy of 'old' universities in the 1980s (not only a vital period for HE politically but also one with a mercifully consistent statistical record in the UGC's *University Statistics* series) is recorded in figure 14.2. By and large, the league table based on full-time undergraduates remains unchanged within an overall system expansion of 14 per cent. All but four campuses also grew (the exceptions being those hit most savagely by cuts in UGC grant income in 1981 (Hoare, 1981) but only 8 out of 52 changed league table position by 5 or more

Table 14.1   University expansion: post-war mechanisms for growth

Mechanism	Example(s)
'Births': new greenfield establishments	York, East Anglia, Sussex
In situ expansion	Almost all – including Bristol (see section 3.1)
'Branch plants': establishment of subordinate campuses in different locations	Northumbria – new campus established in Carlisle
Transfers: movement of main centre of HEI to new location	University of the West of England; New University of Ulster
Acquisitions & Mergers	Exeter, of Cambourne School of Mines; Manchester Metropolitan, of Crewe and Alsager College; Queen Mary College with Westfield College
Joint Ventures	Establishment of University College Stockton by Durham and Teeside
Independence of previously subordinate establishments	Southampton (from London); Newcastle (from Durham); Dundee (from St Andrews)
Franchising: licensing of other institutions to teach courses approved by institution on its behalf	Plymouth (of other sites in South West); Hull (of HEI in Hong Kong)
Outworking: away from HE location	Wolverhampton providing workplace-based teaching; Open University – sole distance learning-based HEI in UK
Reclassification	Colleges of Technology and Polytechnics as universities in 1960s and 1990s respectively

places. The biggest change – Ulster's rise from 48th to 11th – was the artificial consequence of the first 'polyversity' merger between its predecessor, the New University of Ulster, and the Northern Ireland Polytechnic.

This same theme of stability and consolidation arises in a second way too, that of the geographical accessibility to expanding university provision nation-wide.[3] In the 1960s the UGC had favoured new universities in small centres, with no such previous presence, whereas Robbins preferred larger towns and cities for the mutual benefit of institution and host city, even if this meant some doubling up. The decision of the equivalent committee in Northern Ireland to establish its second university in the small town of Coleraine has also been interpreted in terms of the Province's sectarian divide (Osborne and Singleton, 1982). In contrast, many of the later new universities have duplicated existing provision, rather than in-filling the significant remaining interstices in the HE map. Large underserved swathes remain, beyond Plymouth, astride the English/Welsh borders and in Scotland outside the central lowlands.[4] Figure 14.3 shows how the hinterlands of pre-Robbins universities had little mutual overlap, whereas the 1960s generation only partly penetrated unserved territory and the poly-conversions have effectively reinforced the previous provision. Only 4 out of 39 add anything to the areal coverage of the 30-mile radii mapped, all the more significant a distribution given the role HEIs can play in their surrounding economies (section 3.4). Of course, this is a crude index of any university's

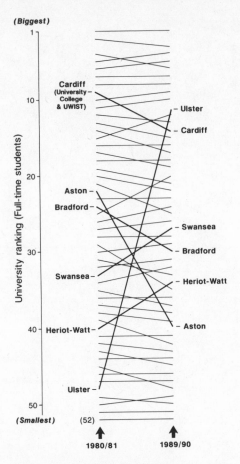

Figure 14.2 A largely unchanging
hierarchy: British universities 1980–1990

realistic hinterland, and the equivalent 30-mile proportion of the *population* so served is much greater than the 'area-covered' values in figure 14.3b). But the tendency for post-war HE expansion to have shifted from penetrating fresh territory to doubling-up on existing provision is still very clear.

While they may not have kept their distance from older HEIs spatially, the newest (1992) universities have been forced to in another respect, that of their titles adopted upon redesignation. Since they serve a particularly image-conscious age cohort their choice of names is a far from trifling aspect of an enhanced status. For new universities with an established university neighbour Privy Council approval of a new title hinges on avoiding confusion between the two. The name-selection process would likely prove an intriguing research project in its own right: space allows only a few comments here. Many new universities with no local competitor can simply substitute *University* for *Polytechnic* – as at Kingston, Portsmouth, Huddersfield, Wolverhampton and Sunderland, while Brighton Polytechnic could safely become Brighton University since its nearby sixties university took the county name. Others had to

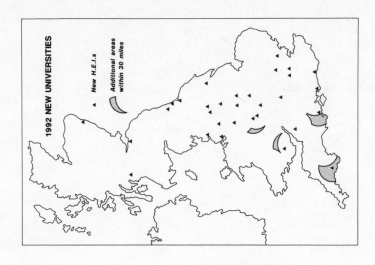

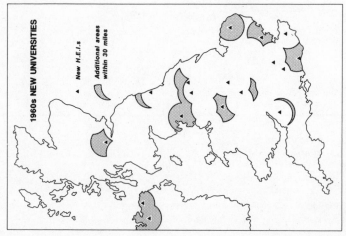

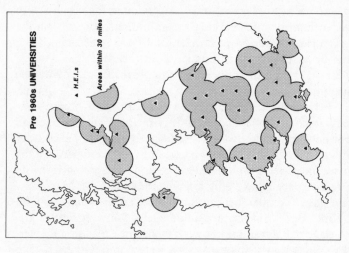

Figure 14.3(a) A geography of consolidation: new universities 1960–1992

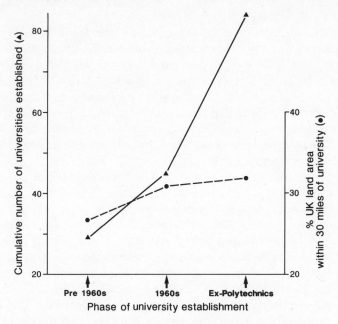

Figure 14.3(b)   A geography of consolidation: new universities
1960–1992

navigate, sometimes verbosely, around an established place-named neighbour. So Birmingham Polytechnic became *The University of Central England in Birmingham* and the equivalent in Bristol the *University of the West of England, Bristol*, while Leeds and Manchester incorporate 'Metropolitan' in their titles and Liverpool and Oxford the names of local worthies. For yet others an unforced shift of areal identity has been preferred. Hatfield Polytechnic is now the University of Hertfordshire, the Polytechnic of the South West became Plymouth University and Thames and Central London Polytechnics changed respectively to the Universities of Greenwich and Westminster. Perhaps most intriguing of all is the decision of the Polytechnic of West London (based in Ealing and Slough) to become the elusive Thames Valley University, of Leicester Polytechnic to become even more hard-to-locate De Montfort University and Napier Polytechnic of Edinburgh to drop any mention of one of Britain's grandest cities, as Napier University.

Expansion at the local level. The spatial interplay of public policy and university expansion is not confined to this broad-brush, nationwide scale, but can arise at a local level too. However, this can still implicate central government. Within a six-month period in 1992, the Department of the Environment apparently opened and then closed the door on the London School of Economics' hopes of moving as a transfer (in terms of table 14.1) from its cramped Aldwych premises across the Thames to County Hall, effectively empty since its predecessor Conservative administration disbanded the Greater London Council in 1986. At other times the political links of HEI expansion are directed towards local government, as with the experience of Peter's own university's recent *in situ* expansion.

By 1980 the scattered premises of the University of Bristol's Faculty of Social Sciences were variously at operational capacity and working inefficiently for staff and students alike. Departments were both separated from each other and also remote from the campus Library and other academic facilities (figure 14.4a). Consolidation at a central site already owned by the University, at the junction of Priory and Woodland Roads, offered the only hope of improvement. This was an area of substantial, free-standing Victorian villas, as well as being designated as a Conservation Area where, by statute, the local planning authority (Bristol City Council in this case) must pay due regard to 'preserving or enhancing its character or appearance' when judging planning applications (figure 14.4b). Although a string of villas opposite had been imaginatively converted for Faculty of Arts departments a few years previously (gaining some architectural awards *en route*) the initial scheme for the new Social Sciences site involved demolishing two houses and outbuildings and erecting a single block (figure 14.4c). The University argued this was necessary for internal flexibility over inter-departmental usage, while their design respected the neighbourhood's villaesque environment in its 3-bayed facade and building height. The planners disagreed. In increasingly tetchy correspondence the City Planning Officer variously described the proposal as 'a 5-storey monolith', 'totally alien to the very clearly established character of this part of the Conservation Area', and 'a large step backwards [from the Arts complex]'. He contrasted the University's intentions here, and its piecemeal development proposals in general, with the coordinated and sympathetic projects from the other major neighbourhood employer – the BBC. In this opposition he was fully supported by a number of irate letters and petitions from local residents, conservation and civic groups. Not surprisingly, Scheme A was rejected by the city's Planning Committee on 5 August 1987 as out of keeping with the local built environment.

The University's response was to retain the option of appealing against the refusal decision, but also to prepare a revised Scheme B (figure 14.4d) of a self-evident villa format, preserving the more valuable (in conservation terms) of the houses previously scheduled for demolition (No. 8 Priory Road). Although more rigid in inter-departmental usage by the Faculty, it was better received by the planners in informal discussions and, when submitted, by the previously hostile lobbies as well. Despite some residual local residents' opposition, Scheme B was approved by the Committee on 20 July 1988, whereupon the University withdrew its intended appeal on Scheme A. After points of detail had been resolved what was in essence Scheme B was opened on 23 October 1991, allowing the Vice-Chancellor to remind those invited to the official reception how it demonstrated the University as a good neighbour in respecting its local environment.

3.2 *Academic structure*

No two universities are ever precisely alike in what goes on in their physical premises, but some are more similar than others. In this section I identify two

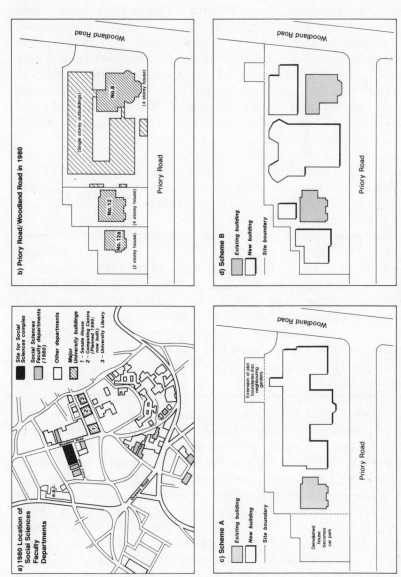

a) 1980 Location of Social Sciences Faculty Departments

Site for Social Sciences complex

Social Sciences Faculty departments (1980)

Other departments

Major University buildings
1 – Senate House;
2 – Computing Centre (Planned 1980; now built)
3 – University Library

b) Priory Road/Woodland Road in 1980

Woodland Road

No.8
(Single storey outbuildings)
(4 storey house)

No.12
(4 storey house)

No.12a
(2 storey house)

Priory Road

c) Scheme A

Existing building

New building

— Site boundary

Woodland Road

Extension of plot boundaries into neighbouring gardens

Demolished house becomes car park

Priory Road

d) Scheme B

Existing building

New building

— Site boundary

Woodland Road

Priory Road

Figure 14.4 *In situ* expansion: Bristol's Social Sciences Faculty

interrelated aspects of these academic structures, exploring in each the logic of their geography and the role played by public policy.

Structure by academic subject. Certain HEIs remain true to their foundation as single-discipline medical, veterinary or business schools. Others, which grew from Colleges of Technology, often preserve a flavour of their former selves, despite subsequently diversifying their academic base. Modern green-field establishments have to resolve which brands of academic scholarship to offer and which to ignore in an increasingly competitive student market. And older universities have to decide how far to adopt new academic specializations, never dreamt of by their Victorian or medieval founders. Not surprisingly, the outcome is a patchwork of subject availability, confusing to university applicants and often lacking much overarching logic as to what is taught where.

There are, of course, some exceptions. It is common sense for Oceanography to be offered at coastal campuses such as Southampton and Bangor, for Leeds to have a Textile Industries department, Bristol one of Aerospace Engineering, and Birmingham an Automotive Engineering Centre, just as Scottish Law, Welsh and Irish have inevitable national confines. Mainstream school subjects like Mathematics and English are more widely available, even if not universally so: Geography, the 7th (out of 112) most popular subject for university applications (in 1991)[5] is offered by only 32 of the 47 pre-1992 universities as a single honours subject, for example. Indeed, differential availability is not a simple response to student demand: were it so there would be currently more veterinary science schools and fewer departments in engineering, physics and chemistry. The other rationale comes from the government's view of national need for graduates of different types, which translates into the 'what', 'where' and 'how many' of places it agrees to support at pre-specified levels, through its funding intermediaries.

Peter was a member of the oldest of these, the UGC, between 1985 and 1989, during which time it became increasingly active in implementing Whitehall demands for 'value for money' from the universities. One response was its series of HE-wide subject reviews, designed to identify the appropriate national provision levels for particular subjects and the case for supporting them at specific institutions. These reviews, which ceased in 1989, covered only certain subjects but their impact on inter-subject resourcing decisions by individual universities, while hard to disentangle, was still significant (Burnett, 1992). Some of the most obvious impacts arose with the rationalization of small departments, sometimes associated with a transfer of staff, such as that bringing displaced academics in threatened small Arts departments elsewhere to Exeter (*Times Higher Education Supplement*, 1 December 1989). Reactions to the Oxburgh Committee on Earth Sciences on campus were long drawn-out and Byzantine in complexity. At Bristol, Oxburgh's first report questioned the very continuation of Geology, so the University's response secured its funding to hitherto unequalled levels! In the reviews of Sociology and Social Administration, the explicit emphasis on the 'where' of academic provision figured higher than in many other reviews (Hoare, 1991a), and a still stronger geographical dimension emerged in the report for Veterinary Science. Discussion of the country's changing agricultural geography dominated its debate over which 4 of 6 pre-existing vet schools should survive. The core of the argument lay in the increasing contrast between an arable east and a pastoral west and the implications this held for providing training for vets in the care of farm animals. Although this may seem an eminently reasonable general approach, the way it was to be translated into policy prescriptions by the UGC-commissioned Riley Report did not bear detailed scrutiny (Hoare 1991b).

Structure by dominant academic activity. Whatever her/his subject specialism, almost all UK academics are contractually required both to teach and to research. But just as the balance between them varies among individuals so some institutions have started to position themselves towards one or other end of the teaching-research spectrum. Periodic Whitehall denials of any secret listing of 'research' and 'teaching' universities have not prevented the exigencies of HE funding nudging universities to one or other such strategy to maximize their public finance. The debate surrounding the Flowers Committee report on extending the teaching year (Flowers, 1993) is a further impetus in the same direction. Teaching and research activity both play a part in government funding formulae, the outcomes of which have increasingly diverged among HEIs in the 1980s (Hoare, 1981; 1986). For the first time, the outcome announced in February 1992 publically separated research and teaching contributions for each university, the former drawing on their peer-group research ratings in 1989 and the latter on the preparedness of HEIs to take fees-only students, beyond their fully funded quotas. By and large, those performing well on one criterion were unimpressive on the other, with only Essex being in the top six of the national league tables on both (and hence excluded from the analysis to follow).

Two aspects of this growing division deserve our attention. First, the regional distributions of the most teaching (*T*) and most research (*R*) orientated campuses are dramatically different: only two of my *R* category (as defined in figure 14.5) are outside England and only four beyond its three southern regions (the South-East, South-West and East Anglia), whereas English universities form only half of the *T* subset, and 'southern' ones less than 20 per cent.

Second, consider the interplay between the *R/T* division and the general relationship whereby bigger HEIs teach more subjects than smaller ones. Most university disciplines have the academic equivalent of a 'minimum economic size' (m.e.s.) of students and staff below which their provision is inappropriate (Hoare, 1994b). This follows partly from the scale economies of capital equipment and other necessary teaching infrastructure, as for training chemists, medics, engineers, and vets, partly from external degree validation by professional bodies, requiring a range of teaching specialisms (as with Law, Planning, and Architecture), and partly from intangible but still potent arguments of critical academic mass, below which scholars suffer from isolation and students from a truncated approach to scholarship. This lumpiness of commitment to particular subjects, addressed by many of the UGC subject reviews (Hoare, 1991a), means that only reasonably large universities can offer effective teaching and research across several departments and faculties. Even if smaller ones concentrate on subjects with lower m.e.s. values they may still select these within

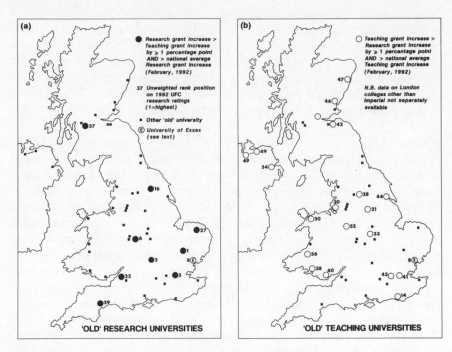

Figure 14.5   The growing divide: research and teaching universities

one or two faculties to maximize research and teaching interaction among them, and develop some brand-image identity in a competitive HE market.

Figure 14.6 compares HEI size with the number of officially recognized subject groupings (excluding Combined Studies) each offers. None achieves the possible maximum of 15 but the two Northern Ireland universities, Manchester, and Edinburgh are each only void in one, whereas St David's Lampeter only registers in 3.[6] The general increase of academic range with size is as foreshadowed earlier, but note the wide HEI size diversity within some provision levels – in three cases by a factor of 2. Furthermore, *R* universities cluster towards the right-hand (larger) end while the *T* locations are disproportionately smaller-than-median (table 14.2), consistent with the thesis of critical mass in stimulating intellectual enterprise and attracting good researchers to 'strong' departments. It seems fair to conclude that universities that spread their endeavours widely by academic subject are less able to pursue a research growth path under current funding strictures than those size-equivalent HEIs which put their resourcing eggs in proportionately fewer departmental baskets.[7]

3.3 Mobility and interaction

Geography is not merely about the distinctiveness of places and spaces but also the interaction and movement among them. Indeed, such distinctiveness often

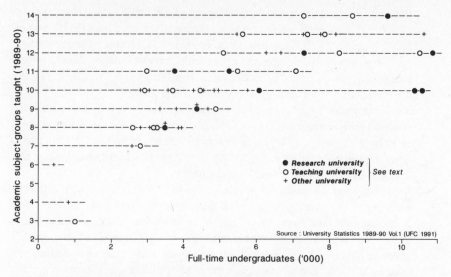

Figure 14.6 Size, academic diversity and the research/teaching divide
(*Source*: University Statistics 1989–1990, vol 1, UFC, 1991)

Table 14.2 Relative sizes of 'research' and 'teaching' universities by subject provision

Category	Below median size for provision level	Above median size for provision level
Research[a]	1	6
Teaching	11	6

[a] Three research universities are median for their provision level.

depends on interaction, as the HE system can demonstrate in two ways, one brought about by mobile students and the other by mobile academics.

Student mobility. Just prior to World War II some 43 per cent of Britain's full-time university students lived at home (Robbins, 1963b). By 1955, when Peter joined the academic staff of University College, London, this had fallen to 28.6 per cent (CSO, 1957), and by 1992 it was only 13.7 per cent (Universities Statistical Record, personal communication). The fact that undergraduates seem more mobile than hitherto is the combined result of more Halls of Residence, the arrival of a nationwide application system, the preparedness of award-granting bodies to fund students away from home and the inter-cohort transmission of positive experiences of living and studying in different localities. A parallel consequence is that the student intake profiles of different institutions have become less dictated by the social mix of their immediate hinterlands. Rather, they represent the interplay among four more general geographical factors:

1   Previous comments notwithstanding, students' willingness to travel increasing distances to study still shows some distance-decay (Fairweather, 1980; Nahkle, 1976; Trotman-Dickinson, 1989). So since the secondary-school geography of Britain has a preponderance of independent (private) schools in the south (Bradford and Burdett, 1989) this inflates the independent school intake of southern universities.

2   Students from 'higher' social class backgrounds are less distance-constrained than those from 'lower' ones. Some reasons for this are suggested elsewhere (Hoare, 1994a), while recent evidence from the CVCP (1991) also reveals more support for the notion of students studying locally and living at home among 'lower' social groups.

3   Irrespective of distance, some campuses have a cultural image differentially attractive to particular social class groups. I remember firm advice from my own (state grammar) school as to the universities and colleges where 'you would feel more at home', and as an admissions tutor over 12 years at Bristol I have been all too conscious that equivalent attitudes a quarter of a century later still control who applies to, and accepts a place in, 'my' department.

4   Strong traditions of studying at university in the region of home residence persist in the Celtic fringes, even if less so than hitherto (UCCA, 1992).[8]

Other work I have published explores these effects as the admissions process winds through from initial application to autumn intake, teasing out the different effects of factor 1 and a rolled-together 2 + 3 effect in enrolment profiles (Hoare, 1991c) as well, more recently, as attempting to segregate 2 from 3 (Hoare, 1994a).

Another consequent geography not yet analysed in detail by anyone is that of live-at-home university students, shown in figure 14.7,[9] a likely amalgam of factors 2, 4 and the high accommodation costs of London. These last 'encourage' students from the South-East who do study in London to live more cheaply at home, the more so if from less affluent backgrounds. As well as London and the other major metropolitan areas, the main concentrations of live-at-homes are again in Scotland and Northern Ireland although, nationwide, levels have declined between the dates mapped, by an average 3.5 percentage points for the 41 HEIs with data for both years.

Overall, the role of public policy is more subtle and complex here than in some other aspects covered in this chapter. Government directives towards HE expansion affect not just the quality but also the likely mix of students in school-background terms coming to universities, given the much higher penetration rates of HE into the independent than the state sector. Its publishing of nationwide school exam results will influence which secondary education parents choose for their able children and hence, indirectly, the HE campus culture these later find attractive. Government funding levels help determine how many bed-spaces universities can build for expanding numbers: limited funding encourages recruiting local students, while real-money cuts in student grants should persuade more to study from home, as well. Finally, the seal of

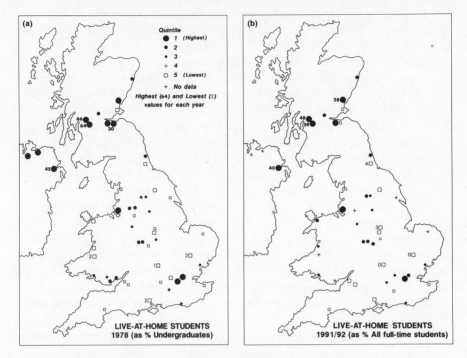

Figure 14.7   Studying at university from home: 1978 and 1991–1992

university approval bestowed on former polytechnics adds another complica-
tion. As we have seen, these usually duplicate existing HE locations (section
3.1) but their much higher commitment to part-time, mature and thereby often
local students, plus their lower status in the perception of some potential
students, their schools and parents, may complicate the comparatively well-
behaved geographies just discussed.

Academic mobility. As a general principle, a high spatial job mobility of academics is to be both expected and welcomed, the first given the general
labour-market relationship between this and educational attainment (for example, Toyne, 1977) and the second from its enabling know-how and viewpoints
to move freely within a community of scholars. Peter's 22 current (1993)
academic colleagues at Bristol gained their (non-Honorary) degrees from 14
different universities and have held previous permanent academic posts at a
further 9, both sets excluding Bristol itself.

However, despite its normality and desirability, geographical movement of
university staff has proven controversial of late in Britain. Any significant net
loss of UK-trained academics overseas, in quantity and/or quality terms, is seen
by lobby groups within the academic trade union and vice-chancellorial ranks
as bad news for the national economy and also indicative of low morale, deficient
government funding, and inadequate remuneration. Independently, the President of Texas A & M University reportedly characterized British academe as

'very big brains running around on very small salaries' (*Times Higher Education Supplement,* 16 February 1990). Certainly, some senior academics have left for lucrative postings abroad, but just as one swallow does not make a summer so one big name departure doesn't constitute a Brain Drain. Nor, argued government ministers, do the more comprehensive data in the *Universities Statistical Record,* which apparently show Britain as a net importer of academic talent (Robert Jackson in letter to *The Times,* 12 February 1990). 'Not so', retort their opponents. Such statistics under-record the volume of out-migration, while the quality of those leaving is also higher than the reverse flow. Equally, accelerated losses of younger dons in the internal brain drain to Britain's non-academic professions must be acknowledged, raising the average age of residual HEI staff, despite government policy initiatives to attract new blood.

With vested interests on all sides of the debating battle, wielding unreliable statistical weaponry, the real state of overseas migration to and from British academe is very elusive. This is not such a problem with a less politically charged aspect of academic migration – that of internal, inter-university movement – which I have explored in two different ways. The first (Hoare, 1981) considered whether those universities where the then members of the UGC had either graduated, were in post or had been in post, fared any better in that same Committee's 1981 selective allocation of (mostly reduced) income and student numbers across the UK's universities. I had confidentially expected no such relationship before looking at the figures, so imagine my surprise . . . .[10]

Second, in a more substantive exercise, and one more akin to the spatial diffusion theme, I examined how far different universities and their constituent parts drew upon their own graduates for academic appointments, and hence were, *a priori,* less open to innovation waves in teaching and research from the outside academic world (Hoare, 1994c). Other things being equal, departments with a high research reputation should attract academic applications from a range of other universities, especially for more senior posts. By appointing better candidates from larger application pools they thus enhance their reputations further. Less senior posts, particularly those for short-term contract research, might draw more on local graduates: applicants have had less chance to develop their research reputations, favouring the devil you know appointing principle.

Empirical analysis of 13 similarly sized UK universities strongly suggested this was so, but also indicated three other important points. Since a broadly similar study 30 years ago for Robbins (1963c), academic mobility, like that of students, appears to have risen nationally. However, an important spatial gradient arises in that universities in southern England depend the least on their local graduates, and those in Scotland and Northern Ireland the most. Furthermore, medical appointments were much more likely to draw upon local graduates than non-medical ones. Further discussion of the possible whys, wherefores and caveats are in the relevant paper but it is worth noting here that the high local dependency universities included some that did singularly poorly in the UFC's latest (1992) research selectivity index, which it would be cavalier of you and unwise of them to dismiss as pure coincidence.

3.4 System health

A healthy, successful university is more than just one with high research ratings in peer-group reviews. In this final section I first consider which are the 'successful' universities conceived of more widely and second, what consequences follow from their existence and their differential success for their surrounding space economies.

Successful universities. That some universities are recognized as of higher status than others, whether among schools, parents, students, academics or the wide community, is uncontentious, but establishing the same empirically is not quite as simple. Not only do academics have invested emotional capital in such evaluations but also many of the likely indicators are open to lively, if inconclusive, debate. Thus, for example, the *University Management Statistics and Performance Indicators in the UK* (CVCP/UFC, annual) statistics can show how much more *per caput* one university spends than another in teaching a given subject,[11] but it is less obvious which is the 'better' end of the spectrum! Equally, assessment of teaching quality across institutions falls foul of complications of value-added from different quality intakes and the inter-institutional comparability of degree results: after all, every academic knows her/his students could obtain a First more easily somewhere else. The same UGC/UFC Research ratings can also be used to construct a family of league tables rather than a single definitive one (Johnston, 1990). However, difficult and controversial though it may be, assessment of the differential performance of HEIs is now part-and-parcel of the much greater accountability demanded of the sector since 1979 by government (Johnes and Taylor, 1990), even though elements of it were still evident before (Piper, 1978).

So, nothing ventured, nothing gained. In the hopes that a multivariate approach might yield some consistency in outcome, I produced a three-fold regional classification of UK universities, which conformed closely to a traditional centre-periphery view of the national space economy (figure 5 in Hoare, 1991d). While primarily derived from a number of measures of the university admissions process, this structure also performed well in terms of the UGC's 1989 research ratings, degree classifications and graduate employability. It also conforms closely to the R/T division on funding yardsticks noted earlier (figure 14.5) and to the 1992 UFC research selectivity rating exercises, both of which data sets became available subsequently. In the latter, a disproportionate number of HEIs with above-average ratings and/or with improvements in their rank-order position since the 1989 exercise are also in the three southern English regions.

Although reservations might be entered against this or that indicator it is hard to gainsay the consistent overall message from this growing body of evidence. Universities in southern England are better at attracting good students from wide geographical catchments, and in sustaining this quality by the output stage to the benefit of their employability. The same universities have also generated high research reputations which show no signs of being eroded and which, in turn, will further their attraction for leading academic teacher/researchers and

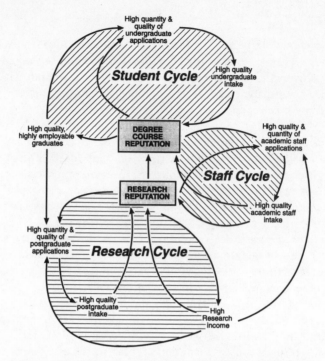

Figure 14.8   Cumulative causation in British Higher Education

for able students. Figure 14.8 represents this Myrdalian process of cumulative growth working through the HE sector, and incorporating distinct but inter-locking cycles of reinforcement based on these same three components. The virtuous positive feedbacks shown would be typical of Britain's *R* universities, able to choose, and successful in choosing, a research-based growth path with an accompanying size-constrained, but high quality, teaching programme. In contrast, while some institutions may deliberately see their mission as based on teaching, for others their versions of figure 14.8 would substitute *low* for *high*, as the cycles conspire to make a high-quantity teaching profile a Hobson's Choice to make ends meet. It is far easier to see how these processes of relative and cumulative change, favouring as they do the already 'have' regions of the UK space economy, can be sustained than to envisage their counteraction, short of a major remedial public sector initiative of which few signs are yet visible.[12]

Economic impulses. Many universities take a keen academic interest in their local economies as research laboratories, or in other ways. As the flip side of the same coin, universities also contribute to their local and regional economy in many ways, typified recently by Bristol City Council for its 'old' university as in table 14.3 (Bristol City Council, 1992). Equally, the possibility that the *R/T* distinc-tions discussed previously will translate into relatively more powerful benefits for the surrounding economies of the former than the latter is a tempting working hypothesis (even if, in the absence of appropriate evidence, no more than this).

Table 14.3   City economy benefits of Bristol University's planned expansion

Item	Type of benefit
1.	Research initiative stimulation to inward and local development, especially in high-technology field
2.	Well-qualified graduates enrich local labour pool and thus stimulate employment growth
3.	Multiplier effects of (i) expenditure of University employees, (ii) construction work at University
4.	Effect on city's image appeal to investors and employees
5.	Tourist benefit from conference and catering facilities

Source: Bristol City Council (1992)

The aspect of table 14.3 most widely studied on both sides of the Atlantic is probably that of universities as a source of innovative capacity for the local economy, thereby boosting employment and other induced (income-spending) or expenditure (input-providing) multipliers. This brain-power resource can entice other firms to locate nearby, or can spin-off into existing or newly-founded local business (Malecki, 1991; Keeble, 1989). However, by no means all industrial research is university-linked in these ways (for example, Malecki, 1980), nor does such as there is necessarily benefit the immediate locality (Smith, 1991). Not surprisingly, attempts to further this symbiosis artificially through near-campus science parks have not proved an unqualified success. By contrast, interest in university multiplier analysis has been more sporadic, at least in Britain, although such evidence as there is suggests HEIs play a major role in direct and indirect local jobs and incomes, as with Lewis and Townsend's (1992) recent study in Durham University and McNicoll's (1993) of Strathclyde (see also Brownrigg, 1973; Lewis, 1988; Bleaney et al., 1992).

Finally, consider two further aspects of table 14.3, through some Bristol-based examples. The first pursues the 'at home' induced multiplier of the spending patterns of those at the university, but in a more disaggregated way than does the published evidence to date. For academic staff, a relatively diffuse geography of home-based spending emerges, and is fairly stable over time (figure 14.9a). The more affluent suburbs and attractive villages beyond the built-up fringe are home to many senior administrators and academics. For other grades of staff only snapshot residence data are available but these show how the city districts most likely to benefit from University-income spending vary sharply with the staff categories under the microscope (figure 14.9b), as with the very different residential geographies of catering and cleaning staff compared to the other categories.

Most (though not all!) undergraduates have lower disposable incomes than those who teach them. However, as Bristol depends less than most on local enrolments the bulk of the student-spend fraction of the local economy is additional, exogenous money, directly attributable to the University (making its omission from table 14.3 the more surprising). No detailed budget diaries of

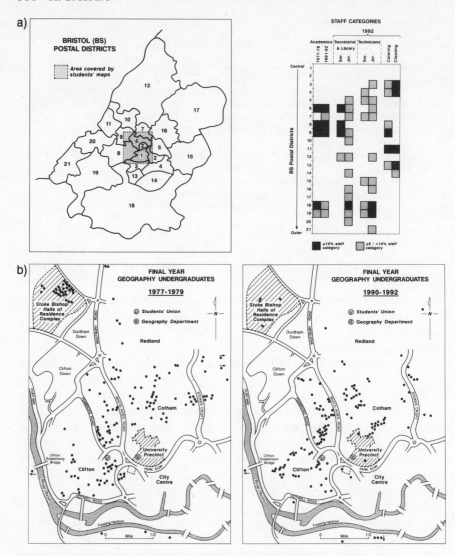

Figure 14.9 Expenditure epicentres: University of Bristol staff and students

these consumers exist (cf. Research Services Ltd, 1989) but we can at least identify the geographical bases from which their expenditures emanate. Most first-year students live in Halls of Residence, most of which provide catering services. Thereafter, many flee to a self-catering life in private flats and shared houses, so raising their average spend in the vicinity of their term-time addresses. If final year Geography undergraduates are typical (figure 14.9b), these expenditure epicentres cluster around the University precinct, and more so than a decade ago, perhaps as peer-group perceptions of smart parts of town ebb and flow or as the worsening renting power of student incomes forces more attention on inner locations.

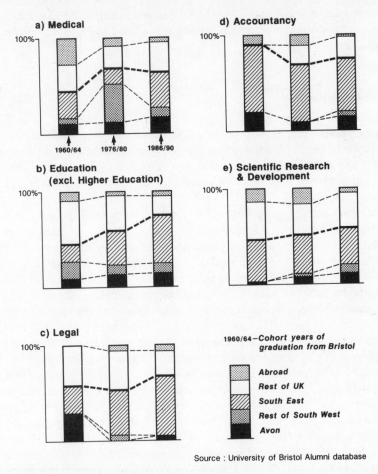

Figure 14.10   Bristol graduates and spatial labour markets
(*Source*: University of Bristol Alumni database)

Second, how do the student cohorts, once they have left the University, enrich the quality and quantity of the work force in particular spatial labour markets? Do they disproportionately obtain local employment, and is there any tendency for a widening diffusion wave of Bristol graduates to occur over space and time since graduation? Drawing on the University's Alumni Association records, the answers to both seem to be 'No', at least among the five professional subgroups and three sets of years analysed in figure 14.10. The dominance of accountancy employment in the South-East and the low retention rate of scientific researchers in the local (Avon) and regional (South-West) labour markets are particularly noteworthy. More generally, in no period and in no profession do more than 30 per cent of the relevant sample work in the South-West region. But, equally, never are more than 50 per cent of the UK-based Bristol graduates employed outside this and the South-East in combination, suggesting the University essentially serves a southern England labour market. Whether this is in any way exceptional could only be judged were comparable figures available for graduates trained at other UK institutions, which, in the published literature at least, they aren't.[13]

4 CONCLUSIONS

Perhaps because it is thought too much like academic navel-contemplation, the geography of Higher Education in this country has been relatively ignored by those geographers working within it, just as the discipline has, until recently, been unrepresented in the sector's authority positions to influence it in other ways.

But things are changing. Five geographers are now (1993) Vice-Chancellors and signs of an emergent geography of HE are becoming clearer, as more academic attention is turned towards it and as government pressures channel the system in distinct geographical directions. I have not attempted a complete overview of this broad topic here, but I have tried to show how it touches upon areas of established academic interest in human geography, the discipline Peter has served with such distinction for 40 years. National-level policies since the war have at once generated spatial consolidation (of places with HEI provision) and spatial segregation (via measures of success and mission), the latter being both responsive to, and generative of, enhanced inter-regional mobility of staff and students. More locally, HE growth impinges on land use planning principles and pragmatics, and also invokes concepts of urban economic analysis of a university as a 'basic' sector, sucking in and then rechannelling wealth and employment within the local system. This can spill over onto a regional scale as well, depending on the geography of commercial application of university research, the employment of graduate and postgraduate-trained labour and the continuing education of in-post professionals. And to the extent that a university can draw upon the most able academic researchers and most promising undergraduate and graduate talent from a wider area still, the region that benefits does so at the expense of other parts of the national, and even international, economy. Indeed, the emerging spatial centre-periphery structure of the national HEI sector, evident in student and academic staff attractiveness, in university 'successfulness' and restructuring towards either research or teaching, is the most impelling of the patterns and changes reviewed here.

Such university-space economy interactions are not unindirectional. The university still depends disproportionately upon its region and locality for its research and educational raw materials, and where these are limited or in decline – as with arable England's alleged shortages of farm animal patients for trainee vets or Tomlinson's transfer of human ones from London teaching hospitals – this can have a sharp implication for the dependent universities.

As explained at the outset, the precise interplay between the details of government policy and those of university geography often defy easy dissection. Equally, certain aspects of the latter owe little or nothing to such policy, like the entrenched regionalism in the UK's periphery, evident in staff and student recruitment patterns, and the distinctiveness of campus cultures. But few would dismiss as coincidence the simultaneous clarification of a university geography on the one hand and the tightening of central government control of what universities are doing, and the financing of their doing it, on the other. As never before, universities have had to examine their own academic destinies within a changing and uncertain political economy. That the net outcome of their several 'independent' responses is a logical geography of Higher Education is not fully appreciated, nor was it ever intended or foreseen by government. But it is not the less real for all that and may in turn call for public policy recognition and response if its consequences are not to run unchecked through the nation.

NOTES

1 The semi-autonomous colleges of the Universities of Wales and London are not included as separate 'universities' in these totals. Figures for graduates in the relevant years are drawn variously from three series: the Department for Education's *Statistics of Education: Further Education and Higher Education in polytechnics and colleges*, and the University Grants Committee's *Statistics of Education Universities (UK)* [a superseded series] and *University Statistics vol. 1 (Students and Staff)*, plus some best estimates by myself for Scottish (ex)Polytechnics.

2 In Northern Ireland the contemporaneous Lockwood Committee fulfilled a similar role to Robbins in mainland Britain, and recommended the formation of a second university for the Province. This was established as the New University of Ulster with a greenfield campus at Coleraine, but evolving from the long-established Magee College in Londonderry (Osborne and Singleton, 1982).

3 The most obvious example of this, of course, is the Open University, which opened its airwaves to students in 1971 and whose distance learning brought higher education into the family lounge if not, as popularly portrayed, the kitchen as well.

4 The yet-maybe University of the Highlands has been mooted both as a private investment project and as an initiative by the (Scottish) Highland Regional Council (Highland Region of Scotland, nd). Whether as a single campus site at Inverness or as a set of federal campuses it would occupy one of the largest empty spaces of figure 14.2. Furthermore, the Higher Education Funding Council in England also established a fund of £3.6m partly to finance the extension of HE courses by franchising or outworking 'to desolate [sic] locations' (*Times Higher Education Supplement* 7 May 1993, p. 1).

5 These figures amalgamate the Science and Social Sciences entry streams separately identified in UCCA statistics for Geography and for Psychology, with consequences for the total number of subjects.

6 Specialist HEIs, such as medical and business schools, are excluded from these figures.

7 At Swansea, for example, its poor showing in the 1986 UGC research assessment exercise caused the Principal to conclude the college was 'trying to do too much with too few resources', heralding the closing and merging of some departments in a rationalization programme (Dykes, 1992, p. 213).

8 Thus the location quotients (Haggett, 1965, p. 236) relating to students accepted for a university place in their region of domicile in 1991 were above 1.0 for all UK regions, but with the highest by some way being Wales' 6.5, Scotland's 6.8 and Northern Ireland's massive 18.1. While only 5.2 per cent of all home students

accepted nationally through UCCA that year were from homes in Northern Ireland the equivalent for the Province's two universities was 94.1 per cent.

9 Unfortunately, since 1980 these data are no longer made available at the individual university level by the *Universities Statistical Record*.

10 By the equivalent exercise in 1986 this *prime facie* support for the pork-barrelling hypothesis in inter-university grant dispersal was much weaker (Hoare, 1986).

11 *The Times Higher Education Supplement* (28 May 1993) made public the Higher Education Funding Council for England's league tables of English universities and Further Education colleges, based on their supposed teaching efficiency (that is, cheapness) per student, and noted the criticism both of their methodology and of the interpretations placed on them.

12 One exception is the decision in 1993 of the Welsh Higher Education Funding Council to offer more generous financial support than their English counterpart to HEIs of identical research rating, to bolster the low research base of Welsh universities.

13 However, Thexton and McGarrick (1983) did find some clustering of dentists in practices around the university dental schools where they had trained.

REFERENCES

Allington, N.F.B. (1990). 'The governance and funding of university education in Britain: retrospect and prospect.' In R. Watts and J. Greenberg (eds), *Post-Secondary Education: Preparation for the World of Work*. Aldershot: Dartmouth, 89–110.

Bleaney, M.F., Binks, M.R., Greenaway, D., Reed, G.V., & Whynes, D.K. (1992). 'What does a university add to its local economy?' *Applied Economics*, 24, 305–11.

Bradford, M.G. & Burdett, F. (1989). 'Spatial polarisation of private education in England.' *Area*, 21, 47–57.

Bristol City Council (1992). *University of Bristol – Strategy: Issues and Opportunities*. Report by the Acting City Planning Officer, agenda item paper for Planning and Development Committee, 16 December.

Brownrigg, M. (1973). 'The economic impact of a new university.' *Scottish Journal of Political Economy*, 20, 123–39.

Burnett, J. (1992). 'The universities of the United Kingdom.' In *Commonwealth Universities Yearbook, 1992*, vol. 1, London: Association of Commonwealth Universities, 384–93.

CSO [Central Scottish Office] (1957). *Annual Abstract of Statistics*, No. 94. London: Her Majesty's Stationery Office.

CVCP [Committee of Vice-Chancellors and Principals] (1991). *Public attitudes towards universities*. London: CVCP, survey conducted for CVCP by MORI.

CVCP/UFC [Committee of Vice-Chancellors and Principals and Universities Funding Council], (annual, since 1988), *Universities Management Statistics and Performance Indicators in the UK*. Cheltenham: Universities Statistical Record.

Dykes, D. (1992). *The University College of Swansea: an Illustrated History*. Stroud: Sutton.

Fairweather, M. (1980). *University Enrolment Patterns in England and the United States*. New York: State University of Plattsburgh, Department of Geography, (mimeo).

Flowers, Lord (1993). *Review of the Academic Year, Committee of Enquiry (under Chairmanship of Lord Flowers): Interim Report for Consultation* (unpublished).

Haggett, P. (1965). *Locational Analysis in Human Geography*. London: Edward Arnold.

Highland Region of Scotland (no date). *A University in the Highlands*. Inverness: Highland Regional Council.

Hoare, A.G. (1981). 'UGC: unequal geographical cuts.' *Area*, 13, 256–62.

Hoare, A.G. (1986). 'UGC: more unequal geographical cuts.' *Area*, 18, 315–25.

Hoare, A.G. (1991a). 'Reviewing the reviews: the geography of university rationalisation.' *Higher Education Quarterly*, 45, 234–53.

Hoare, A.G. (1991b). 'Riley's report: geography (mis)applied?' *Applied Geography*, 11, 91–103.

Hoare, A.G. (1991c). 'Bias in university enrolments: a regional analysis.' *Regional Studies*, 25, 459–70.

Hoare, A.G. (1991d). 'University competition, student migration and regional economic differentials.' *Higher Education*, 45, 234–53.

Hoare, A.G. (1994a). 'School type as a discriminant in the geography of university applications in Great Britain.' *Geoforum*, 25, 87–104.

Hoare, A.G. (1994b). 'Big is excellent: the importance of departmental size in academic research ratings.' *Higher Education* (forthcoming).

Hoare, A.G. (1994c). 'Academic mobility and the dependence on local graduates in British universities: a geographical analysis.' *Geografisker Annaler B*, 76 (forthcoming).

Johnes, J. & Taylor, J. (1990). *Performance indicators in higher education*. Guildford: The Society for Research into Higher Education.

Johnston, R.J. (1990). 'University league tables.' *Environment and Planning A*, 22, 285–90.

Keeble, D.E. (1989). 'High technology industry and regional development in Britain: the case of the Cambridge phenomenon.' *Environment and Planning C, Government and Policy*, 7, 153–72.

Lewis, J.A. (1988). 'Assessing the effect of the Polytechnic of Wolverhampton on the local community.' *Urban Studies*, 25, 53–61.

Lewis, J.R. & Townsend, A.R. (1992). *The local economic impact of the University of Durham: summary of interim findings*. Department of Geography, University of Durham, Durham (mimeo).

Malecki, E.J. (1980). 'Corporate Organization of R and D and the location of technological activities.' *Regional Studies*, 14, 219–34.

Malecki, E.J. (1991). *Technology and Economic Development: the Dynamics of Local, Regional and National Change*. Harlow: Longman.

McNicoll, I.H. (1993). *The Impact of Strathclyde University on the Economy of Scotland*. Glasgow: University of Strathclyde.

Nahkle, T. (1976). 'Influences of geographical location on university admissions.' *Times Higher Supplement*, 30 July 13.

Osborne, R.D. & Singleton, D. (1982). 'Political processes and behaviour.' In F.W. Boal & J.N.H. Douglas (eds), *Integration and Division: Geographical Perspectives on the Northern Ireland Problem*. London: Academic Press, 176–94.

Piper, D.W. (ed.) (1978). *The Efficiency and Effectiveness of Teaching in Higher Education*. London: University of London Teaching Methods Unit, Institute of Education.

Research Services Ltd (1989). *Student Income and Expenditure Survey*. Wembley: Research Services Ltd.

Richardson, J. (1981). 'Geographical bias.' In D.W. Piper (ed.), *Is Higher Education Fair?* Guildford: Society for Research into Higher Education, 40–56.

Robbins, Lord (1963a). *Higher Education: Report of the Committee under the Chairmanship of Lord Robbins 1961-63*. London: Her Majesty's Stationery Office, Cmnd 3154.

Robbins, Lord (1963b). *Appendix 2A (Students and their Education)*. Part V of main report (Robbins, 1963a).

Robbins, Lord (1963c). *Appendix 3 (Teachers in Higher Education)*. Part I of main report (Robbins, 1963a).

Smith, H.L. (1991). 'Industry–academic links: the case of Oxford University.' *Environment and Planning C. Government and Policy*, 9, 403–16.

Sultan, R.G.M. & Sultan, P.E. (1990). 'The struggle for higher education resources.' In R. Watts and J. Greenberg (eds), *Post Secondary Education: Preparation for the World of Work*. Aldershot: Dartmouth.

Thexton, A.J. & McGarrick, J.C. (1983). 'The geographical distribution of recently qualified dental graduates (1975–1980) in England, Scotland and Wales.' *British Dental Journal*, 154, 71–75.

Tomlinson, B. (1992). *Report of the Inquiry into London's Health Service, Medical Educational Research under the Chairmanship of Sir B. Tomlinson*. London: Her Majesty's Stationery Office.

Toyne, P. (1977). *Organization, Location and Behaviour: Decision-making in Economic Geography*. London: Macmillan.

Trotman-Dickinson, A. (1989). 'East or west, hame's best.' *Times Higher Education Supplement*, 20 October, 3.

UCCA [Universities Central Council on Admissions] (1992). Statistical Supplement to the 29th Report 1990–1991. Cheltenham: UCCA.

15

The Business of British Geography

R.J. Johnston

1 ON THE HISTORY OF GEOGRAPHY

Historians of science no longer believe in its linear progress – if they ever really did (Livingstone, 1992). Despite what some accounts tell us, science does not proceed straightforwardly through the production of findings, from which new hypotheses are deduced and then critical tests are devised and conducted to produce the next round of discoveries. One might, perhaps somewhat unkindly, associate this idealized, almost idealistic, view with the 'young Peter Haggett': the 'model of models' with which he structures the first edition of *Locational Analysis in Human Geography* (Haggett, 1965) comprises a feedback loop involving theory, deduction, empirical test and reappraisal, for example, and in their introductory chapter to the seminal *Models in Geography* he and Dick Chorley present their 'new geography' as a continuous exercise in puzzle-solving (Haggett and Chorley, 1967, p. 39).

Of course, Haggett always realized that this was a very simple view: in the first sentence of *Locational Analysis,* he notes that 'Geographical writing, like any other, inevitably reflects the assumptions and experience of the writer' (Haggett, 1965, p.1). Furthermore, he and Chorley championed Kuhn's concepts of paradigm and 'revolutionary' paradigm-shifts, with the latter involving practitioners making 'leaps of faith' as they switch from one organizing framework to another – a practice which is far from the idealized state which some portray as scientific practice (see Johnston, 1991a).

The 'mature Peter Haggett' was even clearer in recognizing that what geographers do is complexly determined. His own career to date has been characterized by a 'search for spatial order', he tells us, but while he pursued that goal 'Other geographers would have chosen to emphasize other things, to see other patterns' (Haggett, 1990, p.19).

If individual geographers influence the nature and course of their discipline, what factors lead them to follow some routes and to ignore others, to promote certain ideas and relegate (even denigrate) alternatives? Historians of science have stressed that individual personalities may be important. Charismatic academics may be more able to promote their ideas than relatively retiring and self-effacing people, but Peter Haggett's own career indicates that this is an insufficient account, for he has rarely trodden the international conference scene in the manner so well satirized in David Lodge's novels. More importantly, however, historians have stressed the roles of context and culture. Geographers are socialized into their discipline, both in a general sense in that they adopt widely accepted definitions of what geography is, and in the local sense that they are influenced by the other members of their academic social networks with whom they may well work closely, in the physical as well as the intellectual sense. And so if your network is weak and your context thinly populated you may have little influence, whatever the quality of your ideas – a point well illustrated by Duncan's (1974) discussion of the belated discovery and adoption of Hägerstrand's pioneering ideas regarding spatial diffusion – a theme close to Peter Haggett's heart (see also Johnston, 1993d).

Context is crucial, therefore, as those influenced by Anthony Giddens's (1984) theory of structuration argue and those promoting the rediscovery of place, or locality, as a central geographical concept have claimed (Johnston, 1991b). As a discipline, in Giddens's terminology, geography is a locale; situated within it are many subsidiary locales where individual geographers create and re-create their disciplinary practices. Three sets of influences on the content of those sublocales and their members' actions are suggested here: (1) the individuals themselves; (2) the flows of information within and between sublocales; and (3) the ruling ideas in the wider societies within which those sublocales are situated and on which they depend for their sustenance. In this chapter, my main interest is in the last of the three.

The importance of a society's ruling ideas as an influence on the practice of academic disciplines, and on geography in particular, is excellently illustrated in Taylor's (1985) essay on the relative strengths of 'pure' and 'applied' geography over time. Applied geography, he contends, is especially strong in periods of economic recession. That is when societies, through those elements of the state apparatus which direct expenditure on science and higher education, call for greater academic contributions to 'solving the problems of the day' than is usual in the more quiescent periods of relative economic plenty, when 'pure' geography can better flourish (see also Taylor, 1992). This societal pressure may be direct, as experienced in the state socialist societies of the ex-USSR and Eastern Europe for much of the twentieth century (Johnston, 1992a); it may involve pressures through financial and other incentives; and it may involve crusading individuals (like Bennett, 1989; Openshaw, 1991, and Stoddart, 1987: see Johnston, 1992b) arguing that their fellow academics should orient their scientific activities so as to serve 'the nation's (or the world's) needs'.

1.1 The ruling ideas of the late 1980s–early 1990s

The call for applied geography was strong in the 1980s and the state apparatus in the United Kingdom made substantial efforts to dragoon its universities into becoming both more 'relevant' and more 'efficient' in their teaching and research activities. Geography as a discipline was rarely identified separately in these attempts to restructure and reorient British higher education (though see Joseph, 1985). It was far from insulated from the storms that raged for much of the decade, however, with universities caught between two 'counter-revolving whirlpools' (Sanderson, 1991, p. 429): one required them to respond to student demand, which was strongest in the social sciences and humanities; the other expected them to respond to employers' demands for more and better-trained technologists. Critics from the 'New Right', who dominated political discourse throughout the decade, accused the universities of 'failing the nation' by promoting liberal, anti-business and anti-vocational attitudes rather than contributing to a 'continuing supply of wealth creating instruments' (as summarized in Sanderson, 1991).

Peter Haggett had the misfortune to be at the centre of the universities' response to these pressures in the late 1980s – though it was undoubtedly the good fortune of academia in general and geography in particular that he was willing to give so much of his time to attempts to tame the whirlpools. From 1985 until 1989 he sat on the University Grants Committee (UGC), a buffer between government on the one hand and the autonomous universities on the other. The UGC's roles were to distribute the government block grant for universities among the various institutions and to advise the government on the system's needs. Because it was also accountable to the House of Commons Public Accounts Committee for the efficient use of that money, the UGC became increasingly interventionist during the decade: it conducted a number of subject reviews, for example, which led to departmental closures and many premature retirements. (Fortunately there was no review of geography, which suggests that the discipline was perceived as in relatively good heart and presenting no system-wide problems – a view for which British geographers undoubtedly owe Peter Haggett a debt of gratitude, given the nature and outcome of many of the other reviews, most notably that of earth sciences: see Hoare, 1991.)

One cannot identify Peter Haggett's influence in all of these activities, but one can look at how well geography rode out the policy storms in whose direction, if not generation, he was unfortunately implicated. Thus, after a brief presentation of the political context within which those storms were generated, the remainder of this chapter looks at geographers' 'performance' during the 1980s and early 1990s ('performance indicators' are part of the 1980s 'newspeak' of educational management: Cave et al., 1988: Johnston, 1989).

2 THATCHERISM AND HIGHER EDUCATION

For the whole of the 1980s the United Kingdom was governed by the Conservative Party led by Margaret Thatcher. Her governments were characterized by a crusading, radical zeal and a determination to achieve substantial change in British economy, polity, and society (a concept whose existence she denied). As followers of the arguments of the economic 'New Right', who stressed the superiority of markets over states in promoting wealth, efficiency, and individual well-being, these governments attacked spending on higher education from their first budget (May 1979) and were relentless in their pressure for better performance, more in tune with national (that is, market capitalism's) needs. Although 'Thatcherism' (on which there are many books: among the best is Gamble, 1988) had many much larger targets than the universities, its demands on them were several (see Scott, 1989) and the outcomes substantial. Thatcherism thus provides the context for appreciating what happened in British universities during the 1980s.

2.1   The 'Thatcherism' project

The basic goal of 'Thatcherism' was to make the UK more efficient and effective in wealth-creation through the operation of markets, with the minimum of interference from a strong state. This was founded on a searching critique of the welfare and corporate state arrangements which had developed over the previous half-century, some of which had direct effects on higher education. (This section draws heavily on Johnston, 1992c.)

The welfare state, which expanded rapidly from 1945 on, created a 'general culture of expectations' (Bennett, 1989, p. 277); calls on the state to correct relative deprivation experienced by substantial segments of the population, over a wide range of 'entitlements', generated ever-expanding demands, requiring the state to increase its tax demands. The Thatcher governments were strongly influenced by Hayek's (1944) arguments regarding the incompatibility of liberty and state direction of the economy, and sought to reduce dependency on the state by encouraging self-reliance. Thus many welfare state programmes were cut. University students, for example, saw the value of their maintenance grants reduced in real terms throughout the decade; from 1990 to 1994 the value of the grant was frozen, with any increase provided as a long-term loan from a government-guaranteed company, and from 1994 to 1996 the grant will be reduced by 10 per cent per annum, with compensating increases in the size of the available loan, until grant and loan are equal in value. From 1990 also, students were denied access to housing benefits, which many had previously used to cover their part of their living costs, especially during vacations. An attempt to insist on students (or their parents) meeting part of the costs of tuition was withdrawn in 1986 in the face of Conservative Party back-bench opposition in the House of Commons, though the Secretary of State for Education again raised the issue with the Vice-Chancellors in 1993: later in the year he indicated that the government had no intention of raising the issue again for a further three years.

The welfare state has a very large bureaucracy, attacked as inefficient because it lacked the stimulus of competition; that inefficiency increased, it was claimed, as the culture of dependency grew and the system became overloaded. A variety of measures was thus introduced to increase efficiency, many of which involved opening up large parts of the state apparatus to the operation of market, or quasi-market, forces. Schools, for example, were urged to opt out of local government control and hospitals were encouraged to operate as separate trusts within the National Health Service. All components of the welfare state, including universities, were required to be more accountable for their spending (thereby demonstrating their efficiency), and also to raise increased proportions of their income from sources other than the state. For universities, it was argued, freeing them from over-dependence on the state for their teaching and research income would enhance their independence and sustain their academic freedom.

The five central planks of the 1980s policies were reducing the culture of dependency, eliminating bureaucratic inefficiency, ending monopolies, enhancing incentives, and minimizing inflation. Public spending had to be cut; state bureaucracies had to be efficient; people had to be encouraged to invest, which required inflation to be low; individuals had to become more self-reliant and take greater control over their own futures – which they were more likely to do in a competitive market that offered them choice and the potential for self-advancement with low taxation rates than if living under the wide embrace of a welfare state. The state has to be strong, to protect market operations and ensure that they remain free, but it should intervene as little as possible, with people controlling their own destinies rather than relying on the state to do it for them in what would certainly be a more inefficient and ineffective way.

2.2 Higher education

Higher education was far from immune from the goals of reducing public expenditure, making the recipients of such money more accountable for and efficient in its use, and promoting an 'enterprise economy'. Four particular aspects of changes in the universities can be identified as they responded to those pressures, largely channelled to them by the UGC which found itself increasingly subordinated to the demands of the state (Scott, 1989).

2.2.1 Leaner and fitter. This catch-phrase, widely used in the early 1980s, was applied to many British institutions. It was believed within the government, and publicly stated by Secretaries of State for Education and Science (notably by Sir Keith, now Lord, Joseph), that the universities were inefficient institutions, far from business-like in their management and operations let alone in their accountablility for the expenditure of public funds; it was also argued that many individual academics were far from efficient and productive in using their time. The British taxpayers were getting a poor return on their investment, it was claimed, and so the block grant to the UGC was cut substantially in 1981 – which led to it implementing cuts of up to 40 per cent in the annual budgets of some universities, with immediate effect. Substantial staff losses were inevitable and government funds were provided to facilitate voluntary redundancy and premature retirement schemes in most institutions.

Although funds were cut – as they were again in 1986 (Hoare, 1981, 1986) – universities were expected to recruit about the same numbers of students in total, in order to make efficiency gains. (Institutions were penalized for failing to recruit their target numbers but, paradoxically, they were also, for a few years, penalized for over-recruiting!) More efficient management was promoted through the recommendations of an inquiry – the Jarratt Report (1985) – commissioned by the Committee of Vice-Chancellors and Principals (CVCP), eager to demonstrate that the message had been received and understood by the new breed of university 'chief executives'.

Some initiatives were fostered by special government-provided funds for the employment of 'new blood' lecturers. Allocation of this money was by competitive bidding to the UGC and the majority of the new posts went to scientific, technological and other vocationally oriented disciplines. Of the 638.5 posts created in the years 1983–5, just over half went to the physical sciences, engineering and technology: geography departments received just 11.5 posts, of which five were concerned with remote sensing and digital mapping, three were in relatively sophisticated mathematical modelling (two of them in physical and one in human geography), two related to the economic geography of technological change, and one was in historical-cultural geography. Commentators saw this as UGC selection of applications likely to be attractive to the government (Cosgrove, 1985) and evidence of a 'new philistinism' (Smith, 1985, p.242):

The outcome of the new blood scheme is profoundly depressing to those who see the research frontier as involving the direct rather than remote sensing of human experience, using qualitative as well as quantitative methods, informed by and contributing to critical social theory rather than by the technology of cybernetics, and dedicated to the enhancement of human welfare conceived far more broadly than economic performance.

In response, Clayton (1985a), a UGC member at the time, pointed out that the initial proposals from the Secretary of State allowed for no 'new blood' posts outside science and technology, but that the UGC insisted upon some. Regarding Smith's charge of state interference, he claimed that

if this [the 'new blood' allocation] is all the interference geography suffers we shall be lucky – it is likely that the UGC's move towards more strongly differentiated funding and overt recognition of research will have far greater effects both between and within institutions. (p. 321)

(Events proved him correct!) Earlier, in his Presidential Address to the IBG, Clayton (1985b) had criticized geographers for the low priority that they gave to research and counselled that to prepare for the forthcoming funding environment we should 'pull in our geographical horns and try to do fewer things, though each on a larger scale' (p. 16), a change of orientation which called for 'more determined management and highly motivated staff' (p. 11).

2.2.2 Accountability. In reaction to the government's requirement for greater accountability for the expenditure of public money, the UGC instituted a formula-driven methodology for allocating moneys among the universities: by the end of the 1980s, most details of that formula were public and the 1990s successor organizations (the Higher Education Funding Councils for England, Scotland and Wales) were entirely open about the formulae employed.

The government had: (a) queried whether universities were efficient in their teaching function (with the lower costs per student in the expanding polytechnics quoted as the comparator); and (b) wondered whether it was getting value-for-money from the large annual sum (*c.* £600m per annum in 1990 figures) allocated for distribution among the universities to support research. Following that lead, which was stimulated to some extent by the government's scientific advisers drawn from academia, the UGC decided that for British researchers to compete internationally – and so contribute the ideas which would lead to technological breakthroughs – it was necessary to concentrate its allocations on the main centres of excellence. This was initially done in an *ad hoc* manner – by, for example, the allocation of large sums of money for equipment to research groups of international status by a committee of experts, who called for no bids – but in 1986 a formal system of assessing all departments in terms of their research performance and potential was introduced.

This first Research Assessment Exercise required universities to submit a 'research profile' for each of their departments, including a research plan. These were considered by panels of experts, who graded them on a four-point rating scale: 'outstanding', 'better than average', 'about average', and 'below average'. The composition of the panels was not divulged (though it is generally assumed, and not contested, that Peter Haggett, by then a member of the UGC, chaired the geography panel). Of the 42 geography departments assessed, in a procedure which generated substantial unease and anger (Smith, 1986; Cosgrove, 1987; Bentham 1987; Gleave, Harrison and Moss, 1987), 11 were judged 'outstanding' (at least in part), 5 as 'better than average', 16 as 'about average', and 10 'below average'.

The assessment was conducted to provide a parameter for the UGC's allocation formula which rewarded universities having higher ranked departments with a larger share of the research money. (It was up to the individual, autonomous universities to decide how to allocate their money internally, since it came to them as a block grant with no earmarked funds for named departments, but in each year since 1986 universities were required to report to the UGC on their progress in achieving greater selectivity in the distribution of research funds.) A second exercise was conducted in 1989, when departments were rated on a five-point scale: of the 36 geography departments rated, 5 received a grade 5 (the highest), 11 a grade 4, 10 got grade 3, 8 a grade 2, and 2 a grade 1. (This assessment was undertaken by a panel of four academic geographers – Peter Haggett, Ken Gregory, Ron Johnston, and David Sugden – plus two other members of the UGC, a town planner and an economic historian: Edwards, 1991.) The exercise was repeated in 1992, when the 'new universities' (the former polytechnics) and the Colleges of Higher Education were invited to participate: the geography submissions were assessed by a panel of eight (Ken Gregory, David Bowen, Peter Daniels, Ron Johnston, Richard Munton, David Rhind, Edmund Penning-Rowsell, and David Sugden: see Gregory, 1993). The outcome was 6 grade 5 departments (all in the 'old' universities), 12 with grade 4 (again, all in the 'old' universities), 22 (20) in grade 3, 11 (4) in grade 2, and 9 (0) in grade 1 (for more details, see the symposium edited by Thorne, 1993).

It was announced in 1989 that a greater proportion of the research money would be allocated according to the gradings and less as a 'floor' provision for research, the latter being distributed to all universities according to their size. This made the striving for high gradings even more important and increased the pressure on individual universities to reward their better-performing departments. After the 1992 assessment exercise, which used the same five-point scale, all of the research money was to be distributed selectively to universities, with no floor money to support some research by all, and no research money associated with departments graded only 1. (See Johnston 1993a, b, c.) Money distributed to universities for equipment purchase was also to be allocated according to a formula in which the research grading was a significant component.

From 1986 until 1992, the UGC (and its successor the UFC) also distributed research money to universities by matching their research grant earnings from the government Research Councils and various charities (at an initial rate of 40p in the £ but reduced to 29p by 1991–2). This was part of the block grant also, although universities were expected to use it to sustain the research activity in the departments which earned the grants. (It was paid two years in arrears.) From 1992 on that money has been transferred to the Research Councils and much of it will be used to meet the direct costs of research projects which formerly were met by universities from their block grants. This shift circumvents the universities' autonomous decisions on where to spend their block grants and channels more of the government's money selectively to those obtaining external support for their research.

2.2.3 The reduction of dependency and the promotion of services. As part of its anti-monopoly drive, the government pressed the universities very hard to reduce their dependence on the block grant and to earn larger proportions of their income from a range of other sources. It also pressed them to enlarge their contributions to the country's economic restructuring by, for example, more consultancy work, more 'technology transfer', and more vocational education courses aimed at continuing professional development (CPD). Pump-priming funds were made available – the PICKUP programme for CPD, for example – but universities were instructed that in the long term such work had to be self-supporting and not subsidized from public funds. There was also strong encouragement (supported by the CVCP) to ensure that all research contracts and consultancies met their full direct and indirect costs through the proper calculation of overheads.

Universities were thus launched into a variety of market-places. Among the main ones exploited were:

1   Overseas students. In the late 1970s the government ended the practice whereby students from whatever origin paid the same fee for a course of study as a 'home' (that is, UK-resident) student. The 'home' fee was well below what the government estimated as the 'full economic cost' and universities were required to charge at least that latter cost (which was calculated in three bands – for non-laboratory, laboratory, and medical disciplines) to all students coming from outside the European Community. (Community regulations prevented non-UK students being unfavourably discriminated against and so all 'Home/EC' students, as they became known, pay the same fee: for most UK-resident undergrad-

uates, payment of their fee is part of the mandatory award that they receive when obtaining a university place, and this – unlike their maintenance grant – is not subject to a means test of their parents' income.) Overseas students – both undergraduate and postgraduate – thus represented major potential sources of additional income (on average over £6000 each in fees, in 1990 values). Further, their recruitment was not limited in the same way that numbers of Home/EC students were determined by the UGC. They were virtually the only source of student growth available to universities in the mid-1980s, which responded with extensive recruitment campaigns and the development of initiatives such as distance-learning degrees franchised overseas.

2   Industrial, commercial and other potential sources of research income. Although the Research Councils and some of the major charities (such as Leverhulme, Nuffield, Wellcome, and Wolfson) offer the most 'prestigious' funding for 'pure' research activities, their money was limited and success rates for applicants often low. Thus universities directed their academic staffs' attention to other sources, and employed liaison officers to assist in the search for money and in the sale of intellectual property rights in the consultancy market. 'Applied' research was thereby given a major boost, because it was both consistent with the 'culture of the times' and – especially if overheads were properly costed – could underpin some of the universities' basic expenditure (on research and support staff, for example).

3   Continuing education. There was substantial expansion of both 'liberal adult education' (LAE: courses open to the general public and not leading to a university qualification) and, especially, 'continuing vocational education' (CVE) courses designed for specific (usually professional or quasi-professional) markets. Many of the latter were offered at substantial prices, thereby yielding a 'profit' as well as providing introductions to potential commercial sponsors for later research and development work. Increasingly, such short courses were offered in modular form, which could be aggregated to create a postgraduate qualification.

Universities were also encouraged to introduce their undergraduate students to the new 'enterprise culture' by ensuring that all courses exposed them to the commercial world beyond academia. A Department of Employment 'Enterprise in Higher Education' initiative offered pump-priming funds, much of which was spent on developing 'student-centred learning' approaches, including the greater use of Information Technology (see Clark, 1991).

2.2.4 Growth 'on the cheap'. After a decade or more of virtually no growth in the number of Home/EC students at British universities, the government performed a U-turn at the end of the 1980s. It had been convinced by an argument that, compared to its main industrial competitors, the UK had an inadequately trained workforce, as evinced by the small percentage of its school-leavers who participated in further and higher education. It determined to more than double that participation rate by the end of the century, and encouraged universities to plan for expansion. In 1989 the UGC – just before its replacement by the Universities Funding Council (UFC) – invited universities to submit plans for their teaching activities, including the number of students they wished to recruit, for the period 1991 to 1995. Most universities proposed substantial growth, with a wide range of new initiatives at both undergraduate and postgraduate levels, although because the markets for students in science and technology were relatively weak, most growth was planned for the humanities and social sciences (including business and management studies and law).

In preparing those bids for extra government-funded student numbers, universities were given a 'guide price' above which they should not bid for a student place in each discipline. They were encouraged to bid below that price by the UGC, thereby demonstrating that they could achieve efficiency gains and admit extra students at marginal costs below the average. In addition, they were told that there would be no separate money for capital expenditure: if universities needed new buildings, equipment, books, and so on, to cater for the growth they bid for, these would have to be paid for out of: (a) their reserves (some, though by no means all, universities have substantial cash reserves); (b) other sources of income (such as donations); (c) the grant received to teach the students; and (d) realization of other assets through, for example, better management of their land and buildings.

Very few universities bid for growth below the guide price, and the UFC abolished the practice: all growth was funded at the full price (basically the average amount spent per student per discipline in the previous few years, partially compensated for inflation since). But the volume funded was considered insufficient (it certainly was less than the demand for HE at the time), and universities were immediately pressed to grow even further. They would no longer be constrained in the number of Home/EC students they could admit, only in the number which would be fully funded through the UFC. They could take more, for which they would get the fee element of the funding only. (On average, the fee at that time was about two-thirds of the total funding per student. Thus a fully funded geography student might bring a university some £3200 per annum, whereas a 'fees-only' student would bring only about £1900: all students, whether fully funded or not, were eligible for the means-tested maintenance grant.) Universities were told that more fully funded numbers would be allocated each year (18,000 for the first year, 1992–3), based on each university's record in recruiting fees-only students. Only those recruiting above-average percentages of fees-only students – by subject category – received more fully funded numbers, and they were expected to recruit the same percentage the following year, thus growing even further and faster (without additional capital funds, indicating a general government belief that the universities had unused physical capacity). Most universities felt impelled to participate in this exercise and recruit substantial fees-only percentages, because without such growth the stability of their budgets was under threat (Johnston, 1993e, satirizes this policy).

The government also required the UFC (and its successors, the Higher Education Funding Councils for England – HEFCE, Scotland – SHEFC, and

Wales – HEFCW) to obtain an annual 'efficiency gain' in the universities' teaching function (a lower rate of gain was required in medicine and dentistry), and in addition when calculating the UFC allocation it used an inflation estimate (the GDP deflator) which invariably underestimated the increase in the retail price index, let alone the 'real' inflation in university costs. Initially the efficiency gain was set at 1.5 per cent per annum; by 1993 it had reached an average across all universities of 2 per cent; and for 1994 it was increased again to 4 per cent. Thus without growth of Home/EC student numbers of at least several per cent per annum in the early 1990s, universities found that their real incomes were declining, which meant that they were unable to sustain existing staff levels let alone invest in more (plus other resources) to educate the larger student population.

Despite, or perhaps because of, these stern financial constraints, British higher education expanded very rapidly over the period, with the number of full-time-equivalent students increasing by almost 50 per cent between 1981 and 1991 (most of it between 1987 and 1991): the participation rate in higher education for 18-year-olds shifted from 12 per cent at the start of the 1980s to 27 per cent by 1992, and in 1993 it exceeded the government's target of 30 per cent by the end of the century. Clearly, there was a pent-up demand for higher education, which was met in part (especially, but not only, in the 'new universities') by the expansion of part-time and other innovative degree schemes.

In 1992–3, however, faced with a public spending crisis, the government decided that it could no longer fund this rate of expansion, especially in the more popular arts and social science disciplines. It didn't seek to restrain growth directly, but by cutting the fee for non-laboratory disciplines to £1300 it much reduced the incentive for universities to grow at the fees-only margin. (The laboratory fee was left at £2700, but recruitment of science and engineering students was difficult and little growth was feasible.) But universities continued to grow – they increased their intakes by 7 per cent in 1993 over 1992, for example – and at the end of 1993 the government introduced further measures to halt the expansion. The fees were slashed by 33 per cent and the Funding Councils were instructed to ensure that numbers fell by 3.5 per cent in the 1994–5 academic year: they were also required to penalize severely those universities which nevertheless continued to grow. Student numbers were to decline slightly until 1996–7, and then increase by about 20 per cent over the following four years.

All of this growth in the late 1980s and early 1990s was to be achieved with no diminution in the quality of British higher education: indeed the government and the UFC pressed for improvements in standards. Staff appraisal and training programmes were demanded as part of the price to be paid for a relatively favourable pay award for academics in 1988; government insisted that at least 1 per cent of the pay bill each year should be distributed selectively as performance-related pay rises, rather than as normal increments obtained by all; and the CVCP introduced an Academic Audit Unit to conduct a four-yearly cycle of visits to all institutions to check on the presence of and full adherence to quality control mechanisms. The Funding Councils introduced regular Quality Assessment of Teaching from 1993 on, as required of them by the 1992

Education Act. Every department's performance is to be rated on a scale of 'excellent', 'satisfactory' and 'unsatisfactory' at least once every four years. The assessments are being done discipline-by-discipline: by the end of 1993 geography departments had been assessed only in Scotland. (For more details, see Johnston, 1994a.)

These four aspects of change in the nature of British universities during the 1980s and early 1990s placed great demands on individual academics, and in particular on those with responsibility for the management of academic life: the head of department's role changed both qualitatively and quantitatively, for example (Smith, 1988a; Gregory, 1988; Rhind, 1988). And still the challenges come. In 1991 the government announced – to general approval – that the UK's two higher education sectors, the universities and the polytechnics, were to be merged under a single funding council which would allocate all government higher education funds to over 100 separate institutions, and that polytechnics could, if they wished, adopt the title university: all did, and several Colleges of Higher Education were also granted university status. New funding methodologies are thus being devised for both teaching and research, and all institutions face substantial further change in their financial milieux.

3 GEOGRAPHY'S PERFORMANCE

How well has geography performed in this changing context? Although some performance indicators are available, they only cover the 'old university' sector and are far from ideal (and the whole concept of 'management statistics and performance indicators' is a topic of debate: Smith, 1988b; Johnston, 1989).[1] The following sections briefly describe trends within British geography in those institutions having the title of university prior to April 1992, using data published by the Universities Statistical Record for the 1970s and 1980s and, for the last few years only, the CVCP–UFC (now CVCP–HEFC). Geography as a discipline is separately identified in those collections, although there are problems of consistency (for example in counting student numbers doing geography courses). Where relevant and possible, geography's performance is compared with that of the university system as a whole.

3.1 Student numbers

Between the academic years 1965–6 and 1991–2, USR data show that the numbers registered as full-time geography Home/EC degree students changed from 3395 undergraduates and 312 postgraduates to 7686 and 611 respectively (figure 15.1):[2] the undergraduate population increased by 126 per cent, and postgraduate numbers almost exactly doubled. This compares with growth rates of 115 and 148 per cent respectively for undergraduate and postgraduate numbers in the university system as a whole: geography has slightly outpaced all other disciplines in undergraduate numbers, and substantially so in the growth of postgraduate studies.

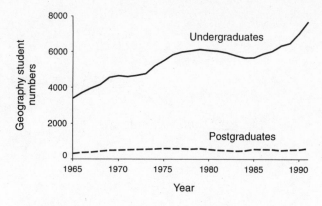

Figure 15.1   Changes in the number of students registered for degrees in geography in the 'old universities', 1965–1966 to 1991–1992

There were three periods of rapid growth in undergraduate numbers, in the late 1960s, the mid 1970s and the late 1980s–early 1990s. Numbers reading for geography degrees fell from the 1979 peak of 6120 to a low of 5650 five years later, however, slightly in advance of the decline in all disciplines (which occurred between 1981 and 1984). There was very rapid growth (some 25 per cent) from 1988 on (figure 15.2).

The number of registered geography postgraduates fell from the 1975 peak of 603 to a low of 463 in 1983, and only exceeded the former figure again in 1991: indeed the number of geography postgraduates in 1988 was less than that in 1969 (figure 15.3). For all disciplines, the period 1976 to 1984 saw a decline in postgraduate numbers also, but these rapidly recovered from then on, with a 50 per cent increase since 1983. In this aspect of their work, geography departments clearly lagged behind many others: they have been unable (presumably not unwilling) to expand postgraduate numbers during the 1980s.

Data for enrolment of part-time Home/EC and of overseas students are available from 1980 only. Since then, the number taking undergraduate geography degrees part-time increased from 55 to 123, whereas the number of part-time postgraduates fell from 374 to 240. In all disciplines, the numbers of undergraduates increased from 4491 to 9758, and of postgraduates from 27,448 to 49,276. Clearly, geography departments have not participated in this aspect of the system's growth in terms of postgraduate numbers. Their part-time undergraduate numbers have increased slightly more rapidly than the national percentage, but starting from a very low base.

The number of overseas students registered for undergraduate geography degrees increased from 24 to 76 over the same period; for postgraduates the figures were 159 and 174. Again, the proportionate increase in undergraduate numbers was greater than for the system as a whole (15,313 to 22,493), but this was not so in postgraduates for which the national figures were 15,855 and 22,432. In general, therefore, geography departments contributed relatively little to the expansion of part-time provision and the attraction of overseas

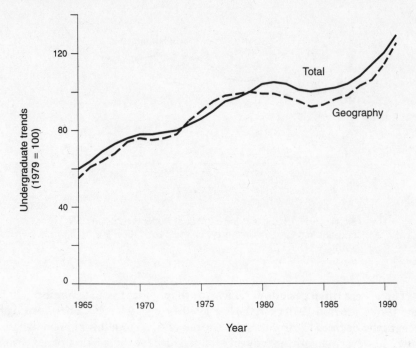

Figure 15.2   Trends in undergraduate numbers – total and reading for geography degrees – in the 'old universities' 1965–1966 to 1991–1992

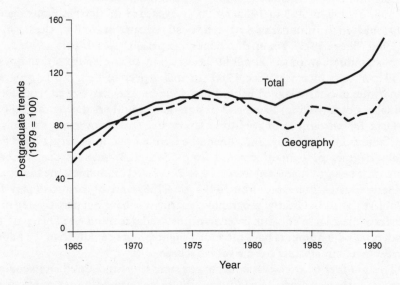

Figure 15.3   Trends in postgraduate numbers – total and reading for geography degrees – in the 'old universities' 1965–1966 to 1991–1992

numbers, though it is not clear whether this was because of supply (lack of offerings) or demand (insufficient market opportunities) considerations.

Finally, with regard to continuing education activity, the number of LAE courses provided by geographers increased over the period 1979–80 to 1990–1 from 128 to 251 while the number of CVE courses grew from only 2 to 39: student numbers enrolled per annum on the two types of courses increased from 3150 to 7628 and from 21 to 1278 respectively. The growth in activity by geographers was very substantial, therefore, but again from a very small initial base.

3.2 Staff

The number of teaching staff in geography departments fell from 657 to 591 over the period 1980–1 to 1991–2, a decrease of 10 per cent: the national fall was 6 per cent. There were 75 geography professors at the start of the period, and 82 at the end (all but two of them male). The percentage of geography staff aged under 35 fell from 31 to 21: the national figures were 24 and 17. Thus in relative terms geography suffered more cuts than the average in staff numbers.

Data for research staff, virtually all of them employed on short-term contracts, are available for the three years beginning in 1987–8 only. For geography the numbers were 120, 145, and 161 respectively: the percentage growth in geography was 34 and the national figure was 10 – but again geography departments started from a low base.

3.3 Student:staff ratios

Workloads in university departments are usually calculated as the ratio of the number of students to the number of staff. Three ratios have been calculated here, for 1980–1 and 1991–2: for all Home/EC full-time students (under- and postgraduate); for all Home/EC full-time and part-time students (with the latter counted as 0.5, according to normal conventions); and for all Home/EC plus overseas students (table 15.1).

At the start of the decade, the student:staff ratio (SSR) was higher for geography than for the university system as a whole. Over the period, it increased by just under 40 per cent, at about the same rate as that for all disciplines (see also Jenkins and Smith, 1993). By recruiting fewer overseas students than is the norm (only 3 per cent of geography's total load in 1989–90 comprised overseas students, compared with 10 per cent for the total university system), geography departments have, it seems, stemmed the worsening SSR compared with the general pattern, but at the expense of not gaining the additional income which overseas students bring. This may reflect deliberate policy decisions on behalf of geographers: it is more likely to record difficulties in recruiting both postgraduates and undergraduates from overseas, but especially the latter because the discipline is well represented in most university systems of the English-speaking world.[3]

Table 15.1   Student:staff ratios, 1980–1981 and 1991–1982

	Geography	Total
Home/EC full-time		
1980–1	10.08	8.96
1991–2	14.04	12.26
Per cent change	39.28	36.83
Home/EC full- and part-time		
1980–1	10.41	9.44
1991–2	14.35	13.20
Per cent change	37.85	39.84
Home/EC plus Overseas		
1980–1	10.69	10.38
1991–2	14.77	14.64
Per cent change	38.17	41.04

3.4 Research outputs

The most commonly used output measure of research performance is volume of publication (see Clayton, 1985b). Nationwide data were only collected for the first time in 1991, however (CVCP, 1993). These show that staff in geography departments in the 'old universities' produced 2986 publications in 1991, of which 70 were authored books, 91 were edited books, 468 were contributions to edited books, and 684 were contributions to refereed academic journals.

Of more interest than these raw totals are the publication rate data. The CVCP published the data for 37 separate cost centres, and for each calculated the number of publications per academic staff member during the year, the number of publications per £1000 of block recurrent grant research income, and the number per £1000 of external research income. For geography these three ratios were 2.97, 0.24 and 0.35 respectively. The frequency distribution for the publications per staff member variable shows only four cost centres (planning; law; humanities; and creative arts) with higher rates than geography (the average was 1.8). Geography's publication rate per £1000 of research funding was also well above the average of 0.17, though nine cost centres exceeded it: the average rate of publication per £1000 of external research income was 0.14, so geography was again well above it – though also well exceeded by six other humanities and social science cost centres, among others.

The implication is that geographers are relatively productive scholars, and that their productivity (relative to the amount spent on their research) is high. The validity of such comparisons is questionable, however, and while noting the data we should not draw too many firm conclusions from them.

The only quantitative publications information available for more than one year is that supplied by geography departments in 1989 for the assessment exercise then. Over the five years a discipline comprising some 600 academic staff members (that is, those under contract to teach and research), supported by about 150 research staff, published a total of 4764 refereed articles, 2304 chapters in edited volumes, and 792 books. The average rate of publication was 1.53 articles per staff member per annum, 0.74 chapters, and 0.26 books: these rates did not vary substantially over the five-year period, with no evidence of a trend to more publication.

3.5 Research assessment

The only available measures of research quality which compare both within and between disciplines are the results of the three Research Assessment Exercises conducted by the UGC/UFC in 1986, 1989 and 1992. These are given in table 15.2. The 1986 and 1989 gradings are not comparable, because they used different scales and different grade-point descriptions. Those for 1989 and 1992 are comparable, because of the standard descriptors used in both exercises, as follows:

5   Research quality that equates to attainable levels of international excellence in some subareas of activity and to attainable levels of national excellence in virtually all others.
4   Research quality that equates to attainable levels of national excellence in virtually all subareas of activity, possibly showing some evidence of international excellence, or to international level in some and at least national level in a majority.
3   Research quality that equates to attainable levels of national excellence in a majority of the subareas of activity, or to international level in some.
2   Research quality that equates to attainable levels of national excellence in up to half of the subareas of activity.
1   Research quality that equates to attainable levels of national excellence in none, or virtually none, of the subareas of activity.

(Full details of the 1992 Exercise are available in: Universities Funding Council, 1992; Higher Education Funding Council for England, 1993.)

Table 15.2 shows that the great majority of UK geography departments fell in grades 3 and 4 in both the 1989 and the 1992 exercise: for the 36 departments assessed in both, the average grade increased from 3.25 to 3.53 – it increased in all other disciplines in the 'old universities'. Compared to the outcome across all disciplines, geography had fewer grade 5 departments (10 per cent of geography departments in England, for example, compared to 15 per cent in all disciplines) but no substantial differences in the other grades.

3.6 Research income

Research income data (that is, on specific earnings for research grants and contracts, as against the research component of the block recurrent grant obtained from the UFC–HEFC) are only available for the short period covered by the CVCP/UGC indicators. They show that earnings per staff member in

Table 15.2   The results of the Research Assessment Exercises for Geography

Grade	1986	Grade	1989	1992(C)	1992(A)
Outstanding	11	5	5	6	6
Better than		4	11	9	11
average	5	3	10	19	22
About average	16	2	8	2	9
Below average	10	1	2	0	9

1992(C) gives the grades for the 36 universities also graded in the 1989 exercise; 1992(A) gives the grade for all 57 institutions, excluding the three 'non-geography departments' which were graded by the geography panel then.

geography departments averaged £5390 at the start of the period (ranging from £0 in two departments to £26,390 in the highest earner): at the end of the period, the UK figure was £15,260, with a range from £80 to £45,630 per head.

Further information about research grant and contract income in geography departments alone for the five-year period 1984–8 is given by the data provided to the UGC for the 1989 Research Assessment Exercise and separately analysed for the Conference of Heads of University Geography Departments. Over the five years the number of Research Council grants won per annum remained virtually constant at 55 (an average of 0.08 grants per staff member per annum), though their average value increased from £13,000 to £32,000. The number of 'Other Research Grants' (that is, from sources other than the Councils) more than tripled, however, from 67 in 1984 to 220 in 1988 (an average of 0.24 per person per year): the majority were small grants, however, and they averaged only £9000 in the final year (though their total value over the five years was £5,568,000). Research contracts more than quadrupled in number (from 53 to 221); their average value remained almost constant at c.£21,000. As before, there was substantial variability in grant- and contract-winning success rates: in every year at least one department obtained no grants and contracts and the distribution of success rates (both number of grants and their value) was very positively skewed, with a small number of departments (generally the same ones from year to year) substantially outperforming the rest.

The size of the research component of the block recurrent grant from the UGC and its successors was not initially clear, and the proportion notionally 'earned' by geography departments could not be separately identified until the late 1980s: it was generally assumed that about two-thirds of the total grant was to fund teaching activities and one-third to fund research. (This component provided the 'basic infrastructure' for research – such as staffing, space, and libraries. Specific project funding – to employ contract researchers, for example – had to be won from the Research Councils and other bodies.) For the financial year 1993–4, however, the separate Funding Councils have provided very full data.

The HEFCE has published data for the 1993–4 allocations which allow the *Unit of Council Funding for Research* (UCFR) in each subject to be calculated.

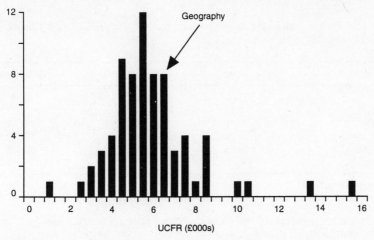

Figure 15.4 Frequency distribution of the Unit of Council Funding for Research values, by discipline

Given the way that the formula works, the UCFR is equivalent to the amount of block grant research income earned by one research-active staff member in a grade 2 department (grade 1 departments get no research component funding). For geography the figure was £6810, which was the seventeenth largest (and larger than that for several other sciences, including physics) of the UCFRs for the 72 different units of assessment used in the exercise (figure 15.4: a Unit of Assessment is equivalent to a separate discipline in most cases): the comparable figure for geography in Scotland was also a high £6800.

There has been much debate about the construction of the formula which produced these UCFRs and their very substantial variation (see Johnston 1993a, c, 1994b): they ranged from £15,642 in Pre-Clinical Studies and £13,604 in Veterinary Science to £2925 in Communication and Media Studies and just £1437 in Art and Design – with a mean of £6151 and a standard deviation of £2204. Six basic reasons for the differences have been identified: (1) the average amount being spent per student in each discipline in the mid-1980s in all universities; (2) the results of an assessment then into the proportions of that money spent on research and on teaching; (3) the numbers of postgraduate research students, and of postgraduate research assistants relative to the number of research active staff; (4) the average grade allocated to departments in each discipline – weighted by department size; (5) the percentage of the departments getting a grade 2 or higher in the 1992 Research Assessment Exercise which came from the 'new university' sector, and so were not involved in the previous ratings; and (6) the amount of Research Council income earned in the discipline and transferred to the Research Councils under the 'dual support transfer' which was shifting money away from the block recurrent grant and into project-specific grants.

So why did geography get a high UCFR? In part, it was because it was allocated a relatively large amount of money from the outset. In the distribution of that sum in 1993, its UCFR came out large because of geography's low

Table 15.3 Performance on the key indicators influencing the HEFCE Unit of Council Funding for Research

Indicator[a]	Mean	Standard deviation	Geography
TEpc	65.00		63.00
PGRatio	1.18	0.63	0.90
RARatio	0.47	0.50	0.34
WTGrade	2.66	0.37	2.58
NONUFCpc	19.21	7.80	21.95
Transfer	4.50	5.24	3.47

[a] Key to indicators:

TEpc – the percentage of the amount spent per student in the mid-1980s going on teaching rather than research

PGRatio – ratio of postgraduate research students to research active academic staff numbers

RARatio – ratio of postgraduate research assistants to research active academic staff numbers

WTGrade – the average grade obtained in the 1992 Research Assessment Exercise (departments getting grade 2 or over only), weighted by staff size

NONUFCpc – the percentage of all departments getting grade 2 or over in the 1992 Research Assessment Exercise which came from the 'new university' sector

Transfer – the volume of money transferred from the discipline's block grant research fund to the Research Councils, as a percentage of that fund.

average performance on several of the key variables, as shown in table 15.3. Its low average grade (weighted by staff member – on average, the larger the department the higher the grade; Unwin, 1993), low transfer to the Research Councils, and low ratios of postgraduate students and assistants to staff all meant a relatively high UFCR: only on the percentage of the grades above 1 going to 'new universities' did geography 'outperform' the average discipline, and so have its money relatively widely distributed. (For more details on this formula, see Johnston, 1993c.)

As a discipline, therefore, geography is relatively well funded per staff member for research through the block recurrent grant formula: the amount of money 'earned' per individual in a grade 5 department is some £27,000 (although whether the university authorities allow all of this to be expended in and/or for the geography department is a separate, internal management issue, because the moneys are not earmarked for use by geography alone: Johnston, 1993b). But this high UCFR is, paradoxically, the result of both a lack of success in winning external funds (the more research grants and research students, the lower the UCFR) and relatively low overall achievement (the lower than average mean grade). Among geography departments, the amount of money is allocated according not only to grade but also to these other measures of 'success' (grants and studentships etc.), so departmental heads and other 'managers' will be constructing strategies to enable them to benefit most from a declining UCFR. And it is unlikely that the funding formula will remain unchanged for long: greater emphasis is likely to be give to 'external success', with the potential that geography's UCFR could be substantially reduced.

Departmental managers have to make a number of strategic decisions in the context of this new method of block recurrent research grant funding. The amount of money allocated is a function of the grade achieved and the number of research-active staff returned in the Research Assessment Exercise. It is generally assumed that the larger a department's 'tail' of research-inactive staff members returned (that is, the proportion with few or no research publications) the lower the department's grade will be. Thus there is a potential trade-off between size and grade: if a department gets a higher grade by returning fewer of its staff, does it nevertheless earn more money? Simulations (Johnston, 1993b) suggest that with geography's current UCFR the answer is 'yes': if a department's grade increases by a point as a consequence of excluding up to one-quarter of its staff, its grant will increase (*ceteris paribus*). Thus sooner or later, each department and its managers will have to decide whether it is to be an 'all-research' outfit or whether some of its staff will be identified as 'teachers only', with clear consequences for not only their job descriptions but also, in all probability, their promotion prospects.

4 IN SUMMARY

Much changed in British universities during the 1980s, and much more change is likely in the 1990s following the amalgamation of the polytechnic and university sectors of higher education in 1992 and then the re-election of a Conservative government intent on achieving further efficiency gains and selectivity in the allocation of research funding both among institutions and among disciplines within them. Some of the 1980s ideological zeal to change British society may no longer be present, but the country's financial difficulties (as exemplified by the very large Public Sector Borrowing Requirement) are resulting in strong government pressures to reduce costs and increase efficiency in higher education, among other policy areas, because of its great reluctance to increase direct taxation.

During the 1980s, British university geography departments were not the focus of particular attention from either politicians or the UGC/UFC. They took their 'fair share' of the cuts and reduced their staff while increasing their student numbers – thereby increasing their workloads. They had become more entrepreneurial – in line with the 'culture of the times' – and had pressed their claims to provide research and consultancy services which met national needs (as in the claims made for GIS – Openshaw, 1991 – and in the success of ventures such as the GMAP Company based on the School of Geography at the University of Leeds). In comparative terms, however, geography departments have been less successful at winning large research grants and contracts, attracting overseas students, and developing new markets for courses – though the peer review of their research rates them highly (see also ESRC, 1989). Whether this reflects on the nature of the discipline or of its practitioners remains an open question.

Peter Haggett was at the centre of much of this activity during the turbulent 1980s, first in his role as acting Vice-Chancellor of the University of Bristol and then during his four years at the University Grants Committee. Posing the counter-factual question as to what might have happened if he had not been there then is as difficult as asking what would have happened in British universities if: (1) the Conservatives hadn't been in power throughout the decade; (2) Margaret Thatcher hadn't been their leader throughout that period; and (3) the graduates of the University of Oxford hadn't publicly rebuffed her by rejecting the proposal that she be awarded an honorary degree! Suffice it to note that in his quiet, dignified and entirely non-judgemental way Peter undoubtedly played an important role in ensuring the protection of all that he identified as good in British universities, and especially their geography departments, within the constraints set by the radical political zeal of the decade.

But what of the future – recalling Peter Haggett's interest in forecasting? Writing in late-1993, storm clouds are gathering on the horizon for geography in the UK; they are for all disciplines, but perhaps more so for geography. The apparently never-ending supply of undergraduates may be under threat from proposed changes in the National Curriculum at school level (calling for more heroics in lobbying by the Geographical Association); the high UCFR for research is likely to be challenged, and geographers will have to earn more from outside the block recurrent grant than they have done to date; there will be at least two more Research Assessment Exercises this decade; and the possibility of students having to meet part at least of their tuition costs may lead them to concentrate more on vocationally-oriented degrees rather than more generalist ones such as geography, whatever its rigour, breadth and general interest. The 'business of geography' in the UK universities for the rest of the century will be hard, as we do what Peter presses on us and seek to preserve that disciplinary heritage which 'we are priviliged to pass on to the next generation' (Haggett, 1990, xvii).

NOTES

1 Nearly all of the data quoted here are taken from two sources: (1) Universities Funding Council, *Universities Statistics* vol. 1: *Students and Staff*. Published annually by the Universities Statistical Record, Cheltenham; (2) Committee of Vice-Chancellors and Principals, and Universities Funding Council, *University Management Statistics and Performance Indicators in the UK*. Published annually by the Universities Statistical Record, Cheltenham. Other, unpublished, data are taken from a report I produced (in collaboration with Ken Gregory, Peter Haggett, and David Sugden) for the Conference of Heads of University Geography Departments. *Research Activity in Departments of Geography in British Universities, 1984–1989: A Statistical Profile.* January 1990.

2 All of the data for geography students taken from the USR refer only to the numbers registered for geography degrees. They exclude students registered for joint degrees including geography, and so are not true measures of the total student load handled in university geography departments.

3 Other sources give different SSRs because they are based on total student load per department rather than the numbers registered for degrees only (see note 1 above). Using the former, the CVCP/UGC publications (1987ff) record the SSR for UK geography departments in 1984–5 as 11.3 (varying across institutions from 7.1 to

18.2) and for 1991–2 as 16.9 (varying from 11.9 to 25.0). Over that shorter period, therefore, geography's SSR worsened by just 50 per cent.

REFERENCES

Bennett, R.J. (1989). 'Whither models and geography in a post-welfarist world?' In B. Macmillan (ed.), *Remodelling Geography*. Oxford: Blackwell Publishers, 273–290.

Bentham, G. (1987). 'An evaluation of the UGC's ratings of the research of British university geography departments.' *Area*, 19, 147–54.

Cave, M., Hanney, S., Kogan, M., & Trevett, G. (1988). *The Use of Performance Indicators in Higher Education*. London: Jessica Kingsley Publishers.

Clark, G.L. (1991). 'Enterprise education in geography at Lancaster.' *Journal of Geography in Higher Education*, 15, 49–56.

Clayton, K.M. (1985a). 'New blood by (government) order.' *Area*, 17, 321–2.

Clayton, K.M. (1985b). 'The state of geography.' *Transactions, Institute of British Geographers*, NS10, 5–16.

Cosgrove, D.E. (1985). 'Present fears for the future of the past: report of a survey into academic recruitment of historical geographers.' *Area*, 17, 243–6.

Cosgrove, D. E. (1987). 'UGC rankings, IBG Council and the future of geography in the universities.' *Area*, 19, 155–9.

CVCP (1993). *Research Performance Indicators: Annual Survey of Publications*. London: CVCP.

Duncan, S.S. (1974). 'The isolation of scientific discovery: indifference and resistance to a new idea.' *Science Studies*, 4, 109–34.

Edwards, R.A. (1991). 'UK geography departments: a perspective on UFC ratings.' *Area*, 23, 197–208.

ESRC (1989). *Horizons and Opportunities in the Social Sciences*. Swindon: ESRC.

Gamble, A.M. (1988). *The Free Economy and the Strong State*. London: Macmillan.

Giddens, A. (1984). *The Constitution of Society*. Cambridge: Polity Press.

Gleave, M.B., Harrison, C., & Moss, R.P. (1987). 'UGC research ratings: the bigger the better?' *Area*, 19, 163–6.

Gregory, K.J. (1988). 'Managing geography departments.' *Area*, 20, 366–7.

Gregory, K.J. (1993). 'The 1992 UFC Research Assessment Exercise for geography.' *Journal of Geography in Higher Education*, 17, 169–74.

Haggett, P. (1965). *Locational Analysis in Human Geography*. London: Edward Arnold.

Haggett, P. (1990). *The Geographer's Art*. Oxford: Basil Blackwell.

Haggett, P. & Chorley, R.J. (1967). 'Models, paradigms and the new geography.' In R.J. Chorley & P. Haggett (eds), *Models in Geography*. London: Methuen, 19–42.

Hayek, F.A. (1944). *The Road to Serfdom*. London: Routledge.

Higher Education Funding Council for England (1993). *A Report for the Universities Funding Council on the Conduct of the 1992 Research Assessment Exercise*. Bristol: HEFCE.

Hoare, A.G. (1981). 'UGC: unequal geographical cuts.' *Area*, 13, 257–62.

Hoare, A.G. (1986). 'UGC: more unequal geographical cuts.' *Area*, 18, 315–25.

Hoare, A.G. (1991). 'Reviewing the reviews: the geography of university rationalisation.' *Higher Education Quarterly*, 45, 234–53.

Jenkins, A. & Smith, P. (1993). 'Expansion, efficiency and teaching quality: the experience of British geography departments 1986–91.' *Transactions, Institute of British Geographers*, NS18, 500–15.

Johnston, R.J. (1989). 'Do you use the telephone too much? A review of performance indicators, evaluation and appraisal in British universities.' *Journal of Geography in Higher Education*, 13, 31–44.

Johnston, R.J. (1991a). *Geography and Geographers: Anglo-American Human Geography since 1945* (4th edn). London: Edward Arnold.

Johnston, R.J. (1991b). *A Question of Place: Exploring the Practice of Human Geography.* Oxford: Blackwell Publishers.

Johnston, R.J. (1992a). 'Foreword'. In L. Mazurkiewicz, *Human Geography in Eastern Europe and the Soviet Union.* London: Belhaven Press, 1–3.

Johnston, R.J. (1992b). 'Meet the challenge: make the change.' In R.J. Johnston (ed.) *The Challenge for Geography – A Changing World: A Changing Discipline.* Oxford: Blackwell Publishers, 151–80.

Johnston, R.J. (1992c). 'The rise and decline of the corporate-welfare state: a comparative analysis in global context.' In P.J. Taylor (ed.), *Political Geography of the Twentieth Century: A Global Analysis.* London: Belhaven Press, 115–70.

Johnston, R.J. (1993a). 'Formulaic follies: funding research in English universities.' *Environment and Planning A*, 25, 601–5.

Johnston, R.J. (1993b). 'Removing the blindfold after the game is over: the financial outcomes of the 1992 Research Assessment Exercise.' *Journal of Geography in Higher Education*, 17, 174–180.

Johnston, R.J. (1993c). 'Formulaic follies revisited: or, why geography researchers get twice as much as town planners in English universities.' *Environment and Planning A*, 25, 1527–1534.

Johnston, R.J. (1993d). 'The geographer's degrees of freedom: Wreford Watson, postwar progress in human geography, and the future of scholarship in UK geography.' *Progress in Human Geography*, 17, 319–332.

Johnston, R.J. (1993e). 'Some fables for our times.' *Journal of Geography in Higher Education*, 17, 200–208.

Johnston, R.J. (1994a). 'Quality assessment of teaching: inputs, processes and outputs.' *Journal of Geography in Higher Education*, 18 (forthcoming).

Johnston, R.J. (1994b). 'Funding research through the block recurrent grant in English universities: an exploration of inter-discipline differences.' *Higher Education Quarterly* (forthcoming).

Joseph, Sir K. (1985). 'Geography in the school curriculum.' *Geography*, 70, 290–9.

Livingstone, D.N. (1992). *The Geographical Imagination: Episodes in the History of a Contested Enterprise.* Oxford: Blackwell Publishers.

Openshaw, S. (1991). 'A view on the GIS crisis in geography, or, using GIS to put Humpty-Dumpty back together again.' *Environment and Planning A*, 23, 621–8.

Rhind, D. W. (1988). 'Leadership and management of university geography departments.' *Area*, 20, 368–71.

Sanderson, M. (1991). 'Higher education in the post-war years.' *Contemporary Record*, 5, 417–32.

Scott, P. (1989). 'Higher education.' In D. Kavanagh and A. Seldon (eds), *The Thatcher Effect: A Decade of Change.* Oxford: Clarendon Press, 198–212.

Smith, D.M. (1985). 'The "new blood" scheme and its application to geography.' *Area*, 17, 237–43.

Smith, D.M. (1986). 'UGC research ratings: pass or fail?' *Area*, 18, 247–9.

Smith, D.M. (1988a). 'The management of geography departments.' *Area*, 20, 363–6.

Smith, D.M. (1988b). 'On academic performance.' *Area*, 20, 3–13.

Stoddart, D.R. (1987). 'To claim the high ground: geography for the end of the century.' *Transactions, Institute of British Geographers*, NS12, 327–36.

Taylor, P. J. (1985). 'The value of a geographical perspective.' In R.J. Johnston (ed.), *The Future of Geography*. London: Methuen, 92–110.

Taylor, P.J. (1992). 'Full circle: or new meaning for the global?' In R.J. Johnston (ed.), *The Challenge for Geography – A Changing World: A Changing Discipline*. Oxford: Blackwell Publishers, 181–97.

Thorne, C.R. (ed.) (1993). 'Arena symposium. University Funding Council Research Selectivity Exercise, 1992: implications for higher education in geography.' *Journal of Geography in Higher Education*, 17, 167–99.

Universities Funding Council (1992). *Research Assessment Exercise 1992: The Outcome*. Bristol: UFC.

Unwin, D.J. (1993). 'Matthew writes again: size and the RAE.' *Institute of British Geographers Newsletter*, 20, 7–8.

16

Simplicity, Complexity, and Generality: Dreams of a Final Theory in Locational Analysis

A.G. Wilson

1 INTRODUCTION

Haggett's work in locational analysis (for example, Haggett, 1965) is characterized by an ambition which is unusual. Too often, a combination of narrow and reductionist perspectives combine to produce 'research' which offers little. He has managed to avoid this by confronting all the major problems of locational analysis – including some of the most difficult – which remain difficult to this day – for example, the evolution of networks (Haggett and Chorley, 1969). I would like to take this opportunity to do two things: to offer a particular modeller's perspective on the agenda defined by Haggett in broad terms; and then to illustrate what is now possible by the application of the approach to a new problem area.

An ambitious approach can contribute to a number of objectives which are reflected in the title of this essay: powerful but essentially *simple* insights; means of handling the formidable *complexity* of the systems – typically, cities and regions – which are the laboratories of locational analysis; and a *generality* of approach – so that *methods* are available to tackle new problems as they arise. The prime goal is analysis – understanding; but if this can be achieved, with power and simplicity, then utility will follow also.

2 SYSTEMS, SCALES AND PROBLEMS

Throughout his long career in Bristol, Peter Haggett has been Professor of Urban and Regional Geography (a title I purloined for my own chair in Leeds). Urban and regional systems have provided the main examples for the development of locational analysis. They intersect with the other major fields of human geography through concerns with people (social geography) on the one hand and the economy (economic geography) on the other. The variety of kinds of system can be illustrated by the following list:

- agriculture
- industry
- the service sectors
- population, residential location and housing
- land use

It is important to recognize at the outset that different kinds of problems present themselves to the locational analyst at different spatial scales. If an area is considered as a single spatial unit – a whole city or region, say, then the appropriate analytical methods are those of the demographer or the economist. Even at this scale, the analytical problem becomes essentially geographical if a *system* of cities or regions is considered. At this point, difficult issues of analysis start to present themselves: any geographical model of such a system should be compatible with the single area unit models of the demographer or the economist. There is yet another kind of problem if a finer level of resolution is introduced to the city or a region – whether by the *continuous* treatment of space, as in a Cartesian coordinate system, or through the *discrete* structure represented by a zoning system. Questions can be posed about geographical structures of the elements in any of the systems defined earlier: residential location, industrial location, services, land use mixes.

Each of the problems of locational analysis formulated in this sketch is complex. Even more complex is the problem which can be formulated by arguing that each of these systems is interdependent with the rest: what is needed is an *integrated* theory of urban and regional systems – the ultimate goal of a large part of locational analysis. Indeed, it can be argued that this interdependence is mediated by a variety of spatial flows and that a sixth set of systems should be added as part of the goal of building up a comprehensive theory:

- interactions

To what extent do we have a set of methods available for tackling this huge spectrum of problems which constitutes locational analysis? If, as we are, we are seeking *theory*, then we are seeking *explanation*; and this already takes us into the realms of controversy. As noted earlier, the argument here represents a modeller's perspective. I will indicate how the modellers' tools for locational analysis connect to accepted cannons of theory. Needless to say, there are imperfections of fit. This is inevitable and progress can be made by a judicious choice of approximations which still allow effective insight to be generated.

That the problem agenda presented above is a reasonable one can be argued by a brief review of the way in which the 'classical' authors have covered the field:

- agriculture – von Thünen (1826)
- industry – Weber (1909)
- services – Christaller (1933) and Lösch (1940)
- residential location – Alonso (1964)

- land use – perhaps as in rent theory – von Thünen (1826) and Alonso (1964) again
- interactions – Reilly (1931)

It is interesting from a modern perspective to see how an author with a particular focus sometimes produced a method which had more general applicability. von Thünen's approach to agriculture was the basis for a more general theory of land rent (Alonso, 1964), for example; Christaller and Lösch, focused on interaction and services, also found themselves tackling the broader issues associated with systems of cities – or was it the other way round!?

3 THEORY AND METHODS

If understanding and explanation are to be represented as theory, what kinds of things can constitute theory? If we want to be fundamental then we have to look to cognate disciplines of the social sciences for help – particularly to economics, politics and sociology. Our elements are individuals and households on the one hand and the great variety of organizations which make up the rest of the economy on the other. Economics helps us at least to provide descriptions of the problem at the micro-scale: utility-maximizing approaches for individuals, profit-maximizing approaches for firms; different kinds of maximizing formulations for, say, public services. Politics focuses on power and the distribution of costs and benefits. Sociologists perhaps make us focus on the classifications modellers might adopt through such concepts as social class – with the implication that behaviour is different in different classes. All approaches demonstrate the complexity of the social sciences: even if we have an effective theory of the individual or firm or other organization, the real agenda involves all these elements in interaction. These interactions create other kinds of features or *structures* – such as buildings, transport networks, or social structures. The theorist then has to confront some version of the agency-structure problem: how much of the structures can be taken as given when approaching a theory of the behaviour of individual elements? To what extent can individual agents, or collections of agents, affect structures – and over what periods of time? From a modeller's point of view, this aspect of theory building often presents itself as an aggregation problem: how do you aggregate micro theories into system theories? Many ingenious approximations have been used to solve this problem – and it is interesting to review the work of the classical theorists from this perspective. There is also an interesting task for the future historian of geographical thought to analyse Haggett's contributions in this respect. What will be found is a refusal to be put off by the difficulty of a problem – and the deployment of whatever analytical methods are available at the time. These range from a battery of statistical techniques through simple but ingenious modelling approximations to the sophisticated modelling methods of the epidemiologist.

Fortunately for this author, this paper can be restricted to a modeller's perspective, and a very particular one at that. This section is concluded therefore with an indication of how certain pieces of mathematical equipment can be used to solve the different kinds of model building task. This set provides the basis for one approach to handling the problems of complexity – and indeed provides clues as to how far it is possible to expect to go in particular cases. It is argued that this is sufficient to generate both generality and considerable insight – and utility in a variety of planning contexts based on that insight.

The agenda is as follows: to seek ways of modelling the key urban and regional subsystems in such a way that they can be linked together into a comprehensive model system. For this author, this has been an ambition for over 25 years.

Since cities and regions have large numbers of elements – people and organizations – the first task is to be able to count properly. It turns out that the development of appropriate accounting methods for either the demographic half of the system or the economic half is not simple (Rees and Wilson, 1976; Wilson, 1970, ch. 3). When these problems are solved, it is possible to approach the task of constructing useful indicators more effectively. This will be illustrated in the example to be introduced in section 4.

The second component of the argument is that many interesting geographical components of systems can be captured if there is an initial focus on interaction. This has two advantages: a model building method is available which works very well; and it facilitates linking submodels in a more general urban model. The method is that of entropy maximizing (Wilson, 1967, 1970) and it works because (a) it is a certain kind of statistical averaging procedure which allows the aggregation problem to be solved; and (b) it relies heavily on constraints to specify the *structures* of the system – so that the interaction patterns generated in these models are consistent with these structures. It can be made consistent with micro-level economic theory – though this remains a matter of some controversy. It also offers an effective separation of two problems – one more difficult than the other: that of interaction from that of structure.

In the early days of this programme, there were no methods available for systematic modelling of structure. This changed in the mid-1970s when mathematicians made a number of breakthroughs in non-linear systems research – beginning with the ideas of catastrophe theory and then more generally as dynamical systems modelling (beginning perhaps with Thom, 1975). This has proved very fruitful for certain modelling problems in geography (Harris and Wilson, 1978; Wilson, 1981). It was particularly important to be able to represent in dynamical models phenomena which were partly understood intuitively: that there were critical parameter values at which the development of a system could bifurcate – follow one of a number of alternative paths. The choice of the path might then be determined by a small perturbation. It then becomes possible to reconcile what had appeared to be conflicting views: those of the modellers, with the implication that forecasting was possible; and those who argued that forecasting was impossible because, for example, of the 'irrational' behaviour of individual decision-makers. It was now clear that the small perturbations could in a significant way determine the course of the development of a system – until the next perturbation, of course. The modellers could show that detailed forecasting was indeed impossible. However, there were two consolations: modelling could be used *after* the event and so was a powerful historical tool; and secondly, a kind of forecasting was possible – for instance to predict the *type* of system which would develop in certain circumstances, if not the detail.

The two methodologies together (spatial interaction combined with dynamic structural modelling) offer a basis for improving and extending the solutions to the classical problems of locational analysis (Wilson, 1986). Many of the restrictions imposed on the classical authors by the tools available to them can be removed. Some of the power derives from using a discrete zone system rather than a continuous one and this enables the restriction to a single 'centre' to be avoided (as in von Thünen's and Alonso's models – or restriction to a single firm in Weber's). Reilly could only analyse competition between two centres; this can be generalized. The geometries of Christaller and Lösch were too rigid; this too can be avoided. These developments will not be pursued in detail here – but references which match the earlier list are as follows:

- agriculture – Wilson and Birkin (1987)
- industry – Birkin and Wilson (1986a, b)
- services – Wilson and M. Clarke (1979)
- residential location – M. Clarke and Wilson (1983a)
- land use – M. Clarke and Wilson (1983b)
- interactions and networks – Wilson (1983)

Needless to say, even if this claim is accepted, this still leaves an enormous programme of research – and perhaps almost insuperable difficulties. Some of the difficulties remain theoretical – as argued through the concept of configurational analysis in Wilson (1988). But perhaps the main thrust of ongoing research should be in the empirical development of this programme. This should include such development at a variety of spatial scales. Economic geography, for example, would become dramatically more interesting if it were possible to develop systems of interacting input–output models for urban and regional systems – and at even finer spatial scales. The insuperable difficulties relate to data availablility. This is not the place for a detailed review, but three observations can be made. First, there will be continuous improvement – fuelled by computing capacity. Secondly, when all the data are not available for a particular problem, it is possible to progress by estimating what is missing – cf. Jin, Leigh, and Wilson (1991) for such an approach in relation to small area input–output modelling; or by the use of a more general missing data-integration methodology such as micro-simulation, whose time will surely come (Wilson and Pownall, 1976; M. Clarke and Wilson, 1985). Thirdly, in particular sectors, enormous progress is being made – as with GMAP's work in the service sectors. So, we are still a long way short of the geographers' dreams of a final theory but – as in physics – we at least have enough understanding to make it sensible to pose the question.

4 AN EXAMPLE: UNIVERSITIES IN ENGLAND

The particular modelling approach can be illustrated by outlining the application to a new area: a system of universities – and, for the sake of the argument, we will say in England, since that enables us to address some of the policy issues which are the concern of the Higher Education Funding Council for England, the HEFCE.

We can proceed as follows: (a) define the underpinning spatial interaction model; (b) examine examples of performance indicators which can be calculated once this conceptual basis is established and we can show how these illuminate particular policy issues; (c) explore a range of more ambitious and difficult questions concerned with dynamics (market forces and planning).

The principles of building spatial interaction models are well known and of long standing (see, for example, Wilson, 1971). The essence is to define an interaction array which connects an origin zone, i, one of a set, to a destination zone (or point), j, also one of a set. In this case, the origin zones can be taken as the areas of residence of actual or potential students (say specified as local authority districts) and the destination zones as universities. This would give a matrix of around 200×100, which is perfectly manageable with modern computers.

The students can be characterized by an index, m (which can itself be a list, $\{m, n, \ldots\}$), and what is offered to students in universities can be called 'courses' and labelled g. Again, this can be itself a list. The main array is then S_{ij}^{mg}, the number of students of type m who live in area i and study on course g in university j. The spatial interaction model to be built is based on three hypotheses: that S_{ij}^{mg} is proportional to:

1 the demand at i, say $e_i^{mg}P_i^m$, where e_i^{mg} is the per capita demand and P_i^m is the population;
2 the attractiveness of university j for course g for type m students. Call this W_j^{mg}. It will also be useful to specify the capacity at j for type g courses – say D_j^g;
3 an inverse function of the travel impedance between i and j, say c_{ij}.

As usual, the description immediately raises many of the problems of theory building with this kind of framework. Demand will be, to an extent, a function of availability. How do we measure attractiveness? How do we handle the distinction between a subject like *medicine* which is essentially supply-constrained with the universities exercising the choice and one like *Italian*, which is essentially demand-constrained, with the student making the choice? These questions can be answered – though in this case, the responses will demand hybrid models which are partially demand-constrained, partially supply-constrained. For immediate purposes, a functional representation will suffice:

$$S_{ij}^{mg} = S_{ij}^{mg}[e_i^{mg}, P_i^m, W_j^{mg}, c_{ij}]. \tag{16.1}$$

It can be said with some confidence that such a model could be calibrated. It would be necessary, for example, to distinguish between post-18 full-time students on the one hand, and mature (full-time or part-time) students on the other – because their spatial interaction behaviour – and there will be an appropriate parameter varying with m within the model – will be very different.

This kind of model system can be thought of as a new and extended 'data' base – an information system – on top of which we can build concepts which add intelligence. One way to do this is through the concept of performance indicators. There are essentially two types: those measuring *effectiveness of delivery* at a residential location; and those measuring *efficiency* at facility locations. It is particularly important to make this distinction when, wherever the boundaries are drawn, there are many cross-boundary flows. Another way of putting this is to say that it is particularly important when there are overlapping catchment populations.

This can be illustrated by our universities example: most universities have extensive catchments, and therefore these overlap. The HEFCE is currently looking at areas where it is believed that the provision of higher education is poor. There will be a temptation to formulate this question in terms of local universities in 'poor provision' regions; but the issue may be much more complicated: many types of student in such areas may in fact be adequately served; other types of student in 'well provided' areas may be badly served. The indicators we can now construct show how these situations can be identified – and then appropriate action taken.

To construct these new indicators, we first need to define two new concepts. The first is 'effective delivery' at a residential location; the second is the 'catchment population' of a facility. Consider

$$X_i^{mg} = \sum_j S_{ij}^{mg} / S_{*j}^{mg} \cdot D_j^{mg}, \tag{16.2}$$

and

$$Y_j^{mg} = \sum_i S_{ij}^{mg} / S_{i*}^{mg} \cdot P_i^m. \tag{16.3}$$

Each term in the sum on the right-hand side of equation (16.2) is a proportion of capacity at j which is delivered to i – the delivery being measured through the spatial interaction array. Similarly, each term in the sum on the right-hand side of equation (16.3) is the proportion of the m-type population actually served at j. Note, however, that we need to calculate effective delivery *for each type of student* and we need to calculate catchment population both *for each type of student and each type of course*; see G. P. Clarke and Wilson (1987a,b; 1994) for the detailed argument. Typical indicators are

$$X_i^{mg} / P_i^m \tag{16.4}$$

and

$$D_j^{mg} / Y_j^{mg}. \tag{16.5}$$

What are virtually meaningless are the traditional indicators

$$D_i^{mg}/P_i^m \tag{16.6}$$

and

$$D_j^{mg}/P_j^m. \tag{16.7}$$

The value of the indicators in (16.4) and (16.5) relative to those in (16.6) and (16.7) arises because they are properly based on spatial interaction concepts and adequately take account of cross-boundary flows. In each of (16.6) and (16.7), the numerators and the denominators do not match.

There are, of course, other more traditional efficiency indicators which retain their value. For example:

$$C_j^g/D_j^{*g} \tag{16.8}$$

is the cost per student on a type g course at j, where of course, C_j^g is the total cost of the course at j. If a planner, either in an institution or for the system as a whole, is trying to optimize provision, then it is a *multiple* indicator optimization problem which probably does not have a unique solution. Extensive experience in other contexts has shown that the best way to find good solutions is to integrate the planner with an *intelligent information system* in which he or she can manipulate provision – viewing the whole battery of indicators for each 'what if?' run. There are now a number of systems of service provision for which such systems have been developed, tested and deployed.

In the universities case, the policy issues which should be addressed extend beyond the 'deprived locality' which has been used as an example (cf. Hoare in ch. 14, section 3.1). For example, for courses where it is not sensible to have them in every university (because demand is too low for efficient provision – and this is most subjects), optimal patterns of provision could be explored. It would also be possible to address the question of under-represented student groups.

Finally, we can address the issue of dynamics and more ambitious theory building questions. A differential equation which indicates likely directions of change is

$$D_j^g = \in [\, p_j^g \, S_{*j}^{*g} - C_j^g \,] \tag{16.9}$$

where p_j^g is the income derived (that is, the 'price' charged) by the university at j from a course g student. In other words, if income exceeds costs, there will be a tendency to increase the capacity. (Alternatively, of course, in some cases there will be a tendency to adjust the price – cf. Birkin and Wilson, 1989.) We will neglect for the time being the complications of 'quota' subjects such as medicine where the university cannot act unilaterally (this can easily be dealt with by having a special equation for such cases).

Equation (16.9) is deceptively simple at first sight. Recall S_{ij}^{mg} from equation (16.1). The term S_{*j}^{*g} in (16.9) is a function of W_j^{mg} which is in turn a function of D_j^g. What is more, the functional form of the interaction model in equation

(16.1) ensures that D_j^g appears in a highly nonlinear form, reflecting not simply the ability of university j to attract students to course g but also the competition of all other universities. There is now much experience of this kind of model in, for example, retail studies. These show that the nonlinearities generate significant bifurcation points at which the nature of the system might change – as in the corner-shop to supermarket transition in the early 1960s (Wilson and Oulton, 1983; Wilson and M. Clarke, 1979, G.P. Clarke,1984).

This formulation also reveals the difficulty of, and the interest in, the specification of the attractiveness function W_j^{mg}. We have to make hypotheses and test them empirically – seeing to what extent the best calibrated models for each functional form representing the hypotheses fit the data. Again, there is much experience of this kind of development, but this example provides a new area for empirical research. The attractiveness term, for example, will contain elements other than simply the capacity of provision for a particular course; overall size may be a proxy for a number of features, and it will also be necessary to build in measures which represent 'reputation' – though it may be possible to do this also with proxies – for example by using a measure of the types of student attracted. There are also in fact 'complications' associated with every term of the equation: the 'demand' term e_i^m should be elastic, partly a function of access to provision; the population distribution, P_i^m, will be a function of the effectiveness of the economy in the neighbourhood of i. All this adds to the ongoing research agenda.

Dynamic modelling is at the stage where it can provide considerable insights into the nature of system development. It is unlikely in the near future to offer a detailed forecasting capability – indeed, we have already indicated that this may be inherently impossible because of the nature of the nonlinearities in the system. What is more feasible, and it would be nice to think likely, is the use of the comparative static model as a 'what if?' planning tool.

5 CONCLUDING COMMENTS

Peter Haggett has immensely encouraged the rest of us by the ambition of his theory. He has charted the problems to be solved in locational analysis. He has solved many of them and made considerable inroads into the rest. Inevitably, a subdiscipline of the complexity of locational analysis will be open to a variety of approaches, none of them complete. This essay has given this author an opportunity to show how one agenda is influenced by another and how a discipline rumbles forward, occasionally with significant lurches!

The example which has been used, universities in England, shows that there are far more potential opportunities for empirical research which would be valuable in a planning context than are being taken. We have lived for almost two decades in a period when planning was unfashionable. There are signs that the climate is changing. If it is, and the discipline can develop to harness both theory and the power of modern computers, then we will see a very exciting future.

REFERENCES

Alonso, W. (1964). *Location and Land Use: Toward a General Theory of Land Rent*. Cambridge, Mass.: Harvard University Press.

Birkin, M. & Wilson, A.G. (1986a). 'Industrial location I: a review and an integrating framework.' *Environment and Planning A*, 18,175–205.

Birkin, M. & Wilson, A.G. (1986b). 'Industrial location theory II: Weber, Palander, Hotelling and extensions in a new framework.' *Environment and Planning A*, 18, 293–306.

Birkin, M. & Wilson, A.G. (1989). 'Some properties of spatial-economic-dynamic models.' In J. Hauer et al. (eds), *Urban Dynamics and Spatial Choice Behaviour*. Dordrecht: Kluwer Academic Publishers, 175–201.

Christaller, W. (1933). *Die Centralen Orte in Suddeutschland*. Jena: Gustav Fischer. English translation by C.W.Baskin, *Central places in Southern Germany*. Englewood Cliffs, NJ: Prentice-Hall.

Clarke, G.P. (1984). 'The expansion of service outlets across the city: a review.' School of Geography, University of Leeds, Working Paper 379.

Clarke, G.P. & Wilson, A.G. (1987a). 'Performance indicators and model-based planning I: the indicator movement and the possibilities for urban planning.' *Sistemi Urbani*, 2, 79–123.

Clarke, G.P. & Wilson, A.G. (1987b). 'Performance indicators and model-based planning II: model-based approaches.' *Sistemi Urbani*, 2, 138–65.

Clarke, G.P. & Wilson, A.G. (1994). 'A new geography of performance indicators for urban planning.' In C.S. Bertuglia, G.P. Clarke, and A.G. Wilson (eds), ch. 5, forthcoming.

Clarke, M. & Wilson, A.G. (1983a). 'Exploring the dynamics of urban housing structure: a 56–parameter residential location and housing model.' School of Geography, University of Leeds, Working Paper 363.

Clarke, M. & Wilson, A.G. (1983b). 'Dynamics of urban spatial structure: progress and problems.' *Journal of Regional Science*, 21, 1–18.

Clarke, M. & Wilson, A.G. (1985). 'A framework for dynamic comprehensive urban models: the integration of accounting and micro-simulation approaches in urban modelling.' School of Geography, University of Leeds, Working Paper 443.

Haggett, P. (1965). *Locational Analysis in Human Geography*. London: Edward Arnold.

Haggett, P. & Chorley, R.J. (1969). *Network Analysis in Geography*. London: Edward Arnold.

Harris, B. & Wilson, A.G. (1978). 'Equilibrium values and dynamics of attractiveness terms in production-constrained spatial interaction models.' *Environment and Planning A*, 10, 371–88.

Jin, Y-X., Leigh, C.M. & Wilson, A.G. (1991). 'Construction of an input-output table for Yorkshire and Humberside.' School of Geography, University of Leeds, Working Paper 544.

Lösch, A. (1940). *Die Räumliche Ordnung der Wirtschaft*, Jena: Gustav Fischer. English translation by W.H.Stolper (1954), *The Economics of Location*. New Haven, Conn: Yale University Press.

Rees, P.H. & Wilson, A.G. (1976). *Spatial Population Analysis*. London: Edward Arnold.

Reilly, W.J. (1931). *The Law of Retail Gravitation*. New York: G.P.Putnam and Sons.

Thom, R. (1975). *Structural Stability and Morphogenesis*. Reading, Mass.: W.A.Benjamin.

Thünen, J.H. von (1826). *Der Isolierte Staat in Beziehung auf Landwirtschaft und National-ökonomie*, Stuttgart: Gustav Fischer. English translation by C.M.Wartenburg (1966), *The Isolated State*. Oxford: Oxford University Press.

Weber, A. (1909). *Über den Standort der Industrien*. Tübingen. English translation by C.J.Friedrich, *Theory of the Location of Industries*. Chicago: University of Chicago Press.

Wilson, A.G. (1967). 'A statistical theory of spatial distribution models.' *Transportation Research*, 1, 253–69.

Wilson, A.G. (1970). *Entropy in Urban and Regional Modelling*. London: Pion.

Wilson, A.G. (1971). 'A family of spatial interaction models.' *Environment and Planning*, 3, 1–32.

Wilson, A.G. (1981). *Catastrophe Theory and Bifurcation: Applications to Urban and Regional Systems*. London: Croom Helm.

Wilson, A.G. (1983). 'Transport and the evolution of urban spatial structure.' Naples: *Atti delle Giornate do Lavoro*, AIRO.

Wilson, A.G. (1986). 'Spatial dynamics: classical problems, an integrated modelling approach and system performance.' *Papers, Regional Science Association*, 58, 47–58.

Wilson, A.G. (1988). 'Configurational analysis and urban and regional theory.' *Sistemi Urbani*, 1, 51–62.

Wilson, A.G. & Birkin, M. (1987). 'Dynamic models of agricultural location in a spatial interaction context.' *Geographical Analysis*, 19, 31–56.

Wilson, A.G. & Clarke, M. (1979). 'Some illustrations of catastrophe theory applied to urban retailing structures.' In M.J. Breheny (ed.), *London Papers in Regional Science, 10: Developments in Urban and Regional Analysis*. London: Pion.

Wilson, A.G. & Oulton, M. (1983). 'The corner-shop to supermarket transition in retailing: the beginnings of empirical evidence.' *Environment and Planning A* 15, 265–74.

Wilson, A.G. & Pownall, C.E. (1976). 'A new representation of the urban system for modelling and for the study of micro-level interdependence.' *Area*, 8, 256–64.

PART VI

Peter Haggett
A Career in Geography

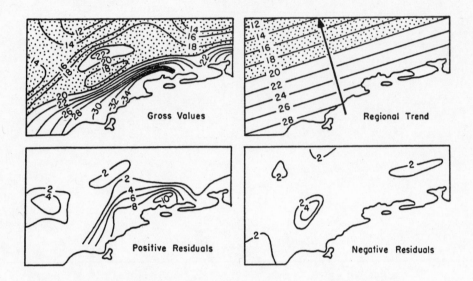

Gross Values

Regional Trend

Positive Residuals

Negative Residuals

Plate VI   Like the geographical phenomena he was so instrumental in mapping in his pioneering work with Dick Chorley, Peter's academic career has had both its ups – such as landmark publications and academic awards – and also occasional downs like the hospital confinement of adolescence. Presentation of the paper containing his famous diagram above (reproduced from the first edition of *Locational Analysis*, p. 271) to show a trend surface analysis of forest cover in south-east Brazil from his time as Leverhulme Research Fellow there, threatened, as chapters 17 and 18 relate, to be a further 'down' when thrust upon an unsuspecting Royal Geographical Society. Thankfully, however, this turned into another milestone in the quiet revolution he wrought in the methodology of geography.

17

Haggett's Cambridge: 1957–1966

R.J. Chorley

Coming events do not only cast their shadows before, sometimes they send out flashes of light. Before I first met Peter Haggett, when I joined the staff at Cambridge in October 1958, two events connected with him occurred to me which proved prophetic. In the early 1950s my family home was in Bridgwater, Somerset, a few doors away from the Headmaster of Dr Morgan's School, the historian of the British Empire, Charlie Key, with whom I became friendly. An amateur astronomer, he invited me to visit his school to see his production of telescope reflectors by grinding the glass from ship's portholes, and to view the heavens. This was the first time I had looked through a large telescope, which he had trained on Saturn (figure 17.1). The geometry of the planet was firmly impressed on my mind when Key then showed me the school honours board which gave pride of place to the Open Scholarship to St Catharine's College, Cambridge, awarded to a pupil from the nearby village of Pawlett. Thus, from the outset, I was to associate Peter with planetary geometry. The second event was much more sudden and unexpected. At 8.45 p.m. on Friday, 29 June 1951 I was passing Pawlett in the train and took the opportunity of pointing out to a casual travelling companion the nearby Royal Ordnance Factory visible across the fields at Puriton. I had no sooner done this when there was a considerable explosion, accompanied by a towering plume of smoke (figure 17.2)! More than a decade later, Peter and I were to write in *Frontiers in Geographical Teaching*: 'Better that geography should explode in an excess of reform than bask in the watery sunset of its former glories.' Peter played as big a part in jolting the geographical profession out of its previous lethargy as that explosion did to that of my railway companion.

Peter Haggett rejoined the Department of Geography at Cambridge as a University Demonstrator in October 1957, was promoted Lecturer in 1962 and left in 1966 to become Professor of Urban and Regional Geography at the University of Bristol. These nine years were very important ones not only for the maturation of Peter as a scholar and teacher but also for the Cambridge Department – indeed, each fed very productively on the other. The Department

Figure 17.1   The planet Saturn

which Peter joined in 1957 was an extremely professional one, having the highest of academic reputations particularly as a training ground for geographers. The College system provided the maximum level of personal support for all students as individuals, and undergraduate and graduate scholarship flowered in the most benign and secure of atmospheres. Students were much more concentrated in certain Colleges than is the case today, and there dedicated teachers considered it their main duty and privilege to bring their students to maturation as scholars – notably Gus Caesar at St Catharine's, Benny Farmer at St John's, Jean Grove at Girton, and Jean Mitchell at Newnham. The Department Head was Professor Alfred Steers, another St Catharine's man, and the other University teaching staff were Gus Caesar, Benny Farmer, Dick Grove, Vaughan Lewis, Jean Mitchell, Cameron Ovey, Clifford Smith, Bruce Sparks, Harriet Steers, Bill Williams, Mike Morgan and the surveyor John Jackson. During Peter's stay at Cambridge, Tony Wrigley and I joined the staff in 1958, Chris Board in 1959, David Stoddart in 1962, David Keeble in 1963 and Rendall Williams in 1965. Peter was soon made a Fellow in the newly designated Fitzwilliam College and was primarily responsible for laying the foundations of its subsequent record of geographical scholarship.

The quality and reputation of the Cambridge Geography Department has always rested to a considerable extent on the quality of its student body which, especially 35 years ago, comprised much of the flower of young British geographers. In 1957 Haggett found an undergraduate body which included C.F.T. Aub, G.R. Elliston, M.C. Gilpin, R.F. Kinloch, R.J.M. More, A.M. O'Connor, R.E. Pahl, P.J. Perry, A. Scarth, D.R. Stoddart, W.H. Theakstone, D.W.G. Timms,

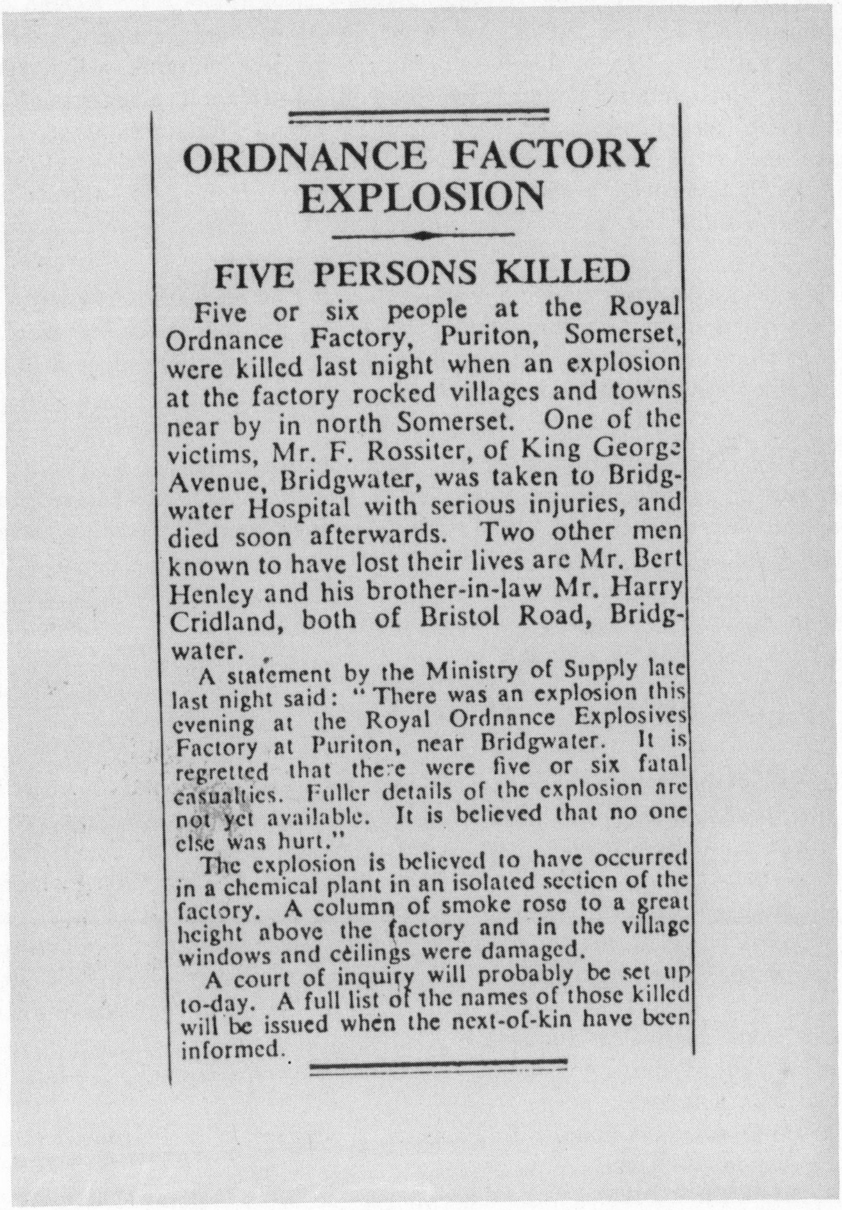

ORDNANCE FACTORY EXPLOSION

FIVE PERSONS KILLED

Five or six people at the Royal Ordnance Factory, Puriton, Somerset, were killed last night when an explosion at the factory rocked villages and towns near by in north Somerset. One of the victims, Mr. F. Rossiter, of King George Avenue, Bridgwater, was taken to Bridgwater Hospital with serious injuries, and died soon afterwards. Two other men known to have lost their lives are Mr. Bert Henley and his brother-in-law Mr. Harry Cridland, both of Bristol Road, Bridgwater.

A statement by the Ministry of Supply late last night said: "There was an explosion this evening at the Royal Ordnance Explosives Factory at Puriton, near Bridgwater. It is regretted that there were five or six fatal casualties. Fuller details of the explosion are not yet available. It is believed that no one else was hurt."

The explosion is believed to have occurred in a chemical plant in an isolated section of the factory. A column of smoke rose to a great height above the factory and in the village windows and ceilings were damaged.

A court of inquiry will probably be set up to-day. A full list of the names of those killed will be issued when the next-of-kin have been informed.

Figure 17.2 An extract from *The Times* of 30 June 1951 reporting the explosion at the Puriton Royal Ordnance Factory the previous day

C. Vita-Finzi and F.F. Zuill. In the following year K.R. Cox, D.E. Keeble, G. Robinson, B.T. Robson, H.O. Slaymaker and D. Turnock, among others, entered the Department. This rich vein continues to be exploited and, as the years passed, the Cambridge undergraduate body remained a roll call of much that was to be excellent and innovative in world geography. Nothing expressed this excellence better than the research students in geography of the period. During the 1950s there were seldom more than 4 or 5 Ph.D. research students in residence in the department. Peter wrote later (1990, p. 182):

> my fellow graduate students in geography at Cambridge in 1954 were small in number, with most working in glaciology . . . only one of the three went on into academic life, the other two dying in independent field accidents in different parts of the Arctic.

In 1957 Peter's contemporaries at St Catharine's, Peter Hall and Ken Warren, had recently completed their research and the few research students in residence included David Grigg and John Hardy. They were joined in 1958 by David Harvey and the Australian Tom Perry, and in 1959 George Elliston, F.C. German, Brian McCann (from Aberystwyth) and Claudio Vita-Finzi came into residence. Both Peter and I were particularly fortunate in this expansion of research, especially as suddenly in 1960 there was an explosion of research numbers from single figures to some 24, to 28 in 1961 and 29 in 1962. These later expansions included:

- **1960** Conrad Aub, Filipe Bezara (from Venezuela), Lucy Caroe, H.D. Dias (from Ceylon), Nick Flemming, Robin Kinloch, Mike Kirkby, Peter Perry, M.R. Postgate, Alwyn Scarth, David Stoddart, Wilf Theakstone, Duncan Timms, Tess Tindal (from Edinburgh – Peter's first research student), and Felicity Zuill.
- **1961** K.A. Gunawardina (from Ceylon), Ken Hewitt, John Hutchinson (from Birmingham), David Keeble, Tony O'Connor, Brian Robson, David Turnock, U.I. Ukwu (supervised by Peter), and Andrew Warren (from Hontine Air Surveys).
- **1962** B.M. Evans, N.F. Large, G.H. Peris, B.M. Welch and Paul Williams (from Durham).
- **1963** A.G.R. Cooke, R.S. Harrison, A.M. Hay, H.O. Slaymaker, and Rendall Williams.
- **1964** Piers Blaikie, Mike Carson, Robert Dilley, Valerie Haynes, and Henry West.
- **1965** Bob Bradnock, Graham Chapman, Ian Evans, David Hauser, Richard Hey (from Bristol), V. Hopkinson, Henry Irving, Elizabeth Lincoln, Tim O'Riordan (from Canada), Brian Plummer (from Australia), Derek Spooner, Celia Washbourn, and John Winslow (from California State College, Hayward).

Peter's teaching at Cambridge was concentrated around the three themes of Brazil, practical work, and locational analysis. As an undergraduate he conducted fieldwork on land-use changes and forestry in north-west Portugal and had gained in his own modest words, 'a smattering of that language'. At University College, London, where he served for a short period until 1957, he was directed to lecture on South America and naturally elected to concentrate on Brazil. During the whole of the succeeding nine years at Cambridge he delivered a first-year, 16-lecture course, variously entitled *Expansion of Europe* and *European Settlement Overseas,* in which Brazil featured strongly. Similarly, he lectured throughout to third-year students of historical geography on Brazil, variously as *Portugal Overseas, Settlement of Eastern Brazil* and *Regional Growth of Brazil.* For the third-year human geographers he offered special options on *Portugal* (1957–9), *Latin America* (1959–63), *Locational Studies of Brazil* (1963–4) and *Regional Development of Brazil* (1964–5). To the second year he delivered *Regional Geography of Eastern South America* (1963–5). As always, his regional interests had an especial focus, and in both Portugal and Brazil vegetation and land-use change were a primary concern. As an undergraduate he had studied the Portugese cork oak and in the summer of 1959 he visited the Sierra do Mar and Fortaleza Basin in south-east Brazil to survey the distribution and changes in forested areas, as well as land use and sediment yields. From this fieldwork resulted many practical exercises for the Cambridge undergraduates (some timed with stop watches!), as well as three important publications (1961, 1963, and 1964). Of these, the most significant was 'Regional and local components in the distribution of forested areas in south-east Brazil' (1964), in which Peter gave a very high-profile demonstration of the value of the use of quantitative techniques in a regional context. This paper was delivered as a lecture to the Royal Geographical Society on 4 March 1963 and caused somewhat of a furore. Peter was introduced on that occasion by the then RGS President, Sir Dudley Stamp (surely the archetypical traditional regional geographer, against whose ilk our energies began to be directed at Madingley the following July), as 'one of a group of young geographers to be found now in this country, the United States and elsewhere, attempting to put a greater precision into some of our geographical studies'. This made us sound rather like a fragile and fleeting species of migrant birds! After the lecture, Stamp summed up with the following words (1964, p. 380):

In thanking Mr Haggett I am reminded of the interest in reading in the *Geographical Journal* the discussion after some of the afternoon meetings of the past. One realizes how, in this hall, or its predecessor, the Royal Geographical Society has had put before it new lines of thought. I think we must say to our lecturer this afternoon, that he has introduced some of us to the modern quantitative approach. Some of us may not like the look of it. We may even feel that here is an enormous steam hammer! How is it working in the cracking of nuts? One does hear that said facetiously, but I remember on one occasion seeing an enormous steam hammer so delicately adjusted that it did the best cracking of nuts I have ever seen. With new statistical techniques we geographers are being given a new weapon. I would only ask this. We have been told in the past that we must make maps and cartograms, and use them as waste paper, being quite content if we get one good one, that really shows something, out of a dozen. I hope that the mathematically-inclined will have the strength of mind to tear up some of their results if necessary. I think then, through such means as we have had this afternoon, we may see important advances in our subject.

Some days later it was reported that Professor Steers, Peter's Head of Department at Cambridge, called him into his office and told him that, in his opinion, Peter was bringing the subject of geography into disrepute by applying such mathematical methods. I have no reason to disbelieve this and, consequently, took an especial pleasure in Peter's gold medal which he received from the RGS in 1985. What is much more important than the views of elderly academics at that time was that Peter's teaching on Brazil showed him to be the kind of true polymath which our discipline has now largely lost – a quantitative, regional, historical, and economic geographer with biogeographical interests. All this was despite the fact that he entered Cambridge as a student intending to specialize in physical geography. This regionally directed teaching also encapsulated three of Peter's deeply underlying concerns: his love of trees (one of his sons is now a forestry expert); his historical feel – he has always been deeply moved by thoughts of the carnage of World War I which so affected his home area; and his love of place. It is characteristic of his 'geopiety' that he recently chose to link the concept of love of place with the Germanic idea of 'Heimat' (1990, p. 90).

When Peter and I joined the Cambridge Department as University Demonstrators (that is, non-tenured Assistant Lecturers) it was one of the jobs of the three such post-holders to organize and conduct the 6 hours per week of practical laboratory work for first-year students, as well as some of the undergraduate fieldwork. In this we were assisted by certain post graduates (Student Demonstrators). As Professor Steers insisted that everyone should be present during all laboratory sessions, irrespective of who was primarily concerned in conducting a particular project, there were (potentially!) some 120 hours per year for Peter and I to chat with one another and with the other University Demonstrators – initially with the very agreeable and practically talented Mike Morgan and later with the puckish cartographic expert, Chris Board. There was also a succession of Student Demonstrators, including the flat-mates David Grigg and David Harvey, Brian McCann, Claudio Vite-Finzi, Mike Kirkby, Alwyn Scarth, David Keeble, Brian Robson and, most especially, David Stoddart. Steers' edict turned out to be a blessing in disguise in that over those few years we discussed everything under the sun, usually in a spirit of irreverent levity, and in the presence of some 80 talented undergraduates who readily entered into the spirit of the occasions. I now see in retrospect that some very productive intellectual chemistry took place there. At that time the Department was, despite the natural personal disharmonies endemic to academics, a very convivial and agreeable place, made all the more stimulating by the intellectual tensions which were rapidly building up. If the Department could be likened to a small town, the first-year practical laboratory was its market place. Here lecturers such as the mercurial Vaughan Lewis, Gus Caesar, Benny Farmer, and

Dick Grove dropped in from time to time to chew the fat and, especially, Bruce Sparks who had an office the only access to which was via the laboratory. Indeed, this bluntly-stimulating and reactionary man seemed to regard the laboratory as an extension of his office and for many years was a centre of sociability there as he sieved his Pleistocene snails in the laboratory sink. Consequently, for all these reasons, as the students sat on their high stools along the four heavy wooden benches which ran the length of the large room, grappling with their assignments, there was a constant coming and going, and exchange of ideas, gossip and scandal. Here assignations were made, plans discussed and expeditions planned; the whole forming a microcosm of the kind of democratic academic interaction, involving everyone from the most apprehensive new undergraduate to the middle-aged established scholar, which has long given Cambridge much of its intellectual fire. In this connection it must be remembered that, despite his intellectual apprehensions, Professor Steers' stewardship of the Department coincided with one of its genuine high points.

In 1957 the Cambridge examination structure (the Tripos) and its teaching formed a distinctly monolithic and inflexible structure governed by decisions of Staff Meetings largely dominated by very traditional attitudes. Nevertheless, syllabus discussions did occur, generating their customary acrimony, which commonly led to the prolonged suspension of such gatherings – I recall Chris Board asking me, after being many months resident in the Department, whether we ever held Staff Meetings! However, every situation can be turned to advantage and Peter and I were able little-by-little to introduce new ideas into the Department via the first-year laboratory teaching which was largely in our hands, thereby injecting them deep into the roots of the developing student body. This technique was to be repeated in our planning and conduct of the residential courses 'for teachers and other adult students' which we organized in collaboration with the University Extra-Mural Studies Board at Madingley Hall beginning in July 1963. We arrived as Junior Lecturers in the late 1950s to find a traditional suite of practical exercises which had been presented year after year to incoming undergraduates (and which were consequently on file in many Colleges!) consisting of geological maps, map projections, artistic cartography, graphical techniques, air photo interpretation and the like. We made gradual rather than wholesale changes, indeed Peter was particularly attracted to the teaching of aerial photography which he continued to the first-year in 1963–5 after his promotion to Lecturer, and even introduced it to the newly instituted second-year practical work in 1963. Nevertheless, we introduced little by little an increasing amount of quantitative work into the first-year practicals, mostly to do with statistical methods, matrices, set theory, trend surface analysis, and network analysis. Our enthusiasms undoubtedly exceeded our competence, but we went to considerable lengths to put a sugar coating on what the more 'artistic' students soon came to regard as an unpleasant pill – and still do! Peter, in particular, was especially imaginative in his teaching and, for example, regularly encouraged me to accompany his topological teaching of network methods by a demonstration (learned in a New York bar) of removing my waistcoat (that is, vest) without first taking off my jacket. It was only his translation to Bristol which saved me from even more embarrassing topological excesses, and for that reason alone I was happy to join him in writing *Network Analysis in Geography* (1969).

I had learned such statistical skills as I possessed in America from Art Strahler's applications of the techniques pioneered by Bill Krumbein and John Tukey. Starting with the ideas of D'Arcy Thompson, Hägerstrand, Lösch and some early American regional scientists, Peter's interest in the possibilities of quantitative applications in geography was increasingly fuelled by teaching developments of the 'new mathematics'. At their outset, our efforts at quantitative teaching caused the Head of Department to have the occasional hot flush during which he taxed our senior colleagues as to 'what Haggett and Chorley knew about mathematics'. Loyal as always, they answered 'nothing', which did not ease our position. Periodically, professional mathematicians were imported to conduct non-geographical statistics teaching but, naturally, this was not a great success. In 1963, just after Peter and I had been promoted to Lectureships, we had allayed some of the fears sufficiently to be allowed to take over much of the new second-year practical sessions. These involved the variously-entitled *application of statistical methods, quantitative techniques* or *the analysis of field data*, first for one term and then from 1964 to 1966 for two terms, latterly in the company of David Stoddart and Mike Kirkby. The early 1960s were particularly significant for Peter's mathematical interests, and in the lead up to *Locational Analysis in Human Geography* (1965) with its emphasis on what he was to identify as the weakest third of the 'geographical Venn diagram' – the geometrical sciences (1965, p. 15). At the beginning of the decade the Nuffield Foundation instituted a scheme designed to further the teaching of the new mathematics in Primary schools (that is, to children under the age of 11 years). This involved the setting up of a number of teaching centres to develop teaching texts through interaction with local teachers in adjacent pilot schools. One of these centres was by chance located in Peter's home village of Stapleford, near Cambridge, where his daughter was to be a pupil. Peter married Brenda, a student at Homerton College, Cambridge, in 1956 and while at the Cambridge Department of Geography he produced the 'two *s*, two *d*' now listed in *Who's Who*. How much geography has owed to Peter's growing interest in the prospective mathematical opportunities for these *s*s and *d*s it is difficult to say, but this happy conjunction is not only characteristic of the open-mindedness and lack of conceit on the part of Peter, but also of the way in which geographical vistas were opening up at the time. A fresh wind was blowing through the discipline. No longer was the geographical wagon train drawn up into an academic defensive circle, as in my undergraduate days just after World War II. Increasingly geographers were exploring what seemed to be a limitless intellectual landscape and striking gold often in the most unlikely places.

As well as the mandatory supervision of the first-year surveying classes (chain survey on Coe Fen, and levelling and plane tabling on the Gogs), Peter was especially active in promoting fieldwork, both in the form of day projects conducted from Cambridge (for example, to Hunstanton and Grimes Graves – figure 17.3) and week-long residential courses in other parts of the country. Two of these were particularly memorable. In 1960 we organized a residential field course, naturally in West Somerset. Together with a large group of under-

Figure 17.3   View up the near-vertical ladder at Grimes Graves, Norfolk, a prehistoric flint mine. The departmental instructions of the time were that female undergraduates should descend first and ascend last

graduates, Peter and I stayed in a distinctly seedy Taunton hotel, accompanied by David Harvey, then a research student. Peter, David, and I were assigned a room containing one double and one single bed. I have always been suspicious of the coin Peter used, but as the years have passed I have gained a great deal of kudos among radical circles in geography by being able to claim that I have shared a bed with David Harvey on a number of occasions. At the time David was making free with a product which was marketed under the trade name 'Naughty Fido', and this did little to improve our relations with the Manager. For the sake of all concerned, I will draw a veil over the matter at Horner Water involving the soaked female undergraduate and the transparent plastic macin-

Figure 17.4   The Bell Hotel, Thetford, in the 1960s

tosh. The second notable field occasion of the period was three years later when Peter, David Stoddart, and I organized the second-year practical class to sample sand sizes in the Breckland. The academic results of this appeared (with the valuable participation of Olav Slaymaker) in the *Journal of Sedimentary Petrology* for 1966 and the operation was recently described by Peter (1990, p. 42), who wrote:

> On a day in May 1963 it was the scene of unusual activity as eighty Cambridge undergraduates swarmed over the sands armed with soil augers (and sandwiches) taking borings from the top half-metre of the soil profile. Seen from the air the distribution of the students in their bright anoraks would have seemed puzzling. But in terms of figure 2.9 the logic behind their distribution was clear: they formed part of a carefully thought-out nested sampling design.

My own abiding memory of this field project is of Peter, David, and I eating roast duck in the Bell Hotel at Thetford (figure 17.4) while dozens of students and the rain beat on the windows – but perhaps that was during a subsequent occasion when the nested sampling design was being strengthened! In fairness, I recall that Peter was distinctly embarrassed on that occasion, as he was on many others when he was with David and myself – but he did enjoy the duck.

The third theme of Peter's teaching at Cambridge was, naturally, locational analysis. In the Lent Term 1960 he gave a series of eight lectures to the Second Year entitled *Economic Geography – Studies in Location* which continued for four

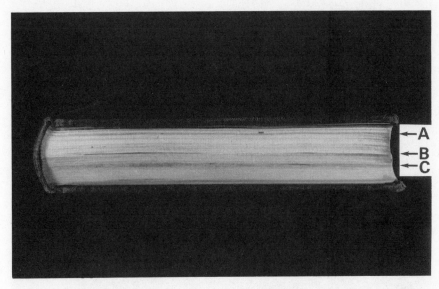

Figure 17.5   One end of a bound library copy of the 1965 *Transactions of the Institute of British Geographers*. Can you spot Peter's trend surface article? Is it A, B or C?

years. In the Michaelmas Term 1963 these were translated into 16 lectures to the Third Year, first as *Locational Studies* and latterly as *Locational Analysis*. In his final year (Lent 1966) he supplemented these by fortnightly seminars on *Quantitative Methods in Regional Geography* to the Third Year. It is noteworthy that, for much of this period, Peter (partly from choice) delivered these innovative locational lectures at 9 a.m. on Saturday morning and it was a measure of their abrasive impact that, like many another hair shirt (a triumph of masochism over common sense), they had such a profound effect. As has been noted, this enterprise was based on a vision of a revived geometrical basis for geography and drew on Peter's wide studies, particularly of foreign work in the discipline. He was kind enough in the Preface to *Locational Analysis in Human Geography* (1965, p.v.) to credit me with encouraging him to write his great book from his 'much-thumbed and much-revised lecture notes'. My recollection, however, is of a meticulous loose-leaf file and of such encourage-ment as I gave to have been in the form of vague admonitions for him to 'pull his finger out' of some non-geographical location. Peter recognized that this general work related to 'rather simple geographical systems' and much of his subsequent thought has been directed towards 'complex sets of relations between man and the land in particular places (implying) a much more complex system' (1990, p. 91). In those early 1960s our interests, in human and physical geography respectively, ran along very parallel general lines, and our common concern with spatial generalization came together in the production in 1965 of 'Trend surface mapping in geographical research' (figure 17.5). This joint effort was first presented verbally at an IBG Symposium on Regression Techniques in Geography at Bristol in January 1965 before an audience of some 80 souls (to give them the benefit of the doubt). As Peter was at the time attending the

Figure 17.6 Haggett and Chorley at Bodie, near the California–Nevada state line, in September 1962

birth of one of his many children, or at any rate that was the excuse he gave, it was left to me to give the presentation which, apart from support from Roger Barry, was received with distinct hostility. This hostility was of a kind which had already surfaced at Cambridge in the person of Professor Steers and which was to become only too familiar – namely that the locational methods outlined were not new, were wrong, and in any event were irrelevant. Afterwards I travelled back to London feeling strangely elated, probably due both to the recognition that such strength of opposition confirmed the rightness of our cause and to the prospect of dinner with my future wife. I must confess here that the latter thought was uppermost, but historians of geography may prefer the former. Peter has always been the first to acknowledge his debt to the quantitative regional work which was carried on during the late 1950s and early 1960s in the United States. This influence was strengthened when in the summer of 1962 Peter spent some weeks at Berkeley, where he taught Summer School and attended a meeting of the Regional Science Association. This visit was to have another consequence which involved myself, who was also on a visit to Berkeley at the time (Haggett and Chorley, 1989, pp. xv–xvi). Peter and I, accompanied by a former Cambridge student, Roger Barnett, borrowed a University station wagon and during Labor Day Weekend drove to Yosemite, over the Sierras and north along the Owens Valley, ending up at Bodie, which had been recommended by Jim Parsons as the best ghost town in North America (figure 17.6). It was there, against the backdrop of empty façades so reminiscent of much geographical teaching in British schools, that the theme of the Madingley Conferences was born.

As our plans evolved, it became increasingly clear that new life had to be breathed into British geography teaching at all levels. Existing teaching seemed to us to be routine, inward-looking, lacking in any real intellectual challenge and resigned to geography remaining a second-rate academic subject. In contrast to more recent movements in the discipline, we were not out to use geographical teaching as a weapon to achieve some supposedly higher socio-political goal. We viewed ourselves as two liberal scholars (although Peter's 'L' was probably more capital than mine) who were aiming at an intellectual revolution in our chosen discipline. It is perhaps not irrelevant that the Bridg-water Parliamentary Constituency, in which we had both been born and had spent our formative years, has historically possessed distinct radical tendencies, nor that Oliver Cromwell was born only 15 miles from Cambridge and was a Fellow Commoner at my own college, Sidney Sussex. It must be understood that the notion of radical change in geography teaching was not unique to us in the early 1960s. For some time previously the massively organized and considerably funded US High School Geography Project had been carrying out experiments in school teaching and producing mountains of proposals and teaching material. However, it was clearly:

> foundering due to the then low status and lack of professionalism associ-ated with the subject in many American schools. Britain possessed in school geography a clearly defined discipline with an established role and status and which was orchestrated by an organized group of well-trained, dedicated and highly professional geography graduates. A substantial proportion of these was clearly dissatisfied with existing syllabuses, rec-ognizing them to be antique, demanding of memory rather than intellect, innocent of any real philosophical overviews, and increasingly divorced from the condition of the real world which was changing so fast after World War II. (Haggett and Chorley, 1989, pp. xvi–xvii)

Peter's studies of World War I convinced us that, when confronting the kind of entrenched, well-organized but essentially static advisory as was represented by the British geographical establishment in the 1960s, the correct strategy was to attack points of critical vulnerability and by-pass the strong points. Accord-ingly we identified a core of intellectually dissatisfied, very active and highly influential sixth-form teachers as our critical point of incursion into the existing system. It was clear that these teachers could be extremely influential in syllabus reform, that their pent-up professionalism could be rapidly unleashed in terms of their teaching and that changes in sixth-form teaching would rapidly diffuse up into the universities and down into the teaching of younger pupils. We were fortunate in that both time and place favoured our enterprise and that it was as if we were opening a safe with a combination time lock having chanced upon the correct combination and the correct opening time. It transpired that the subsequent influence of those involved in the Madingley Conferences as teachers, syllabus builders, textbook writers and HM Inspectors of Schools was

Figure 17.7   Madingley Hall, Cambridge

to give ample justification to our good luck, intuition, and of a military lesson gained from the first three years of a carnage which hung over our childhoods. I can clearly recall, as undoubtedly can Peter, that in Somerset during the 1930s at 11 a.m. on 11 November everything would stop for 2 minutes – people would stand bare-headed in the streets and even cars would stop and their drivers alight. We are, in this respect, both products of a special post-war time and of a special rural place.

If the High School Geography Project had the substantial financial and logistic backing of the American geographical establishment, we had the support of the Cambridge University Board of Extra-Mural Studies! It was fortunate that the Cambridge geographer Ray Pahl (now Research Professor of Sociology at the University of Kent) was an influential member of the Extra-Mural Board and that it was possible for an annual residential course for teachers of a week's duration to be arranged at Madingley Hall (figure 17.7):

> a rambling Elizabethan mansion which had been purchased by the university shortly after the end of World War II. It lies in a small village four miles from Cambridge, surrounded by formal gardens (with a croquet lawn, to be much used by the geographers) on one side; walled kitchen gardens on the other. Altogether very rural, very English, very un-revolutionary. (Haggett and Chorley, 1989, p. xvi)

Peter, in particular, was keen to associate our efforts with Madingley so that they could be rooted in a poetic spot with a magical name:

> And things are done you'd not believe
> At Madingley, on Christmas eve.

> (Rupert Brooke, *The Old Vicarage, Grantchester*
> written at the Café des Westens, Berlin, May 1912)

Figure 17.8 The dust jackets of Peter's three important books published in the two-year period 1965–7

It was, however, not at Christmas but on 27 July 1963 when 28 'teachers and other adult students' gathered at Madingley Hall to attend a course on *Modern Geography*. A similar course entitled *Modern Geography: A survey of developments in methodology and research* was held between 25 July and 1 August the following year for an audience of 24. These and subsequent courses involved lectures, seminars, discussions, practical exercises, and much croquet and banter. As the title suggests, these two initial conferences aimed simply at surveying and interpreting recent scholarly developments in geography and one of the more immediate results was the publication in 1965 of *Frontiers of Geographical Teaching*.

Frontiers carried the following message on the dust jacket:

Although this book is not a teachers' guide to a new syllabus or a pupils' textbook, it may serve to sharpen the appetite of both for some of the changes that must, sooner or later, make their impact on geography as it is taught in our schools.

With this distinctive dust jacket symbolically depicting an Elizabethan print of Madingley Hall on which had been superimposed Christaller's hexagons, *Frontiers* appeared almost simultaneously with Peter's more important *Locational Analysis* (figure 17.8). These works established him at the forefront of British geography and were instrumental in his promotion to the Chair at Bristol which brought the era of Haggett's Cambridge to an end the following year. The table of contents of *Frontiers* indicates something of the scope and eclecticism of the first Madingley Conferences in 1963 and 1964:

PART I: CONCEPTS

I   CHANGES IN THE PHILOSOPHY OF GEOGRAPHY
E.A. Wrigley *(Lecturer in Geography, University of Cambridge)*

II   A RE-EVALUATION OF THE GEOMORPHIC SYSTEM OF W.M. DAVIS
R.J. Chorley *(Lecturer in Geography, University of Cambridge)*

III   SOME RECENT TRENDS IN CLIMATOLOGY
R.P. Beckinsale *(Senior Lecturer in Geography, University of Oxford)*

IV   GEOGRAPHY AND POPULATION
E.A. Wrigley *(Lecturer in Geography, University of Cambridge)*

V   TRENDS IN SOCIAL GEOGRAPHY
R.E. Pahl *(Tutor, Board of Extra-mural Studies, University of Cambridge)*

VI   CHANGING COCEPTS IN ECONOMIC GEOGRAPHY
P. Haggett *(Lecturer in Geography, University of Cambridge)*

VII   HISTORICAL GEOGRAPHY: CURRENT TRENDS AND PROSPECTS
C.T. Smith *(Lecturer in Geography, University of Cambridge)*

PART II: TECHNIQUES

VIII   THE APPLICATION OF QUANTITATIVE METHODS TO GEOMORPHOLOGY
R.J. Chorley *(Lecturer in Geography, University of Cambridge)*

IX   SCALE COMPONENTS IN GEOGRAPHICAL PROBLEMS
P. Haggett *(Lecturer in Geography, University of Cambridge)*

X   FIELD WORK IN GEOGRAPHY, WITH PARTICULAR EMPHASIS ON THE ROLE OF LAND-USE SURVEY
C. Board *(Lecturer in Geography, London School of Economics)*

XI   FIELD WORK IN URBAN AREAS
M.P. Collins *(Lecturer in Town Planning, University College, London)*

XII   QUANTITATIVE TECHNIQUES IN URBAN SOCIAL GEOGRAPHY
D. Timms *(Lecturer in Geography, University of Queensland)*

XIII   GEOGRAPHICAL TECHNIQUES IN PHYSICAL PLANNING
E. C. Willatts *(Principal Planner, Ministry of Housing and Local Government)*

PART III: TEACHING

XIV   GEOGRAPHY IN THE UNIVERSITIES
PART I: GEOGRAPHY IN THE OLDER UNIVERSITIES
C. Board *(Lecturer in Geography, London School of Economics)*
PART II: GEOGRAPHY IN A NEW UNIVERSITY
T.H. Elkins *(Professor of Geography, University of Sussex)*

XV GEOGRAPHY IN THE COLLEGES
PART I: GEOGRAPHY IN THE TRAINING COLLEGES
S.M. Brazier *(Lecturer in Geography, Homerton College, Cambridge)*
PART II: GEOGRAPHY IN THE TECHNICAL COLLEGES
W. Islip *(Lecturer in Geography, Cambridge College of Arts and Technology)*
XVI GEOGRAPHY IN SCHOOLS
P. Bryan *(Senior Geography Master, Cambridge High School for Boys)*
XVII TEACHING THE NEW AFRICA
R.J. Harrison Church *(Professor of Geography, London School of Economics)*
XVIII FRONTIER MOVEMENTS AND THE GEOGRAPHICAL TRADITION
P. Haggett and R.J. Chorley *(Lecturers in Geography, University of Cambridge)*

One of the initial participants in these conferences has written:

My own recollections of that period . . . are mainly of the extraordinary intellectual ferment in the Department and at Madingley. In retrospect it seems one of those rare occasions when people . . . and a rising swell of ideas catch a tide in a conjunction which makes the sum far greater than the parts . . . In my own case, and I know in the case of many, Madingley was a revelation of 'Road to Damascus' proportions, when things suddenly fell into place under the influence not so much of new knowledge as of new ways of looking at knowledge. I think for many of us it was the most exciting and stimulating event of our careers.

After the first two years of Madingley which publicized in *Frontiers* a range of ideas which were so novel to British sixth-form teaching, it was felt that some more coherent and generalized methodological focus was required.

The idea for *Models* had been launched in the Spring of 1964. An initial meeting was held at Cambridge in the Department of Geography's Clark Collection room, a handsome room with its walls lined with classical geographical and exploration volumes. It is not clear that their authors would have approved either of the 'robustly anti-idiographic' aim of the proposed volume, or of the distinctly junior status of its proposed authors. Certainly, they would have considered a veil should be drawn over events late in the day when the anti-idiographic discussions between contributors became so robust as to lead to fisticuffs in a pasture field (located somewhere along the Cambridge–Bristol axis) before a bemused circle of Friesian heifers . . .

In those heady, rather confused months during which the book took shape it would have been difficult to identify our aims clearly, which is perhaps why it did not occur to any of us to write a preface, or to lay down hard-and-fast rules for contributors. However [it] was our desire to begin an active review of the goals of geographical scholarship, its relations with other disciplines, the changing dialogue between human and physical geography, and not least, to try and explore the unifying bonds in the subject at a time when conventional regional geography appeared to have run out of steam. (Haggett and Chorley, 1989, pp. xvi–xvii)

The immediate result of all this talking, laughing, drinking (not, I hasten to add, by Peter), and general mayhem was the third Madingley Conference which took place between 24 and 31 July 1965, entitled *Geography in a changing intellectual environment: Models in Geography*, to an enrolment of 32. More importantly, in 1967 *Models in Geography* was published containing the following contributions:

I: THE ROLE OF MODELS

1   MODELS, PARADIGMS AND THE NEW GEOGRAPHY
    Peter Haggett and Richard J. Chorley, *Departments of Geography, Bristol and Cambridge Universities*
2   THE USE OF MODELS IN SCIENCE
    F.H. George, *Educational and Scientific Developments Ltd, and Bristol University*

II: MODELS OF PHYSICAL SYSTEMS

3   MODELS IN GEOMORPHOLOGY
    Richard J. Chorley, *Department of Geography, Cambridge University*
4   MODELS IN METEOROLOGY AND CLIMATOLOGY
    R.G. Barry, *Department of Geography, Southampton University*
5   HYDROLOGICAL MODELS AND GEOGRAPHY
    Rosemary J. More, *Department of Civil Engineering, Imperial College London*

III: MODELS OF SOCIO-ECONOMIC SYSTEMS

6   DEMOGRAPHIC MODELS AND GEOGRAPHY
    E.A. Wrigley, *Department of Geography, Cambridge University*
7   SOCIOLOGICAL MODELS IN GEOGRAPHY
    R.E. Pahl, *Faculty of Social Sciences, University of Kent at Canterbury*
8   MODELS OF ECONOMIC DEVELOPMENT
    D.E. Keeble, *Department of Geography, Cambridge University*
9   MODELS OF URBAN GEOGRAPHY AND SETTLEMENT LOCATION
    B. Garner, *Department of Geogaphy, Bristol University*
10 MODELS OF INDUSTRIAL LOCATION
    F.E. Ian Hamilton, *Department of Geography, London School of Economics and Political Science, and School of Slavonic and East European Studies, London University*
11 MODELS OF AGRICULTURAL ACTIVITY
    Janet D. Henshall, *Department of Geography, King's College, London University*

IV: MODELS OF MIXED SYSTEMS

12   REGIONS, MODELS AND CLASSES
      David Grigg, *Department of Geography, Sheffield University*
13   ORGANISM AND ECOSYSTEM AS GEOGRAPHICAL MODELS
      D.R. Stoddart, *Department of Geography, Cambridge University*
14   MODELS OF THE EVOLUTION OF SPATIAL PATTERNS IN
      HUMAN GEOGRAPHY
      D. Harvey, *Department of Geography, Bristol University*
15   NETWORK MODELS IN GEOGRAPHY
      Peter Haggett, *Department of Geography, Bristol University*

V: INFORMATION MODELS

16   MAPS AS MODELS
      C. Board, *Department of Geography, London School of Economics and
      Political Science*
17   HARDWARE MODELS IN GEOGRAPHY
      M.A. Morgan, *Department of Geography, Bristol University*
18   MODELS OF GEOGRAPHICAL TEACHING
      S.G. Harris, *Department of Education, Cambridge University*

The Madingley Conferences continued until 1978 and the effects of *Locational Analysis*, *Frontiers* and *Models* have reverberated on. However, the effect was not, as the timid and conventional feared, to signal 'the end of geography'. Instead, this and related work provided a coherent, intellectually-challenging and academically-viable groundswell which raised British geography from its previous trough, providing a summit of achievement for our discipline against which the heights of all subsequent post-modernist revolutions, reactions and fads must be measured. The years 1957–66 witnessed Peter Haggett approaching a peak of his remarkably creative and vigorous scholarship. During this period at Cambridge we were all young, optimistic, full of pep and irreverence, and privileged to be in his company when, probably for the first time in this country, geography achieved some measure of respect within the academic community as a whole. The final word should be reserved for one of the Madingley participants:

I had called in at lunchtime to see Peter, and he suggested a working lunch at the Senate House. In a few minutes walk from the Department to the Senate House, Peter threw out more brilliant ideas . . . than I have ever heard before or since, quite literally off the cuff. It was a 'performance' of quite breathtaking quality, delivered of course with that easy charm and urbanity which is such an agreeable feature of his character . . . To have known Peter then and played even the smallest part in those events was both a privilege and a piece of the most extraordinary luck for me.

I'll drink to that!

REFERENCES

Chorley, R.J. & Haggett, P. (eds) (1965a). *Frontiers in Geographical Teaching.* London: Methuen.

Chorley, R.J. & Haggett, P. (1965b). 'Trend surface mapping in geographical research.' *Transactions of the Institute of British Geographers*, 37, 47–67.

Chorley, R.J., Stoddart, D.R., Haggett, P., & Slaymaker, O. (1966). 'Regional and local components in the areal distribution of surface sand facies in the Breckland, Eastern England.' *Journal of Sedimentary Petrology*, 36, 209–20.

Chorley, R.J. & Haggett, P. (eds) (1967). *Models in Geography.* London: Methuen.

Haggett, P. (1961). 'Land use and sediment yield in an old plantation tract of the Sierra do Mar, Brazil.' *Geographical Journal*, 127, 50–62.

Haggett, P. (1963). 'Regional and local components in land-use sampling: a case-study from the Brazilian Triangulo.' *Erdkunde*, 17, 108–14.

Haggett, P. (1964). 'Regional and local components in the distribution of forested areas in south-east Brazil.' *Geographical Journal*, 130, 365–80.

Haggett, P. (1965). *Locational Analysis in Human Geography.* London: Edward Arnold.

Haggett, P. (1990). *The Geographer's Art.* Oxford: Basil Blackwell.

Haggett, P. & Chorley, R.J. (1969). *Network Analysis in Geography.* London: Edward Arnold.

Haggett, P. & Chorley, R.J. (1989). *Foreword*, in W. Macmillan (ed.), *Remodelling Geography*. Oxford: Basil Blackwell, xv–xx.

18

Peter Haggett's Life in Geography

N.J. Thrift

1 INTRODUCTION

An academic's work takes on a life of its own, yet traces of its origin in a particular person still remain. More than most, Peter Haggett's work bears the traces of his life and milieu. In this concluding essay, I will attempt to summarize Peter Haggett's work and point to some of the ways in which it still bears the marks of his life.

I will make this reckoning through a device that Peter has used on more than one occasion – a progressive mapping of the nodality of a particular phenomenon. In Peter's case, the phenomenon was usually a city region or some other element of the modern landscape. In my case, the phenomenon is Peter himself.

Thus, I will begin by writing of the origins of Peter Haggett as a person. I will then show how he was mapped onto a particular intellectual and institutional field. Finally, I will endeavour to explain why that field was influenced by Peter Haggett – how, in a sense, he redrew a part of its map.

2 ORIGINS: ON BECOMING A GEOGRAPHER

Peter Haggett was born on 24 January 1933 in Pawlett, Somerset. His early life, before he went up to Cambridge at the age of 18, clearly formed much of his character and it is therefore worth pausing to identify some early energies and enthusiasms. Five of these seem to have been particularly important. There was, first of all, his upbringing as a staunch Methodist. To this day, Peter is a teetotaller. Second, there was the deep attachment to family life (an attachment which is attested to by Peter's long-lasting and happy marriage and his four children). Third, there was the value that was placed on the pursuit of knowledge, both by his family and by the schools he attended, especially Dr Morgan's school in Bridgwater. Fourth, there was the abiding love of the Somerset landscape.

Figure 18.1   The young Haggett (extreme right) in his sixth form class photograph (courtesy of the Rt Hon. John Biffen, MP)

> Long ago my father introduced me to the landscape he loved around our Somerset home and there both family finances and petrol-rationing ensured that we followed Carl Sauer's dictum that ' . . . locomotion should be slow; the slower the better'. (Haggett, 1965, p. vi)

This bond to the Somerset countryside has proved a lasting one, constantly reinforced by walks and bird-spotting. Finally, there was his love of cricket. It is difficult to resist the speculation that part of the attraction of the game for Peter arises out of its mixture of rules, arcane knowledge, and the picturesque grounds on which it is often played. John Biffen's memoir of the early Haggett captures all of these energies and enthusiasms (figure 18.1):

> School is supposedly a sunshine period. It certainly was for me. Dr Morgan's School, Bridgwater, was a modest boys' grammar school, but what it lacked in amenities it compensated with quite exceptional teaching staff. The pursuit of learning was an end in itself.
>
> In the austerity of post-war Britain, Peter Haggett and I settled down to our sixth form studies. Our subjects did not entirely overlap and I was a school year ahead, but in the miniscule sixth form we were grouped together for our studies. I am not sure whether modern educationalists would be appalled at such an arrangement or whether they would envy the intimate and repetitive tutorials we received.
>
> Peter was an evident scholar from early school days, and he amply fulfilled his promise of scholarship. In particular I think he gained inspi-

ration from Charles Key, the headmaster who had recently arrived from Cheltenham Grammar School and was both a geographer and a historian.

The passage of over forty years is bound to play mischief with memory, but I recall that Peter combined a natural command of learning with a generally relaxed approach to life. He was not a games zealot, but had the balance of commitment and competence that might have made him an adept cricket umpire. Anticipating modern controversy he wisely withheld his talents. Even so the game had its fascination. Writing in the school magazine in July 1949 he muses with more accuracy than partisanship about 'Somerset's chances of saving the follow on'.

Life was always good-natured in his company. We came to school from different villages, he from Pawlett on the far edge of the 'levels' (where my forebears had farmed) and I from Otterhampton close by the west bank of the River Parrett estuary. Peter was from a family of staunch methodists and I always felt he watched my burgeoning and precocious reactionary political views with some anxiety. At any rate they were halcyon days and Peter's natural aptitude and application deservedly earned him a Cambridge exhibition.

Our paths then crossed again at university. After my national service I had three gilded years of studying history, indulging in undergraduate politics, and generally enjoying myself. Peter was at St Catharine's and I was at Jesus, but we would frequently meet for nothing stronger than coffee, his methodism prevailing over my worldly army experience. We kept in touch, talked of the school and our native Somerset. Rather ponderously we decided we were the Cambridge Old Morganians Club, and there was even a somewhat contrived message sent to the school magazine. One reported that Peter Haggett had splintered his squash racket in 'a life and death struggle' with me. That must have been an aberration of physical exercise.

As I have said, after forty years memory can play mischief, but one thing is quite clear. From the years in the sixth form and onwards it could always be asserted that Peter's quiet intellectual authority and the easy personal manner would secure him a distinguished academic career. He has not disappointed his admirers among whom I am most happy to count myself.

It is no surprise that, given these five energies and enthusiasms, Peter became attached to geography, a discipline that most easily recaptures the sense of something familiar yet still unknown. Peter documents his slow but steady conversion.

Goodness knows what possessed me to become a geographer. Was it some curious alchemy of DNA or some critical experience of childhood? Reading Conrad or *The Riddle of the Sands* at too early an age? Or being given battered 1920s *National Geographics* when recovering from a scarlet fever attack? Or was it simply a built-in curiosity to wonder what lay over the distant ridges of the Quantock Hills (west) and Mendip Hills (east) that bounded my attic bedroom horizons?

Certainly I can remember no Pauline conversion on a road to Damascus nor a Wesleyan warming on a London street. But I can recall precisely when the final die was cast and the odd circumstances that surrounded it. At the age of sixteen I was stupid enough to injure myself in a school rugby match. This set off an old problem and, as a result, I had to spend several months in an orthopaedic hospital before and after a spinal operation. For the initial period I lay encased, pharaoh-like, in a long head-to-toe plaster cast, so that any movement was restricted. The only way I could get to read a book was through a set of mirrors. By reversing a book and laying it flat on my chest the pages could be reflected, the right way up, to a final mirror just above my head. Other adjustments allowed a view of the lawn and trees outside the ward windows.

For that short period of my life the mirrors were critical, and ironically, they were to play an indirect part in determining my future course. For public school examinations (the old Higher School Certificate) were only a year away and although in hospital I was not let off normal school work. But reading through mirrors was tiring and the first 'serious' book I was brought and whose illustrations captured my attention was Charles Cotton's *Geomorphology of New Zealand*. At the time I was uncertain about which subject I would study at university or, indeed, whether I would be fit enough to go on to university at all. Cotton's diagrams of finely-etched landforms and the problems which their morphology and origin posed made up my mind. I resolved to take forward the study of 'physiography' by whatever route was open to me. (Haggett, 1990, pp 5–6)

3 THE INTELLECTUAL–INSTITUTIONAL FIELD

Peter Haggett's mapping on to a particular intellectual–institutional field began when he came up to St Catharine's College, Cambridge, in 1951. He was, by all accounts, a brilliant student. Not only did he gain a First in all three years of his degree, but his work was considered to be so far ahead of others that, at the final examiners' meeting, his case was set aside before other candidates for Firsts were considered. Kenneth Warren recaptures the Haggett of those undergraduate years.

The writer was for four years a contemporary of Peter's as an undergraduate at St Catharine's College Cambridge. Unlike most of the group of eight geography freshman, who had served for up to two years National Service, Peter came from school to university direct. From the first it was clear that he had been deeply influenced by his West Country home background. He spoke with great warmth of the Quantock Hills, and of country walks, as far as I could judge, largely with his father, who obviously had an important influence on his attitudes to his subject – and probably in other ways too, though he did not speak much in my hearing about them. In short, Peter's geography had a firm landscape basis.

The Geographical Tripos involved a Qualifying examination and Part One and Part Two of the Final Honours examination. The syllabus was then still rather 'conventional', but contained more in the way of systematic geography than was common at many British universities. In each of the three annual examinations, Peter was awarded a First class. In his options he chose to take a mix of human – largely economic – and physical geography, an unusual but by no means unique choice. As a physical geographer he was one of those from this period who went to Scolt Head Island to undertake the revisions in James A. Steers' long term survey of the evolution of this prominent Norfolk coastal feature. He also attended Bruce Sparks' Wealden field course, centred on the picturesque Timberscombe House in the west of the region. Generally, even at that time, field work was not prominent in the training of Cambridge undergraduates.

Various departmental occasions come to mind, though it is impossible at this distance in time to recall whether or not Peter was involved in some of them. The surveying classes were memorable – plane tabling on Coe Fen on the afternoon on which the 1951 General Election results were coming through, and some weeks later a compass traverse in the lower parts of the Gog Magog hills – when Peter and his companion were puzzled by their anomalous compass readings until they realised the effect of steadying the instrument against the iron lamp posts. There were Christmas parties in the library of the department in Downing Place and an annual departmental dinner in the Dorothy Café in the centre of Cambridge.

In college we were taught in pairs by 'Gus' Caesar, an outstanding geography tutor, then at the height of his powers. Additionally, for special subjects, we were sent to tutors at other colleges. Gus carefully arranged and changed his tutorial pairs so as to measure students against their academic peers. Each student would take turns to read out his essay, and the other would be expected to join Gus in careful criticism of it – knowing that he would later have to stand up to a similar scrutiny. From the start it was clear that Peter was outstanding, though, given the condition of the subject at that time, and his own background in it, there was no sign of the directions in which he would within a few years be helping to pioneer its further advance.

At St Catharine's undergraduates then lived out in their first year and Peter, along with a modern linguist, was housed just off the Barton Road.

In the second year he occupied an interesting room on the top floor of the Hobson building. During his final year he shared a large sitting room – to which were attached two bedrooms/studies – with the writer.

The St Catharine's geographers were a close knit group. They would meet in each other's rooms for coffee and talk, or on long summer's evenings after dinner go out walking – and talking. Peter was always welcome, but seemed to have wider interests and associations and so was less commonly a member of this group then some of his colleagues. On fine summer evenings we might walk up to the College sport field off Grantchester Meadows, and I recall Peter playing in the cricket nets there.

He was an active member of Meth Soc, the undergraduate association of Methodists, which involved not only meetings for worship or fellowship but social activities as well. He was – as were undergraduates commonly in those days – a keen cinema-goer. The 'Rex', a picture house out of the town centre, was a common place of pilgrimage. I remember him remarking that his favourite film actress was Susan Hayward – what this proves, I am at a loss to speculate.

For all students conditions were in many respects more limiting than they are today. There were still remnants of rationing until the last year of our undergraduate course, and levels of comfort in college accommodation were not up to modern standards. Foreign travel was possible but was of course much more restricted in its range. The first of the two long vacations was partly taken up by work on a dissertation or local study. Even so a party of the St Catharine's geographers managed a long cycling trip through France.

By the end of the final year of the course three of the nine geographers – the number had been increased by the addition of a transfer from the Mathematics Tripos – had secured places for study during the following year at American universities. Peter at that time opted to stay in Britain to begin to follow up his distinguished undergraduate career with what was to prove an even more fruitful one in teaching, research, writing and acting as an ambassador for his subject.

In 1954, Peter commenced graduate work at Cambridge but, in 1955, he was snapped up by University College London Geography Department, then under the leadership of H. C. Darby, as an Assistant Lecturer. However, his sojourn at UCL proved to be short-lived. In 1957 he transferred back to the Cambridge Geography Department, initially to a University Demonstratorship in Geography and then to a University Lectureship and Fellowship of Fitzwilliam College. This period at Cambridge is covered in Chorley's memoir (ch. 17).[1]

What is clear from this memoir is that, by the year 1966, when Peter moved to be the first holder of the Chair of Urban and Regional Geography at Bristol, he was part of a web of contacts spun out of the warp and weft of Cambridge. He was a member of a group of Cambridge undergraduates, many of whom went on to outstanding academic careers. He was part of a generation of Cambridge postgraduates who were to go on to colonize British and North American geography. Finally, he became a member of a group of academic staff at UCL and Cambridge who were, or who would become, the cream of British geography. It is this membership of a multiple geographical elite that accounts for the success of Peter's ideas. He was able to mount an assault on the then geographical establishment in part because he was so firmly located within it. This meant that the geographical establishment could less easily identify him as a foe and, in turn, its younger members acted as willing conductors for his ideas.

Certainly these ideas were legion and through the 1960s they came flooding out. As has already been noted, by Chorley, they sometimes met with opposition. David Stoddart recounts a particularly choice set piece occasion from another viewpoint.

In March 1964 Peter gave a paper at the Royal Geographical Society on 'Regional and local components in the distribution of forested areas in south east Brazil' (*Geographical Journal*, 130 [1964], pp. 365–78). It arose from his fieldwork near São Paulo in 1959 and followed a previous paper in 1960 on land use and sediment yield in the same area (*Geographical Journal*, 127 [1961], pp. 50–8). This latter was Peter's first foray into quantitative geography, replete with maps and even histograms, though the story it told, while beautifully done, was safely traditional. The first paper drew considerable praise: 'a very stimulating attempt to apply quantitative techniques in a field of study which brings together geomorphology and historical geography in a most profitable way', said C.T. Smith; 'the quantitative, statistical approach to geographical problems that he has so ably demonstrated is bound to have applications in all aspects of geography', added B.H. Farmer. Alas, the second lecture proved a different matter.

The meeting was chaired by Professor Dudley Stamp, shortly to become Sir Dudley and already acting the role. He and Alfred Steers (Peter's head of department at Cambridge) sat in the middle of the front row and were its only occupants. Peter analysed the controls affecting forest cover through 'a factorial design based on variance analysis', losing much of the audience immediately, and then looked at regional distributions using trend surfaces and residuals. The paper culminated with a general explanation of forest cover which turned out to be

$$Y = \log 0.16 + 0.161 \log X_1 - 0.07 \log X_2 - 0.08 \log X_3 + 1.10 \log X_4 + 0.05 \log X_5$$

There was a sharp intake of breath around the lecture room at this apparent mumbo-jumbo. Both Stamp and Steers had grown visibly agitated as the lecture progressed, and the regression equations were the last straw.

Stamp introduced the discussion by saying it was all 'too much for some of us'. The technical points about variance analysis raised by Stan Gregory and Roger Barry's suggested use of orthogonal polynomials instead of trend surfaces simply made the situation worse. Steers' face darkened visibly; he did not speak. But it was too much for Stamp. Peter must have found his concluding words a great encouragement:

'I think we must say to our lecturer this afternoon, that he has introduced some of us to the modern quantitative approach. Some of us may not like the look of it. We may even feel that here is an enormous steam hammer! How is it working in the cracking of nuts! . . . I hope that the mathematically inclined will have the strength of mind to tear up some of their results if necessary.'

Worse was to come. Next morning Steers summoned Peter to his room. Glowering as only he could and with his feet drumming on the ground – a not infrequent sight at that time – he dressed Peter down. 'This kind of thing has got to stop', he tetchily demanded: 'You are bringing the subject into disrepute.' The rest, of course, is history.

Yet, in retrospect, what is striking is how quickly Peter's ideas on what came to be known as 'locational analysis', with its vocabulary of surfaces, nodes, networks, and diffusion, and its attention to methods like regression, became a new kind of orthodoxy. In effect, their adoption by the discipline in Britain, and in many countries overseas, took only ten years (Billinge, Gregory, and Martin, 1984; Livingstone, 1992; Taylor, 1976). Why was this? It is possible to fix on five main reasons. First, and as already mentioned, the ideas were rooted in the prevailing geographical establishment. In Bourdieu's (1988) terms, they were heretical ideas but produced by a 'hesiarch'. Second, the ground for these ideas had already been prepared, most especially in North America, but also in Germany and Scandinavia. In North America writers like Isard, Garrison, Berry and Bunge were influential. In Germany, the ideas of Christaller and Lösch could be called upon whilst Scandinavia harboured luminaries like Häger-strand. Third, there was the calculated campaign of proselytizing that Peter Haggett (and Dick Chorley) embarked upon. Through the medium of events like the Madingley Conferences, the new ideas were carefully and effectively disseminated. Fourth, the University system was expanding in many countries in the 1960s and most especially in Britain. This expansion produced posts for new, younger people who were more likely to be drawn to the new ideas. Certainly, in at least one case, Peter was influential in the appointment of another rising star of the 'quantitative revolution', Alan Wilson:

He was a very significant supporter of me in my early days of modelling. He had judged that my work was of importance to Geography – presumably on the basis of hearing me in seminars and at conferences (and in reading my work) long before I could wear a geographer's hat. In particular, he as an external adviser to the Chair Committee, explicitly supported my appointment to my chair in Leeds in 1970 – so through this he has been a major influence on my career. (Incidentally, my chair was originally in *Spatial Analysis* but I thought it would be better to have Geography in the title – so with the Committee's approval, I adopted for myself the same title as Peter's chair in Bristol).

Finally, there was Peter Haggett's (and Dick Chorley's) extraordinary fecundity. To put it in a nutshell, they outproduced their rivals. The roll of honour is still impressive in today's produce-for-the-sake-of-production academic culture – *Frontiers in Geographical Teaching* (1965), *Locational Analysis in Human Geography* (1965), *Models in Geography* (1967), *Network Analysis in Geography* (1969), the *Progress in Geography* series of books (started, 1969) . . . These books, and especially *Locational Analysis in Human Geography*, became, along with Harvey's *Explanation in Geography*, the icons for a whole generation of geographers. Tony Gatrell's reaction was typical of many:

When I was 17, in the lower sixth, my teacher at Haberdasher's, Brian Fitzgerald, was enthusing about this guy called Peter Haggett (I think he must have met him at the Madingley conference) and mentioned a book that we might look at. When I next went into London I bought from Dillons 'Locational Analysis in Human Geography'. It turned out not to be the book that Brian had wanted us to look at; that was 'Frontiers', edited by C&H. Anyway, Brian was impressed! I tried to read it, but could only make sense of fragments. However, it was my pride and joy, simply because the writing was so wonderful; I think I knew the Preface by heart! I knew then that I wanted to study with this man. My twin brother went off to Cambridge to read History; I persuaded my teachers that I wasn't interested in Cambridge, only Bristol.

Peter's move to Bristol had two immediate effects. First, it allowed him to renew the contacts with his beloved Somerset. He and his family moved to Chew Magna and Peter still continues to reside in the village which is remembered with affection by one Scandinavian visitor, Torsten Hägerstrand.

In 1974 I was again invited to come to Bristol in order to receive a honorary degree. Peter acted as orator and presented me to the Madam Chancellor who at that time was the Nobel laureate Dorothy Hodgkin.

After the Degree Congregation Peter spent a couple of days, taking my wife, daughter and myself around his lovely corner of England. He brought us to Bath so my daughter could visit the Costume Museum and all of us enjoy the remarkable city plan. He also brought us across the Severn. Brenda's and Peter's dog – I think maybe a briard – had on the other hand mixed feelings about the visitors from the backwoods. He (she) was very shy and simultaneously very curious about us. When we were sitting on the terrace at Chew Magna the dog vanished behind the corner of the house but stretched out its shaggy head – only the head – now and then in order to check if we had not the good sense to quit the territory.

Ten years later, when Peter acted as Vice-Chancellor, he sent me a book about the history of the University of Bristol and suggested in his dedication that I look on page 147 where to my surprise he had managed to smuggle in a colour picture of me and the Lord Mayor of Bristol, both in red robes.

Second, Peter Haggett's name rapidly became synonymous with that of the Department (Peel, 1975). The reviews of *Locational Analysis in Human Geography* had appeared and they hailed 'the most original and important book from a British geographer for many years' (Peter Hall in *New Society*). The impact of *Locational Analysis* (which in its first edition sold well over 40,000 copies) and the other books of the 1960s continued to reverberate in the years to come. The 1970s saw further publishing projects completed. Most particularly, there was the volume of the proceedings of the twenty-second Colston Symposium (Chisholm, Frey, and Haggett, 1970), the volume of essays to mark the fiftieth anniversary of the establishment of a Department of Geography in the

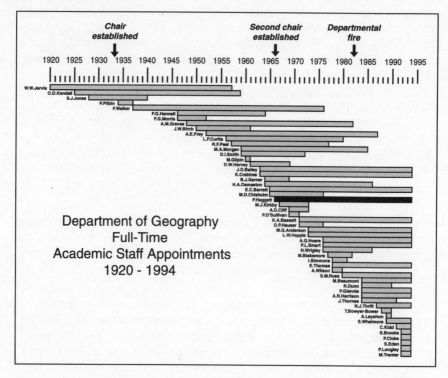

Figure 18.2   Full-time Bristol academic appointments, 1920–1944

University of Bristol (Peel, Chisholm, and Haggett, 1970; see figure 18.2), the second edition of *Locational Analysis in Human Geography* (Haggett, Cliff and Frey, 1977) and, most importantly of all, the publication of *Geography:A Modern Synthesis* in 1972, a textbook which, over the years, and through four editions, has become the standard introduction to geography for numerous English-speaking students around the world, and which is also available in Russian, German, Italian, and Spanish.

In the 1960s, Peter Haggett's interests had already began to turn towards medical geography, partly prompted by involvement with the World Health Organization. By the mid-1970s Peter had focused on epidemiological modelling (for example, Cliff, Haggett, Ord, Bassett, and Davies, 1975). In the 1980s and 1990s, usually in partnership with Andrew Cliff, this work multiplied, rather like the epidemics which were the subject of its study. A series of major volumes have been produced on the characteristics of influenza, measles and AIDS/HIV epidemics (Cliff, Haggett, Ord, and Versey, 1981; Cliff and Haggett, 1985; Cliff, Haggett and Ord, 1986; Cliff and Haggett, 1988; Smallman-Raynor, Cliff, and Haggett, 1992; Cliff, Haggett, and Smallman-Raynor, 1993).[2]

The level of productivity is all the more remarkable because at the same time as these and other volumes – like the retrospective, *The Geographer's Art* (Haggett, 1990) – were appearing, Peter was actively and extensively involved in matters institutional. In the University of Bristol, not only was he head of the Department of Geography for long periods of time but in rapid succession he was also Dean of the Faculty of Social Sciences (1972–4), Pro-Vice-Chancellor (1979–82) and Acting Vice-Chancellor (1984–5). His qualities in these posts were clear from the start and he is remembered with great affection by all those who came in contact with him – not the usual lot of the holders of such posts – as these two memoirs from its present Registrar, Michael Parry, and Vice-Chancellor, Sir John Kingman, make clear.

I first came to know Peter Haggett closely during his period as Pro-Vice-Chancellor from 1979 to 1982, although I had been vividly aware of him as the one professor who, at that time of my own appointment in 1966, both was – and seemed – young. Our initial contacts were largely through the Halls of Residence, when he was Chairman of the Committee on Student Residence and I was its Secretary. For one reason or another, we had to appoint a number of new Wardens over this period and he and I spent long evenings in the Halls, taking soundings and talking to various interested parties – JCR, SCR and staff – about the qualities required in the Warden of that particular Hall. Peter had the capacity to listen in such a way as to make the speaker feel he was the centre of attention and to bring out the views of the shyest and most incoherent member of the Hall.

From time to time I would drive him back to Chew Magna at the end of these evenings and, although always a private person, he would sometimes talk about his love of cricket and about his farming origins in Pawlett. He would tease me, too, in the nicest possible way, about my own keenness for fishing – a bug from which he seemed totally immune. When my father died suddenly in the States in 1982 and I had to go over at short notice Peter gave me the firm sympathy I needed at the time.

Another memory is when Gordon Moon retired in 1980 after a lifetime of service in the University, at first in the Department of Geography and latterly in the Personnel Office, Peter delivered the main speech. It was in some ways not the easiest of occasions, but Peter's combination of charity, integrity and understanding has stuck in mind ever since.

And so, when Alec Merrison retired in 1984 and John Kingman was not available to take up the post of Vice-Chancellor until 1985, Richard Hill, who was then Chairman of Council, telegraphed Peter in Australia to ask if he would serve as acting Vice-Chancellor for the year. Peter was then on sabbatical following his period as Pro-Vice-Chancellor and he can have wanted nothing less than to return to University administration, but typically of him he consented to take up the reins for a year.

His consent gave great pleasure to us in the Senate House and his tenure of the Vice-Chancellorship was in some ways for me a golden period. Not that it was in any way an easy time. We had just come through the three year period of cuts from 1981 to 1984 and believed that we had been promised a level of funding thereafter. We were all perhaps slightly pleased with ourselves and were looking forward to emerging on the plateau, when it became apparent that level funding was not to be and that we had entered into the long, difficult time from which we have yet to emerge.

Peter, though, had the capacity to draw his team together and make every member of it feel valued and important. I loved working for him and I know he brought out the best in me. His membership of the old, impenetrable UGC had given him considerable insight into the arcane world of university funding, and some of the beliefs of the administrators who worked with him must have seemed gauche in the extreme, but he never let us feel this.

He gave his all to the job and worked far too hard. For this reason sadness at losing him from Senate House had to be tempered with relief for his sake. He handed over a team that pulled together and that felt itself to be one. The friendship has lasted and will last.

It would not have been a surprise to anyone if, when Sir Alec Merrison announced that he would retire as Vice-Chancellor in 1984, the University of Bristol had chosen Peter Haggett to succeed him. Peter's combination of great scientific distinction with a remarkable record of success as Dean and Pro-Vice-Chancellor, and his national and international experience, must have made him a front runner. But he felt that he could contribute more in other ways, and Bristol had to look outside.

In the event the chosen candidate had commitments which meant that there would be an interregnum for the academic year 1984–85, and Peter readily agreed to be Acting Vice-Chancellor for that year. It was not an easy assignment; an Acting Vice-Chancellor has all the pressures of a permanent incumbent, but without the length of time to see his decisions through. He must leave his permanent successor to take long-term decisions, but maintain the momentum of the University's development.

Peter started with the immense advantage that he was trusted by the University community and by the lay Council members, and he amply justified that trust. He did not evade the difficult decisions which reached his desk, but he left options open for his successor where this could be done without damage. As a result, the new Vice-Chancellor came to a university which was moving ahead strongly, and which was ready for fundamental thinking and planning about its future.

In the University, this year was the culmination of many years of loyal and wise service. The outside world, however, was already seeing him as a member of the UGC (and later the UFC), and as the chief planner of social sciences within the universities at large. This combination of tasks, all undertaken with the thoroughness which he always brings, must have stretched even Peter's talents, but he never allowed himself to be over-whelmed with detail. His judgement remained true and impartial. His reputation for wisdom and integrity was soon as high in all the universities as it had long been in Bristol.

Yet to say that Peter is respected and trusted and admired is only part of the story. He wears his distinctions with a modesty which is entirely genuine. He is a friend to all those who work with him. Even when he has to say no, he can do it with a warm humanity that takes away the sting of refusal. The most numerate of geographers is no desiccated calculating machine, but a human being who inspires great affection as well as honour.

As Sir John Kingman's memoir makes clear, more institutional service was to follow, but now outside the University. From 1985 until 1989 Peter was a member of the University Grants Committee, later University Funding Council, during a stormy period in British academic history, and was involved in three major subject reviews (of Earth Sciences, Sociology, and Social Administration), two of which he chaired. From 1986 he has also been a member of the National Radiological Protection Board.

Thus, in some ways, one might describe Peter Haggett as an archetypal member of the British establishment, as offers of the Chair of Geography at Oxford, and of the provostships and masterships of several Oxford and Cambridge Colleges, also attest.[3] Yet, what is interesting is that Peter has always stood slightly to the side. As has been demonstrated, throughout the period when he was most deeply involved in University and public service, he maintained an academic output that others without such social responsibilities would be proud of. Equally, it is clear that many of the onerous responsibilities he has undertaken have resulted from his commitment to a strongly felt idea of service to the community. In other words, Peter has remained an academic at heart.

4 DIFFUSION

One might well ask why Peter Haggett's work has been so influential. There are of course, a myriad of reasons, and not least the quality of the work itself. But, ultimately, five reasons seem to stand out.

The first of these has been the matter of timing. Peter Haggett's most influential work, the work from the 1960s, both summarized and took forward a developing intellectual movement in geography. In this sense, Peter Haggett was the right person in the right place at the right time. But there is more to it than this.

The second reason for the success of 'Haggettry' was that, from an early time, Peter Haggett was locked into the North American scene. His visits to the United States, from 1962 onwards, allowed him to gain new knowledge, cement relationships, and become known (see the recollections in Billinge, Gregory, and Martin, 1984). From an early stage, Peter was a transatlantic geographer and his audience was similarly placed.

A third reason for success has been Peter's frenetic travelling, which meant that he rapidly become known all over the world (figure 18.3). On his travels he has built up an enormous world wide contact network[4] and a day has rarely gone by without a string of incoming overseas telephone calls or one of his famous postcards winging its way overseas. As Pip Forer, one of his former postgraduate students in Bristol, remembers, this contact network meant that

> meetings with Peter always had a special flavour. For some reason the recently departed David Harvey had left an anorak on the back of Peter's door, almost like the Siege Perilous waiting for an occupant. It brooded

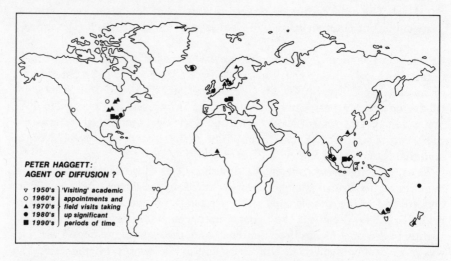

Figure 18.3   Peter Haggett: agent of diffusion (courtesy of Tony Hoare)

there while consultations went on, punctuated by frequent calls from exotic places – in one session, Geneva, Reykjavík, Canberra (I guess Gerry Ward couldn't sleep), Berkeley and somewhere in Latin America.

Some of his network of contacts were made on brief academic visits. Others were made on visits taking place over more extended periods – to teach, carry out field work, and so on.[5] Increasingly, the visits have been to take on heavyweight advisory duties. For example, Peter was an adviser on the setting up of a new Department of Geography at the Chinese University of Hong Kong, and the University of Brunei Darrusalam. The tenor of these visits is suggested by the reminiscences of the former head of the Geography Department at the University of Canterbury, with which the Department of Geography at Bristol has had a longstanding connection.

From a handwritten inscription in *Geography: A Modern Synthesis,* 3rd edition, 1979.

> 'To a senior Dean in the Canterbury Connexion
> from a newly enrolled Creyke Road Curate!!'
> (signed) Peter
> Christchurch, March 30, 1979
> 'It is a special privilege to write as a member, albeit
> a very junior member of the 'Canterbury connexion.'[6]

Peter Haggett spent 'two idyllic' (to use his words) months at the University of Canterbury in Christchurch, New Zealand, in early 1979 as the fourth in a distinguished line of visiting Erskine Fellows in Geography. Two outstanding features are in the quotations: intellectual modesty and geographical thinking.

But his visit provided other memories. The gift of a photographic

Figure 18.4   Haggett teaching in the field, Majorca (courtesy of Keith Crabtree)

memory appeared to be balanced by a degree of numerical imperfection – he could not remember the numerical combination for the lock of his bicycle. He left this warrior steed to the Department on his departure. From the Canterbury archives comes this Haggett gem:

> 'For the record, the code number of the very old –
> but trusty – bicycle is 3241 (CBD1 might be a
> suitable mnemonic!). You might like to caution
> others lucky enough to be visitors here the brakes
> are applied by pedalling backwards. Doubtless
> this is a Southern Hemisphere invention.'

A fourth reason for success, and one not to be downplayed, is Peter's ability to communicate. This ability to communicate has taken three forms. To begin with he is, and always has been, an excellent lecturer (figure 18.4). His lectures have undoubtedly inspired generations of undergraduates – and many wider audiences too. As Tony Gatrell remembers:

> I never missed a lecture by PH, simply because they were always great fun
> and I always left feeling that I'd learnt something. Peter always apologized
> for his blackboard sketches, but his circles were immaculate, with never a
> hint of ellipticity!

The carefully modulated tones, the myriad slides and the constant jottings on the blackboard wrapped together in an enthusiastic whole have been bettered by few other lecturers.[7] Peter also communicates through his writing. In an age when academic writing has all too often become a mass-produced sludge, Peter writes with style. His writing manages to be crystal clear and economical. It is the same kind of clarity and economy found in baroque music – ringing, rhythmic and robust. As Torsten Hägerstrand notes:

> I participated in the IGU conference in Montreal in August 1972. And among the notes from that occasion I read that on August 17 I glanced through 'Geography, a Modern Synthesis' at the book-exhibition. It is the only book-title I wrote down from that exhibition, so it no doubt impressed me very much. When I came back home I was happy to find that Peter had sent me a private copy.
>
> The book was included as a textbook in my department and became very popular among the students. And more even than that. The university has a study program called International Economics which, beside economics and management, also includes Economic Geography and English. Teachers in the English department found Peter's book so well written that they adopted it also among their textbooks. This means that students in the program read the book two times, one for its geography and one for its language.
>
> I once congratulated Peter for his masterly way of writing English – a strange thing to do for an outsider. The reaction was a bit surprising. He said that he was not so sure that the language was exactly his own, since the text was heavily edited by all sorts of experts. I suspect this was too modest to judge from the essays in 'The Geographers' Art'.
>
> The various editions of Peter's *Geography* have been, and are, so widely used at Swedish universities that Peter is included with a short biography in the new National Encyclopedia of Sweden in order to give students and others a chance to find out the when and where of its author.

There is one more facet of Peter's ability to communicate. That is his constant use of maps and diagrams. This mixture of the visual and the verbal is, of course, a fundamental part of what distinguishes geographical texts from others in the social sciences and humanities. But Peter has raised it to something of an art form. Few pages of his books and papers ever go by without a map or diagram. It is a part of Peter's strongly visual sense of the world.

The final reason for the success of Peter Haggett's work is undoubtedly his personality. He is, to put it straightforwardly, a very nice person. Without exception, all the contributors to this piece wanted that fact stressed. As one correspondent (Ian Simmons) put it succinctly Peter has 'a total lack of malice, something I have found in about three people altogether'. As another correspondent put it even more succinctly, Peter is living proof that 'you don't need to be a rat to come out tops' (Pip Forer).

So what does the Haggett personality consist of? First of all, there is his unflappability. Pip Forer recounts how:

As a Prestige Visitor to the University of Canterbury Peter was allocated to me to deliver to an evening seminar in a poorly signposted part of town. No sooner had Peter sat down in the front seat of my aging Austin Maxi than the seat collapsed backwards, laying him almost horizontal. With a composure that the Queen would have envied Peter expressed no surprise at all, commenting that the angle of repose was very comfortable. We managed to prop him up again (he protested that really he was quite happy on the floor), but then perpetrated the geographer's ultimate sin: we got lost. The light was fading, the deadline was fast approaching, the tension in the car (at least amongst the Cantabrians) got higher and higher as street after street rolled up (often several times). Lights burnt brightly from house windows as the evening settled into night. Frustration and disorientation threatened to simply jam any thought processes we had left, when Peter piped up 'I love driving round town at this time of night. It's so interesting comparing people's living rooms'. The delivery was perfect. We relaxed, we found the critical turning and we arrived with 30 seconds to spare. Of course, Peter uses the same defusing technique all the time in seminars and discussions, both to enable the unsure and to demolish painlessly the unfounded.

Next, there is Peter's diplomacy. He is legendary for his ability to offer charitable opinions on colleagues that the rest of us find trying. A person who has just proved themselves in print to be someone with a psychopathic condition, Peter will describe as 'grumpy'. Someone the rest of us might consider to be a devious careerist Peter will describe as 'not playing a straight bat'. A person who has just ranted on to Peter for an hour about some trivial dent to their ego Peter will describe as, at the very most, 'getting on his pip'. Ian Simmons enlarges on this catalogue:

I would from time to time rail against various individuals high and low, especially in the year in which I was head of department, but Peter always managed to defuse my annoyance with the sort of phrase which indicated that I was quite right to be concerned with them, but it was not much good showering them with invective even at second hand. Of a senior figure in the discipline, ' . . . not known for his keenly tuned sense of humour.' Of another member of the University, spoken lightly ' . . . Of course, Ian, we have to love all God's creatures but some of them do make it difficult for us'.

It is no wonder that a whole industry has grown up around retailing and interpreting these Haggettian phrases! Then there is Peter's integrity. He is known for sticking to the rules but never doing so in such a way that his conscience cannot bear. Two vignettes serve to illustrate this point. One is from Tony Hoare, the other from Allan Frey.

I recall with particular pleasure the Haggettian experience of one former senior colleague who found himself on the same late-night Paddingtonto-Bristol train after both had been at separate meetings in London. Peter's was at the UGC, on the eve of the eagerly awaited announcement in May, 1986, of its selective funding distribution across the UK universities. The train sped westwards, but only after one day had passed into the next did Peter, after carefully checking his watch, feel it proper to vouchsafe to his travelling companion how Bristol had fared in the allocation.

He often had a clearer idea of the future than most, but he had the willingness and good sense to back down when his vision was obviously not being shared by colleagues. An infrequent occurrence I might say, but there was another rather similar conflict of loyalty which arose when the physical chair had to be filled and then re-filled on Ronnie Peel's retirement and Ian Simmons' return to Durham. Most universities are highly conservative institutions, not least the University of Bristol where, quite rightly, professional appointments are regarded as the principal mechanism by which excellence is maintained and the future assured, but where this appointments system is treated as highly confidential and to be shared by only a small group of senior figures. Carried to this length it makes a mockery of the claim that we are all colleagues (all colleagues are equal but some are more equal than others!) and, on these two occasions, left the staff of the geography department in substantial ignorance over who the contenders were, the identity of the short list and even the date of interviews. Whatever the arguments are for and against such secrecy, the level of unhappiness in the department grew to the point where Peter took it upon himself, against all university rules, to end the lengthy uncertainty by releasing a good deal of information and then holding himself accountable to the Vice-Chancellor for the breach. None of us underestimated the conflict of loyalty he must have experienced between duty to the Institution and duty to the department, but we were all profoundly glad that his ultimate concern was for the well-being of the department.

Last of all, there is Peter's generosity of spirit. He is simply the kindest and gentlest of all people, always willing to help or encourage others as Michael Chisholm makes clear.

Some examples. 1971 saw the appearance of two books, *Regional Forecasting* (Butterworth) and *Spatial Policy Problems and the British Economy* (CUP). Peter was absolutely central in formulating the idea, and then running the Colston Symposium which resulted in the appearance of *Regional Forecasting*. But he then made sure that two of his colleagues, Allan Frey and myself, could fully share any permanent glory by making sure we had a prominent role in the editorial process. As for *Spatial Policy Problems*, the idea of a collection of essays by former students of Gus Caesar, to appear 20 years after a group of us went up to Cambridge as a form of 'festschrift', was one that I recalled Peter suggesting when we were in Ronald Peel's office for some meeting. The suggestion having been made he stood back and allowed others to pick it up – in the event, the book was edited by Gerald Manners and myself.

Over the last few years, Peter Haggett has obtained some of the highest awards and distinctions. In geography, these have included the Association of American Geographers Meritorious Contributions Award, the Royal Geographical Society Patron's Gold Medal ,the Gold Medal of the Royal Scottish Geographical Society, the Anders Retzius Gold Medal of the Swedish Anthropological and Geographical Society, the Prix International de Géographie and the Laureat d'Honneur of the International Geographical Union. More generally he has received a string of honorary degrees – from York University, in Canada, from Bristol University, and from the University of Durham. Recently, he was made a Fellow of the British Academy and awarded the CBE for his contributions to public service. It is impossible to think of anyone who would begrudge him these honours and for two good reasons. First, because they are a measure of not just a professional but also a personal success. Second, because they mark out how, in the right hands, 'geographical study can enrich all the remaining years of one's life' (Haggett, 1990, p xvii).

ACKNOWLEDGEMENTS

The following people have kindly contributed reminiscences of Peter Haggett to this piece: The Rt Hon John Biffen, MP, Professor Michael Chisholm, Dr Pip Forer, Mr Allan Frey, Dr Tony Gattrell, Dr Tony Hoare, Professor Torsten Hägerstrand, Professor Barry Johnston, Sir John Kingman, Dr Bill Macmillan, Mr Michael Parry, Professor Ian Simmons, Professor David Stoddart, Dr Kenneth Warren, Professor Alan Wilson. I would like to thank Tony Hoare for gathering these reminiscences together.

NOTES

1 However it is impossible to resist an extra memoir from David Stoddart recounting Haggett as Demonstrator.

> Peter came back to Cambridge as University Demonstrator in 1957 (the year before Richard Chorley); I was then a second-year undergraduate. After some years on coral islands in the Caribbean I too was appointed to a similar position in 1962. The shock was immense: not only had I forgotten most of what my mentors had taught me but I was expected to teach things I never knew. Peter with alacrity abandoned his practical class on Map Projections as soon as I was appointed, and I took that on, together with Geological Maps and Introductory Statistics. While nowadays no student knows what a map projection is, then they all had to construct them. We worked our way through the Zenithal, the Cylindrical, the Conical with Two Standard Parallels, and similar delights. It was all made possible by Peter's lab handouts which he generously bequeathed to me. And then we got to the most difficult yet – the Mollweide. The students worked assiduously for

over an hour in total silence. Peeking over their shoulders I saw with consternation that instead of a smooth bounding ellipse the outline was coming out zig zag. I ran at once to Peter as mumbles of discontent began. He seized his copy of Alfred Steers' *Introduction to the Study of Map Projections*. Feverishly riffling through the pages we found the problem: Peter's handout had the equation wrong. By now the murmurs of discontent had become a distant thunder down the corridor. I went back into the lab long enough to close the class down, then Peter and I ran down the stairs and out into the street, closely pursued by the mob. I have always taken heart from the knowledge that even so distinguished a quantitative luminary as Peter could screw things up. And as soon as I could I passed the subject on to someone else and went back to my coral islands.

2　Peter has been ill-served by published citation analyses. His recent contribution has been systematically under-reported because he has generally been involved in cooperative work with co-authors whose names begin with letters earlier in the alphabet.

3　A number of correspondents suggested that the most impressive list we could compile would be of all the jobs that Peter Haggett had turned down!

4　This contact network has not just been compiled through travel, of course. It is also important to note Peter's many editing activities, including founding co-editor of the journal *Progress in Human Geography*, and his participation in international academic institutions like *Academia Europaea*.

5　For most of these journeys Peter has kept a log and detailed record in diary format.

6　Peter Haggett, 'Emerging Trends in Regional Geography: a View from the Touch Line'. In P. Forer (ed.), *Futures in Human Geography*, Canterbury Branch, NZ Geographical Society, Christchurch, 1980, 1.

7　This is to ignore Peter's other lecturing abilities. Most especially these include orations and perorations on all public occasions, and fieldwork. Allan Frey describes Haggett in the field:

> Good staffwork is Peter's forte, nowhere better illustrated than when planning and executing novel exercises in the field for students at all levels. His preparation and attention to detail is phenomenal, so that each field group is equipped with a separate portfolio of materials and a set of aims and objectives, all to be reconciled and interpreted at prolonged, but always enjoyable, de-briefing sessions afterwards. Even the Spanish Language was not allowed to get in the way of this process and the opportunity it brought for the close informal contact with staff and students that he so much enjoys.

REFERENCES

Billinge, M., Gregory, D., & Martin, R.L. (eds) (1984). *Recollections of a Revolution. Geography as Spatial Science*. London: Macmillan.

Board, C., Chorley, R.J., Haggett, P., & Stoddart, D. (eds) (1969, 1976). *Progress in Geography*. London: Edward Arnold (9 vols).

Bourdieu, P. (1988). *Homo Academicus*. Cambridge: Polity Press.

Chisholm, M.D.I., Frey, A.E., & Haggett, P. (1970). *Regional Forecasting*. London: Butterworth.

Chorley, R.J. & Haggett, P. (1965). *Frontiers in Geographical Teaching*. London: Methuen.

Chorley, R.J. & Haggett, P. (1967). *Models in Geography*. London: Methuen.

Cliff, A.D. & Haggett, P. (1985). *The Spread of Measles in Fiji and the Pacific: Spatial Components in the Transmission of Epidemic Waves through Island Communities*. Australian National University, Department of Human Geography, Publication HG 18.

Cliff, A.D. & Haggett, P. (1988). *Atlas of Disease Distributions. Analytic Approaches to Epidemiological Data*. Oxford: Blackwell.

Cliff, A.D., Haggett, P., & Ord, J.K. (1986). *Spatial Aspects of Influenza Epidemics*. London: Pion.

Cliff, A.D., Haggett, P., Ord, J.K., Bassett, K., & Davies, R.B. (1975). *Elements of Spatial Structure: a Quantitative Approach*. Cambridge: Cambridge University Press.

Cliff, A.D., Haggett, P., Ord, J.K., & Versey, G.R. (1981). *Spatial Diffusion: an Historical Geography of Epidemics in an Island Community*. Cambridge: Cambridge University Press.

Cliff, A.D., Haggett, P., & Smallman-Raynor, M.R. (1993). *Measles. An Historical Geography of a Major Human Virus Disease from Global Expansion to Local Retreat, 1840–1990*. Oxford: Blackwell.

Haggett, P. (1961). 'Land use and sediment yield in an old plantation tract of the Serra Do Mar, Brazil.' *Geographical Journal*, 127, 50–9.

Haggett, P. (1964). 'Regional and local components in the distribution of forested areas in South-East Brazil: a multivariate approach.' *Geographical Journal*, 130, 365–78 (Discussion, 378–90).

Haggett, P. (1965). *Locational Analysis in Human Geography*. London: Edward Arnold.

Haggett, P. (1972). *Geography: A Modern Synthesis*. New York: Harper and Row (2nd edn, 1975; 3rd edn, 1979; 3rd edn, revised, 1983).

Haggett, P. (1990). *The Geographer's Art*. Oxford: Blackwell.

Haggett, P., & Chorley, R.J. (1969). *Network Analysis in Geography*. London: Edward Arnold.

Haggett, P., Cliff, A.D., & Frey, A.E. (1977). *Locational Analysis in Human Geography* (2nd edn). London: Edward Arnold.

Harvey, D.W. (1969). *Explanation in Geography*. London: Edward Arnold.

Livingstone, D. (1992). *The Geographical Tradition. Episodes in the History of a Contested Enterprise*. Oxford: Blackwell.

Peel, R.F. (1975). 'The Department of Geography, University of Bristol, 1925–1975.' In M.D.I. Chisholm & P. Haggett (eds), *Processes in Physical and Human Geography: Bristol Essays*. London: Heinemann, 411–17.

Peel, R.F., Chisholm, M.D.I., & Haggett, P. (eds). (1975). *Processes in Physical and Human Geography: Bristol Essays*. London: Heinemann.

Smallman-Raynor, M.R., Cliff, A.D., & Haggett, P. (1992). *The London International Atlas of AIDS*. Oxford: Blackwell.

Taylor, P.J. (1976). 'An interpretation of the quantification debate in British geography.' *Transactions, Institute of British Geographers*, NS1, 129–42.

Contributors

M.D.I. CHISHOLM is Professor of Geography and Fellow of St Catharine's College at the University of Cambridge, Cambridge, UK.

R.J. CHORLEY is Professor of Geography and Fellow of Sidney Sussex College at the University of Cambridge, Cambridge, UK.

A.D. CLIFF is University Reader in Theoretical Geography and Fellow of Christ's College at the University of Cambridge, UK.

P. CLOKE is Professor of Geography at the University of Bristol, Bristol, UK.

P.C. FORER is Lecturer in Geography at the University of Canterbury, Christchurch, New Zealand.

A.C. GATRELL is Reader in Geography at the University of Lancaster, Lancaster, UK.

P.R. GOULD is Evan Pugh Professor of Geography at Pennsylvania State University, State College, Pennsylvania, USA.

T. HÄGERSTRAND is Emeritus Professor of Geography at Lund University, Lund, Sweden.

D.W. HARVEY is Professor of Geography at the Johns Hopkins University, Baltimore, Maryland, USA.

A.G. HOARE is Senior Lecturer in Geography at the University of Bristol, Bristol, UK.

J.H. HOLMES is Professor of Geography at the University of Queensland, Brisbane, Australia.

R.J. JOHNSTON is Vice-Chancellor of the University of Essex, Colchester, UK.

W.D. MACMILLAN is Lecturer in Geography and Fellow of Hertford College at the University of Oxford, Oxford, UK.

J.K. ORD is Evan Pugh Professor of Statistics and Business Administration at Pennsylvania State University, State College, Pennsylvania, USA.

M.R. SMALLMAN-RAYNOR is Lecturer in Geography at the University of Exeter, Exeter, UK.

N.J. THRIFT is Professor of Geography at the University of Bristol, Bristol, UK.

R.G. WARD is Professor of Human Geography, Research School of Pacific and Asian Studies, Australian National University, Canberra, Australia.

A.G. WILSON is Vice-Chancellor of the University of Leeds, Leeds, UK.

N. WRIGLEY is Professor of Geography at the University of Southampton, Southampton, UK.

Author Index

Index

Related Titles: List of IBG
Special Publications

Also published by Blackwell for the IBG

Atlas of Drought in Britain
Edited by J. C. Doornkamp and K. J. Gregory